Interfaces

# Personal Computer Interfaces

## Macs to Pentiums

## Michael Hordeski

**McGraw-Hill, Inc.**

New York   San Francisco   Washington, D.C.   Auckland   Bogotá
Caracas   Lisbon   London   Madrid   Mexico City   Milan
Montreal   New Delhi   San Juan   Singapore
Sydney   Tokyo   Toronto

**Library of Congress Cataloging-in-Publication Data**

Hordeski, Michael F.
    Personal computer interfaces / Michael Hordeski.
      p.  cm.
    Includes index.
    ISBN 0-07-030419-X—ISBN 0-07-030424-6 (pbk.)
    1. Computer interfaces. 2. Microcomputers. I. Title.
TK7887.5.H668   1995
004.6'16—dc20             94-24427
                          CIP

1 2 3 4 5 6 7 8 9 0  DOC/DOC  9 0 9 8 7 6 5 4

ISBN 0-07-030419-X (HC)
ISBN 0-07-030424-6 (PBK)

*The sponsoring editor for this book was Stephen S. Chapman.*

*Printed and bound by R. R. Donnelley & Sons Company.*

*Many thanks to Dee, who worked very hard to organize the chapters and worked on many of the diagrams, and to Bob, Bill, Don, Frank, Joe, Larry, Linda, Marge, Paul, Ron, Rowland, Steve, and all the others who have helped me over the years.*

# Contents

# Chapter 3. 32-Bit Microprocessors

## Chapter 5. Serial Interfaces

# Preface

Microcomputer interfaces do not have to be a mystery. The computer interface allows the communication among products from different manufacturers. Printers, plotters, scanners, page readers, keyboards, and many other peripherals are often connected to personal computers. This book shows how this is done and explains the standards used in interfacing personal computers to a variety of equipment.

Interfacing allows us to get information out of the computer (the output) and get information into the computer (the input). The subject of interfacing (which is also called I/O for input/output) is of interest in many fields. Both hardware and software are involved, along with engineering and economics. The basic methods used in modern interfacing have their roots in the previous century, when binary numbers were invented.

Both hardware and software are explained. This book includes parallel system hookups to the computer bus structure, as well as connections using different forms of serial, distributed serial, and virtually any type of personal computer interface. Interfaces require detailed knowledge of specific pinouts, line functions, polarities, and timings. In this book, the required details for the most popular interfaces are described in detail in a straightforward way. This includes parallel, direct, bus-connected, serial and other examples in the spectrum of personal computer interfaces. This book explains how the encoding and decoding are accomplished. The multiple serials hookup options include the RS-232 standard, RS-422, and 20 mA current loops.

This book includes examples of software routines including real time software control.

Step by step, this book takes you through general-purpose input/output, analog-to-digital interfaces and digital-to-analog interfaces for connecting different types of external hardware such as switches, lamps, LEDs, relays, solenoids, digital circuits, and motors.

The approach taken results in a step-by-step treatment of interfacing using readily available products with the personal computer. It should make the understanding of interfaces a straightforward topic to a broad range of readers. With this book, the reader should be able to develop a working knowledge of interface connections and concepts. This includes the full complement of required information for understanding personal computer interfaces. Applications include personal computer security systems, monitoring and control of laboratory experiments, lighting control, data acquisition, machine control, automated testing, material handling, games, simulators, and robotics.

The key highlights and rationale of each chapter follow. Chapter 1 serves as an introduction to digital electronics. It discusses basic terminology, digital circuits, gates, and integrated circuits. It also introduces digital codes, which are the language of interfacing. Basic microprocessor concepts are introduced as are the basic types of interfaces. Although Chap. 1 is introductory, it will be helpful to more experienced readers who will want to refer to it to clear up some of the gray areas in interface concepts.

Chapter 2 examines the modern microprocessor structure and architecture. In a book about interfacing to microprocessors, it is important to study microprocessors and how they are designed to talk to other devices. You will learn the differences between memory-mapped and plain I/O beginning in this chapter and continuing in Chap. 3 which covers 32-bit microprocessors including the 386 and 486 machines and 64-bit microprocessors such as Pentium.

Chapter 4 is concerned with microcomputer buses. This includes the buses which have become standardized through their use like the different IBM PC buses (8, 16, and 32 bits). These are critical to an understanding of microcomputer interfaces.

Chapter 5 covers serial interfacing. The serial interface is the oldest type of electrical communication and it has many years of experience and standards behind it. In practice, these interfaces are more likely to give the computer user more problems because of the timing requirements. The uninformed user can rarely plug two devices with standard serial interfaces together and get them to communicate the first time. Chapter 5 explains why this can happen and how it can be avoided so the computer and a serial peripheral can communicate properly.

Chapter 6 explains parallel I/O, which is one of the simpler types of interfaces (although some variations of the parallel interface can be quite complex). Integrated circuits have been available the last several years for making these complex parallel interfaces. These are covered in this chapter.

Chapter 7 examines analog interfaces which are sensitive to the amount of signal present. Digital devices are only concerned with the presence or absence of the signal at a particular time. Analog interfaces create a bridge to the real world allowing the computer to sense and control analog equipment.

Chapter 8 goes on to advanced interfacing concepts. Interrupts are one example since the computer is diverted from what it was doing. If this is not done properly, the processor may lose itself and the computer will hang up. We will examine the various interrupt schemes that are available and show the differences between hardware and software interrupts.

Chapter 8 also covers one of the most complex concepts in interfacing: *direct memory access,* or DMA. A microprocessor cannot perform DMA by itself; additional hardware is required. This hardware, which can be more complex than some processors, is explained in this chapter.

Chapter 9 introduces the concept of time in microprocessor control. Many real processes depend on time, such as heating a material at a specific temperature for a specific period of time. Time is divided into two types: real and absolute. We will examine how to sense both types of time with a microprocessor and how to interface to time.

Anyone who uses a personal computer will want this readily accessible source. The information provided in this book should meet all of your interface needs.

# Interfacing Basics

An interface refers to the connections between different electrical circuits or equipment. The circuits could be located in the same enclosure, like a computer, or they could be located in two separate pieces of electrical equipment. Interfaces are encountered when one connects a printer, keyboard, mouse, or monitor to a computer. The interface circuitry must provide the means to allow these different pieces of equipment to communicate with each other.

These interface circuits use digital electronics which have roots that go back to the work of a nineteenth-century mathematician, George Boole. In 1854 Boole created a type of algebra to allow problems in logic to be precisely stated. These problems existed in philosophy. Electronics as we know it would not exist for another 100 years.

Boolean algebra was devised for philosophic logic, which is concerned with the truth of statements based on other statements. Logical algebra is a method of symbolically expressing the relationship between logic variables. Ordinary algebra is the symbolic expression for relationship of number variables. Logical algebra is different from ordinary algebra in two ways:

1. The symbols, which are usually letters, do not represent numerical values.

2. Arithmetic operations are not performed.

Logical algebra owes much to the *Laws of Thought* written by George Boole in 1854. In recognition of his work, the term *boolean algebra* is often used. Boolean algebra is useful for analyzing the many forms of logical thought as well as describing the action of switching circuits.

This application is important in computer design, since a switch can represent ON and OFF states in the computer. The operation of the digital circuits can be described by logical equations using boolean symbols. These equations are often referred to as the computer logic.

## Computer Logic

Two discrete states may exist in logical algebra. Any pair of conditions different from each other can be used. The states are usually described as TRUE or FALSE. Any dissimilar set of values or states may be used to represent TRUE and FALSE as long as the set is consistent in the use of the selected values. Every logical quantity must exist in one or the other of the two chosen states and no other value is allowed.

Every logical quantity is single-valued, so no quantity can ever be simultaneously both TRUE and FALSE. Any quantity that is TRUE is equal to any other quantity that is TRUE. Any FALSE quantity is equal to any other FALSE quantity.

Every quantity has an opposite, so if the quantity is TRUE, then the inverse, or complement, is FALSE. If the quantity is FALSE, then the opposite is TRUE.

A logical quantity may be either constant or variable. If it is a constant, it will remain at the TRUE or FALSE state. If it is a variable, it can switch between the TRUE and FALSE states, but it must not be at any level between these two states.

Logical quantities may be physically represented in different ways. Common techniques include:

1. Electrically, by two different voltages

2. Mechanically, by the position of a switch

3. Optically, by the presence or absence of light

## Logic Notation

As in ordinary algebra, the letters of the alphabet are commonly used to represent logic variables. The letter $A$ could represent the condition of a logic variable. Then, the allowed values for $A$ would be only TRUE or FALSE, since these are the only values that a logic variable can represent. In ordinary algebra, the letter $A$ could represent any value.

The following symbols are all used to represent the inverse or complement of $A$:

$A'$     $A$-prime

$\bar{A}$     $A$-bar

$A*$     $A$-asterisk or $A$-star

The definitions of logic states tell us that $A$ and $A*$ cannot have the same value at the same time. So, if $A$ is FALSE at any given time, then $A*$ must be TRUE at this time; and the opposite is also true.

If two or more logic variables are present at the same time, one might be represented by $A$, another by $B$ and so on. If, at one time, $B$ is TRUE and $A$ is TRUE, then $B = A$ since a TRUE equals a TRUE. At the same time, the opposite of $B$ is $B*$ and the opposite of $A$ is $A*$ and $B* = A*$, since a FALSE equals a FALSE. At a later time, the variable represented by $A$ may change state and $A$ then becomes FALSE and $A*$ (the complement) becomes TRUE.

$$A* \text{ (now equal to TRUE)} = B \text{ (still TRUE)}$$

and

$$A \text{ (now FALSE)} = B* \text{ (still FALSE)}$$

Notice that symbols like $A$, $B$, or $B*$ simply represent logic variables and that, at any given time, any symbol can be TRUE and at some time later the same symbol may be FALSE.

The letter $T$ is often used to denote the TRUE state and $F$ is used to denote the FALSE state. The number 1 is also used to represent the TRUE state and 0 to represent the FALSE state. Although 1 and 0 like binary numbers, 1 is not necessarily equal to the number 1, and 0 is not necessarily equal to the number 0 unless it is stated to be so. The symbols, 1 and 0, only denote TRUE and FALSE states in logical variables.

For example, the logic for a digital circuit might be defined with the following conditions:

| | |
|---|---|
| TRUE state | Represented by $T$ or 1 and equal to +5 V. |
| FALSE state | Represented by $F$ or 0 and equal to 0 V. |

Under these conditions, a binary number like 10101 might be electrically represented on five different lines as shown in Fig. 1.1. Line C might be given the logic notation $C$. If line C has a true voltage on it

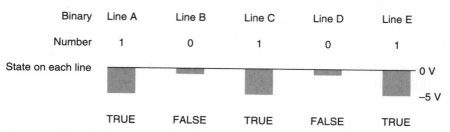

**Figure 1.1** Electrical representation of logical states. Negative true logic; false is close to zero.

$$C = T = 1$$
$$C* = F = 0$$

If line C switches to false

$$C = F = 0$$
$$C* = T = 1$$

These boolean variables may only have one of two values: TRUE or FALSE. Boole decided that TRUE and FALSE were too clumsy for use in an algebra of logic and reassigned the numeral 1 to true and the numeral 0 to represent false. In doing so, he forged an unbreakable link between boolean algebra and the binary number system which only has the numerals 1 and 0. The mathematics of computers was devised over 100 years before the logic circuits were developed that would allow wide use of Boole's theories.

Arithmetic operations like add, subtract, multiply, and divide can be accomplished in the binary number system as accurately as in the decimal system. The results are the same in either system.

## Decimal and Binary Systems Compared

In the decimal system we have fewer places for the same quantities but must deal with 0 through 9 digits. Electrically we could represent the digits of the decimal system by voltage levels such as 0 through 9 volts or 1 volt per digit. The electronic circuits needed to create and test for these voltage levels would be expensive and difficult to calibrate.

In the binary system, the electrical quantities 1 and 0 can be represented by two simple electrical states or voltage levels. The two voltages representing the binary 1 and 0 can be degraded as much as 50 percent during transmission, reception, and storage, and still be recognized. Circuits for restoring the binary levels are easily implemented, and can be done as they are processed.

## Binary States and Logic Polarity

The two binary states are the digits 1 and 0. They can be represented by zero volts for 0 and a positive voltage for 1. This is called *positive logic* since the 1 level is represented by the more positive voltage. If the 1 level is the more negative voltage, then it is known as *negative logic*. This is illustrated as follows:

| Digit | Negative | Positive | Positive | Positive |
|-------|----------|----------|----------|----------|
| 1 | –5 V | 0 V | +5 V | +6 V |
| 0 | 0 V | –12 V | 0 V | –6 V |

To avoid problems in using the terms *one* and *zero,* since 0 volts may not always be binary 0, the terms *high level* and *low level* or *true* and *false* are also used in place of 1 and 0. The use of these logical terms is shown as follows:

| Positive logic | Common logic terms | | |
|---|---|---|---|
| +5 V | 1 | High | True |
| 0 V | 0 | Low | False |

## Digital Signal Duration

In a computer, there is constant transmission, reception, and process-ing of signals between the different components and subsystems. All of this is done with representations of binary numbers. Some of these are control signals and others may represent letters or punctuation. The use of the term signal means that there is some intelligence transmit-ted in the form of changes in the 1 and 0 levels.

These changes or pulses are of very short duration. In a computer system they are controlled by a clock, which is actually a pulse gener-ator that generates periodic voltage pulses at a fixed frequency. The frequency is usually divided for the digital operations which occur in cycles. The read-and-write operations of a computer memory occur in cycles of so many clock pulses. The add cycle of the arithmetic unit is another example.

The term *leading edge* is the change between 1 and 0 that occurs at the beginning of the pulse. The term *trailing edge* is the change between 1 and 0 that occurs at the end of a pulse. The clock period is measured between the leading edge of one clock pulse and leading edge of the next.

A time measurement between like edges of two zero pulses is the cycle time. This can also be obtained by multiplying the clock period by the number of clock pulses per cycle. The clock period can also be obtained by the reciprocal of the clock frequency. The clock pulse is directly or indirectly used in generating the signals within the com-puter. For example, if a clock line is obtained from a 20-megahertz gen-erator. The clock period is

$$t_{cp} = \frac{1}{20 \text{ MHz}} = \frac{1}{20 \times 10^6} = 0.05 \text{ microseconds}$$

$$\text{clock frequency} = 20 \times 10 \text{ Hz}$$

and if the cycle uses six pulses, the cycle time is

$$t_{cy} = t_{cp} \times 6 \text{ pulses per cycle} = 0.05 \text{ sec} \times 6 = 0.3 \text{ microseconds}$$

## Serial and Parallel Numbers

Signals representing binary numbers may use parallel or serial formats. In serial numbers the binary places or powers of 2 are represented by clock or time periods. They use either pulse trains or level trains. Figure 1.2*a* shows a pulse train representing the binary number for 19.

The LSB (least significant bit) occurs on the left because it is first in time. The same number might also appear as a level train, as Fig. 1.2*b* shows. In this signal, the 1 level remains for the full period. If two or more adjacent ones occur, there is no change in level between them. These serial numbers have the advantage of requiring only one line or channel for processing them, but they require a separate clock period for each binary place. For some applications, this makes them too slow.

A parallel number requires a separate wire or channel for each binary place. The entire number can be transferred in one clock period, making it many times faster than the serial number. Figure 1.2*c* shows the waveforms that would occur simultaneously on the five lines or parallel channels of a five-bit number.

## Digital Switches

The 1 and 0 levels of voltage are not the only electrical states that may be used for binary values. A lamp may represent a 1 when turned on and a 0 when turned off. A switch can be in the 1 state when on, the 0 state when off. A relay may be a 1 when energized, a 0 when not energized. Several electrical devices and the states that may be assigned a binary number value are shown below.

| Value | Lamp | Switch | Relay | Diode | Vacuum tube | Transistor |
|-------|------|--------|-------|-------|-------------|------------|
| 1 | On | Closed | Energized | Forward bias | Saturation | Saturation |
| 0 | Off | Open | Not energized | Reverse bias | Cut off | Cut off |

## The Ideal Switch

An ideal switch for digital machines would have the following characteristics:

1. Easy to turn off and on with binary 1 or 0 levels

2. High-speed, almost instantaneous transition from off to on state

3. High, almost infinite, off resistance

4. Low or 0 on resistance

5. Be isolated from the signal turning it on and off

6. Consume very low power in the off and on states

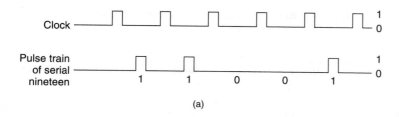

(a)

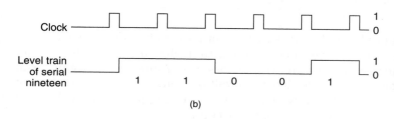

(b)

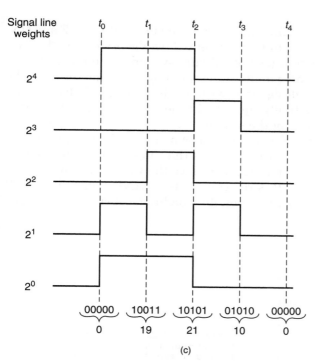

(c)

**Figure 1.2**(*a*)  Pulse train of serial nineteen; (*b*) Level train of serial nineteen; (*c*) Five bit parallel transmission.

Following is a list of these characteristics for common electrical devices:

| Device characteristic | Mechanical switch | Relay | Diode | Transistor |
|---|---|---|---|---|
| Easy to switch | O | X | X | X |
| Speed | Low | Low | High | High |
| OFF resistance | Infinite | Infinite | High | High |
| ON resistance | Low | Low | Medium | Medium |
| Isolation | Good | Good | None | Medium |
| Power consumption | None | High | Medium | Low |

The manual switch and relay have other disadvantages, like contact bounce and large size in comparison to diodes and transistors, especially when the diodes and transistors are in integrated circuit form. Contact bounce produces irregular voltage spikes during the instant of contact. These spikes may appear like a group of pulses and will cause erroneous operation of the digital circuits.

## Manual Switches

A manual switch has an input and output and two states, OFF and ON. The state of the switch can be represented by algebraic term *A*. If we assume the switch to be a part of a digital system, the input will have either a 1 or 0 level and can be represented by algebraic term *B*. The output, which can be designated with algebraic term *X*, depends on both *A* and *B* and is actually equal to *A* times *B*. Figure 1.3 shows this algebraic representation of the switch.

This particular type of algebra is known as *boolean algebra* and is also called *switching algebra*. It follows the rules of ordinary algebra, but there are some special conditions since the values are limited to 1 and 0. The term $X = A \cdot B$ is referred to as an *AND function* or *AND multiplication*. It has only four possible conditions. A chart known as a

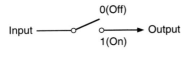

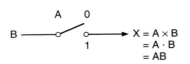

**Figure 1.3** A toggle switch may be represented as an algebraic term and can be part of a boolean algebra equation.

*truth table* is used to show the possible conditions for a given switching function.

As can be seen from the truth table, of the four conditions, only if a 1 exists on both *A* and *B* does the value *X* equal 1. This is the AND function. The switch (*A*) alone is not an AND function. It is an AND function only in conjunction with the variable (*B*). If the input of the switch were connected to a power supply (a constant one), the function would be

$$X = A \times 1$$

and, as in ordinary algebra, anything multiplied by 1 equals itself,

$$X = A$$

If the input of the switch is tied to ground (a constant 0),

$$X = A \times 0$$

and, as in ordinary algebra, anything multiplied by 0 equals 0. The following truth table shows these conditions.

| A | B | X |
|---|---|---|
| 0 | 0 | 0 |
| 1 | 0 | 0 |
| 0 | 1 | 0 |
| 1 | 1 | 1 |

If several switches are combined in the same circuit, we can use the Boolean functions to construct the truth table. These same procedures can be used on complex arrangements of series and parallel switching circuits.

## Relays

The relay was one of the first switching devices in computing devices. In a two-pole relay the sets of contacts are similar to a double-pole, double-throw switch. The terminals are usually designated as *common*, *normally open*, or *normally closed*. The contacts and coil are shown with the symbols in Fig. 1.4. The individual contacts or the coil may appear at separated areas on the drawing, as long as they are marked. Following is the truth table for the two-pole relay:

| A | B | X |
|---|---|---|
| 0 | 0 | 0 |
| 1 | 0 | 0 |
| 0 | 1 | 1 |
| 1 | 1 | 0 |

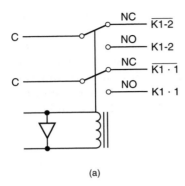

(a)

**Figure 1.4a** Schematic diagram of relay K1-1. K1-1 and K1-2 have values of 1 when K1 is energized. $\overline{K1\text{-}1}$ and $\overline{K1\text{-}2}$ have values of 1 when K1 is deenergized.

The relay is high-speed compared to human reaction time, but the relay pull-in and drop-out time is usually measured in milliseconds, as compared to microsecond or even nanosecond delay time for semiconductor switches. Miniature relays with low power consumption have been developed. Relays require more power than semiconductors and occupy much more space. Early computing systems have been built with relays, but this was before the availability of low-priced reliable semiconductors.

### Boole's Legacy

Boole's algebra meshes with digital electronics and allows low-cost computers to be based on binary numbers. The binary number system is based on the numerals zero (0) and one (1) while the decimal number system we normally use is based on the numerals zero (0) through nine (9). Binary numbers are particularly useful in electronics.

A single binary digit, which is called a *bit,* can be used to represent a true or false state, as used in Boole's logic. Binary numbers can also be used to represent numeric quantities, just as is done with decimal numbers.

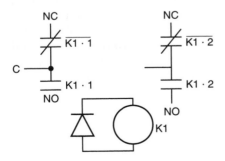

(b)

**Figure 1.4b** Logic symbol for the same relay.

Several bits can be grouped together and used to represent characters for transmitting text between different pieces of equipment. Many of these codes use eight bits, called a *byte,* which allow the representation of up to 256 different characters or text operations.

## Boolean Operations and Computer Circuits

Mathematical operations of addition, subtraction, multiplication, and division are a part of simple arithmetic. Boolean algebra has its own operations called AND, OR, and NOT. These fundamental operations are combined for more complex operations in digital logic circuits.

Computers are made up of circuits that are capable of a great many AND, OR, and NOT operations. This gives computers the power that they have. Modern electronic technology allows thousands of boolean operations to take place at a very high rate on a single integrated circuit or chip. The three basic boolean operations are simple enough in concept.

## NOT Operation

The NOT operation is very simple. The boolean variable operated on by NOT is inverted. So NOT TRUE is false and NOT FALSE is true. Note that a boolean variable must have one of two values. If one value does not exist then the other must.

Writing the NOT statements in boolean equations we get:

$$\text{NOT } 0 = 1$$
$$\text{NOT } 1 = 0$$

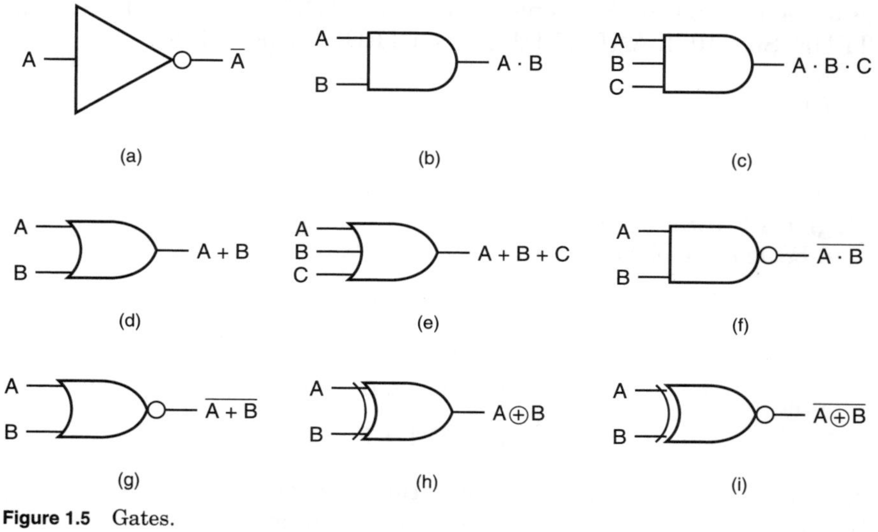

(a)　　　　　　　　　　(b)　　　　　　　　　　(c)

(d)　　　　　　　　　　(e)　　　　　　　　　　(f)

(g)　　　　　　　　　　(h)　　　　　　　　　　(i)

**Figure 1.5**　Gates.

Since boolean algebra was originally designed for philosophical logic, the NOT operation is shown as a bar over the variable. For example, if A is a variable, then

$$\text{NOT A} = \overline{\text{A}}$$

The NOT operation is also called negation, so placing a bar over A negates it and makes it NOT A. The electrical device that performs the negation is called a *NOT gate,* or simply an *inverter.* The symbol for an inverter is shown in Fig. 1.5. The input to the inverter is on the left side of the symbol and the output is on the right. A logic signal applied to the inverter's input is transformed by the device and the inverse of the signal is available at the output.

## Truth Tables

A truth table shows the output function for all possible inputs. An inverter has a single input which can have only one of two values, 0 or 1. Thus, there are only two entries in the truth table of an inverter as listed below

| Inverter input | Inverter output |
| --- | --- |
| 0 | 1 |
| 1 | 0 |

## AND Operator

This operator involves two or more inputs. In a two-input AND, if a statement using the AND operation is to be TRUE, both inputs must be TRUE. So, TRUE AND TRUE gives a TRUE output while

```
TRUE AND FALSE
FALSE AND TRUE
FALSE AND FALSE
```

all give a FALSE output.
In boolean algebra:

$$0 \text{ AND } 0 = 0$$

$$0 \text{ AND } 1 = 0$$

$$1 \text{ AND } 0 = 0$$

$$1 \text{ AND } 1 = 1$$

The symbol used for the AND operation is a centered dot (·), which is the same symbol used in computers for multiplication.

If we have two arguments called A and B, then the AND operation on those two arguments is written as

A · B

Sometimes the dot is not used, then the AND of A and B is simply

AB

## Gates

The electrical device which performs the AND operation is called the *AND gate*. The symbol for a two-input AND gate is shown in Fig. 1.5*b*. The AND truth table is shown below. The two inputs are on the left and the output is on the right. Since this AND gate has two inputs and each of these can have one of two values applied to them, there are four entries in the following truth table:

| Input | | Output |
|---|---|---|
| A | B | A · B |
| 0 | 0 | 0 |
| 0 | 1 | 0 |
| 1 | 0 | 0 |
| 1 | 1 | 1 |

A three-input AND gate would have three inputs labeled A, B, and C (Fig. 1.5*c*). The truth table has eight entries as shown below. This occurs because each of the three inputs may have one of two values, which results in eight input possibilities.

| Inputs | | | Output |
|---|---|---|---|
| A | B | C | A · B · C |
| 0 | 0 | 0 | 0 |
| 0 | 0 | 1 | 0 |
| 0 | 1 | 0 | 0 |
| 0 | 1 | 1 | 0 |
| 1 | 0 | 0 | 0 |
| 1 | 0 | 1 | 0 |
| 1 | 1 | 0 | 0 |
| 1 | 1 | 1 | 1 |

So far, we notice a definite pattern to the number of entries in the truth table that a boolean operation may have. The single-input inverter had two, a two-input AND gate had four, and a three-input AND gate had eight. The number of entries in a truth table is equal to two raised to the power of the number of inputs. This is illustrated as follows for up to four inputs:

| Number of inputs | Number of entries |
|:---:|:---:|
| 1 | $(2^1) = 2$ |
| 2 | $(2^2) = 4$ |
| 3 | $(2^3) = 8$ |
| 4 | $16 \ (2^4) = 16$ |

## OR Operation

This operation can also have two or more arguments. If a statement using the OR operator is to be TRUE, then only one of the arguments has to be TRUE. So, for a two-argument OR operation,

```
TRUE OR FALSE
FALSE OR TRUE
TRUE OR TRUE
```

are all TRUE statements.
   Only

```
FALSE OR FALSE
```

is FALSE.
   In boolean algebra, the statements become

```
0 OR 0 = 0
0 OR 1 = 1
1 OR 0 = 1
1 OR 1 = 1
```

The symbol used for the OR operation is a plus sign (+), which is the same symbol used for addition in arithmetic. The plus symbol is used in both philosophic and electric circuit logic statements.
   Figure 1.5d shows the symbol that is used for a two-input OR gate. The truth table appears as follows. The two inputs to the gate are on the left and the corresponding output is on the right.

| Inputs | | Output |
|:---:|:---:|:---:|
| A | B | A + B |
| 0 | 0 | 0 |
| 0 | 1 | 1 |
| 1 | 0 | 1 |
| 1 | 1 | 1 |

The symbol for a three-input OR gate is shown in Fig. 1.5e and the truth table is shown as follows:

| Inputs | | | Output |
| --- | --- | --- | --- |
| A | B | C | A + B + C |
| 0 | 0 | 0 | 0 |
| 0 | 0 | 1 | 1 |
| 0 | 1 | 0 | 1 |
| 0 | 1 | 1 | 1 |
| 1 | 0 | 0 | 1 |
| 1 | 0 | 1 | 1 |
| 1 | 1 | 0 | 1 |
| 1 | 1 | 1 | 1 |

## More Complex Boolean Operations

All logic functions can be built up from the basic AND, OR, and NOT operations. It is common in electric circuits to use a few slightly more complex operations. These new operations include a negated AND and OR, a variation of the OR operation and a negated version of this operation. These four boolean operations are the NAND, NOR, Exclusive OR, and Exclusive NOR.

## NAND Operation

This operation is formed by negating the AND operation. NAND is a contraction of NOT and AND. In the AND operation,

```
TRUE AND TRUE is TRUE
```

while

```
FALSE AND FALSE
FALSE AND TRUE
TRUE AND FALSE
```

are all

```
FALSE
```

Negating the AND function with a NOT produces opposite results.

```
TRUE NAND TRUE
```

is

```
FALSE
```

while

```
FALSE NAND FALSE
FALSE NAND TRUE
TRUE NAND FALSE
```

are all

```
TRUE
```

In boolean algebra, we write

```
0 NAND 0 = 1
0 NAND 1 = 1
1 NAND 0 = 1
1 NAND 1 = 0
```

The symbol for a two-input NAND gate is shown in Fig. 1.5*f*. It is similar to the AND gate, except for the dot at the output. This dot is the same as the dot at the output of the inverter and is used to represent negation. The NAND operation is written as the inverted AND of the arguments as shown in the truth table below.

| Inputs | | Output |
|---|---|---|
| A | B | $\overline{A \cdot B}$ |
| 0 | 0 | 1 |
| 0 | 1 | 1 |
| 1 | 0 | 1 |
| 1 | 1 | 0 |

## NOR Operation

This operation is formed by negating the OR operation with a NOT. NOR is a contraction of NOT and OR. In the OR operation,

```
FALSE OR FALSE
```

is

```
FALSE
```

while

```
FALSE OR TRUE
TRUE OR FALSE
TRUE OR TRUE
```

are all

```
TRUE
```

Negating the OR with a NOT produces opposite results.

```
FALSE NOR FALSE
```

is

```
TRUE
```

while

```
FALSE NOR TRUE
TRUE NOR FALSE
TRUE NOR TRUE
```

are all

```
FALSE
```

In boolean algebra, we write

```
0 NOR 0 = 1
0 NOR 1 = 0
1 NOR 0 = 0
1 NOR 1 = 0
```

The symbol for a two-input NOR gate appears in Fig. 1.5*g*. The NOR gate is similar to the OR gate except that it has an inversion dot at the output. The NOR operation is written as the inverted OR of the two arguments as shown in the following truth table.

| Input | | Output |
| A | B | $\overline{A + B}$ |
| --- | --- | --- |
| 0 | 0 | 1 |
| 0 | 1 | 0 |
| 1 | 0 | 0 |
| 1 | 1 | 0 |

## Exclusive OR Operation

This operation differs from an OR in that the operation has a true result if only one of the inputs is true. If all inputs are false or more than one input is true, then the output is false.

```
FALSE EXCLUSIVE OR FALSE
TRUE EXCLUSIVE OR TRUE
```

are

```
FALSE
```

while

```
TRUE EXCLUSIVE OR FALSE
FALSE EXCLUSIVE OR TRUE
```

are

```
TRUE
```

In boolean algebra, we write

```
0 EXCLUSIVE OR 0 = 0
0 EXCLUSIVE OR 1 = 1
1 EXCLUSIVE OR 0 = 1
1 EXCLUSIVE OR 1 = 0
```

The symbol for EXCLUSIVE OR is the symbol for OR with a circle around it. The symbol for a two-input EXCLUSIVE OR gate is shown in Fig. 1.5$h$. It is similar to the symbol for that of the two-input OR gate. An extra line is added on the input to show that this gate is exclusive. The truth table is shown as follows:

| Inputs | | Output |
|---|---|---|
| A | B | A + B |
| 0 | 0 | 0 |
| 0 | 1 | 1 |
| 1 | 0 | 1 |
| 1 | 1 | 0 |

## Exclusive NOR Operation

This operation differs from a NOR gate in that the operation has a true result if the inputs match each other.

```
FALSE EXCLUSIVE NOR FALSE
TRUE EXCLUSIVE NOR TRUE
```

are

```
FALSE
```

In boolean algebra, we write

```
0 EXCLUSIVE NOR 0 = 1
0 EXCLUSIVE NOR 1 = 0
1 EXCLUSIVE NOR 0 = 0
1 EXCLUSIVE NOR 1 = 1
```

The symbol for the EXCLUSIVE NOR operation is shown as the inversion of the EXCLUSIVE OR of the arguments. The symbol for a two-input EXCLUSIVE NOR gate is shown in Fig. 1.5$i$. This symbol is similar to that of the two-input NOR gate. An extra line is added to the input to indicate that the operation is exclusive. EXCLUSIVE NOR gates are often used for making comparisons since the output is true if the inputs match. This is shown in the following truth table.

| Inputs | | Output |
| --- | --- | --- |
| A | B | $\overline{A + B}$ |
| 0 | 0 | 1 |
| 0 | 1 | 0 |
| 1 | 0 | 0 |
| 1 | 1 | 1 |

## Noninverting Buffer

This device takes an input and reproduces at the output, so in a noninventing buffer, FALSE IS FALSE and TRUE IS TRUE, just like a piece of wire. The need for a noninverting buffer is a condition found in logic circuitry. Logic gates can provide only a certain amount of current. When the output of the gate becomes overloaded, the signal is distorted and the difference between a 0 and a 1 may be difficult to detect.

Noninverting buffers act like repeaters; they take a 0 or 1 and amplify it so that the inputs of more gates can be driven with the signal. Noninverting buffers are usually built so that they can drive more inputs than normal gates.

The symbol for the noninverting buffer is the same as an inverter except there is no inversion dot on the output.

## Flip-Flops

Logic gates simply provide an output signal determined by any logical combination of inputs. The output state of a logic gate depends only on the current state of the gate's inputs. The circuits that are made from gates are formed using combinatorial logic.

In computers, there is a need to remember when an event happens so that if another related event happens, this will cause a third event to occur. A logic device that remembers events includes the circuits called flip-flops. The output of a flip-flop may be either a 0 or a 1 and it does not depend on what the current inputs are. The output of a flip-flop can be either set (logic 1) or cleared (logic 0) and it will remain that way until changed.

There are different types of flip-flops. Each type is able to remember events, with the main difference being how the output is set or cleared. These flip-flops include RS (reset-set), D, and JK.

## RS Flip-Flops

This is the simplest type of flip-flop. The logic symbol is shown in Fig. 1.6a. Normally, both the S and R inputs are at 0. When a 1 is applied to the S input, the flip-flop is set and the Q output goes to a 1 state. The Q output remains in the 1 state even after the 1 applied to the S input is removed. The flip-flop is reset by applying a 1 to the R input; this causes the Q output to go to the 0 state. You are not allowed to apply 1 states to both the S and R inputs at the same time since the results of doing this are not defined.

The flip-flop has a second output, marked $\overline{Q}$. This output has a negation dot and is called the INVERTED Q, Q-BAR, or NOT Q output. It always has an opposite state to that of the Q output.

An RS flip-flop can be built with two NOR gates as shown in Fig. 1.6b. If both the S and R inputs are in the 0 state and the flip-flop is in the reset state, then the Q output is in a 0 state. Then, both inputs to the top NOR gate are in a 0 state, so the output of the top NOR gate is

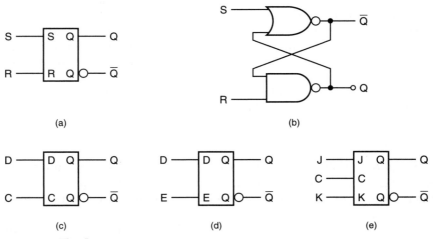

**Figure 1.6**   Flip-flops.

in the 1 state. This is applied to one of the inputs of the bottom NOR gates. Since the input of the bottom NOR gate is 1, the output of that gate is in the 0 state. This is one stable state for the RS flip-flop and as long as both the S and R inputs are in the 0 state, the flip-flop will remain in the reset state.

If the RS flip-flop is in the set state, then the Q output will be in a 1 state. This is the other stable state of the flip-flop.

When the flip-flop is in the reset state, the $\overline{Q}$ output is in the 0 state and the Q output is in the 1 state. If a 1 is applied to the R input, nothing changes since one input to the lower NOR gate was already in the 1 state. The output of the lower NOR gate is 0 whether one or both inputs is a 1. But, if we apply a 1 to the S input, the output of the lower NOR gate changes from a 1 to 0. This causes the output of the lower NOR gate to change from a 0 to 1 and the flip-flop is set. Removing the 1 from the S input does not change the outputs since the 1 at the output of the lower NOR gate holds the 0 at the output of the upper NOR gate. The state of the flip-flop has switched from reset to set.

The set flip-flop is cleared by applying a 1 to the R input. A reaction takes place similar to setting the flip-flop, except the two NOR gates are interchanged. The sequence of events then causes the flip-flop to switch back to the reset state.

Since Q and $\overline{Q}$ must have opposite values, the flip-flop must be either set or reset. The input that is last returned to a 0 will determine which state the flip-flop is left in.

## D Flip-Flop

This type of flip-flop has the same outputs as the RS flip-flop but the inputs are different. There are two types of D flip-flops; the positive-edge-triggered D and the transparent D.

The symbol for a positive-edge-triggered D flip-flop is shown in Fig. 1.6c. The Q and $\overline{Q}$ outputs are like the RS flip-flop but the inputs are different. The D input is the DATA input and the C input is the CLOCK input.

Edge-triggered flip-flops function from transitions on the C input. The Q output takes on the same state as that applied to the D input at the time that the signal applied to the C input changes from 0 to 1. After the 0 to 1 transition, the Q output will not change, even if the signal applied to the D input changes. The Q output will not change until the next 0 to 1 transition on the C input, when it will again take on the same state present at the D input.

A transparent-D flip-flop is shown in Fig. 1.6d. It has a D input for data and an E input for enable. When a 1 is applied to the E input, the Q output will take on the same state as the D input. If the signal on the

D input changes while a 1 is applied to the E input, the Q output will follow the change. If the signal on the E input is changed to a 0, the Q output will hold its state and not follow the level on the D input.

Note that, as long as the E input has a 1 on it, the flip-flop is transparent and passes along the state of the D input to the Q output. When the E input has a 0 applied to it, the flip-flop is not transparent and the Q output has the same state as the D input had before the E input was changed from 1 to 0.

## JK Flip-Flop

This type of flip-flop has three inputs along with Q and $\overline{Q}$ outputs. Fig. 1-6e shows the symbol for the JK flip-flop. The three inputs are J, K, and C for clock. The JK flip-flops are edge-triggered, like edge-triggered D flip-flops. Both positive and negative edge-triggered JK flip-flops are used.

The J and K inputs specify what the flip-flop will do when the appropriate transition is applied to the C input. If both J and K have zeroes applied to them when the transition occurs, the flip-flop does not change state, whether it is set or reset. If 1 is applied to J and O to K when the transition occurs, the flip-flop will be set. If 1 is applied to K and O to J when the transition occurs, the flip-flop will be reset.

If 1 is applied to both J and K when the transition on the clock input occurs, the flip-flop will toggle. That means if it was set before the transition, it will be reset. If the flip-flop was reset before the transition, it will be set.

## Digital Circuits

In an actual system, some physical quantity is used to represent the logic ones and zeroes. In electrical systems, this quantity may be a voltage or current, or it might be a magnetic spot on a disk or tape. Mechanical systems may use air or water pressures.

## TTL Logic Levels

TTL stands for *transistor-transistor logic,* a popular family of integrated logic circuits. TTL circuits were introduced in the late 1960s for military and space systems. Commercial products shortly followed. TTL operates on five volts. This means that the power supply that powers the circuitry must supply five volts.

We need two binary-valued signals: one voltage level will represent logic 0 and the other, logic 1. In TTL circuits and other logic families, there is a range of allowable voltage levels.

In the TTL family the low logic level is defined as a voltage between 0.0 and 0.8 volts and the high logic level is defined as a voltage between 2.0 and 5.0 volts. The area between 0.8 and 2.0 volts is not defined and voltages in this region are not allowed except for voltage transitions, when a signal is changing from high to low or low to high. When a logic gate has this undefined voltage applied to one of the inputs for a longer period of time, the output of the gate cannot be predicted. Voltages below 0.0 or above 5.0 volts should not be applied to TTL circuits. Some improved TTL families will not be harmed with slightly higher or lower voltages, but these voltages should not be applied in normal practice.

### Input and Output Currents

Logic gates have limits to the current that can be applied to their outputs. Each gate input must have a certain amount of current at the specified voltages. Each logic gate output must be able to supply a certain amount of current at the specified voltages.

There are several subfamilies in the TTL family. Besides the standard TTL, there are the low-power and high-speed TTL subfamilies. Schottky and low-power Schottky logic families are also considered as TTL. A numbering system indicates which subfamily a part is from as well as other characteristics. The basic series starts with a package containing four 2-input NAND gates, numbered as 7400 and called a *quad 2-input NAND*. The low-power version is the 74L00; the high-speed version is the 74H00; the high-speed version is the 74H00; the Schottky version is the 74S00; the low-power Schottky version is the 74LS00; the advanced Schottky version is the 74AS00; and the advanced, low-powered Schottky version is the 74ALS00. Each of these subfamilies has different input current requirements and output drive capabilities.

When you control a TTL input to a low logic level, you need to consume or sink current out of it. If you control a TTL input to a high logic level, you need to supply or source current into it. The amount of cur-

**TABLE 1.1    Input Current Levels for Digital Logic Families**

| | Input current | |
|---|---|---|
| | Maximum High-level (microamps) | Maximum Low-level (milliamps) |
| Standard 7400 | 40 | 1.6 |
| High speed 74H | 50 | 2.0 |
| Low power 74L type 1 | 10 | 0.18 |
| type 2 | 20 | 0.8 |
| Low-power Schottky 74LS | 20 | 0.4 |
| Schottky 74S | 50 | 2.0 |

TABLE 1.2    Output Current Levels for Digital Logic Families

| | Output current | |
| | Maximum High-level (microamps) | Maximum Low-level (milliamps) |
|---|---|---|
| Standard 7400 | 400 | 16 |
| High speed 74H | 500 | 20 |
| Low power 74L | 100 | 2 |
| Low-power Schottky 74LS | 400 | 4 |
| Schottky 74S | 1000 | 20 |

rent needed to sink or source depends on the subfamily of the logic circuit. Table 1.1 lists the high- and low-level input currents for the different families and Table 1.2 shows the different output drive capabilities.

Most of the logic family gates can drive ten inputs from its own subfamily. The low-power subfamily can drive eleven. Gates from different families can be mixed, as long as the gate output currents match. Note that a low-power output can only drive one Schottky input.

Many interfacing circuits are not fabricated with TTL technology, but the TTL voltage levels are popular and many of these circuits have been designed to be compatible with TTL levels. Sometimes this compatibility means only that the outputs can drive one and only one low-power TTL input.

## Logic Polarity

Besides defining the two signal levels used to represent logic levels, we need to define which level to represent a logic 0 and a logic 1. We could use the lower voltage level (0 to 0.8 volts) to represent logic 0 and the high voltage level (2.0 to 5.0 volts) to represent logic 1. This is called *positive-true logic* since the more positive voltage represents the logic 1 or TRUE state.

The lower voltage level could be used to represent logic 1 and the higher voltage level as logic 0. This is called *negative-true logic*. The more negative voltage represents the logic 1 or TRUE state.

In most device data sheets, the truth table uses Hs and Ls instead of zeros and ones. H and L represent the actual voltage levels instead of just the logic states. An H stands for the high-voltage level (2.0 to 5.0 volts) and an L stands for a low-voltage level (0.0 to 0.8 volts). The truth table specifies the output of the gate depending on the inputs. It does not specify if we are using positive or negative-true logic. We could interpret this type of truth table either way. An example of this type of truth table is shown as follows for a two-input NAND gate:

| Inputs | | Output | |
|---|---|---|---|
| A | B | C | |
| L | L | H | H = High-level voltage |
| L | H | H | L = Low-level voltage |
| H | L | H | |
| H | H | L | |

If we call this part a positive-true NAND gate, then all the Ls in the truth table are interpreted as zeroes and all the Hs are interpreted as ones. This converts the above truth table to the standard table for a two input NAND gate.

In an interface, we have a set of signals. Some may be positive-true and others will be negative-true. If we have the flexibility to use logic gates as either positive or negative-true devices we reduce a lot of inversion steps that would be necessary to make every signal positive-true or negative-true. This reinterpretation does not change how the part functions; it makes it easier for you to trace the logic. For example, if you want to produce a signal that is TRUE when the equation A OR B is true, you must use a positive-true OR gate. If the negative-true signals A or B are available however, A NAND B is equivalent, as we have shown in the truth table.

We could also say that we will interpret the inputs as negative-true and output as positive-true. That means that the inputs are now called $\overline{A}$ and $\overline{B}$ instead of A and B. The overscore means that the signals are negative-true. With this interpretation, we get the following truth table. This is the truth table of an OR gate, because the output is a logic 1 (high voltage) if either of the inputs is a logic 1 (low voltage).

| $\overline{A}$ | $\overline{B}$ | $\overline{Y}$ |
|---|---|---|
| 1 | 1 | 1 |
| 1 | 0 | 1 |
| 0 | 1 | 1 |
| 0 | 0 | 0 |

By simply reinterpreting the voltage truth table, we now have OR gates with negative-true inputs and a positive-true output. We could also place inversion bubbles on the inputs. These would remind us that the inputs are negative-true, that a low-voltage signal represents a logic 1.

### Demorgan's Theorems

These are formal theorems that simplify logic transformations. The first DeMorgan theorem states:

$$(\overline{AB}) = \overline{A} + \overline{B}$$

This equation says that a positive-true NAND gate is equivalent to an OR gate with negative-true inputs. That is what we showed above.

$$(\overline{A + B}) = \overline{A} + \overline{B}$$

This second equation says that a positive-true NOR gate is equivalent to an AND gate with negative-true inputs.

| $\overline{A}$ | $\overline{B}$ | $\overline{Y}$ |
|---|---|---|
| 1 | 1 | 1 |
| 1 | 0 | 0 |
| 0 | 1 | 0 |
| 0 | 0 | 0 |

By interpreting the TTL voltage levels with negative-true logic, the TTL NOR gate becomes an inverted-input NAND gate with a negative-true output.

## TTL Output Circuits

Logic circuits provide TTL-compatible signals with the following levels;

1. A low level between 0.0 and 0.8 volts.
2. A high level between 2.0 and 5.0 volts.

A circuit that is used to supply these levels is shown in Fig. 1.7a. This is called a *totem-pole output structure*. The two transistors are tied together forming a stack or totem pole. If the bottom transistor is on, current will flow from the output terminal to ground through that transistor, pulling the terminal to ground potential. If the top transistor is on, current can flow from the 5-volt power supply to the output terminal, pulling the output terminal toward the 5-volt level.

In a normal totem-pole output, one of the transistors will be on and there will be either a high- or low-voltage level at the output pin. When the circuit is switching from one level to another, both transistors are connecting for a short time. The 50-ohm resistor will limit the current from the +5 volt supply, so the circuit will not be damaged.

If the output terminals from two totem-pole devices are connected, (Fig. 1.7b) one of the totem-pole outputs may be in the high-voltage state and the other may be at the low-voltage state. This allows a large amount of current to flow through the top transistor of one output and the bottom transistor of the other as long as these transistors are on. The 50-ohm resistor will not prevent damage for these longer periods of time.

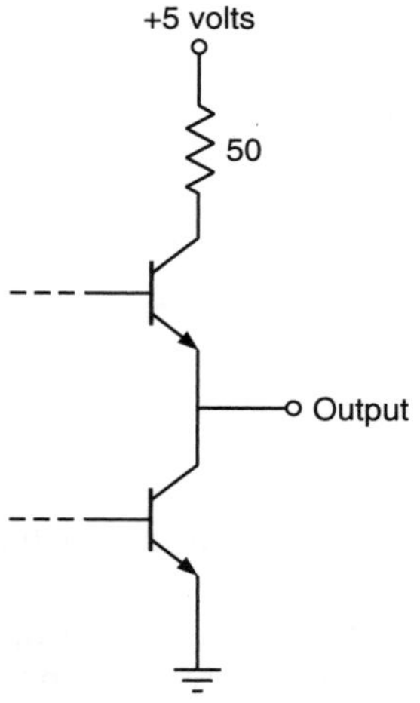

**Figure 1.7a**  TTL totem-pole output circuit.

When it is necessary to connect more than one output together, alternative output configurations like the open-collector and three-state output are used.

An open-collector circuit as shown in Fig. 1.7c does not have the top transistor and 50-ohm resistor like the totem-pole circuit. Only the bottom transistor is used and it can only supply a low TTL signal. When this transistor is off, the output terminal is at the supply voltage. An external resistor is used to clamp or pull the output to the supply voltage. This resistor is called the *pull-up resistor* and it limits the current flowing in the output terminal when the transistor is turned on to the

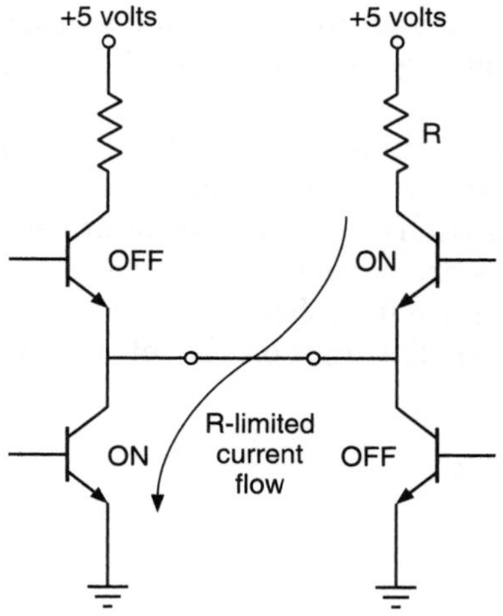

**Figure 1.7b**  Two totem-pole devices connected together.

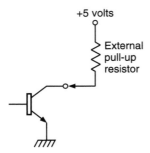

+5 volts

External
pull-up
resistor

**Figure 1.7c** TTL open collector output circuit.

limits specified for the device. Several open-collector outputs can be connected together with a single pull-up resistor.

The disadvantage of open collector outputs is that the switching times from low to high are slower than the totem-pole outputs, since the pull-up resistor has a higher value than 590 ohms. The smaller current supplied by the larger pull-up resistor cannot change the output voltage as fast.

Another output configuration is the three-state output. It is similar to the totem pole except that a special input is used to switch both transistors off. If both transistors are off, no current will flow into or out of the output terminal. The output stage becomes disconnected and acts like an open-circuit.

Three-state outputs can be connected together, but only one output stage is allowed to change at any one time. If two or more outputs are allowed to change, the problem of high currents occurs.

## Number Systems

Computers are involved in the computation, manipulation, and storage of large quantities of numeric data. This is generally done with some type of binary number system.

The decimal number system is very familiar to us and we use it every day. Computers use some type of switch to count, since the switch must be open or closed; a single switch or circuit can count from 0 to 1. To count any higher, more circuits are needed.

In a decimal number like 345, we recognize it as three hundred forty-five. There are three digits in this number. The digit on the left is multiplied by one hundred.

$$3 \times 100 = 300$$

The next digit is multiplied by ten

$$4 \times 10 = 40$$

and the next digit is multiplied by one.

$$5 \times 1 = 5$$

These are summed to obtain the result.

The position of the digit provides a weight to that digit. The right-hand digit has a weight of 1 ($10^0$, the next to the left has a weight of 10 ($10^1$) and the next 100 ($10^2$).

In the decimal system, the base is 10. So the right-hand position has a weight of 1, which is 100 raised to the zero power. The next position to the left has a weight of 10, which is 10 raised to the first power. The third position has a weight of 100 which is 10 raised to the second power.

In the binary number system, the base is 2. The right-hand position weight is 1, like the decimal system. The right-hand position for any base has a weight of 1 since any number raised to the 0 power is 1. The next position to the left has a weight of 2, which is 2 raised to the first power. The next position has a weight of 4, then 8, and so on. Each binary digit is called a *bit,* which is a contraction of *binary digit.*

In a binary number like 10010, there are five digits in the number, so the weight of the leftmost digit is 2 raised to the fourth power, or 16. The 0 power starts at the rightmost position and to determine the power of a position, subtract 1 from the position. There is a 1 in this position, so multiply 16 by 1.

There is a 0 in the next position so we multiply this by 2 raised to the third power, or 8. Since this is 0, we do not need to add it to 16.

There is a 0 in the next position. Multiply this by 2 raised to the second power, or 4. Since this is 0, we do not need to add it to the sum.

The next position has a 1, multiply this by 2 raised to the first power, or 2. Add 2 to 16 to get 18.

The right position has a 0, multiply this by 1. Since this is 0, it does not add anything to the sum and the converted number is 18.

There are two other number bases that are easier to use: the octal (base 8) and hexadecimal (base 16) number systems.

If you break up a decimal number three digits at a time, we are working with thousands. If we break up a binary number 3 bits at a time, we are working with eights which is the octal number system.

The octal numerals are 0 through 7. Then 3 bits will represent the numbers 0 through 7. The octal numbers act like a shorthand notation for binary numbers.

A binary number like 110010 can be written as 62 in octal. We can convert this number to decimal by multiplying 6 (decimal value of 110) by 8 to get 48 and adding 2 (decimal value of 010) to get 50. This is much faster than converting each bit.

Since many computers deal with 8-bit quantities, octal notation is not always best. It has been used in some 12-bit machines. Eight bits is two and two-thirds octal digits. A common number base that is used with microcomputers is 16, called *hexadecimal*. This represents an 8-bit byte as two hexadecimal digits, called *hex* for short.

Base 16 requires 16 numerals, 0–9 plus 6 numerals more. The 6 extra numerals are borrowed from the first 6 letters of the alphabet. Thus, we use the 0–9 and *A–F. A* is worth ten, *B* eleven, *C* twelve and so on until F which is worth fifteen. Table 1.3 lists the first 31 equivalents for decimal, binary and hex.

A binary number like 110010 converts to 32 hex. The 3 is multiplied by 16 raised to the first power

$$16^1 \times 3 = 16 \times 3 = 48$$

**TABLE 1.3    Number Systems**

| Decimal | Binary | Hexadecimal |
|---|---|---|
| 0 | 0 0000 | 00 |
| 1 | 0 0001 | 01 |
| 2 | 0 0010 | 02 |
| 3 | 0 0011 | 03 |
| 4 | 0 0100 | 04 |
| 5 | 0 0101 | 05 |
| 6 | 0 0110 | 06 |
| 7 | 0 0111 | 07 |
| 8 | 0 1000 | 08 |
| 9 | 0 1001 | 09 |
| 10 | 0 1010 | 0A |
| 11 | 0 1011 | 0B |
| 12 | 0 1100 | 0C |
| 13 | 0 1101 | 0D |
| 14 | 0 1110 | 0E |
| 15 | 0 1111 | 0F |
| 16 | 1 0000 | 10 |
| 17 | 1 0001 | 11 |
| 18 | 1 0010 | 12 |
| 19 | 1 0011 | 13 |
| 20 | 1 0100 | 14 |
| 21 | 1 0101 | 15 |
| 22 | 1 0110 | 16 |
| 23 | 1 0111 | 17 |
| 24 | 1 1000 | 18 |
| 25 | 1 1001 | 19 |
| 26 | 1 1010 | 1A |
| 27 | 1 1011 | 1B |
| 28 | 1 1100 | 1C |
| 29 | 1 1101 | 1D |
| 30 | 1 1110 | 1E |
| 31 | 1 1111 | 1F |

Then

$$16^0 \times 2 = 1 \times 2 = 2$$

Adding these we get 50. So, the number 50 converts to the following:

| Decimal | Binary | Octal | Hexadecimal |
|---------|--------|-------|-------------|
| 50 | 110010 | 62 | 32 |

If we want to check an operation in one of these number systems, we can convert the number to decimal, perform the arithmetic, and then convert back. There are also calculators that operate with these different number bases. The Texas Instruments (TI Programmer) and Hewlett-Packard (HP-16C) are examples. There are also conversion programs available in BASIC and other languages that can convert from one number base to another.

Most interfaces deal with the transfer of information between devices, and numbers are just one type of information. Since computers operate with binary information, printable characters need to be coded into binary format. This is done with character codes.

## Character Codes

Codes are used to replace written characters in many different applications. One example of a communications code includes the Morse code for the telegraph. This involves the transmission of two symbols, dots and dashes. Each letter of the English alphabet and each Arabic numeral has a unique string of dots and dashes. Morse code allows text messages to be sent from one telegraph station to another. This code was developed between 1832 and 1838.

Attempts were made at developing mechanical devices for transmitting and receiving Morse code messages, Morse code is a variable-length code. Some characters use two symbols and some three. Variable-length codes are difficult to mechanize.

A constant-length code was developed by Baudot in 1874. In the Baudot code, each character has five symbols. The symbols can be considered as binary, being dots and dashes. Baudot code is a five-bit code and was used in the French telegraph system in 1877.

By 1900 Murray had refined the Baudot code, which was called the International Telegraph Alphabet Number 2. The original Baudot code was Number 1.

A five-bit code can represent 32 different characters. This is not enough to represent all the letters of the alphabet plus the Arabic numerals. So, the Baudot and Murray codes have two special characters for entering letters and figures. After typing a *letters* character, all subsequent characters are interpreted as letters of the alphabet. After typing a *figures* character, all of the following characters are interpreted as numerals and punctuation marks.

These are known as *shift codes* since they cause a shift between two different sets. Shift codes are important, because if a shift code is lost or garbled in transmission, all of the following codes are wrong until another shift code occurs.

In a 5-bit code only capital letters can be represented, so there was a need for a better character code. Two competing codes were developed, the American National Standards Institute (ANSI) developed the American Standard Code for Information Interchange (ASCII) also known as ANSI standard X3.4-1977. This is a 7-bit code which is a worldwide standard. It can represent all of the capital and lowercase letters, numerals, and common punctuation marks. There are also special control codes like *carriage return* and *line feed* along with seven shift codes.

IBM developed its own character set called the Extended Binary Coded Decimal Interchange Code (EBCDIC). This is an 8-bit code introduced with IBM's 360 computer. EBCDIC has one more bit than ASCII, so it could represent twice as many characters; but not all of the EBCDIC codes are used.

## ASCII

The ASCII code is set up as eight columns of sixteen characters each, for a total of 128 characters. Four columns are used for the alphabet. This includes all the letters (upper- and lowercase) and a few punctuation marks. Some computer and peripheral manufacturers modify the punctuation mark definitions.

Two columns are used for numbers, the rest of the punctuation marks, and the space. There is a wide variation in punctuation marks among different countries. The dollar sign is used in North America, while many other countries have their own monetary denominations. International codes use an international monetary symbol called a scarab.

## Control-Characters

Two columns are used for the control characters. These characters do not cause a mark to be placed on the paper or screen. They are designed to control the operation of the receiving device. For example, a carriage return moves the printing position to the first column of the current line.

Many manufacturers have modified the standard definitions of the control characters because they had a function in their device that needed a special code to activate it. It is always best to check the operations manual for a peripheral device whenever you are first interfacing to it.

The ASCII control codes are divided into five groups:

1. Logical communication control

2. Physical communication

3. Device control

4. Field separation

5. Set changing

## Logical Communication Control

These control characters are designed to control the communication channel and label storage media. The 10 logical control characters are normally used only for communications that are block-oriented. They are as follows:

1. *SOH (Start of Header).*   Indicates that an information header follows (the header provides information about the message, which is to follow).

2. *STX (Start of Text).*   Is used to separate the head from the information block.

3. *ETX (End of Text).*   Indicates the last character in a text message block.

4. *EOT (End of Transmission).*   Indicates the last character to be transmitted in the message block.

5. *ENQ (Enquiry).*   Asks for a return identification message or a return-status message.

6. *ACK (Acknowledge).*   Answers yes to an inquiry.

7. *DLE (Data Link Escape).*   Provides a set of communications control characters to be for an alternate set of character definitions.

8. *NAK (No Acknowledge).*   Answers no to an inquiry.

9. *SYN (Synchronous Idle).*   Used for synchronous data communications; used to synchronize the receiver to the sender and is sent when there are no messages to send.

10. *ETB (End of Transmission Block).*   Separates blocks of information in a message block.

Logical Communication Control characters can cause problems when binary data is sent over the same communications link used for ASCII characters. If a modem is used to convert the computer signals so they may be transmitted over telephone lines, a character like EOT can stop the transmission.

### Physical Communication Control

The following four control characters are used for communicating information on the communications channel or recording medium.

1. *NUL (Null).*   Is used to hold a channel open or make space in stored data blocks (DEL can be used in a similar way).

2. *CAN (Cancel).*   Indicates that the receiver should ignore everything received before the reception of the CAN character.

3. *EM (End of Medium).*   Is used in data storage to tell the device that no characters are to be stored beyond the point where the EM character exists.

4. *SUB (Substitute).*   Is substituted for other characters when there is a problem in recognizing the original character which may have been garbled in transmission and received in error.

### Device Control

The device control characters are typically used to move the current character position. The eleven device control characters are as follows:

1. *BEL (Bell).*   Is used to cause an audible signal to be generated.

2. *BS (Backspace).*   Causes the current character position to move back one position.

3. *HT (Horizontal Tab).*   Causes the current character position to move to the next predetermined position.

4. *LF (Line Feed).*   Causes the current character position to move down one line.

5. *VT (Vertical Tab).*   Moves the current position to the same column on the next predetermined line; some terminals move the current active position to the first column of the next predetermined line.

6. *FF (Form Feed).*   Causes a form to eject and places the active character position at the beginning of the next form.

7. *CR (Carriage Return).*   Moves the character position to the beginning of the current line.

8. *DC1–DC4 (Device Controls).* The functions of the device control characters are not specified by the ASCII standard; a common use of DC1 and DC3 is starting and stopping transmissions in the XON/XOFF protocol.

## Field Separators

These four control characters are used to indicate separate fields of data. The following four separators are used:

1. FS (File Separator)
2. GS (Group Separator)
3. RS (Record Separator)
4. US (Unit Separator)

Field Separators are not often used in microcomputer systems.

## Set-Changing Control

The three set-changing control characters are used to alert a pierpheral that the ASCII characters are about to take on different definitions. These can include Greek letters for scientific papers, math symbols, legal characters, and foreign characters. The following set-changing control characters allow other character sets to be selected and activated:

1. ESC (Escape) is placed at the beginning of a string of characters in an escape sequence that can alter the way a peripheral will interpret incoming characters. Escape sequences can be used to select foreign language or other special character sets. Escape sequences are also used for extended control functions such as cursor positioning.

2. SO (Shift Out) causes a selected alternate character set to become active. The escape sequence only designates an alternate character set but SO activates it.

3. SI (Shift In) causes the peripheral to return to the standard ASCII character set from an SO.

## ASCII Variations

As the world becomes smaller, ASCII is no longer sufficient for computing on a worldwide scale and other extended codes are needed. As a 7-bit code, ASCII has space for 128 characters ($2^7$). In 1977, ASCII was certified by ANSI (American National Standards Institute), and the

International Standards Organization (ISO) adopted an almost identical code known as ISO 646.

Since ASCII codes are 7 bits long, ASCII can only represent 128 possible characters. Latin1, known as the European ASCII, adds a bit, providing for 256 characters. A standard called Unicode is 16 bits long, providing for 65,536 characters. The characters in another ISO standard numbered 10646 are 4 bytes (32 bits) long. This standard could use compaction methods that would let you send only 1, 2, or 3 bytes when the initial byte or bytes are redundant.

### Latin1

ISO later added a 1-bit extension to the 646 standard which was called Latin1. It provided space for another 128 characters ($2^8 = 256$). The Latin1 8-bit code includes letters used by European languages such as French, German, and Spanish. ASCII is often used to refer to an 8-bit code, but this is not technically accurate; true ASCII is a 7-bit code. Countries in Africa and the Near and Far East adopted ISO 646 to their native character set, or developed similar standards under groups such as the European Computer Manufacturers Association (ECMA) and the Japanese Industrial Standards Committee. Different standards evolved to represent the thousands of characters in Chinese, Japanese, and Korean writing systems. Some hardware and software manufacturers also developed their own standards. The use of these different character-encoding standards became a problem.

### ISO 10646

In 1983, ISO began work on a new standard for character encoding, ISO 10646. ISO 10646's original goal called for a 2-byte (16-bit) character set, with room for 65,536 characters. The new 16-bit standard would also be compatible with the other international standards. The first 128 characters would be standard ASCII, with other character sets following this.

One problem was that each of the existing international standards included control codes. These are used to control peripheral equipment using messages such as *carriage return* or *formfeed*. Much of the existing communication equipment checks for those control codes.

Removing the control codes would make the new code incompatible with the codes already in use. Setting aside space for the characters that could be interpreted as control codes took up 40 percent of the 65,536 available spaces, even before any characters had been assigned.

Another problem had to do with the characters in the Chinese, Japanese, and Korean writing systems. These have a great number and variety of characters. Although these languages use alphabetic systems, the largest number of characters are *pictographic* (meaning picture writing) or *ideographic* (meaning concept writing). Both of these are also referred to as *logographic* (word writing) since each character represents a word.

Most Japanese and Korean characters are derived from Chinese and are referred to as *Han* characters from the Chinese Han dynasty. In many cases, these characters are similar and mean the same thing in all three scripts. To save space, the 10646 committee wanted to develop a unified Han character set, in which no character would appear more than once.

This would remove thousands of similar characters and provide the character sets of all nations in a single 2-byte code. China agreed to this scheme but Japan and Korea did not. So the committee ended up including all characters from each of the languages.

This resulted in a 4-byte (32-bit) code set, with room for 4 billion characters and codes. Sending the full four bytes for every character did add a lot of overhead to the communications. Instead of sending 1 byte for every character, we need to send 4; so it takes four times as long to send a file. But, since the first 3 bytes of any alphabet's assigned codes will be the same, you do not need to transmit them for each character. The letter *c* in ASCII is

```
01100011
```

In ISO 10646, it is similar, but with 3 bytes of 00100000 in front of it:

```
00100000 00100000 00100000 01100011
```

In the 8-bit code, 00100000 represents a space. All zeros are not used because 00000000 is a control code—nul—and it was decided that these codes would be retained from earlier codes. Other letters look like their ASCII counterparts, except for the same 24 bits in the three high-order bytes.

There are several compaction schemes that can be used for transmission. The sending modem can indicate to the receiving modem that the first three bytes of every character are 00100000. Then, the modems are essentially operating in 1-byte mode. This technique can be used for any language, since all characters in that part of the code would have the same first three bytes. However, this scheme complicates the transmission and can affect data integrity. The effort to develop a single, international character set was beginning to take several paths.

## Unicode

A code that was simpler and more consistent than ISO 10646 was needed. The Xerox Star Computer, which was the forerunner of the Macintosh, used a 16-bit multilingual code. A new standard, called Unicode, for unique, universal, and uniform character encoding, was developed from this code. In 1991, a Unicode consortium was incorporated as Unicode, Inc., and as a result of this group's work Unicode 1.0 was released.

Unicode's design goals included the following. (The resulting code should be completed to eventually cover the full range of characters used in text creation. This includes alphabets with characters that are still evolving, as well as dead languages.)

1. Unicode's first spaces contain standard alphabetic characters from around the world. The lowest Unicode spaces are compatible with the current ASCII standard. The next block is for punctuation, mathematical operators, and symbols. Next, there is a block of spaces reserved for Chinese, Japanese, and Korean nonideographic alphabets and punctuation, and a large space for unified Han characters.

2. Each code represents a single character, unambiguously. A problem with reading a single character should not carry forward so that the characters following it becomes garbled. Every character encoded in the standard should be a real character as recognized by experts in linguistics. Textual data integrity should remain when conversion into or out of other character-encoding standards takes place. This means when an $a$ is transmitted the receiver must get an $a$.

3. Every character code should be the same length (16 bits) and each represents a character. There should be no control codes or embedded escape sequences.

Unicode reserves spaces for the initial control codes of ASCII, although these codes are not used in Unicode. Unicode distinguishes between a character's code and its glyph—what the symbol actually looks like. A character's glyph can change depending on the font use, but the essential shape remains the same.

Table 1.4 shows how the codes are assigned. The first 8192 spaces are used for the standard alphabetic characters, with some room for characters that may be added later. The next 4096 codes are for punctuation, mathematical operators, technical symbols, shapes, patterns, and dingbats. These are decorative characters that can represent religious symbols, smiling faces, chess pieces, and other symbols. These are followed by 4096 spaces reserved for Chinese, Japanese, and Korean alphabets and punctuation.

**TABLE 1.4    Character Space in Unicode**

| Code space | Character use |
|---|---|
| 65,025 to 65,536 | Compatibility area |
| 59,392 to 65,024 | User area |
| 16,384 to 59,391 | Chinese/Japanese/Korean ideographs<br>Unified Han characters<br>Future use |
| 8192 to 16,383 | Chinese/Japanese/Korean auxiliary<br>Alphabets and punctuation |
| 8192 to 12,287 | Symbols:<br>Punctuation, mathematical operators, technical symbols, dingbats |
| 0 to 8191 | Alphabets:<br>English, Latin1, European, Extended Latin, Phonetic, Greek,<br>Cyrillic, Armenian, Hebrew, Arabic, Ethiopian, Devanagari,<br>Bengali, Gurmukhi, Gujarati, Oriya, Tamil, Telugu, Kannada,<br>Malayalam, Sinhalese, Thai, Lao, Burmese, Khmer, Tibetan,<br>Mongolian, Georgian |

A large part of the code space is allocated for the unified Han characters. These 27,000 characters are specified by the Chinese National Standard GB 13000. There is also space for future expansion of other code sets.

Unicode has 5632 spaces in its private user area. This is for users to implement as needed under private agreements. There are also 495 spaces in a compatibility area to help developers convert to Unicode.

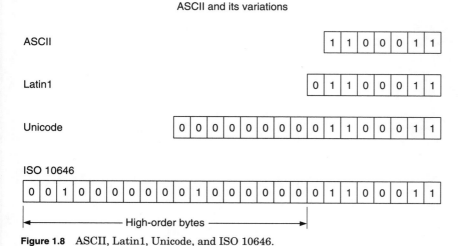

**Figure 1.8**   ASCII, Latin1, Unicode, and ISO 10646.

## Comparison of Unicode and ISO 10646

Although both standards are designed for multilingual character encoding, there are some major differences. ISO 10646 stores characters in 4 bytes, although compaction methods would allow 1, 2, or 3 bytes. Unicode characters are always 2 bytes (16 bits) long (Fig. 1.8). Unicode eliminates duplicate Han characters, but 10646 does not. ISO 10646 leaves spaces for all control codes from previous international code sets; this area accounts for 28,672 spaces.

ISO 10646 has codes for accented letters. Unicode also provides these codes, but it also has a code for each accent mark and builds compound letters by combining the accents with unaccented letters. There are also differences in the way these standards handle bidirectional text that goes from right to left, such as Hebrew and Arabic.

# Microprocessor Interfaces

## Microcomputers

In a microcomputer, the central processing unit (CPU) is fabricated on a single integrated circuit, and is called a *microprocessor*. A microcomputer uses other microcircuits, but the microprocessor is the most complex. The use of microprocessors meant that the computer manufacturer no longer had to design the CPU. It was a standard, off-the-shelf component.

As newer, more powerful microprocessors become available, they are quickly implemented into smaller, more powerful, low-cost microcomputers. The microprocessor provides a complete computer processor, with a standardized instruction set and standardized signals. The semiconductor manufacturers standardized on TTL signal levels.

Miniaturization of the central processing unit and other microcircuits allowed major reductions in power requirements. Microcomputers allow computing power into areas like automobiles, games, and appliances.

## Microprocessor Components

The four major components in a microprocessor are listed as follows:

1. A bank of registers for holding information
2. An *arithmetic logic unit* (ALU) for processing the information
3. A bus interface for moving information into and out of the microprocessor
4. Control logic for managing the operation of the microprocessor (The control logic instructs the bus interface to get an instruction.)

The microprocessor is connected to external memory by the bus. The microprocessor bus is the set of wires and connectors that carry the signals used by the microprocessor to move data between itself, memory, and I/O devices. Each microprocessor bus uses designated signals for accomplishing certain tasks for the devices connected to the bus. These signals must be general enough so they can meet the needs on a variety of input/output devices.

The external memory holds the instructions. When instructed to do so, the bus interface obtains an instruction from the external memory and gives it to the control logic. This is called an *instruction fetch*.

The instruction may require information in one of the registers to be processed by the ALU, and then returned to another register. There are other instructions that may cause information to be moved from

1. External memory to a register

2. A register to external memory

3. One register to another

4. One memory location to another

The control sequencer must issue signals to allow the operation. This is the *instruction execution*. After this instruction is executed, the next instruction is fetched.

Most of the early microprocessors used separate fetch and execute cycles. This means that an instruction is fetched, then executed, and then another instruction is fetched and executed. Some instructions may not need the services of the bus interface. These instructions may move data only between the ALU and register bank. When these instructions are being executed, the bus is free.

## Microprocessor Interfaces

The microprocessor bus carries a collection of signals that the microprocessor needs to perform its required functions. This depends on the particular processor. Buses cannot be extended for great distances since it takes a longer time for the signals to travel over longer conductors. If the distance is great enough, the time lag interferes with the bus signal timings and communications is lost. Most buses are less than a few feet long because of this.

Most peripheral devices are located at a greater distance than this and do not use the same collection of signals to communicate as microprocessors. The problem of distance and signal timing incompatibility between microprocessors and peripherals is solved with specialized circuitry between them that we call an *interface*.

## Interface Tasks

Interface circuits allow a diverse group of peripheral devices to interact with microprocessors. The interface may take the form of a circuit board which plugs into the processor bus. The circuit board connector which plugs into the bus allows the interface access to the microprocessor signals. At the other end of the board is a cable connector for the peripheral device. The interface may perform the following tasks:

- Change the microprocessor signal levels, voltage or current, into signal levels compatible with the peripheral device

- Change the signal durations on the microprocessor bus to speeds that are more compatible with the peripheral device

- Change the signal levels so that the peripheral cable may be used

- Change data formats, the digital coding, so the processor and peripheral are compatible

You can see that the overall task of the interface is to transform the signals to allow communication.

In a microcomputer, the interfaces are usually connected directly to a microprocessor bus. These microprocessor-based computers use the microprocessor bus as the main connection point for most of the other computer elements. The bus is used to carry signals between the three major parts of the system: the processor, memory, and the input/output (I/O) devices. The processor acts as the computational engine of the computer system. It handles the data processing tasks and calculations. Memory is needed to hold the software programs as well as the information that needs to be processed. The input/output devices are needed to move information *into* the system for processing and results *out* after processing.

The local microprocessor bus is also known as the *component-level bus*. This means that it originates at the pins of the microprocessor-integrated circuit and is routed to local components on the same circuit board. Since most microprocessors have limited signal-drive capabilities, a component-level bus is usually routed off the main or system board.

The microprocessor defines the component-level bus because it originates at the microprocessor. Each type of microprocessor uses its own blend of signals, which is designed to be optimum for the applications of the microprocessor. In most systems, until 1976, the clock was external to the microprocessor. Since 1976, the clock circuitry has been incorporated into the microprocessor chip itself. So recent products do not require this external clock, but they always require an external crystal or oscillator which is connected to the clock.

The microprocessor uses three buses:

1. A bidirectional *data bus* which is implemented with tristate logic devices to allow the use of a direct-memory-access controller, or other similar chips.

2. A monodirectional *address bus,* connected internally, within the microprocessor, to address pointers and the program counter. The address bus is also implemented in tristate logic.

3. A *control bus,* which carries the various synchronization signals to and from the microprocessor. Control lines are not necessarily tristate.

All the usual system components are connected to these three buses. The basic components are shown in Fig. 2.1. They include the ROM, the RAM, and the I/O chips.

The ROM is the *Read-Only Memory.* It stores the programs that the microprocessor needs to power-up. The RAM is the Random-Access Memory. It is a read-write MOS memory which stores temporary data and programs. The input-output chips are used for such functions as multiplexing the data bus for two or more input-output ports. These ports may be connected directly to input-output devices, or to device controllers, which may require the use of interface circuits.

The interface circuits or interface chips required to interface this basic system to the I/O devices will be connected to these buses, which include the microprocessor buses or special input-output buses.

Interfacing techniques are the methods required to connect this system to the various input-output devices. The basic interfacing techniques required to connect any microprocessor system to input-output devices are similar.

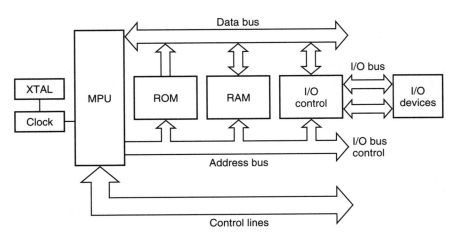

**Figure 2.1**   Typical microprocessor system.

At the level of the microprocessor itself, the logical and electrical interface required is similar. Many standard microprocessors of the same data width have essentially the same data bus and the same address bus. The main difference is the control bus. It is the specific characteristics of the control bus which make input-output interface chips compatible or incompatible from one microprocessor to the next. As an example of these basic interfacing characteristics, the interfacing characteristics for several early microprocessors are shown in Table 2.1.

## Microprocessor Control Signals

We have seen that the microprocessor uses three buses: a bidirectional data bus, a monodirectional address bus, and a control bus with the needed signals. The data bus is essentially identical for microproces-

**TABLE 2.1    Comparison of 8-bit Microprocessor Signals**

| Function | 8080 | 8085 | Z-80 | 6800 | 6502 |
|---|---|---|---|---|---|
| Address | A0-A15 | AD0-AD7 +ALF A8-A15 | A0-A15 | A0-A15 | AB0-AB15 |
| Data | D0-D7 | AD0-AD7 | D0-D7 | D0-D7 | DB0-DB7 |
| Control | HLDA | HLDA | BUSAK | BA&VMA | |
| | Hold | Hold | BUSRQ | Halt | RDY |
| | 02 | CLK | | 02 | 02 |
| | INT | INTR | INT | IRQ | IRQ |
| | INTE | | | | |
| | Wait | | | | |
| | Ready | Ready | Wait | | RDY |
| | Reset | Reset | Reset | Reset | Reset |
| | SYNC | | MI | | SYNC |
| | INTA | INTA | MI&IORQ | VMA | |
| | MEMR | RD&IO/M | RD&MEMRQ | R/W&02 | R/W&02 |
| | MEMW | WR&IO/M | WR&MEMRQ | R/W&02 | R/W&02 |
| | I/O RD | RD&IO/M* | RD&IORQ | R/W&02 | R/W&02 |
| | I/O WR | WR&IO/M* | WR&IORQ | R/W&02 | R/W&02 |
| | BUSEN | | | Halt | |
| | SSTB | | | | |
| | | RST 5.5–7.5 | | | |
| | | Trap | NM1 | NM1 | NM1 |
| | | Out | | | |
| | | SID | | | |
| | | SOD | | | |
| | | ALE | | | |
| | | | RFSH | | |
| | | | Halt | | |
| | | | | TSC | |
| | | | | DBE | |
| | | | | | SO |

sors with the same data width. It is a bidirectional bus, normally implemented in tristate logic. The address bus is a monodirectional bus, used to select memory or a device external to the microprocessor. The third bus, the control bus, is the most complex. It carries the microprocessor control signals (the interface signals). The control bus has four functions:

1. Memory synchronization

2. Input-output synchronization

3. Microprocessor scheduling—interrupts and DMA control

4. Utilities, including clock and reset

Memory and input-output synchronization are similar. A handshake procedure is used. In a read-operation, a ready status or signal is needed to indicate the availability of data. Data can then be transferred on the data bus. In some types of input-output devices, an acknowledge signal is generated to confirm the receipt of data. In a write operation, the availability of the external device is verified through a status bit or signal, and the data is then placed on the data bus. An acknowledge signal may also be generated by the device to confirm the receipt of data.

The use of an acknowledge signal or handshake is typical in an asynchronous procedure. In a synchronous procedure, all events take place in a specified period of time; so there is no need to acknowledge a transmission. In an asynchronous system, an acknowledge signal is needed to verify a transmission.

The use of synchronous versus asynchronous communication depends on a number of factors. A synchronous bus has the potential for higher speed and a lower number of control lines, but, it places speed requirements on the external devices. An asynchronous bus is more complex and requires more logic, but allows more flexibility for device speeds in the system.

## Microprocessor Bus Characteristics

The microprocessor component-level bus is made up of the three subbuses: data bus, address bus, and control bus. Each of these three subbuses has a critical task which is needed for the proper operation of the microprocessor.

All data entering or leaving the microprocessor does so over this bus, so a data bus is needed. This bus is used to move information to be processed into the microprocessor and move the processed information out of the microprocessor. The data bus has bidirectional data lines so data may flow either into or out of the processor, but only in one direction at a time. The direction that the information flows is controlled by the control bus.

Microprocessors can be characterized by the size of their data buses. If the data bus of a microprocessor is 8 bits wide, the microprocessor is known as an 8-bit microprocessor. The Intel 8080 and 8085, the Motorola 6800, 6801, and 6802, and the Zilog Z80 microprocessor are all 8-bit microprocessors since they have 8-bit data buses and internally they process information in 8-bit chunks.

The 32-bit chips include Motorola's 68020 and 68030 and Intel's 80386 and 80486. The Motorola 68000 series is used in the Apple Macintosh. The Macintosh IIfx, which was introduced in 1990, uses a 68030 running at 40 MHz. The Intel Pentium has a 64-bit data bus and a 32-bit address bus. There are also smaller microprocessor which have 4-bit data buses. These are often used in dedicated control applications.

The size of the data bus used by the microprocessor usually indicates the size of the data word the processor is designed to manipulate. An 8-bit data bus generally indicates that the microprocessor processes data 8 bits at a time.

Some microprocessors like the Motorola 6809 and Intel 8088 have 8-bit data buses but internally they are designed to work with 16-bit data chunks.

The reason for limiting the size of the data bus while the processor works with larger quantities internally is cost. The chips are less expensive to make.

### 8-Bit Microprocessors

Introduced in 1974, the 6800 was the first microprocessor to use a single 5-volt power supply. Earlier microprocessors needed two or three power-supply voltages for operation. The 6800 also has a simple bus structure, shown in Fig. 2.2 which makes it easier to visualize as a first example.

Table 2.2 lists the signals for the 6800 microprocessor along with the signals for several other microprocessors. The 6800 uses a relatively simple 40-pin package. Most of the other 8-bit processors also use 40-pin packages.

The bidirectional data bus is made up of D0 through D7, pins 33 through 26. The address bus uses lines A0 through A15 which are on pins 9 through 20 and 22 through 25. Two pins for used for ground connections: (1) the power supply ground, pin 1 and (2) the signal ground, pin 21. Power is supplied through the Vcc pin which is pin 8. Pins 35 and 38 are marked NC which means there is no connection to the microprocessor.

Table 2.2 also lists the signals for several other 8-bit microprocessors. While there is some similarity in many of the signals, other signals are unique to particular microprocessors.

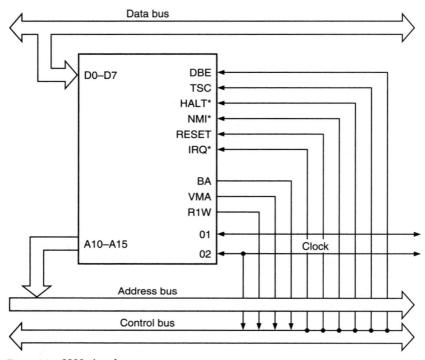

**Figure 2.2**   6800 signals.

## 86 Family Evolution

The Intel 86 family of microprocessors has evolved toward faster processing, simpler, lower-cost interface features, and compatibility with existing software. Tradeoffs have been made to achieve progress from one generation to the next since the introduction of the 8086 processor in 1978 (Table 2.3). The length of processor bus cycles is shorter and more functions have been placed on the chip with each new generation. This has released processor bus bandwidth for other uses. The introduction of burst cycles in the 486 is a factor in improved performance.

The interface system is simpler in some ways due to the following:

1. The address and data buses have been demultiplexed.

2. The internal clock rate is now the same (1×) frequency as the external clock input.

3. Address pipelining on the processor bus has been dropped.

4. The floating point, cache, and parity logic are now on the chip.

**TABLE 2.2   Control Signal Functions of Several 8-bit Microprocessors**

| Signal | Function |
|---|---|
| **8080** | |
| HLDA | Hold acknowledge |
| HOLD | Allows another device to gain control of bus |
| 02 | Phase 2 timing signal |
| INT | Interrupt request |
| INTE | Used interrupts |
| WAIT | Used to signal external circuits |
| READY | Used with WAIT to synchronize devices |
| RESET | Processor restart |
| SYNC | Used to start a new instruction |
| INTA | Interrupt acknowledge |
| MEMR | Memory-read—initiates memory-read cycle |
| MEMW | Memory-write |
| I/O RD | Input/output read |
| I/O WR | Input/output write |
| BUSEN | Bus enable |
| **8085** | |
| HOLD | Allows another device to take over the bus |
| HLDA | Hold acknowledge—the CPU received a HOLD request and relinquished the next clock cycle |
| CLK | Clock timing signal |
| INTR | Interrupt request, general-purpose interrupt |
| READY | CPU being reset |
| INTA | Interrupt acknowledge; used instead of $\overline{RD}$ during instruction cycle after INTR is accepted |
| RD | Read input/output or memory, perform a read operation |
| WR | Write input/output or memory |
| RST5.5 | Restart interrupts; same as INTR except it causes an internal RESTART to take place |
| RST6.5 | Same as above |
| RST7.5 | Same as above |
| TRAP | Trap interrupt; a nonmaskable RESTART interrupt; recognized at same time as INTR or RST 5.5–7.5 |
| RESET IN | Reset processor, program restarted |
| RESET OUT | Reset indication |
| SID | Serial input data line |
| SOD | Serial output data line |
| ALE | Address latch enable—enables address in on-chip latch |
| S0 | Memory write status |
| S1 | Memory read status |
| IO/M&S0 | I/O write |
| **Z-80** | |
| BUSAK | Bus acknowledge—output signal goes high; indicates when lines go high-impedance state |
| BUSRQ | Bus request—releases bus for another device |
| INT | Interrupt microprocessor |
| WAIT | Wait until next clock |
| RESET | Processor reset |
| M1 | Synchronizes transfers of information |
| IORQ | I/O request, used with M1 to request that an interrupt vector be applied to the data bus |

**TABLE 2.2     Control Signal Functions of Several 8-bit Microprocessors (*Continued*)**

| Signal | Function |
|---|---|
| **8080** | |
| MEMRQ | Memory request, used with instruction fetches |
| WR | Write, used for memory or I/O operation |
| RD | Read, used for memory or I/O operation |
| NMI | Nonmaskable interrupt—cannot be ignored by the processor |
| RFSH | Refresh signal for dynamic memory |
| HALT | Causes processor to complete execution of current instruction, then stop and give up control |
| **6800** | |
| HALT | Causes processor to wait |
| 02 | Phase 2 of clock |
| IRQ | Interrupt request line—can be ignored by processor |
| RESET | Starts 6800 from power-down |
| VMA | Valid memory address—high enables RAM |
| R/W | Read/write control—low causes memory read |
| NMI | Nonmaskable interrupt—cannot be ignored by processor |
| TSC | Three-state control—causes processor to release control of the address and R/W pins |
| DBE | Data bus enable—low forces data bus into high impedance mode |

**TABLE 2.3     86 Family of Microprocessors**

| Chip | Year | Bus size Internal | Bus size External | Transistors | Characteristics |
|---|---|---|---|---|---|
| 8086 | 1978 | 16 | 16 | 29K | 16-bit processor, with segmentation for protection |
| 8088 | 1979 | 16 | 8 | 29K | Same as 8086, with 8-bit processor bus |
| 80186 | 1982 | 16 | 16 | 56K | Same as 8086, with more on-chip functions |
| 80188 | 1982 | 16 | 8 | 56K | Same as 80186, with 8-bit processor bus |
| 80286 | 1982 | 16 | 16 | 130K | More segmentation protection, task switching, and greater speed |
| 386 DX | 1985 | 32 | 32 | 275K | Paging, 32-bit extensions, on-chip address translation, and greater speed |
| 386 SX | 1988 | 32 | 16 | 275K | Same as 386, with 16-bit processor bus |
| 486 | 1988 | 32 | 32 | 1200K | On-chip cache, floating-point unit, and greater speed |

The number of clocks per instruction has been reduced and improvements in address computation have made execution faster. In the 486 processor, the internal processing speed is greater due to the on-chip cache and floating point.

## Some History

The first microprocessor was the 4-bit 4004 which appeared in 1971. The 8-bit version was the 8008. The next Intel microprocessor was the 8-bit 8080 which was introduced in 1974. It was more of a general-purpose unit with its larger address space of 64 Kbytes and bus arbitration. The 8085 was introduced in 1976. It was software-compatible with the 8080 and allowed a simpler system.

The third-generation microprocessor was the 16-bit 8086 in 1978. This was the first in the Intel 86 family. The 8086 had an expanded memory address space, instruction set, and bus operations. It included address-space segmentation for protection against software errors and was code-compatible with the 8080.

The 16-bit 80286 processor was introduced in 1982. It had task switching, protected virtual address modes, 16 Mbytes of physical memory, and 1 Gbyte of virtual memory. Address pipelining was used and programs can be run in the real-address mode to emulate the 8086 environment.

The 32-bit 386 processor appeared in 1985. It added 32-bit data types and instructions, demand paging, address translation registers, and a nonpipelined option for bus cycles. The 386 also allows DOS execution under UNIX or OS/2 along with expanded testability and debugging features.

The 32-bit 486 processor appeared in 1989. It has the same architectural features as the 386 along with an on-chip cache and floating-point processor. It dropped address pipelining on the processor bus, although instruction pipelining is still done internally. It supports both 8- and 16-bit data buses and uses burst cycles for faster cache-line fills.

The functions that have changed during this evolution of the 86 family include the definition of I/O space and the way in which interrupts are handled.

The 486 processor is downward-compatible with the rest of the 86 family. The 486 can execute any software written for the 8086, 8088, 80286, or 386 processors. But, the reverse is not true, since the 486 instruction set is a superset of the instruction sets of earlier processors. There are small differences among the processors in shift and divide operations as well as locking.

Each unit of the 86 family has an associated numerics coprocessor. The 8087 and 80287 can perform arithmetic, logical, and transcendental operations on 32-, 64-, and 80-bit floating point operands, 32- and 64-bit integers, and 18-digit BCD operands. The 80387 coprocessor and the i486 processor's on-chip floating-point unit have more transcendental operations than the 8087 and 80287 coprocessors.

In each generation, the bus cycle has been shortened to free up bus bandwidth for other uses. Bus utilization in the 486 is better. In the 486, burst cycles are used to fill the cache so that read requests only access the cache and do not generate bus cycles.

In the 486, bus arbitration is different; the processor can request access to the bus with a BREQ output. In the earlier processors, there is no output to indicate a pending need for the bus.

Bus locking requests are done with the LOCK* output on all processors, but the 486 adds a pseudo-locking (PLOCK*) output for multiple cycles of aligned data. (The * indicates a negative true signal.) A bus backoff input is used to avoid bus deadlock, and another new signal, the address hold input, is used for invalidating the on-chip cache in the 486.

The number of clocks needed for each instruction has decreased. The segmentation and paging units of the 386 processor can do an address computation for every two clocks. The 486 reduced this to one address computation for each clock. The 486 processor also improved performance with its on-chip cache and floating-point units. The cache can perform one access per clock. There were other improvements in address pipelining and instruction decoding.

## Pipelining

The microprocessor fetch/execute process is more efficient if the bus interface is kept busy. This resulted in the concept of pipelining. A pipelined microprocessor makes use of an instruction queue, which holds several consecutive instructions (Fig. 2.3). When the bus interface is free, it fetches additional instructions from external memory and places them in the queue. When the control sequencer needs another instruction, it goes to the instruction queue instead of external memory. Using a queue is faster, and overlapping of the fetch and execute cycles also provides a faster machine.

## Microprocessor Bus

The internal structure of the microprocessor, called the architecture or the system architecture, affects interfacing since it affects the microprocessor bus. The bus is a group of signal lines designed to move information between the microprocessor and the peripheral interface circuits. The typical microprocessor bus has three components: an address bus, a data bus and a control bus (Fig. 2.4).

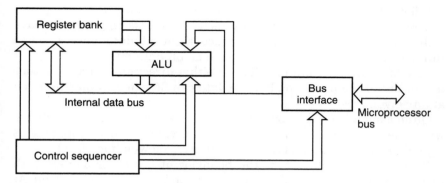

(a) Simplified microprocessor block diagram

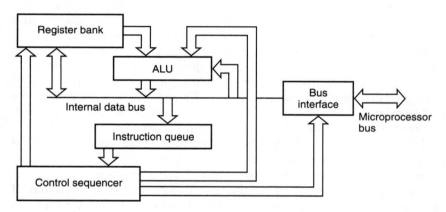

(b) Pipelined microprocessor with an instruction
queue added to speed up instruction fetches.

**Figure 2.3** Pipelined and nonpipelined microprocessors.

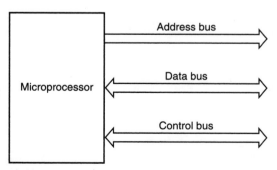

**Figure 2.4** The three major component buses of a
microprocessor bus are the address bus, data bus, and
control bus.

Information is moved over the data bus. Eight-bit processors generally have eight-bit data busses. Sixteen-bit processors generally have sixteen-bit busses although some use eight-bit data busses. Some thirty-two bit microprocessors use sixteen bit data busses.

In a data bus, the data may flow in either direction. It may go either into or out of the processor, but the data can flow in only one direction at any given time.

Often a signal, which is sometimes called a strobe is used to indicate when the other signals on the diagram are valid. An overscore on this signal means the signal is true when it is at a low-voltage level.

Figure 2.5 will then show the behavior of the other signals with respect to the strobe line. At some time period, the signals are valid. At other times, the strobe line makes these signals invalid.

The timing diagram (Fig. 2.5) is often used to indicate a microprocessor cycle. The strobe line would then show when the address and data buses are valid and when these buses become invalid.

The address bus controls the direction and location of the data flow. The microprocessor uses an address to specify the hardware it needs to communicate with. Each memory location has a unique address and each interface port also has an address. These addresses are sent to the address bus by the microprocessor when communication is needed. Address buses are unidirectional and 8-bit processors usually have a 16-bit address bus which limits the addressing range to 65536 addresses. Sixteen-bit processors have address buses of 16 to 24 bits, which means they can access up to 16,777,216 addresses.

The control bus sequences the flow of information over the data bus. If the microprocessor needs to output data, it tells the external hardware when the information is valid on the data bus. When the microprocessor

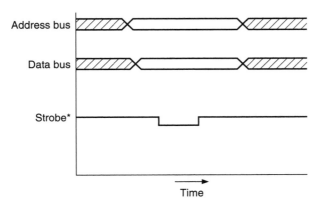

**Figure 2.5** A simple timing diagram. The negative-true strobe signal is used to indicate that the address and data buses have valid information.

wants to input information, the control bus allows the external hardware to tell the microprocessor when that data will be available.

## Timing Diagrams

The signals that the microprocessor and the peripherals use must have a precise timing relationship. A timing diagram is used to show these relationships. The horizontal axis of the diagram is labeled *time*. Events occurring on the right side of the diagram always happen after those shown on the left.

A cross-hatched area indicates that the signals do not matter at this point in time; they are in a don't-care state. Areas with no cross-hatching means the signals must be at valid levels.

## Data Bus Operation

The microprocessor data bus is a bidirectional, three-state bus. It is the same as a single-line bus except that there are eight lines instead of one. To use all of the data bus lines, each talker must have eight drivers, there must be one for each line, and each listener must have eight inputs.

The microprocessor and RAM act as both talkers and listeners. Input ports act as talkers since they take inputs from outside the system and place them on the bus. Output ports act as listeners since they take data off the bus and send it outside the system. A ROM acts like only a talker.

The microprocessor, ROM, RAM, and input ports use three-state drivers on their outputs. Chip Select (CS) inputs are used to enable the drivers and allow the data from the selected device to appear on the data bus.

The microprocessor acts as the main controller for the system. It allows only one device to use the bus at any given time. When the microprocessor needs to read data from ROM, it first disables its own data outputs and then generates the control signals needed to enable the ROM. The ROM's outputs then appear on the data bus and the microprocessor reads the data. Reading RAM or an input port is done in a similar way.

To write data to a device, such as RAM or an output port, the microprocessor first places the data to be written onto the data bus. It then generates control signals that send a write pulse to the device. This write pulse causes the device to internally latch the data.

In most cases, data flows through the microprocessor. In a data transfer from an input port to RAM, the microprocessor will first read the data from the input port and then write it to RAM. Since the data cannot be transferred directly from the input port to the RAM, it is temporarily stored in the microprocessor.

To summarize, the data bus is used for all transfers of data within the microprocessor system. All devices share the same bus. The control logic, operating from signals generated by the microprocessor, directs each device as to when it should place data on the bus or read data from the bus.

## Address Bus Operation

A set of lines is used by the microprocessor to specify where information will come from or go to on the data bus. This is the address bus used by the microprocessor. The memory is divided into locations and each data storage location has a unique address. This address is specified on the address bus when the microprocessor needs to get or place information at that location.

The address bus is controlled by the microprocessor. Addresses are never sent to the microprocessor over the address bus by another device. But, the microprocessor may be asked to release the address bus so that other devices may use it. This capability is required for *direct memory access* (DMA). DMA is an input/output technique designed to speed up certain types of data operations.

Eight-bit processors usually have 16-bit address buses made up of 16 individual address lines. These 16 bits give the processor an addressing capability of 65,536 locations. In an 8-bit processor, this allows a storage capacity of 65,536 bytes of information. In the early microprocessors, memory was expensive and this was more than most microprocessor systems could afford to use. This amount of memory is very inexpensive today and many current programs require much more than this to function properly.

Sixteen-bit processors offer a greater addressing range. Some 16-bit processors, such as the Intel 8086, use 20 address lines, giving them an addressing capability of 1,048,576 locations, while others have 24 address lines and provide 16,777,216 locations. Although these seemed more than adequate when these processors were introduced, PCs with several megabytes of memory are common.

Thirty-two-bit processors with 32-bit address buses have address spaces in excess of 4 billion locations.

## Control Bus Operation

The control bus uses the timing information to synchronize the other devices with the internal operation of the microprocessor. Memory devices are told when the address bus has a valid address and when to place data on the data bus. The processor can then read this data. The memory and I/O devices also need to know when the processor has placed information on the data bus so it can be accepted.

Some lines of the control bus are bidirectional, while others are not. Some of the signal lines on the control bus are driven by the microprocessor, while other signal lines are driven by other devices in the system. The control bus is not as uniform as the data lines in the data bus or the address lines in the address bus. It is a mixture of timing, data direction, and functions.

Each microprocessor operates with its own set of control lines, but most have two signals, the interrupt and DMA lines. These two groups of lines on the control bus have control over the microprocessor in certain situations. They are able to take over control of the microprocessor when they are called upon.

Interrupts allow external devices to stop the normal operation of the processor so that another task can be started. This task can be the transfer of small amounts of data or large routines or programs.

DMA (direct memory access) is a hardware technique where special hardware takes control of the bus from the processor for the required period of time to complete a data transfer. This special hardware can usually perform the data transfer much faster than the general-purpose processor, so this technique is often used for high-speed input/output transfers.

## Microprocessor I/O Techniques

The three types of I/O techniques which the microprocessor uses to communicate with the external world are programmed I/O, interrupt I/O, and Direct Memory Access (DMA). Programmed I/O is a microprocessor-initiated I/O transfer. The data transfer between the microprocessor and an external device is controlled by the microprocessor. A program must be executed by the microprocessor to accomplish this.

Interrupt I/O is device-initiated. An external device is connected to the interrupt pin of the microprocessor. In order to transfer data, the device changes the state on the interrupt pin. The microprocessor completes execution of the current instruction, saves the rest of the program in its memory, and executes an interrupt service routine to complete the transfer.

Direct memory access is also device-initiated. Data transfer between the microprocessor memory and the I/O device occurs without the microprocessor. Special DMA control circuits are used to complete the transfer.

## Microprocessor Hardware

Factors that affect the basic microprocessor system hardware include the bus structure and address decoding. The emphasis is on understanding the basic parts of a typical microprocessor system.

Microprocessor systems are designed around buses, which are not usually found in random logic systems. In a microprocessor system, many devices must exchange data with the processor. Without a bus the processor would need a set of data outputs for each device and a selector or multiplexer to choose a particular device for the data input. This quickly becomes unwieldy as more devices are added. The data paths usually carry 8 bits of data, so each path needs eight lines. In a three-device system, 48 lines would be needed: 24 for data input and 24 for data output. More complex systems with more memory devices and I/O ports could easily require hundreds of interconnecting lines.

The solution to the interconnection problem is the use of a bus (Fig. 2.6). This makes the interconnections much simpler since a single set of eight lines is used to interconnect all the devices and the same set of lines is used for data traveling into or out of the processor. The number of devices can be expanded greatly with little or no increase in interconnection complexity.

Since all devices share the same data lines, only one can supply data at any given time. The address and control lines, which are driven by the microprocessor, provide the needed controls to select a particular device.

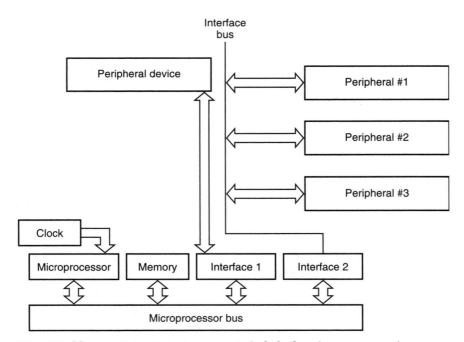

**Figure 2.6**   Microcomputer system components include the microprocessor, microprocessor bus, memory, interfaces, and peripherals.

## Three-State Drivers

The three-state driver makes the shared data bus possible. A single-line bus is given as an example, but the technique is the same regardless of the number of lines in the bus. The typical data bus has eight lines.

The three-state bus works like a telephone party line. The bus may have many talkers and many listeners connected to it. Figure 2.7 shows a bus circuit with four talkers, using three-state drivers and two listeners using logic gates. The control logic selects the driver for a talker to be active. If more than one talker were enabled, the data on the bus would become garbled.

When a driver is enabled, the data at its input are placed on the bus and all of the other drivers are disabled. Their outputs are in a high-impedance, floating state, so they have no effect on the bus.

There can be many listeners on the bus. Since they only listen, more than one of them can be enabled at the same time. Often, the data on the bus is sent to only one of them. The control logic generates signals called *data strobes* that tell selected listeners that the data on the bus is being sent to them.

A data strobe may be used to clock the data from the bus into a flip-flop. The inputs to the control logic are the address and control buses coming from the microprocessor.

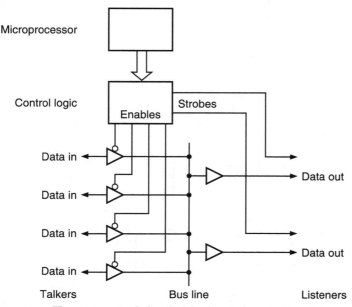

**Figure 2.7**   Three-state, single-line bus for four talkers and two listeners.

These devices are undirectional: they are either talkers or listeners, but not both. Bidirectional devices are also available; these act as both talkers and listeners. See Fig. 2.8.

Each talker/listener has two control signals. There is the output enable signal for the three-state driver and the data strobe for the input. An example of a bidirectional device is a RAM, which can read and write data.

Typically, this works as follows for device 1 to send data to device 2:

1. The control logic sets output enable A true (enabled) and output enable B false (not enabled).

2. After allowing the data to reach device 2's data input, the controller sends a pulse on the data strobe 2 line.

3. This causes device 2 to read the data from the bus, which came from device 1.

If other devices are connected to the bus, as long as their enables are false, they will have no effect.

### Addressing

The data bus is used by different devices to exchange data, so a method is needed by the microprocessor to select the particular device that communicates with the data bus. The address bus (with the aid of the control bus) provides this function.

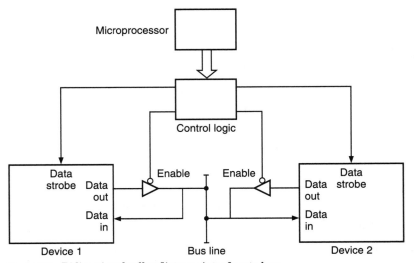

**Figure 2.8**  Bidirectional talker/listener interface to bus.

The address bus is unidirectional, so its operation is simpler than the data bus. Each memory location has a unique address. Before a data transfer can take place on the data bus, the microprocessor sends out an address. This address specifies the memory location that the processor needs to access. This allows the microprocessor to select any part of the system it needs to communicate with.

An address bus with 16 lines allows direct addressing of $2^{16}$ or 65,536 memory locations and I/O ports. The 16 lines are usually labeled from the least significant bit to the most significant as

$A_0$, $A_1$, $A_2$, $A_3...A_{15}$

## Address Decoders

An address decoder, which is a part of the control logic, generates device-select signals when a certain address or range of addresses is present on the address bus. Figure 2.9 shows an address decoder for address 3000 hex (0011 0000 0000 0000 binary). The output of the decoder is TRUE only when this address is present on the address bus. This output is then used to enable the port that is assigned to address 3000.

The address bus selects the memory location or I/O port and the data bus carries the data. The entire process is coordinated by the control bus with its control signals.

The microprocessor will use signals like READ and WRITE.* When READ* is low, it indicates a read operation is taking place, and the

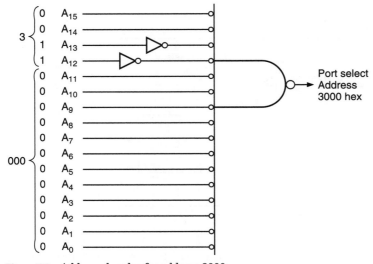

**Figure 2.9**   Address decoder for address 3000.

microprocessor signals the addressed device to place data on the data bus. If WRITE* is low, then a write operation is taking place, and the microprocessor places data on the data bus and signals the addressed device to store this data.

Each wire in the control bus has a unique function; in the address and data buses, each line carries the same type of information—1 bit of the address or data.

The actual control signals in some microprocessors can differ, but the data transfers are the same. They are just achieved in different ways.

### Input and Output Ports

Suppose an output port latch has an address of 2000. The latch is clocked when address 2000 is present on the address bus and a low-to-high switching takes place on the WRITE* control signal. When the latch is clocked, the data from the data bus is stored on it (Fig. 2.10a). The microprocessor causes data specified by the software program to be at the output of the latch by writing the data to address 2000.

Input ports are handled in a similar way: the output of the address decoder is ANDed with READ instead of WRITE to generate the port enable. The input port is usually an eight-line three-state driver. It places the input signals on the data bus when enabled (Fig. 2.10b). The microprocessor can read these input signals on the data bus when enabled. The microprocessor reads these input signals by performing a read operation from the proper address. The processor can then store this data in one of its registers.

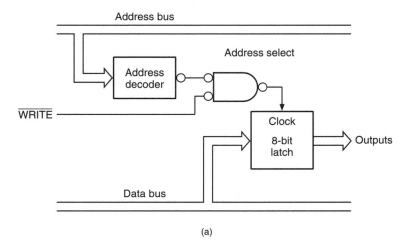

(a)

**Figure 2.10**  Microprocessor write and read operations: (a) data from data bus is stored in a latch when the microprocessor writes to an address.

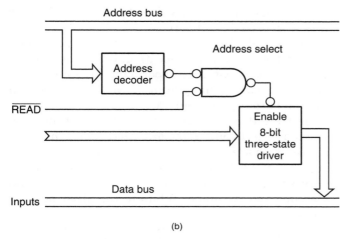

(b)

**Figure 2.10** Microprocessor write and read operations: (*b*) input data is placed on the data bus when the microprocessor reads the address assigned to the three-state driver.

## Multiple Devices

When an address decoder is required to control several I/O ports, several address decoders can be used, but a simpler method is to use an address select decoder to generate select signals. For up to eight addresses only the three low-order address bits are needed, as shown in Fig. 2.10c.

The upper 13 bits are decoded as shown and the output of this circuit is used to enable a decoder such as a 74LS138. This chip generates eight separate outputs, one for each possible combination of the three low-order bits. The decoder is disabled (all outputs are false) when the

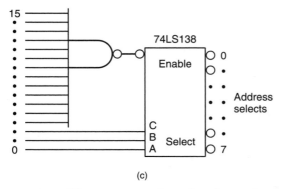

(c)

**Figure 2.10** Microprocessor write and read operations: (*c*) using a decoder to control I/O ports; using a small ROM with decoders; address decoding for RAM.

upper 13 address bits are not of the proper value. Address decoding for memories is similar to that used for I/O ports.

A ROM can be viewed as a device with many 8-bit input ports on a single chip, with one port for each memory location. When the ROM is programmed, the ROM memory locations are permanently set in a pattern of 1s and 0s. In a RAM, each memory location can be viewed with having both input and an output ports combined.

In a ROM system the low-order bits of the address bus are connected to an address decoder that selects one of low-order locations. The high-order 8 bits of the address bus are decoded by another address decoder to enable the ROM when a desired range of addresses is present on the upper half of the address bus. In a 16-bit system, the lower 8 bits would go to one address decoder and the upper 8 bits to the other address decoder. See Fig. 2.10d.

The READ signal is ANDed with the address decoder output to generate the ROM enable. This is the same technique used for input ports.

Most microprocessor systems use more than one memory chip. Table 2.4 is a memory map showing how four small 256-byte ROMs can be connected together for address decoding. More complex arrangements with larger memory chips can be built up using this same technique.

The address lines must indicate which memory chip should be selected and which word within that chip should be addressed. The addresses are shown in binary. The lower 8 bits of address designate the location within each chip, and the upper 8 bits designate which chip is being addressed. Bits 8 and 9 are used for decoding one chip from the other. The lower 8 bits of address would be connected to the

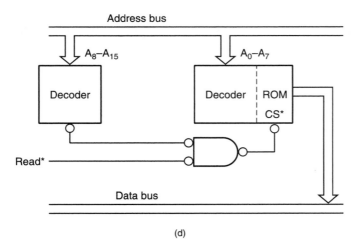

(d)

**Figure 2.10**  Microprocessor write and read operations: (d) using a decoder to control I/O ports.

TABLE 2.4    Addresses Assigned to Four 256-byte ROMs

| Address | Address | bit | 15 | 14 | 13 | 12 | 11 | 10 | ROM no. 9 | 8 | Location within ROM 7 | 6 | 5 | 4 | 3 | 2 | 1 | 0 |
|---|---|---|---|---|---|---|---|---|---|---|---|---|---|---|---|---|---|---|
| 0 | ROM 0 | 0 | 0 | 0 | 0 | 0 | 0 | 0 | 0 | 0 | 0 | 0 | 0 | 0 | 0 | 0 | 0 | 0 |
| 1 | | 1 | 0 | 0 | 0 | 0 | 0 | 0 | 0 | 0 | 0 | 0 | 0 | 0 | 0 | 0 | 0 | 1 |
| 2 | | 2 | 0 | 0 | 0 | 0 | 0 | 0 | 0 | 0 | 0 | 0 | 0 | 0 | 0 | 0 | 1 | 0 |
| . | | | | | | | | | | | | | | | | | | |
| 255 | | 255 | 0 | 0 | 0 | 0 | 0 | 0 | 0 | 0 | 1 | 1 | 1 | 1 | 1 | 1 | 1 | 1 |
| 256 | ROM 1 | 256 | 0 | 0 | 0 | 0 | 0 | 0 | 0 | 1 | 0 | 0 | 0 | 0 | 0 | 0 | 0 | 0 |
| 257 | | 257 | 0 | 0 | 0 | 0 | 0 | 0 | 0 | 1 | 0 | 0 | 0 | 0 | 0 | 0 | 0 | 1 |
| . | | | | | | | | | | | | | | | | | | |
| 511 | | 511 | 0 | 0 | 0 | 0 | 0 | 0 | 0 | 1 | 1 | 1 | 1 | 1 | 1 | 1 | 1 | 1 |
| 512 | ROM 2 | 512 | 0 | 0 | 0 | 0 | 0 | 0 | 1 | 0 | 0 | 0 | 0 | 0 | 0 | 0 | 0 | 0 |
| 513 | | 513 | 0 | 0 | 0 | 0 | 0 | 0 | 1 | 0 | 0 | 0 | 0 | 0 | 0 | 0 | 0 | 1 |
| . | | | | | | | | | | | | | | | | | | |
| 766 | | 766 | 0 | 0 | 0 | 0 | 0 | 0 | 1 | 0 | 1 | 1 | 1 | 1 | 1 | 1 | 1 | 1 |
| 767 | ROM 3 | 767 | 0 | 0 | 0 | 0 | 0 | 0 | 1 | 1 | 0 | 0 | 0 | 0 | 0 | 0 | 0 | 0 |
| 768 | | 768 | 0 | 0 | 0 | 0 | 0 | 0 | 1 | 1 | 0 | 0 | 0 | 0 | 0 | 0 | 0 | 1 |
| . | | | | | | | | | | | | | | | | | | |
| 1023 | | 1023 | 0 | 0 | 0 | 0 | 0 | 0 | 1 | 1 | 1 | 1 | 1 | 1 | 1 | 1 | 1 | 1 |

address lines of all four ROMs, since these bits specify the location within the chip. The address decoder then checks the upper 8 bits of address and generates the chip selects.

There are variations to this approach, but the basic principles remain the same:

1. The low-order address bits are connected to the memory's address lines.
2. The high-order bits are decoded to generate the chip selects. No more than one chip can be selected at any given time.

## RAM Addressing

RAMs are decoded in a similar way, but additional control signals are needed to write input to the RAM and to read output from the RAM. RAMs have a WRITE* input in addition to the CS* input (chip select). In order for the RAM to be controlled, CS* must be low for either a read or write to take place. If WRITE* is high (not TRUE) when CS* is low, the RAM outputs data to the data bus so the processor can read it. This is done when CS* enables the RAM's three-state output drivers. If WRITE* is low, CS* will not turn on the RAM's output drivers. Instead,

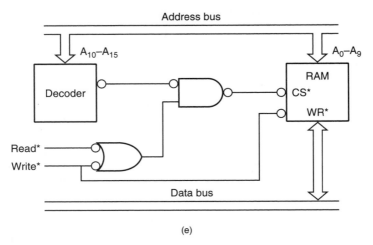

(e)

**Figure 2.10** Microprocessor write and read operations; (e) address decoding for RAM.

the data on the data bus is written into the memory at the location designated by the address bus.

The bus gating is shown in Fig. 2.10e. Chip select (CS) is low when the RAM address select and either READ or WRITE are low. The WRITE* line is connected to the RAM's WRITE* input. The WRITE* input is internally gated with the CS* input, so it will be ignored unless CS is low.

## Decoding Techniques

All devices that communicate with the microprocessor have specific addresses assigned to them. The address decoding circuits ensure that the correct device is on the bus when it is addressed by the microprocessor. This can be done with a 741S138 decoder. Three lines can be used to specify which of eight sections is addressed.

These three lines are used to provide the binary select inputs to the 74LS138 one-of-eight decoder. This device provides eight separate outputs. The 74LS138 has three enable inputs: two active low and one active high. All three must be true to allow any of the outputs to be true. Connecting the READ* and WRITE* lines to the enable inputs ensures that the bus devices can be enabled only during a read or write operation.

The 74LS138 decoder's other enable input is connected to an OR gate that generates the OR of READ* and WRITE*. This allows the device select outputs to be true only when either a read or a write is in progress. The address bus contains useful information only during these periods.

The ROM and the input ports must be selected only if a read is being performed. If they responded to either a read or a write, a bus conflict could occur. If the ROM is enabled during the write operation, it will also attempt to put data on the data bus. This is a dangerous situation which could result in integrated circuit damage.

To prevent this, the READ* signal is ANDed with the ROM device select. This is done by connecting READ* to one of the ROM's enables. A similar situation can occur with output ports.

A RAM's device select is different. It must be TRUE when either a read or a write to the RAM's address space is in progress. The RAM's device-select lines are sent to a write protect circuit, which helps prevent the RAM's contents from being accidentally destroyed.

A simple error may cause the microprocessor to interpret data as instructions. This often results in the storage of useless data in the entire RAM. To prevent this problem, a latch can be used for protecting the RAM. When the latch is set, the RAM is protected. It can be read but not written to. Since you may need to use the RAM to store data during program execution, only part of the RAM may be protected.

The technique used for performing address decoding depends on many factors, including the amount of memory, the number of peripherals, the need for expandability, the type of memory and I/O devices used, and the speed requirements. In some cases these devices have their own enable pins which can be used as a part of the address decoding.

Linear decoding is the simplest decoding technique since it uses no address decoding logic. The high-order address bits are used as chip selects. This method wastes a large amount of address space since there is overlap among the different devices.

The program is not allowed to read any address where there is overlap. This results in some waste in address space. This technique is found only in very small systems.

Another technique is to use a logic comparator to select a portion of the address fields. In the logic comparator, each comparator set of inputs is compared when they all match the comparator output switches. This technique is used on some memory and peripheral boards that have switches or jumpers to set the address of each board in a system. The switching may also be done by software as in the IBM PS2 series. Exclusive OR gates may also be used to accomplish the actual comparator function.

In small systems with limited decoding requirements, standard logic gates can be used. A four-input NAND gate preceded by inverters has an output that goes low when the address lines are in the state 1, 0, 0, 1. By complementing or not complementing the address inputs to the gate, any one of 16 ($2^4$) devices can be enabled.

Microprocessors like the Intel 8080 use a separate control line to specify if the address is for either I/O or memory. In the 8085, this line is called IO/M∗. The instruction being executed controls this line. During memory transfers, IO/M∗ is low. When one of the two I/O instructions (IN or OUT) is executed, IO/M∗ goes high, enabling the I/O ports. When IO/M∗ is low, the memory is enabled. When IO/M∗ is high, the I/O is enabled, and eight of the address lines contain the I/O port address. This method allows memory and I/O to have separate address spaces, increasing the total addressable space in a system.

## Static and Dynamic RAMs

RAMs are used for holding data and running programs in microcomputer systems. ROMs provide a means of storing programs and data. RAMs lose their contents when power is removed.

The two different types of RAMs are *static* and *dynamic*. Static RAMs (SRAMs) use a flip-flop circuit for each memory element. Each 1K of RAM has 1024 flip-flops. Each flip-flop can be set to store a 1 or reset to store a 0.

Address decoding circuits in the RAM chip select the particular flip-flop specified by the address lines. The state of the flip-flop does not change until different data is stored in it or power to the RAM is interrupted.

Dynamic RAMs (DRAMs) use a storage capacitor. When a charge is stored in the capacitor, this indicates a 1; no charge indicates a 0. This technique reduces the size of the storage cell, and allows denser memory chips. Since the charge leaks off the capacitor, it must be refreshed. Refreshing consists of rewriting the data. All of the 1 bits are restored to full charge and the 0 bits to no charge.

## DRAM Refreshing

Since dynamic MOS RAMs store bits of information as charges on MOS capacitors, one capacitor is required for each bit. A read operation causes the capacitor to discharge as it compares the voltage to a reference voltage. A rewrite is then needed to preserve the contents of the RAM.

The normal leakage in the MOS circuit will discharge these capacitors within a few milliseconds. So the charge must be restored, generally every 2 milliseconds. This refreshing must take place for all locations in the RAM within 2 milliseconds.

This is different than the operation of a static RAM, where a bit is stored in a flip-flop. No clock is required and the RAM will conserve information as long as power is applied.

The dynamic RAM cell can be implemented with a single MOS transistor, resulting in a higher density. Typically, a dynamic RAM is four times as dense as a static RAM, resulting in a significantly lower cost.

Dynamic RAMs are also characterized by a lower power consumption. Their disadvantage is that they require a refresh controller, which is often complex. Dynamic RAMs are often used for larger memories while static RAMs tend to be used in much smaller systems.

In order to reduce the number of refresh cycles required for a RAM memory array, the typical RAM is structured in rows and columns of memory cells and a single row or column is refreshed at once. Since many cells in the memory array are accessed simultaneously, less refresh cycles are required.

## Refresh Control

A refresh controller is used for refreshing the RAM within a few milliseconds. A burst mode may be used where the refresh controller refreshes the rows in sequence. This makes the RAM unavailable to the processor for this time period. In the distributed or single-cycle mode the refresh controller takes over the memory every few microseconds to refresh the next row. This technique has the potential for less delay to the processor, provided that each memory access can be kept small. Both of these techniques require getting access to the memory when it is not busy, and at a higher priority than the processor. Two main techniques are used to achieve the synchronization needed.

1. *Asynchronous access.*   Here the requests are generated at a fixed rate, independently of the microprocessor state. This method is microprocessor-independent, but requires complex control and has some access delay. The controller may have to wait for the completion of a RAM cycle in progress. This is a refresh delay, not a delay of the microprocessor.

2. *Hidden refresh.*   This method refreshes the RAM when the microprocessor is not using it. Hidden refresh is also called *transparent refresh,* or *synchronous access.* In every microprocessor, situations normally exist where the memory in not needed for one or more cycles. If these states can be identified, a refresh cycle can be started. The microprocessor is not aware of the refresh, so the name *hidden* or *transparent* is used. One example occurs when the microprocessor decodes and executes an internal instruction and does not require the memory.

Other methods that may be used are combinations of the above techniques which take advantage of the characteristics of the particular microprocessor.

## Refresh Logic

The refresh controller needs several elements, including the following:

1. A refresh counter used to count the addresses.
2. An address multiplexer to supply the RAM chips with a row address. This will originate either from the refresh counter during a refresh cycle, or from the address bus during a regular memory cycle.
3. A request arbitration unit to grant a memory cycle to the refresh unit or to the microprocessor.
4. A baud-rate generator timing circuit to supply pulses at the required rate, every 2 milliseconds.
5. Latches to hold the status.

## Refresh-Controller Chips

Refresh-controller chips are used to implement dynamic RAM controllers. These generally require external timing for its signals. Typically, a single chip includes latches, an oscillator that requires an external R-C circuit, address multiplexer, refresh counter and arbitration unit. It supplies a row address along with the proper timing needed.

These refreshing circuits must be added to the system, so small systems often use static memories; but dynamic memories are less expensive than static RAMs of the same size and consume less power. The larger RAMs are dynamic.

Dynamic memories are usually 1 bit wide. This means that eight chips are needed for one 8-bit data word. All the address and control lines are bused together.

# 32-Bit Microprocessors

## 68020 Microprocessor

The 68000 family uses internal registers that are 32 bits wide and the processors perform 32-bit operations. A 32-bit microprocessor like the Motorola 68020 has 32 address bits and 32 data bits along with the needed control signals as shown in the following list.

| | | | |
|---|---|---|---|
| FCO-FC2 | Function codes | CDIS* | Cache control |
| AO-A31 | Address bus | IPLO-IPL2* | Interrupt priority |
| D0-D31 | Data bus | IPEND* | Interrupt control |
| | | AVEC* | Interrupt control |
| SIZ0 | Transfer size | BR* | Bus arbitration control |
| SIZ1 | Transfer size | BG* | Bus arbitration control |
| | | BGACK* | Bus arbitration control |
| ECS* | Asynchronous bus control | RESET* | Bus exception control |
| OCS* | Asynchronous bus control | | |
| RMC* | Asynchronous bus control | HALT* | Bus exception control |
| AS* | Asynchronous bus control | BERR* | Bus exception control |
| DS* | Asynchronous bus | | |
| R/W* | Asynchronous bus control | CLK | Clock timing |

DBEN*    Asynchronous bus
         control

DSACK0*  Asynchronous bus
         control

DSACK1*  Asynchronous bus
         control

Since all of these cannot fit in a standard 68-pin package, a microprocessor like the 68020 uses a 114-lead pin grid array (PGA) package. The PGA package stacks the pins in a 2-dimensional array, so the pins are marked with a letter and a number.

In the 68020, the address, data, and function-code buses are similar to the other 68000 chips, except the data bus is 32 instead of 16 bits and the address bus is 32 instead of 24 bits.

The 68020 address bus contains bit A0 (like the 68008 but unlike the 68000 and 68010); the bus arbitration signals BR, BG, and BGACK work like the 68000 signals; and the interrupt lines are similar (IPL0, IPL1, and IPL2). AS (address strobe), R/W (Read/Write), RESET, HALT, and BERR are also similar.

Like the 68008, the 68020 microprocessor has only one data strobe, but it can perform 8-, 16-, 24-, and 32-bit data transfers. In order to differentiate among the different-sized transfers, two transfer-size outputs are used. These are called *SIZ0* and *SIZ1* and indicate the width of the transfer as shown in the following table:

| SZ | SIZ0 | Transfer size |
|----|------|---------------|
| 0 | 1 | Byte |
| 1 | 0 | Word (16 bits) |
| 1 | 1 | 3 bytes (24 bits) |
| 0 | 0 | Long word (32 bits) |

If a 32-bit number is not aligned on a 32-bit, long-word boundary, then the 68020 has to transfer the number in two parts. Depending on the alignment of the number in memory, these parts may be 16 bits each or there may be a 24-bit part and an 8-bit part. Generally, the 32-bit words would be aligned on 32-bit boundaries, but the microprocessor needs to be able to handle them if they are not.

Microprocessors with 32-bit data buses also need to talk to 8-bit, 16-bit, and 32-bit devices. The 68020 tells the microprocessor how large the data path is to a device for a data transfer, using a feature called *dynamic bus sizing.*

This is done with two signals called *DSACK0* and *DSACK1*. These are used to acknowledge the bus transfer and indicate how the transfer will be accomplished, as shown in the following table:

| DSACK | DSACK0 | |
| --- | --- | --- |
| 1 | 1 | No Acknowledge |
| | | Insert Wait States |
| 1 | 0 | 8-Bit Transfer Acknowledge |
| 0 | 1 | 16-Bit Transfer Acknowledge |
| 1 | 1 | 32-Bit Transfer Acknowledge |

ECS is the external cycle start output. It indicates that the 68020 microprocessor is starting a bus cycle and appears before OCS, the operand cycle start signal. It also indicates the start of a bus cycle, but is used only during the first bus cycle of an operand transfer.

The 68020 performs a read-modify-write data transfer as a transparent operation. In a multiprocessor system, another processor could take over the bus and access the same location between the read and the write operations of the first microprocessor.

A read-modify-write cycle (RMC) pin is used to prevent the loss of the bus by a processor until it completes the instruction. The 68020 also uses a data bus enable (DBEN) pin to control external data-bus buffers. This pin will prevent bus contention during transitions of the R/W pin.

IPEND (interrupt pending) is used to acknowledge an interrupt. The 68020 uses this pin when it receives an interrupt at a level higher than the current interrupt level or when it receives a nonmaskable interrupt request.

AVEC (autovector) input allows the 68020 to generate an interrupt vector internally. In the 68000, this is done with the VPA input. Since the 68020 does not support 6800 bus cycles, the E, VPA, and VMA signals are not used.

Another pin, CDIS, disables the 68020 instruction cache. Instructions fetched by the 68020 are stored in this instruction cache. When the processor enters a loop of instructions after the first execution of the loop, the instructions making up the loop are stored in the cache. Then, the 68020 does not need to execute external bus cycles to get the loop instructions. It gets them directly from the on-chip cache which is much faster.

The 68020 read-and-write cycles use a minimum of three clock cycles, along with wait states. A read cycle takes place as follows:

1. The 68020 sets the R/W, FC0-3, A0-31, and SIZ0-1 output pins to the proper values.

2. It then sets ECS and OCS during the first cycle of an operand transfer for one-half of the clock cycle.

3. It then sets AS, DS, and DBEN.

This sequence completes the first part of the cycle. The cycle is completed at acknowledgement of the bus transfer on the DSACK0 and DSACK1 inputs.

The 68030 is an enhanced version of its 68020. The 68030 has a data cache along with an instruction cache. The 68030 performs bus cycles the same way as the 68020.

## Cache Basics

High-performance processors like the 68020 and 68030 place a great demand on the bandwidth of memory systems. The newer integrated circuit implementations have greatly reduced the cycle times of processors. Although computer memories have improved in performance, the ratio of memory speed to processor cycle time has continued to increase.

Shared-memory, multiple-processor systems have also become more common and have increased the bandwidth requirements of system memories and the buses that connect them. This has resulted in the increasing use of cache memories.

Caches are high-speed buffer memories that hold the most frequently used instructions and data for quick access by the processor. Caches operate the locality of memory references. Computer programs tend to execute instructions stored in close proximity to each other. Programs also exhibit a locality in that they tend to access a small subset of the entire data set a number of times in any time period. The cache hardware tracks the data accessed by the processor and saves it with the likelihood that it will be requested again. Typically, the cache memory is 20 to 1000 times smaller in size than the system memory and 5 to 20 times faster.

Cache memories have been used in many computers. A cache memory was used in the IBM System 360, and the DEC PDP-11/70 followed. The Motorola 68030 processor uses two on-chip caches.

The cache memory is made up of a number of lines or blocks that can hold the contents of the corresponding elements of the system memory. When the processor issues a memory reference, it is checked with the contents of the cache. If the data is already in the cache due to a previous access to system memory, it is sent back to the processor. This is called a *cache hit*. A *cache miss* requires that the data be fetched from the system memory and sent to the cache.

The cache is made up of two parts. One memory array is for the cached data, and each element in the array is a cache line or block. The other array is used for the cache directory. The memory addresses from the processor have fields: tag, index, and byte number. The index allows access to both the directory and data arrays.

The contents of a previously stored tag are compared with the present tag. A match indicates a hit and a nonmatch indicates a miss. In a miss the address is forwarded to the system memory and the data returned from memory overwrites the data in the cache. The tag in the directory is also updated.

## Associativity

A simple cache like the previous one forces a one-to-one correspondence between the blocks of system memory and the lines in the cache. This relationship is called the *associativity* of the cache and for the cache above, the associativity is one. The cache is described as a one-way set-associative cache or a direct-mapped cache.

The associativity of a cache can also be two-way, four-way, or fully associative. The associativity of the cache tells us the number of lines that can be referred through a single index. As the associativity of the cache increases, so does the number of possible lines where the cached data can be stored. Every processor address must be compared with the tags of all these locations simultaneously to determine a hit. In a fully associative cache there are no restrictions on the mapping of memory blocks to cache lines and the entire directory must be searched for a cache hit.

In a cache with an associativity greater than one, the cache hardware must determine which of the possible lines in the set must be replaced in a cache miss. Three different schemes are used. The *least recently used* (LRU) scheme replaces the line in the set which was accessed furthest back in time. This increases the chances of that line being no longer actively used by the processor. The LRU technique is the best choice among the three methods, but it is the hardest to implement in hardware for caches with a high degree of associativity. Another technique is random selection among the lines in the set. This is not as optimal as LRU but it is a good compromise between implementation complexity and performance. The third scheme is to consider the lines in the set as a FIFO (First-In First-Out) stack replacing the next one in sequence. This is the easiest to implement, but the performance is poor for some types of programs.

The cache hardware may handle the write traffic as either write-through or write-back. In write-through all writes update the cache and are also written through to the system memory. When a line is selected for replacement, it is written back to memory if it has been marked as dirty.

The cache memory must also be able to deal with updates to memory by I/O devices or direct memory access channels. The cache hardware must monitor the system bus traffic and invalidate any lines in the cache that have been updated by I/O devices. This is called *bus watching*.

## 80386 Microprocessor

The Intel 386 DX microprocessor is a true 32-bit microprocessor with multitasking support, memory management, pipelining, address translation caches, and a high-speed bus interface on one chip. The integration of these features on one chip improves performance and reduces the overall cost of the system. Both paging and dynamic data bus sizing are used. While the 386 DX microprocessor is a significant improvement over earlier generations of microprocessors, there is still compatibility with existing 8088 and 80286 software. Hardware compatibility is also preserved through the dynamic bus-sizing feature. The 386 DX microprocessor is supported by the components described in Table 3.1.

## 386 Characteristics

A 33-MHz 386 DX microprocessor can execute over 16 million instructions per second. This is equivalent to 8 million VAX instructions per second, so it operates at speeds comparable to that of a super minicomputer. This is possible because of the pipelined internal architecture, address translation caches, and high-performance bus. The 386 microprocessor has 32-bit wide internal and external data paths and eight general-purpose, 32-bit registers. The instruction set allows 8-, 16-, and 32-bit data types, and the processor outputs 32-bit addresses for a memory capacity of 4 gigabytes. Separate 32-bit data and address paths are used and a 32-bit memory access takes two clock cycles, providing the bus with a throughput of 40 megabytes per second at 20 MHz.

**TABLE 3.1    386 System Components**

| Component | Function |
| --- | --- |
| 386 DX microprocessor | 32-bit microprocessor with on-chip memory management and protection |
| 387 math coprocessor | Performs numeric operations in parallel with 386 microprocessor; expands the instruction set |
| 82380 peripheral chip | Provides 32-bit direct memory access (DMA), interrupt control, and interval timers |
| 82385 cache controller | Provides cache directory and management logic |
| 8259A programmable interrupt controller | Provides interrupt control and management |
| 82350 EISA chip set | Extends the 32-bit transfer capability of the 386 DX microprocessor to the I/O expansion bus |
| 82311 MCA chip set | Provides a microchannel-compatible PS/2 system |
| 82596DX LAN coprocessor | Performs high-level commands, command chaining, and interprocessor communications via shared memory |

The pipelined architecture allows the 386 to perform instruction fetching, decoding, execution, and memory management functions in parallel. The 386 prefetches instructions and queues them internally so instruction fetch and decode times are absorbed in the pipeline and the processor does not have to wait for an instruction to execute.

Pipelining was used in other microprocessors, but including the *memory management unit* (MMU) in the on-chip pipeline was a unique feature of the 386. By performing the memory management on-chip, the 386 eliminated the access delays that occur with off-chip memory management.

## Cache Functions

A 386 microprocessor running at 33 MHz can complete a bus cycle in only 60 nanoseconds. This provides a bandwidth of 66 megabytes per second. At these higher speeds, the 386 microprocessor must be matched with a high-speed memory system. It must be fast enough to complete bus cycles without wait states.

Most memory systems use dynamic RAMs (DRAMs), which give you a large amount of memory in a small space. DRAMs that can complete random read-write cycles in 60 nanoseconds are not typically available. Faster static RAMs (SRAMs) can meet the bus timing requirement, but they are smaller chips that are available at a higher cost.

A cache memory system uses a small amount of fast memory (SRAM) with a large amount of slower memory (DRAM). The system acts like a large amount of fast memory. The cache memory approaches the performance of SRAMs at the cost of DRAMs. The cache places the fast SRAMs between the processor and the slower main memory with the DRAMs. A cache controller contains the logic to implement the cache.

In a cache memory system, all the data is stored in main memory and some data is duplicated in the cache. When the processor accesses the memory, it checks the cache first. If the desired data is in the cache, the processor can access it quickly, since the cache is a fast memory. If the data is not in the cache, it must be fetched from the main memory.

A cache reduces average memory access time if it is organized so that code and data that the processor needs most often is in the cache. Programs execute faster when most operations are transfers to and from the faster cache memory.

If the requested data is found in the cache, the memory access is called a *cache hit;* if not, it is called a *cache miss*. The hit rate is the percentage of accesses that are hits. It depends on the size and organization of the cache, the cache algorithm and the program being run. Programs usually access memory in area of locations accessed most recently. This is known as *program locality* or *locality of reference*.

It allows cache systems to work, and on a larger scale, demand paging systems. In many programs, code execution is sequential or in
small loops. The next few accesses are always nearby. Data variables
are usually accessed several times in succession. Jumps and switching
between programs do not allow program locality.

## Block Fetch

A block fetch uses program locality to increase the hit rate of a cache.
The cache controller partitions the main memory into blocks. Typical
block sizes are 2, 4, 8, or 16 bytes. A 32-bit processor usually uses two
or four words per block. When a desired word is not in the cache, the
cache controller moves the block that contains the needed word.

A block fetch can retrieve the data located before the requested byte,
called *look-behind,* or after the requested byte, called *look-ahead.* Both
of these are sometimes used. The blocks are aligned as 2-byte blocks on
word boundaries or 4-word blocks on double-word boundaries. An
access to any byte in the block copies the whole block to the cache.

When the memory locations are accessed in ascending order, an
access to the first byte of a block in main memory produces a look-
ahead block fetch. When memory locations are accessed in descending
order, the block fetch becomes look-behind.

Block size is an important parameter in a cache memory system. If the
block size is too small, the look-ahead and look-behind are reduced, and
the hit rate is smaller. Larger blocks reduce the number of blocks that fit
into a cache. Each block fetch overwrites the older cache contents and a
smaller number of blocks results in more data being overwritten.

As a block becomes larger, the additional word is further from the
requested word and less likely to be needed by the processor (less program locality). Larger blocks require a wider bus between the cache
and the main memory, as well as more static and dynamic memory.
This tends to increase the cost.

## Cache Organization

Programs need to reference to segments, subroutines and buffers
located in different parts of the address space. An effective cache must
therefore hold several noncontiguous blocks of data. An ideal cache
would hold the blocks most likely to be used by the processor regardless of the distance between these words in main memory.

A fully associative cache provides maximum flexibility in determining which blocks are stored in the cache at any time. In a direct-mapped
cache, only one address comparison is needed to determine whether
requested data is in the cache. Many address comparisons are needed in

the fully associative cache since any block from the main memory can be placed in any location of the cache. Every block of the cache must be checked for the requested address. The direct mapped cache reduces the number of comparisons needed by allowing each block from the main memory to have only one possible location in the cache.

A direct mapped cache address has two parts. The first part is called the *cache index field*. It has enough bits to specify a block location in the cache. The second part is called the *tag field*. It has enough bits to distinguish a block from other blocks.

## Performance Improvement

A 386 running at 33 MHz can perform a bus cycle in 60 nanoseconds, for a bandwidth of 66 megabytes per second. The memory system must be fast enough to complete bus cycles with no wait states. Dynamic RAMs (DRAMs), can provide a large amount of memory in a small space. These low-cost DRAMs cannot usually complete random read-write cycles in 60 nanoseconds. The faster static RAMs (SRAMs) can meet these bus timing requirements, but they are available in smaller packages at a higher cost.

A cache memory system uses a small amount of fast memory (SRAM) with a larger amount of slower memory (DRAM). The system acts like a large amount of fast memory since the cache memory approaches the performance of SRAMs at a lower cost. A cache memory (Fig. 3.1) has the faster SRAMs between the processor and the slower main memory which is made up of DRAMs. A cache controller is needed with the logic circuits to operate the cache.

A request for the byte of data in the main memory is handled as follows:

1. The cache controller determines the cache location from the 14 most significant bits of the index field.

2. The controller compares the tag field with the tag stored at location in the cache.

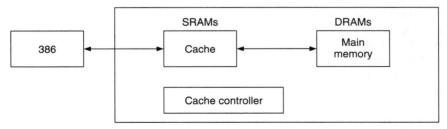

**Figure 3.1**   386 cache memory system.

3. If the tag matches, the processor reads the least significant byte from the data in the cache.

4. If the tag does not match, the controller fetches another block in the main memory and loads it into the cache, replacing the current block.

5. The controller changes the tag and the processor reads the least significant byte from the new block.

The cache controller makes only one comparison to determine if the requested word is in the cache. The address comparison requires only the tag field of the address. The direct-mapped cache uses direct addressing to eliminate all but one comparison operation.

The direct-mapped cache has some drawbacks. The processor may make frequent requests for several locations. However, only one location can be in the cache at a time, so the processor must access the main memory for the other. This means that the direct-mapped cache offers poorer performance than the fully associative cache, although it usually provides an acceptable performance level at a much lower cost.

## Set-Associative Cache

A set-associative cache is a hybrid of the fully associative and direct-mapped caches. In this type of cache, several sets (or groups) of direct-mapped blocks are used. These operate as several direct-mapped caches in parallel. For each cache index, several block locations are allowed, one in each set. A block of data from the main memory can go into a block location of any set. Compared to the direct-mapped cache, the set-associative cache contains half as many locations, but allows two blocks for each location.

Since the set-associative cache has several places for blocks with the same cache index in their addresses, the main memory traffic of the direct-mapped cache is reduced and the hit rate is increased. A set-associative cache is more efficient than a direct-mapped cache.

The set-associative cache is more complex than the direct-mapped cache. In a two-way set-associative cache, there are two locations in the cache in which each block can be stored. So, the controller must make two comparisons to determine in the block where the requested data is located. A set-associative cache also uses a wider tag field, and a larger SRAM to hold the tags. Also, a decision must be made as to which block will receive the information.

The controller also needs to decide which block to overwrite when a block fetch takes place. Three techniques are used:

1. Overwriting the least-recently accessed block. This requires the controller to keep the least-recently used (LRU) bits. These bits must be updated by the cache controller for each cache transaction.

2. Overwriting the blocks in sequential order, first-in first-out (FIFO).

3. Overwriting a block selected at random.

All of these are used, but the LRU technique provides the highest hit rate.

## Cache Updates

In a cache system, two copies of the same data can exist, one in the cache and one in the main memory. If one copy is modified and the other is not, two different data sets exist at the same address. The cache must have an updating system to prevent the old data sets, called "stale" data, from being used.

## Write-Through Updating

In write-through system updating, the controller copies the data to the main memory just after it is written to the cache. This forces the main memory to always contain valid data. The write-through approach decreases performance due to the time required to write the data to main memory and the increase in bus traffic.

In a buffered write-through system, the write accesses to the main memory are buffered, which allows the processor to begin a new cycle before the write cycle to the main memory is completed.

When a write access is followed by a read access that is a cache hit, the read access can take place while the main memory is being updated. So, the decrease in performance of the write-through system is avoided. Usually, only a single write access is buffered, so two consecutive writes to the main memory forces the processor to wait. A write followed by a read miss will also require the processor to wait.

## Write-Back Updating

In write-back updating, a section of the block in the cache, (called the *tag field*) uses a bit called the *altered bit*. This bit is set when the block is written with new data. Before overwriting a block in the cache, the cache controller checks the altered bit. If it is set, the controller writes the block to main memory before loading any new data into the cache.

Write-back is faster than write-through since the number of times an altered block must be copied into the main memory is usually less than the number of write accesses. But, the write-back cache controller logic is more complex than write-through. The write-back system must reconstruct the write address and perform the write-back cycle in addition to the requested access. All of the changed blocks must be written to the main memory before another device can access these blocks and in a power failure, the data in the cache is lost. This means the data in the cache is volatile.

## Coherency

Write-through and write-back eliminate stale data in the main memory caused by cache write operations. But, when more than one device has access to the main memory, (more than one processor) there is another problem. If new data is written to main memory by one device, the cache maintained by another device can contain stale data. This problem is solved with cache coherency. Several techniques are used.

Bus watching or snooping occurs when the cache controller monitors the address lines while other devices are accessing the shared memory. If another device writes to a location in memory which also resides in the cache memory, the controller invalidates the cache entry. The 82385 uses snooping for cache coherency.

Hardware transparency is another technique for cache coherency. This forces all accesses to memory to be known by the cache. This can be done by routing the accesses of all devices to the main memory through the same cache or by copying the cache writes both to the main memory and to the other caches that share the same memory. The copying technique is known as *broadcasting*.

If a noncacheable memory is used, all accesses to shared memory are cache misses and the shared memory is never copied into the cache. Software can offset the drop in the hit rate by copying data between noncacheable and cacheable memory and mapping the shared memory accesses to the cacheable locations.

Cache flushing occurs when any altered data is written to the main memory, if this has not been done with write-through, and then clears the contents of the cache. If all the caches in the system are flushed before a device writes to shared memory, there should be no stale data.

Combinations of the different techniques can be used. Hardware transparency may be used for time-critical I/O operations such as paging and a noncacheable memory for slower I/O such as printing.

## Coprocessors

The performance of many applications is improved by the use of specialized coprocessors. A coprocessor provides the hardware to perform functions that would otherwise be performed in software. The coprocessor extends the instruction set of the 386 microprocessor. The 386 DX microprocessor has a numeric coprocessor interface designed for the 387 math coprocessor. In applications that need high-precision integer and floating-point calculations, the numeric coprocessor provides support for these operations. The 387 DX coprocessor is software-compatible with the 80287 and 8087 earlier numeric coprocessors.

## Peripheral Chips

A DMA (Direct Memory Access) controller performs DMA transfers between main memory and an I/O device. This is typically a hard or floppy disk, or a communications channel. In a DMA transfer, a large block of data can be copied from one location to another without the intervention of the CPU. The 82380 peripheral chip has a 32-bit DMA controller. This chip provides a high data throughput with more efficient bus operation. The 32-bit DMA controller provides eight independent channels that can transfer data at the full bandwidth of the 386 microprocessor bus. A 40-megabyte-per-second data transfer rate is possible at 20 MHz. It also has a 20-source interrupt controller that will handle 15 external and 5 internal interrupt requests. There is a built-in DRAM refresh controller where the refresh request always has the highest priority among the DMA requests.

## Cache Controllers

A cache memory subsystem provides faster storage for frequently accessed instructions and data. This results in faster memory access for the microprocessor and reduces the traffic on the system bus. The 82385 cache controller supports a 32-kbyte cache memory and has an integrated cache directory with management logic.

## EISA Chips

EISA (Extended Industry Standard Architecture) expands the 32-bit capability of the 386 microprocessor to the I/O expansion bus. The 82350 chip set consists of 3 components:

1. The 82358 EISA bus controller
2. The 82357 integrated system peripheral
3. The 82352 EISA bus buffer

A 82355 Bus Master Interface Controller (BMIC) is needed for add-in board support. The BMIC provides all of the necessary control signals, address lines, and data lines for an EISA bus master to interface to the EISA bus. The EISA specification and the 82350 chip set are both compatible with the ISA (Industry Standard Architecture) AT-bus. So, software and expansion boards designed for the ISA bus can also be used in the higher performance EISA systems. The 82350 can also be used with the 486 DX and 386 SX microprocessors.

## MCA Chips

The 82311 chip set consists of peripheral components for IBM PS/2-compatible system boards. This chip set supports the Micro Channel Architecture and includes the following:

1. The 82303 and 82304 local I/O support chips

2. The 82307 DMA/CACP controller

3. The 82308 micro channel bus controller

4. The 82309 address bus controller

5. The 82706 VGA graphics controller

6. The 82077 floppy disk controller

The 82311 chip set has all the peripheral functions needed to interface to the CPU, micro channel bus, I/O peripheral, bus and the graphics channel.

## LAN Coprocessor

The 82596DX is a LAN coprocessor that provides high-level commands, command chaining, and interprocessor communications via shared memory. This relieves the CPU of many tasks used in network control. Time-critical functions are performed independently of the CPU, which improves performance. The 82596 is also available for the 386 SX and 486 DX CPUs.

## Clock Generator

A clock generator circuit generates timing for the 386 microprocessor and its supporting components. The circuit provides the 386 microprocessor clock (CLK2) and a half-frequency clock (CLK) to indicate the internal phase of the microprocessor. The half-frequency clock can be used to operate 80286 devices that may be in the system. It may also be used to generate the RESET signal for the 386 microprocessors.

With the appropriate interface, the 386 microprocessor can use 8086/80286 family components. The 8259A Programmable Interrupt Controller manages interrupts for the 386 microprocessor system. Interrupts from up to eight external sources are handled by one 8259A and up to 64 requests can be handled by cascading 8259A chips. The 8259A resolves priority between active interrupts. It then interrupts the processor and passes a code to the processor to identify the interrupting source.

## 386 Bus Signals

The 386 uses a 132-lead PG package. The 80386 address bus has 30 lines. A0 and A1 are not part of the bus as indicated in the following list.

| | | | |
|---|---|---|---|
| 2X clock | CLK2 | Address bus | A2-A31 |
| | | Byte enable | BE3* |
| | | Byte enable | BE2* |
| 32-bit data bus | DO-D31 | Byte enable | BE1* |
| | | Byte enable | BEO* |
| Bus control | ADS* | Bus cycle | W/R* |
| Bus control | NA* | Bus cycle | D/C* |
| Bus control | BS16* | Bus cycle | M/I0* |
| Bus control | READY* | Bus cycle | LOCK* |
| Bus arbitration | HOLD | Coprocessor | PEREQ |
| Bus arbitration | HLDA | Coprocessor | BUSY* |
| | | Coprocessor | ERROR* |
| Interrupts | INTR | | |
| Interrupts | NMI | | |
| Interrupts | RESET | | |

## Bus Operations

The 386 performs a variety of bus operations in response to internal and external conditions. One of these is interrupt servicing. The function and timing of the signals that make up the local bus interface are designed to provide the sequences needed for the particular local bus operations.

At 33 MHz, the 386 DX CPU bus transfers up to 66 Mbytes/seconds of data. The 386 DX microprocessor communicates with external memory, I/O, and other devices through a parallel bus interface. This interface consists of a data bus, a separate address bus, five bus status pins, and three bus control pins as follows:

1. The bidirectional data bus consists of 32 pins (D31-D0). Either 8, 16, 24, or 32 bits of data can be transferred.

2. The address bus, which generates 32-bit addresses, consists of 30 address pins (A31-A2) and four byte-enable pins (BE3-BE0). Each byte-enable pin corresponds to one of four bytes of the 32-bit data bus. The address pins identify a 4-byte location, and the byte-enable pins select the active bytes within the 4-byte location.

3. The bus status pins indicate the bus cycle as follows:

Address Status (ADS)        Address bus outputs valid

Write/Read (W/R)            Write or read cycle

Memory/I/O (M/IO)           Memory or I/O access

Data/Control (D/C#)         Data or control cycle

LOCK                        Locked bus cycle

4. The bus control pins allow external logic to control the bus cycle as follows:

READY                       Ends the current bus cycle

Next Address (NA)           Allows address pipelining by emitting address and status signals for the next bus cycle during the current cycle

Bus Size 16 (BS16)          Activates 16-bit data bus operation so data is transferred on the lower 16 bits of the data bus; an extra cycle is provided for transfers of more than 16 bits

Other control pins include:

1. The CLK2 input provides a double-frequency clock signal for synchronous operation. This signal is divided by two internally, so the 386 fundamental frequency is half the CLK2 signal frequency. For example, a 33-MHz 386 uses a 66-MHz CLK2 signal.

2. The RESET input forces the Intel386 DX microprocessor to a known reset state.

3. The HOLD signal is used to request that the 386 release control of the bus. The 386 then activates the Hold Acknowledge (HLDA) signal as it releases control of the local bus.

4. The maskable interrupt (INTR) and nonmaskable interrupt (NMI) inputs cause the 386 microprocessor to interrupt its current instruction stream and begin execution of an interrupt service routine.

5. The BUSY, ERROR, and Processor Extension Request (PEREQ) signals are used to interface with an external numeric coprocessor. BUSY and ERROR are status signals from the coprocessor. PEREQ allows the coprocessor to request data from the 386.

The 80386 decodes A0 and A1 into 4-byte enable lines BE0 to BE3. This allows the 80386 to address any combination of bytes in the 32-bit data word.

The 80386 needs a clock generator, the 82384 which generates both a reset signal and a clock signal. This signal runs at twice the rated microprocessor speed.

Four signal lines are used for the bus cycle. These are W/R, D/C, M/IO, and LOCK. These lines all operate with a low-true signal. W/R is used for a read or write cycle while D/C indicates a data or control cycle. M/O indicates a bus cycle for memory or I/O space. LOCK allows the 80386 to keep control of the bus during the multiple address cycles needed for an instruction queue.

The uses of the M/IO, D/C and W/R signals for the different bus cycles are shown as follows:

| M/IO | DC | W/R | Bus Cycle |
|------|-----|-----|-----------|
| 0 | 0 | 0 | Interrupt Acknowledge |
| 0 | 0 | 1 | Idle Cycle |
| 0 | 1 | 0 | I/O Data Read |
| 0 | 1 | 1 | I/O Data Write |
| 1 | 0 | 0 | Memory Code Read |
| 1 | 0 | 1 | Halt-Shutdown |
| 1 | 1 | 0 | Memory Data Read |
| 1 | 1 | 1 | Memory Data Write |

The actual bus-cycle mechanism uses four bus-control signals: ADS, NA, BS16, and READY. These lines also operate with a low-true signal. ADS is the Address Status line and it is used at the beginning of a bus cycle to indicate that the address, byte-enable, and bus-definition lines are valid. When a bus cycle is started, the 80386 sets the address, byte-enable, and cycle-definition signals at the proper signal levels and then sets ADS.

The port being addressed will set the READY signal, acknowledging the cycle. The 80386 will terminate the cycle after receiving READY. To speed up consecutive cycles, there is an NA (Next Address) signal that allows the peripheral device to accept and acknowledge an address before it acknowledges the cycle. When NA is used, the 80386 can place the next cycle's address on the address bus to speed up the address decoding. The actual cycle cannot be started until READY acknowledges the current cycle.

Another signal called BS16 (Bus Size 16), allows a 16-bit peripheral device to signal that it cannot handle 32-bit bus cycles. The 80386 will then split the 32 bits into two 16-bit sections.

Besides RESET, there is a maskable interrupt request (INTR) and a nonmaskable interrupt request (NMI). The 80386 services a maskable interrupt request by reading an 8-bit interrupt vector and using one of the 256 possible interrupt service routines.

In a multiprocessor environment, the HOLD and HLDA signals allow a common bus to be shared with other microprocessors. There are also three signals that allow the 80386 to work with a coprocessor. PEREQ is a signal that the coprocessor uses to request that the 80386 transfer an operand between the coprocessor and memory. The coprocessor uses

BUSY to tell the 80386 that it is busy executing an instruction. ERROR is used by the coprocessor to signal an error condition to the 80386.

## Types of Bus Operations

The seven types of bus operations include memory read and write, I/O read and write, instruction fetch, interrupt acknowledge and halt/shutdown. A bus cycle is initiated when the address is valid on the address bus. The bus status pins are set and ADS is set low. Memory read and memory write cycles can be locked to prevent another bus master from using the local bus.

The 386 microprocessor uses a double-frequency clock input (CLK2) to generate its internal processor clock signal (CLK); each CLK cycle is two CLK2 cycles wide. Each bus cycle is made up of at least two bus states: T1 and T2. Each bus state in turn has two CLK2 cycles, which can be thought of as Phase 1 and Phase 2 of the bus state. During the first bus state (T1), the address and bus status pins go active. During the second bus state (T2), external logic and devices respond. When no bus cycles are needed by the 386, no bus requests are pending and the 386 remains in the idle bus state.

## Performance Factors

System performance means how fast the microprocessing system performs a given task or set of instructions. Two basic methods are used to match the speed of the 386 to external devices. These are bus cycle timing and caches. Bus cycle timing includes the use of wait states and pipelining.

## Wait States

A system may use devices whose response is slow compared to the 386 bus cycle. Two techniques for handling these slow devices are wait states and address pipelining.

Wait states are extra CLK cycles added to the microprocessor bus cycle. External logic generates the wait states by delaying the READY# input to the 386. In a 386 running at 33 MHz, one wait state adds 30 nanoseconds to the time available for the memory to respond. Each wait state increases the bus cycle time by 50 percent of the zero wait-state cycle time. But, the overall system performance does not suffer in direct proportion to the bus cycle change.

## Address Pipelining

In the 386, the timing address and status outputs can be controlled so the outputs become valid before the end of the previous bus cycle. This technique allows bus cycles to be overlapped and is called *address pipelining.*

It increases the bus throughput without decreasing memory or I/O access time. This allows high bandwidth with relatively inexpensive components. Using pipelining to address slower devices can provide the same throughput as addressing faster devices without pipelining. When address pipeline is activated following an idle bus cycle, performance drops slightly since the first bus cycle cannot be pipelined.

Address pipelining increases the time that a memory has to respond by one CLK cycle without increasing the bus cycle. The extra CLK eliminates the output delay of the 386 address and status outputs. Address pipelining overlaps the address and status outputs of the next bus cycle with the end of the current bus cycle. This increases the address access time by one or more CLK cycles for the accessed memory device. An access that requires two wait states without address pipelining needs only one wait state with address pipelining.

Address pipelining will help in most bus cycles, but if the next address is not available before the current cycle ends, the 386 cannot pipeline the next address, and the bus timing is the same as a non-pipelined bus cycle.

The NA input controls address pipelining. When the system no longer requires the microprocessor to drive the address of the current bus cycle, the system can use the NA input. The microprocessor outputs the address and status signals for the next bus cycle on the next CLK cycle.

Address pipelining is not as effective for I/O devices requiring several wait states. The more wait states required, the less important the elimination of one wait state using pipelining becomes.

Another less common approach to handling memory speed is reducing the microprocessor operating frequency. Since a slower clock frequency increases the bus cycle time, fewer wait states may be required for some memory devices. System performance depends directly on the microprocessor clock frequency since execution time decreases in direct proportion to the decrease in clock frequency.

## Memory Speed

In a high-performance microprocessor system, like the 386, the overall system performance also depends on the performance of the memory subsystems. Most of the bus cycles are used to access memory since the memory holds the programs as well as the data used in processing.

A microprocessor like the 386 must use relatively fast memory. These faster memory devices will cost more than slow memory devices. Suppose we partition the functions and use a combination of both fast and slow memories. Then if the most frequently used functions are handled with the faster memory and all other functions are handled with the slower memory, good performance for most operations will be achieved at a lower cost compared to a completely fast memory subsystem. This is also done with read-only memory devices that are used primarily during initialization. These devices can be quite slow with three to four wait states and they will have little effect on system performance.

## Address Latching and Decoding

Latches hold the address for the duration of the bus cycle and are needed to pipeline addresses since the address for the next bus cycle will appear on the address lines before the current cycle ends. Address decoders, which convert the microprocessor address into chip-select signals, may be located before or after the address latches.

If they are before the latches, the chip-select signal becomes valid as early as possible and must be latched along with the address. The number of address latches depends on the location of the address decoder and the number of address bits and chip-select signals needed by the interface. Chip-select signals may be sent to the bus control logic to set the number of wait states needed for the accessed device.

## Data Transceivers

Standard 8-bit transceivers, like the 74LS245, are used to provide isolation and additional drive capability for the 386 data bus. Transceivers prevent any contention on the data bus that may occur when devices are slow to remove read data from the data bus after a read cycle. If a write cycle follows a read cycle, the 386 may drive the data bus before a slow device has removed its outputs from the bus.

The bus interface must have enough transceivers to handle the device with the most inputs and outputs on the data bus. A 32-bit-wide memory subsystem needs four 8-bit transceivers.

A 74LS245 transceiver uses two input signals:

1. *Data Transmit / Receive (DT / R).*   When this is high, it enables the transceiver for a write cycle. When it is low, it enables the transceiver for a read cycle. This signal is a latched version of the 386 W/R output.

2. *Data Enable (DEN).*   When this is low, it enables the transceiver outputs. This signal is generated by the bus control logic.

## Bus Control

The bus controller decodes the 386 status outputs (W/R, M/IO and D/C) and activates a command signal for the type of bus cycle requested. The memory data read and memory code read cycles will generate an EPROM Read Command (EPRD). This is an output that tells the selected memory device to output data.

I/O read cycles generate a I/O Read Command (IORD) output. This tells the selected I/O device to output data. I/O write cycles generate an I/O Write Command (IOWR) output. This tells the selected I/O device to receive the data on the data bus.

Interrupt-acknowledge cycles generate an Interrupt Acknowledge (INTA) output, which is sent to the 8259A Interrupt Controller. The second INTA cycle tells the 8259A to place the interrupt vector on the bus. The bus controller also controls the READY input to the microprocessor that ends each bus cycle.

### Refresh Cycles

The DRAMs will require periodic refreshing. This is usually done by activating each of the row address signals to refresh the data in every column of the row. The frequency of refreshing and the number of rows to be refreshed depends on the type of DRAM. For large DRAMs, only the lower eight multiplexed address bits must be supplied during the refresh cycle. Larger DRAMs usually require a refresh every 4 milliseconds.

### Distributed Refresh

In distributed refresh, the refresh cycles are distributed equally within the 4-millisecond interval. Every 15.625 microseconds (4 milliseconds/256 rows), a single row refresh takes place. After 4 milliseconds all 256 rows have been refreshed and the pattern is repeated. Refresh requests are always given the highest priority. If a DRAM access is already in progress, it must be allowed to finish before the refresh cycle can start.

A distributed refresh has some advantages over other types of refresh. The refresh cycles are spread out, so the microprocessor access is not delayed for long by the refresh cycles. Most software runs at approximately the same rate. The distributed refresh hardware is usually simpler than that required for other types of refresh.

### Burst Refresh

A burst refresh does all of the row refreshes consecutively once every 4 milliseconds instead of distributing them over the time period. Once this refresh is complete, the next 4-millisecond period is free of refresh cycles. The 82380 DRAM Refresh Controller is designed to perform refresh operations.

## I/O Interfacing

The 386 DX microprocessor supports 8-bit, 26-bit, and 32-bit I/O devices. These can be mapped into either the 64-kilobyte I/O address space or the 4-gigabyte physical memory address space. I/O mapping and memory mapping of I/O devices have the following characteristics: (1) The address decoding needed to generate chip selects for I/O-mapping is usually simpler than memory-mapping, (2) I/O-mapped devices reside in the I/O space of the 386 microprocessor (64 kilobytes), and (3) memory-mapped devices reside in the much larger memory space of 4 gigabytes.

Memory-mapped devices can be accessed using any 386 microprocessor instruction. I/O-mapped devices can be accessed only through the IN, OUT, INS, and OUTS instructions. Memory-mapped devices are protected by the memory management and protection features.

The interface to a peripheral device depends not only upon data width, but also on the signal requirements of the device and its location within the memory space or I/O space.

## Address Decoding

Address decoding to generate chip selects is required if the I/O devices are I/O-mapped or memory-mapped. One technique for decoding memory-mapped I/O addresses is to map the entire I/O space of the 386 into a 64-kilobyte region of the memory space. The address decoding logic ensures that each I/O device responds to both a memory address and an I/O address. Addresses can be assigned to I/O devices arbitrarily within the I/O space or memory space.

Eight-bit I/O devices can be connected to any of the four 8-bit sections of the data bus. If the addresses of two devices lie within the same doubleword boundaries, BE3-BE0 are decoded to provide a chip-select signal that prevents a write to one device from erroneously performing a write to the other. This chip select is generated with an address decoder.

Another technique for interfacing with 8-bit peripherals is shown in Fig. 3.2. The 32-bit data bus is multiplexed into an 8-bit bus to allow byte-oriented DMA or block transfers to the memory-mapped 8-bit I/O devices.

In order to avoid extra bus cycles and to simplify device selection, 16-bit I/O devices are usually assigned to even addresses. If the I/O addresses are located on adjacent word boundaries, the address decode must generate the Bus Size 16 (BS16) signal so the 386 goes to a 16-bit bus cycle. If the addresses are located on every other word boundary (every doubleword address), BS16 is required.

In order to avoid extra bus cycles and to simplify device selection, 32-bit devices are assigned to addresses that are even multiples of four. The chip select for a 32-bit device is controlled with all byte enables (BE3-BE0) being active.

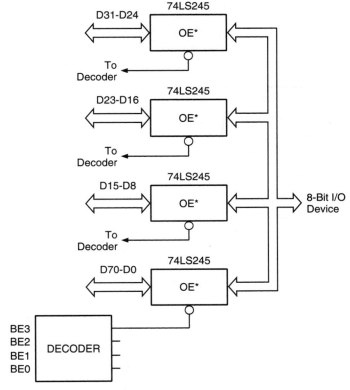

**Figure 3.2**   32-bit to 8-bit interface.

## Linear Chip Select

Systems with less than 14 I/O ports that are only in the I/O space or that require more than one active select can use linear chip selects to access the I/O devices. The latched address lines A2-A15 are connected to the I/O device selects as shown in Fig. 3.3.

## Interfacing

In a 386 system (Fig. 3.4), a number of slave I/O devices may be controlled through the same local bus interface. The I/O interface shown in Fig. 3.5 is used with the 386 for slave peripherals. The following peripherals may be used with this interface: 8259 Programmable Interrupt Controller, 8237 DMA Controller, 82258 Advanced DMA Controller, 8253, 8254 Programmable Interval Timer, 8272 Floppy Disk Controller, 82064 Fixed Disk Controller, 8274 Multi-Protocol Serial Controller, 8255 Programmable Peripheral Interface, and the 8041 or 8042 Universal Peripheral Interface.

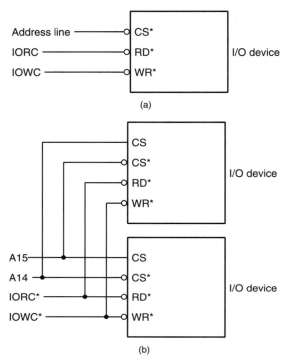

**Figure 3.3** Linear chip selection: (*a*) single chip select;
(*b*) multiple chip selection.

In most systems, the same control logic, address latches, and data buffers are used to access both memory and I/O devices. Latches hold the address for the duration of the bus cycle. If 74LS373 latches are used, the Latch Enable (LE) input is controlled by the Address Latch Enable (ALE) signal from the bus control logic. It goes active at the start of each bus cycle.

The address decoder converts the 386 address into chip-select signals. It can be located before the address latches or after the latches. If it is placed before the latches, the chip-select signal becomes valid as early as possible but it must be latched along with the address. The chip-select signals are sent to the bus control logic to set the correct number of wait states for the accessed device.

The decoder may be made up of two one-of-four decoders. One is used for memory address decoding and one for I/O address decoding. An output of the memory address decoder will activate the I/O address decoder for I/O accesses.

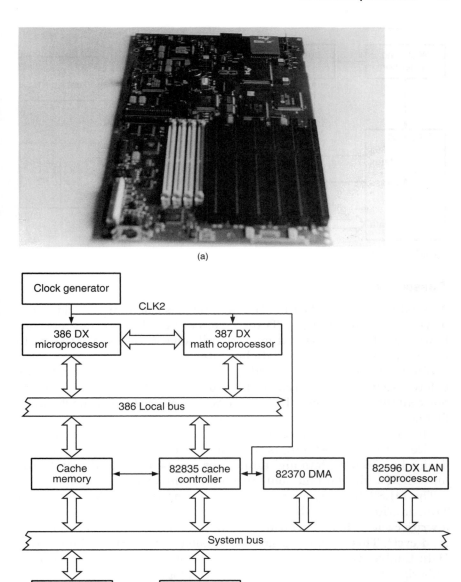

(a)

(b)

**Figure 3.4**    386 System board.

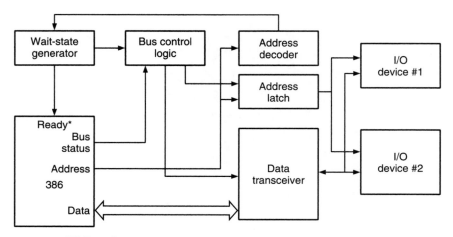

**Figure 3.5**   I/O Interface.

## Transceivers

An 8-bit transceiver like the 74LS245 provides isolation and additional drive for the 386 data bus. Transceivers are used to prevent any contention on the data bus that may occur if some devices take too long to remove read data from the data bus after a read cycle.

If a write cycle follows a read cycle, the 386 can drive the data bus before a slow device has removed its outputs from the bus, resulting in bus contention problems. Transceivers are not used when the device is fast enough.

The bus interface must have enough transceivers to handle the device with the most inputs and outputs on the bus. If the widest device has 16 data bits and all devices can be connected only to the lower half of the data bus, only two 8-bit transceivers are used.

The 74LS245 transceiver is controlled with two input signals. A Data Transmit/Receive (DT/R) is switched high to enable the transceiver for a write cycle. When it is switched low, it enables the transceiver for a read cycle. This signal is a latched version of the 386 W/R output. A Data Enable (DEN) is switched low to enable the transceiver outputs. This signal is generated by the bus control logic.

## Bus Control Logic

The bus control logic for the I/O interface is the same as the logic for the memory interface. The bus controller decodes the 386 status outputs (W/R, M/IO, and D/C) and activates a command signal for the bus cycle selected. The bus controller also controls the READY input to the Intel 386 DX microprocessor that ends each bus cycle. The following bus cycles are used.

1. A data read or memory code read cycle generates the Memory Read Command output. This commands the selected memory device to output data.

2. I/O read cycles generate an I/O Read Command output which commands the selected I/O device to output data.

3. I/O write cycles generate an I/O Write Command output. This commands the selected memory device to receive the data on the data bus.

4. Interrupt-acknowledge cycles generate the Interrupt Acknowledge (INTA) output, which is sent to the 8259A Interrupt Controller.

The added wait states on some devices to match them with other devices does not significantly impact performance. If the response of the device is slow with four wait states already, an additional wait state produces a relatively small delay. Typically, I/O devices are used infrequently so their access time is not critical to system performance.

### 486 Microprocessor

The 486 processor is upward binary compatible with the 8086, 8088, 80186, 80286, 386 DX processor and 386 SX processors. It includes an integer processing unit, floating-point processing unit, memory-management unit, and cache. With these units on a single chip, more signals remain on-chip, running at higher speeds than those using printed circuit board tracks. The increased level of integration also reduces board space, which lowers the cost.

The 486 can provide two to four times the performance of the 386, depending on the clock speeds used and the application. Like the 386, the 486 uses both segment-based and page-based memory protection. The instruction processing time is reduced with instruction pipelining.

The 486 bus is faster than the 386 local bus. Both buses are 32 bits wide, but the 486 bus uses a single-frequency (1X) clock and supports parity checking, burst cycles, cacheable cycles, cache invalidation cycles, and 8-bit data buses.

One advantage of using a 1X clock is that it simplifies the system by cutting in half the clock frequency used by external devices. Other advantages are the reduced RF emission at the higher speeds of the 486 processor and simplified clock generator circuitry.

Burst cycles for read transfers are possible at the rate of one 32-bit (doubleword) transfer per clock cycle. In the 386, a data transfer requires at least two clock cycles. The external cache, interleaved memory banks, or DRAMs with static-column addressing help to achieve zero wait-state memory performance during a burst.

Instructions can also be executed in fewer clock cycles than with the 386. In the 486, streamlined instruction pipelining provides an execution rate of one clock cycle per instruction for most instructions. The internal cache provides a rate of one processor request per clock cycle. There is also a built-in self-test.

The 32-bit integrated math processor performs arithmetic and logical operations on 8-, 16-, and 32-bit data types using a full-width ALU and eight general-purpose registers. Separate 32-bit address and data paths allow four gigabytes of memory to be addressed. An internal write-through cache can hold 8 Kbytes of data or instructions.

## On-chip Caching

The 8K-byte cache stores recently accessed information on the processor chip. This includes both instructions and data. When the processor needs to read data which is available in the cache, the cache is used and the time needed for an external memory cycle is avoided. This speeds up transfers and reduces traffic on the bus.

The cache uses a write-through protocol where all writes to the cache are passed to the external memory which the cache represents, rather than stored for memory updating (write-back). The processor uses a cache line fill to place new information in the on-chip cache. This reads four double words into a cache line, the smallest unit of storage which can be allocated in the cache. Most of the read cycles on the bus result from cache misses, which cause cache line fills.

## Floating-Point Unit

The internal floating-point unit performs floating-point operations on the 32-, 64-, and 80-bit arithmetic formats. Floating-point instructions are executed fastest when they are internal to the processor. This occurs when all operands are in the internal registers or cache. Bus signals are used to monitor errors in floating-point operations and to control the processor's response to these errors.

## System Components

For Ethernet interfacing, the 82596 32-bit LAN coprocessor may be used to handle network data management and physical-layer LAN functions. The 82320 32-bit MCA system peripherals provide interfacing to Micro Channel expansion buses for PS/2 systems and the 82350 32-bit EISA system peripherals provide interfacing to EISA expansion buses.

## 82596 LAN Coprocessor

The 82596 LAN coprocessor is a 32-bit local area network communications processor that supports 80-Mbyte/second transfers at 25 MHz. It implements carrier-sense, multiple-access, and collision-detect (CSMA/CD) link access protocol and can interface the 486 to a variety of networks including: IEEE 802.3 networks (Ethernet, HDLC, Cheapernet, and StarLAN) and IBM PC networks (baseband and broadband).

The 486 processor and 82596 LAN coprocessor talk to each other using a memory-based mailbox. The coprocessor fetches and executes commands for network functions. It handles the interprocessor communication. Since it executes commands without processor intervention, the 486 performance is improved.

In the 82596 coprocessor, a serial subsystem interfaces to the physical-layer device for the network. This subsystem performs the CSMA/CD media-access-control and channel-interface functions.

A parallel subsystem interfaces to the 486 processor. This subsystem contains a data interface unit, bus interface unit, four-channel DMA and command processor. A FIFO (first-in first-out) subsystem connects the serial and parallel subsystems, allowing them to run asynchronously.

The coprocessor can be used in either baseband or broadband networks. It can be configured for any physical cable length operating at data rates up to 20 Mbits/second.

The coprocessor provides several diagnostic and network management functions, including internal and external loopback, exception condition reporting, channel activity, capture of erroneous or collided frames, and time-domain reflectometry for locating fault points on the network cable. The coprocessor has a monitor mode for network analysis. This mode can be used to capture status bytes and update counters of monitored frames.

The 82596 coprocessor is an extension of the earlier 82586 LAN coprocessor, which interfaces an Ethernet network to a 16-bit Intel bus. The 82596 coprocessor can run software drivers written for the 82586.

The coprocessor's bus cycles—including burst cycles, bus interface timing, bus arbitration method, and signal definitions—are compatible with the 486 processor. When the coprocessor is not holding the bus, its bus interface signals are floated.

The similarities between the 486 processor and the 82596 coprocessor simplify bus arbitration when the processor and the coprocessor are the only two bus masters on the processor bus. The HOLD and HLDA signals may be used for handshake arbitration and BREQ from the processor may be used to control the coprocessor's bus throttle timers.

## Turbocache Module

The Turbocache Module is a write-through, second-level cache for the 486 microprocessor. It consists of the 82485 cache controller and 4 to 8 SRAMs. The Turbocache Module is an upgrade that provides 64K or 128 Kbytes of external cache memory. Up to four modules can be cascaded for up to 512 Kbytes of external cache memory. The module is organized as two-way, set-associative, and typically provides a 5 to 30 percent performance improvement.

## EISA Chip Set

The 8235 set of peripherals interfaces the 486 processor to an extended industry standard architecture (EISA) bus. The chips include three system board peripherals (bus controller, integrated system peripheral, and bus buffers) and one peripheral for EISA-bus expansion boards (bus master interface chip).

The EISA standard maintains full compatibility with the existing ISA (IBM-AT) standard. The EISA expansion board connector is a superset of the ISA expansion board connector, allowing existing 8- and 16-bit ISA boards to be installed in EISA slots. Transfers between buses of varying sizes or transfers with misaligned addresses are performed correctly.

## Personal Computers

In a personal computer system, the processor interacts directly with I/O devices and DRAM memory. Most peripherals are on separate plug-in boards. These include memory boards and I/O boards. An industry standard I/O architecture such as MCA or EISA is used. System cost and size are important.

Figure 3.6 shows a typical personal computer configuration. Where an external cache is used, the memory-access speed improves only if the cache uses a write-back system and the memory access has no more than one wait state.

## 486 Bus

The processor bus is the set of pins on the 486 processor chip. It is the bus that the processor uses to communicate with other devices in the system. The signals on the bus can be grouped by their functions:

1. Bus control and arbitration
2. Bus cycle definition and control
3. Address and data
4. Cache control
5. Floating-point error control

The processor bus uses nonmultiplexed 32-bit address and data buses with a single-frequency (1X) clock. At least 50 percent of the pro-

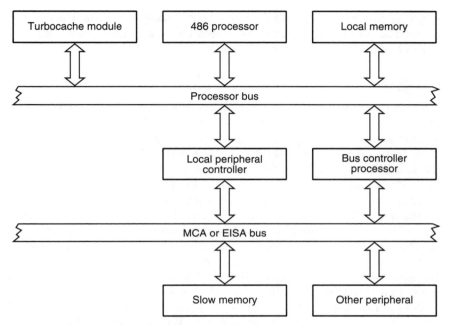

**Figure 3.6** Typical personal computer configuration.

cessor bus bandwidth is needed by the 486. Devices placed on the bus can include a LAN coprocessor or external cache controller.

In many systems, the processor bus will interface with one or more system buses. This distributes the bus traffic across greater bus bandwidth and provides more flexibility for system expansion.

Write cycles are the major 486 processor bus activity. This is different from other systems where read cycles are the major activity and may keep the processor waiting. The 486 uses its internal cache, instruction prefetch unit, support for burst transfers, and a memory system with one data transfer per clock cycle for high-speed computing.

Most of the processor's needs for instructions and data are satisfied quickly by the internal cache and instruction prefetch queue, without having to perform cycles on the processor bus. The processor bus can support multiple external caches.

The 386 processor used address pipelining on the processor bus to minimize the processor waiting time. The 486 processor uses burst reads with the on-chip cache instead of address pipelining on the bus to achieve high performance. This, along with the simpler 1X bus clock and more flexibility in bus-cycling, results in simpler system logic.

Two processor inputs are used to dynamically control the bus size for interfacing 8- and 16-bit devices. There are no problems with byte or word alignment within doubleword boundaries, but data that is not aligned to doubleword boundaries needs more than the minimum number of bus cycles to complete a transfer.

## Bus Cycles

The types of bus cycles show the processor's interactions with the external system. The 486 processor uses the following types of bus cycles: data transfer, prefetch (read) instructions from memory, read data from memory, read data from I/O, write data to memory, write data to I/O, and interrupt acknowledgment. Special bus cycles include halt, shutdown, cache flush, and cache write-back and flush.

Data can be transferred as doublewords, words, or bytes, depending on the bus size specified. All transfers use the 32-bit data bus but some transfers have only certain bytes enabled. Bus cycles that transfer data can be nonburst cycles that transfer up to four bytes at a maximum rate of two clocks per data item. Burst cycles are the fastest way to transfer more than one item of data. These cycles can transfer up to 16 bytes at a rate of one data item per clock cycle.

Transfers internal to the processor, such as reads from the internal cache, are not done on the processor bus. Writes to the cache are done on the bus since the cache uses a write-through technique.

## Bus Signals

Table 3.2 lists the signals on the processor bus.

## Address and Data Buses

The address and data buses are the paths that the bus cycles use to implement the data transfers. The Address Bus (A2-A31) contains bidirectional and output signals. A4-A31 are the bidirectional data bus signals while A2-A3 are for outputs. The A2-A31 signals handle the 30-bit physical address of a doubleword. A4-A31 also specify addresses in the internal cache that are invalid.

A0-A1 are internal. They generate the four byte-enable signals (BE0-BE3). Since the processor is a little-endian machine, the least significant byte of a doubleword is the lowest-addressed byte of that doubleword and the most significant byte is the highest-addressed byte of the doubleword.

The address-bit 20 Mask (A20M) simulates the address wraparound which occurs at 1 Mbyte on the 8086 processor. When A20M goes low, it causes the 486 processor to mask (clear to zero) physical address bit 20 when performing an internal-cache lookup and when writing to memory on the processor bus.

**TABLE 3.2    Processor Bus Signals**

| Group | Pins | Input | Output | Function |
|-------|------|-------|--------|----------|
| Address and | A4-A31 | x | x | Address |
| data buses | A2-A3 | | x | Address |
| | A20M* | x | | Address-bit 20 mask |
| | D0-D31 | x | x | Data |
| | BE0*-BE3* | | x | Byte-enable |
| | BS8* | x | | 8-bit data bus size |
| | BS16* | x | | 16-bit data bus size |
| | DP0-DP3 | x | x | Data parity |
| | PCHK* | | x | Parity error |
| Cycle definition | ADS* | | x | Address status |
| and control | M/IO* | | x | Memory or I/O |
| | D/C* | | x | Data or control |
| | W/R* | | x | Write or read |
| | RDY* | x | | Nonburst data ready |
| | BRDY* | x | | Burst data ready |
| | BLAST* | | x | Last burst cycle |
| | KEN* | x | | Internal-cache enable |
| Bus control | CLK | x | | Clock |
| | RESET | x | | Reset |
| | NMI | x | | Nonmaskable interrupt |
| | INTR | x | | Maskable interrupt |
| | BREQ | | x | Bus request |
| | HOLD | x | | Bus hold request |
| | HLDA* | | x | Bus hold acknowledgement |
| | BOFF* | x | | Bus backoff |
| | LOCK* | | x | Bus lock |
| | PLOCK* | | x | Bus pseudo-lock |
| Cache control | PCD | | x | Page cache disable (internal/ external) |
| | PWT | | x | Page cache write-through or write (external) |
| | EADS* | x | | Cache invalidation (internal) |
| | AHOLD | x | | Address-bus hold (internal) |
| | FLUSH* | x | | Cache flush (internal) |
| Floating-point | FERR* | | x | Floating-point error |
| error control | IGNNE* | x | | Ignore floating-point error |

The data bus (D0-D31) bidirectional signals can carry a doubleword. D0-D7 is the least significant byte. D24-D31 is the most significant byte. The valid bytes on the 32-bit bus are indicated by the byte-enable signals, BE0-BE3. The parity bit for each byte is indicated by the DP0-DP3 signals. The Bus Size (BS8 and BS16) inputs are used with the address of the data being accessed to control the byte-enable signals.

The parity check (PCHK) output will show a parity error, when it goes low, in one of the four bytes sampled during the last clock of a read transfer. Only enabled bytes are checked for parity.

## Cycle Definition and Control Signals

These signals indicate the type and direction of cycles taking place and the times when the data is valid. When the Address Status (ADS) output goes low, it shows when a valid address and cycle definition are on the processor bus. This signal marks the beginning of a bus cycle.

The Memory or I/O (M/IO) output specifies memory space (high output) or I/O space (low output). The Data or Control (D/C) output indicates a data cycle from other cycles when it is high. A Write or Read (W/R) output tells you if the cycle is a write (high output) or read (low output). These signals are used for bus cycle definition.

A low Ready (nonburst) (RDY) input shows when an external device has valid data on the data bus, or that the device has accepted the processor's data. Slow devices may hold back RDY, adding wait states until the data is stable.

The Burst Ready (BRDY) signal replaces RDY during a burst transfer. This signal acts like RDY, but it does not stop a burst cycle in progress. Up to 16 bytes can be transferred during the burst, at the rate of one doubleword, word, or byte per clock. The use of BLAST ends the burst. A low Burst Last (BLAST) output indicates the last transfer of any data transfer cycle.

A low Cache Enable (KEN) input enables the internal cache. When KEN is used, the current read cycle becomes a cache-line fill and 16 bytes are read.

## Bus Control Signals

These affect the basic timing and access to the bus including emergency actions. The Clock (CLK) input controls the timing of the processor and the bus. A Reset (RESET) input forces the processor to initialize in a known state. The reset can initialize registers and run various tests, depending on the conditions during the reset.

The Bus Request (BREQ) output indicates that the processor needs access to the bus, or that it is currently using the bus. A Bus Hold (HOLD) input causes the processor to release the bus. A low Bus-Hold Acknowledge (HLDA) output indicates that the processor has floated most of its bus signals as a result of a HOLD input.

A low Bus Lock (LOCK) output allows the processor to complete several bus cycles without interruption from a HOLD input. Locked read cycles are not cacheable. There is a Bus Pseudo-Lock (PLOCK) output that has a similar function. It is used when the data is aligned to quadword boundaries. This includes transfers of 64-bit floating-point operands and cache line fills.

A low Bus Backoff (BOFF) input is used when another bus master needs to complete a bus cycle. It is used to avoid a contention problem where each processor is waiting for some action by the other.

## Interrupts

A Maskable Interrupt (INTR) input can be masked by software. It interrupts the processor and makes it acknowledge the interrupt by reading an interrupt vector (number). The 486 does not have a separate output for acknowledgment of maskable interrupts like other Intel microprocessors. The 486 uses a special interrupt-acknowledgment bus cycle that reads the interrupt vector from external hardware.

In a Non-Maskable Interrupt (NMI), the input interrupts the processor and makes it execute the interrupt service routine, without reading a vector from external logic. These interrupts are used for conditions which need immediate attention, such as the loss of power.

In a Halt Cycle, the processor suspends operations. The cycle is generated by the HLT instruction. A Shutdown Cycle is used when the processor terminates its operations.

## Cache Control

Cacheable reads are held in the processor's internal 8-Kbyte cache. Cache control maintains consistency between the internal cache, external cache and main memory. Since each 4-Kbyte page of memory can have its cacheability, write-through, and write-back controlled for each cycle, additional outputs are needed. One control is the Page Cache Disable (PCD) output which shows if the page is cacheable.

A Page Write-Through (PWT) output applies a write-through cache for the page. Here, the updates to the external cache are immediately written through to memory. When switched back, this signal can allow a write-back cache to exist. Here, the updates to the cache are written back to memory only when requested. The internal cache is always write-through.

Other inputs are used for validation of the internal cache. The Address Hold (AHOLD) input forces the processor to float its address bus during the next clock cycle. This allows an external device to perform an internal cache line invalidation. For Internal Cache-Line Invalidation the EADS input is used with AHOLD. A low Internal Cache Flush (FLUSH) input forces the processor to flush the complete contents of its internal cache.

## Floating-Point Errors

Two signals are used for compatibility with DOS floating-point errors. One signal alerts the system to errors in the processor's floating-point unit and the other tells the processor what actions to take if errors occur. A low Floating-Point Error (FERR) output indicates that an unmasked floating-point error has occurred. This signal is similar to the ERROR# output on the 287 and 387 coprocessors. A low Ignore

Floating-Point Error (IGNNE) input tells the processor to ignore floating-point errors and continue execution.

## 486 Performance Factors

System performance depends on several factors including CPU speed, clock speed, memory transfer rate and size, disk access rate, and operating system. The CPU clock speed sets the maximum possible performance. Higher is faster, but it requires faster memories to keep the system going at the higher rate. The 486 is faster than most memory systems. It uses caches, write buffers and a prefetcher to allow the execution to go on with slow external memories.

The most important performance characteristic of the memory is the number of wait states needed to read a data item. At 33 MHz, a read operation requires 15 ns memory for no wait states. If slower memories are used, each wait state adds 30 ns to the access time at 33 MHz. Wait states cannot be avoided in practice.

The ideal memory system has no wait states. All bus cycles on the 486 would be completed in two clocks for a single access and five clocks for a cache fill. This would take large amounts of 15 ns memory. Most systems use DRAM with 60 to 100 ns access times.

A parameter called the read transfer rate is important for filling the internal cache of the 486. The 486 processor can transfer data from memory on every clock for most read transfers. This is twice the rate of individual memory cycles. If the memory systems can support this rate, performance is improved by 10 to 20 percent.

The write-cycle time is another important parameter. The 486 write-through cache generates almost twice as many writes as reads. Writes are more important for 16-bit programs since they generate more writes than 32-bit programs. The write-cycle time can limit system performance as the bus usage approaches the allowable maximum.

The on-chip cache of the 486 handles most of the read requests so the performance gain of an external cache is less compared to the 386. This performance gain depends on the application. Some will gain less than 5 percent with an external cache, most gain about 10 to 15 percent, while a few will gain as much as 40 percent.

## Cache Memory

The 486 executes instructions in fewer clocks than 386 microprocessors. This accounts for the heavy write traffic on the 486. The 486 can access instructions and data from its on-chip cache in the same clock cycle. The external bus can access external memory at twice the rate of the 386 CPU. The 486 has an on-chip cache which is organized in a 4-way set-associative manner.

The cache memory is a high-speed memory that is placed between the microprocessor and the main memory. It keeps copies of main memory that are currently in use to speed up the microprocessor access to the requested data and instructions. The cache access time can be three to eight times faster than the main memory. Caches also reduce the number of accesses to main memory.

The cache memory has a directory (or tag), and a data memory. When the CPU needs to read or write data, it first accesses the tag memory and determines if a cache hit has occurred. This means that the requested word is in the cache. If the tags do not match, the data word is not in the cache. This means there was a cache miss.

In a cache hit, the cache data memory allows a read operation to be done more quickly with its faster memory than from a slower main memory access.

The hit rate is the percentage of the accesses that are hits. It depends on the size and organization of the cache, the cache algorithm used, and the program in use.

A zero-wait state cache that has a hit rate of 90 percent will make the main memory appear to be a zero-wait state memory for 9 out of 10 accesses.

## Cache Performance

A number of factors affect a cache's performance. Increasing the cache size allows more items to be contained in the cache, but a larger cache cannot operate as quickly as a smaller one. Increased associativity increases the cache's hit rate but also reduces its speed.

The amount of data the cache must fetch during each cache line replacement (a miss) affects performance. More data takes longer to fill a cache line, but then more data is available and the hit rate improves. The ability to write quickly to the cache and then have the cache write to the slower memory also improves performance. Features like bus watching can also speed up a cache.

## I/O Interface

The peripheral (I/O) interface is an essential part of a microprocessor system. It supports communications between the microprocessor and the peripherals. The peripheral system must allow a variety of interfaces. An important factor are the buses which connect the major parts of the system. Devices like disks must be able to transfer data to a memory with minimal CPU overhead or interaction.

I/O devices may be accessed by dedicated I/O instructions for I/O mapped devices, or by memory operand instructions for memory mapped devices. The 486 microprocessor synchronizes I/O instruction execution with external bus activity. The previous instructions are completed before an I/O operation begins. All writes in the write buffers will be completed before an I/O read or write is performed.

All microprocessor systems include a microprocessor, memory, and I/O devices which are linked by the address, data, and control buses. Figure 3.7 shows the configuration of a typical 486 microprocessor-based system.

The 82596 LAN coprocessor can be used to provide an interface to a variety of networks. The 82596 is a 32-bit LAN coprocessor which implements the carrier-sense, multiple-access, and collision-detect (CSMA/CD) link access protocol. It relieves the processor of all local-network control functions and supports IEEE 802.3 (Ethernet, Ethernet Twisted Pair, Cheapernet, StarLAN, and IBM PC Networks (baseband and broadband). There is on-chip DMA and memory management along with network management and diagnostics.

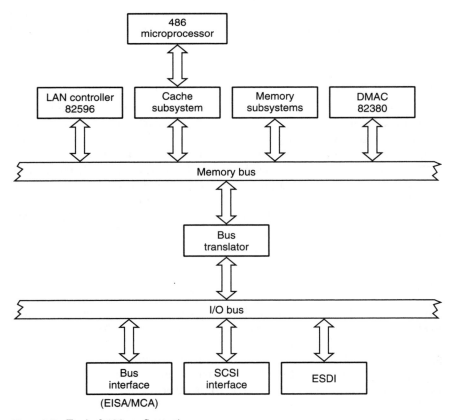

**Figure 3.7** Typical 486 configuration.

The 82350 EISA chip-set provides an interface between the 486 microprocessor and the Extended Industry Standard Architecture (EISA) bus. The chip-set includes a bus controller, integrated system peripheral, and a bus buffer. The basic I/O control logic, wait-state generation logic, and the address decode logic needed for EISA implementation is part of the 82350 chip set.

In most systems, the same control and data logic can access memory as well as I/O devices. The bus interface consists of bus control, data transceiver, byte swap logic, and address decoder.

A typical peripheral device has address inputs which the processor uses to select the devices's internal registers. It also has a chip-select (CS#) signal which enables it to read data from and write data to the data bus as controlled by the READ (RD) and WRITE (WR) control signals. If the microprocessor has separate memory and I/O addressing, either memory or I/O read and write signals can be used.

Many peripheral devices also generate an interrupt output which is asserted when a response is required from the microprocessor. Here, the microprocessor must generate a low interrupt acknowledge (INTA) signal.

The 486 supports 8-bit, 16-bit, and 32-bit I/O devices. These can be I/O mapped, memory mapped, or both. The 486 has a 106 Mbyte/sec memory bandwidth at 33 MHz.

Two techniques may be used to control the transmission of data between the computer and its peripherals. The most straight-forward approach is I/O mapping. The other is memory mapping.

The address decoding required to generate chip selects is much simpler in I/O mapping than memory mapping. I/O mapped devices reside in 64-K I/O space of the 486. Memory mapped devices reside in the much bigger memory space of 4 gigabytes.

## 8-Bit Peripherals

The 486 processor can be interfaced to peripheral devices from the 86 family (like the 8041) and the 8259A. These are universal peripheral interface devices which are used for peripheral device control. These devices have a slave interface on board and include an eight-bit CPU, ROM, RAM, and I/O timer/counter and a clock.

The 32-bit 486 microprocessor needs 32- to 8-bit byte-steering logic to interface to the 8-bit 8042. The bus controller logic will generate the BS8 signals.

## Comparison of 386 and 486

The 486 microprocessor is an integrated chip which is composed of a CPU, a math coprocessor, and a cache controller. It is compatible with the 386 microprocessor, but it has several differences. The 486 uses dynamic bus sizing to support 8-, 16-, and 32-bit bus sizes and requires external swapping logic. The 386 DX microprocessor supports only 16-bit and 32-bit bus sizes and does not require swapping logic.

The 486 has a burst transfer mode which can transfer four 32-bit words from external memory to the on-chip cache using only five clock cycles. The 386 DX microprocessor needs at least eight clock cycles to transfer the same amount of data. The 486 has a BREQ output to support multiprocessors.

The 486 processor bus is much faster than the 386 processor bus. The 486 also has a 1X clock, parity support, burst cycles, cacheable cycles, and cache invalidation cycles.

To support the on-chip cache, new bits were added to one of the control register and new pins were added to the bus along with new bus cycles. The on-chip cache is enabled by clearing these bits.

The 387 math coprocessor instruction set and register set have been added. I/O cycles are not performed during floating-point instruction execution.

The 486 microprocessor supports new floating-point error modes for DOS compatibility. These new modes use a new bit in one of the control registers and new signals FERR and IGNNE.

New instructions include:

1. Byte swap (BSWAP)

2. Exchange and add (XADD)

3. Compare and exchange (CMPXCHG)

4. Invalidate data cache (INVD)

5. Write-back and invalidate data Cache (WBINVD)

6. Invalidate TLB entry (INVLPG).

There are other new bits in the registers for page table and directory entries, page protection, and alignment checking. Three new testability registers have been added for testing of the on-chip cache and the prefetch queue has been increased from 16 bytes to 32 bytes.

## Pentium

This is the next generation of the 386 and 486 microprocessor family. It is binary compatible with the 8086/88, 80286, 386 DX, 386 SX, 486 DX, 486 SX and 486 DX2. The Pentium processor has all of the features of the 486 with the following enhancements and additions; superscalar architecture, dynamic branch prediction, pipelined floating-point unit, improved instruction execution, separate code and data caches, write-back data cache, 64-bit data bus, bus cycle pipelining, and address parity and internal parity checking.

The instruction set of the Pentium includes the 486 instruction set with extensions for the additional functions of the Pentium. Software written for the 386 and 486 can run on the Pentium. The on-chip memory management unit (MMU) is also compatible with the 386 and 486.

The Pentium has two instruction pipelines and floating-point units that are capable of independent operation. Each pipeline issues frequently used instructions in a single clock; the two pipelines can issue two integer instructions in one clock or one to two floating point instructions in one clock. Branch prediction is accomplished in the Pentium with two prefetch buffers. The floating-point unit has faster algorithms to speed some math operations up to 10 times.

## Caches

The Pentium processor has separate code and data caches on the chip. Each cache is 8 Kbytes, with a 32-byte line size and 2-way set associative. Each cache uses a Translation Lookaside Buffer (TLB) to translate linear addresses to physical addresses. The data cache can use write-back or write-through on a line-by-line basis. The cache tags are triple-ported to support two data transfers and an inquire cycle in the same clock.

The data bus is 64 bits which improves the data transfer rate. Burst read and write-back cycles are supported as well as bus cycle pipelining which allows two bus cycles to take place simultaneously.

## Test Functions

The Pentium processor uses functional redundancy checking for error detection. This is done for the processor and the interface to the processor. In functional redundancy checking, a second processor acts as the checker. It runs in parallel with the processor being tested. The checker samples the processor's outputs and compares them for a match. It signals an error condition if a match does not occur.

Since more functions have been placed on the chip, board-level testing becomes difficult. So, the Pentium processor has increased test and debug capability. Like other 486 CPUs, the Pentium uses IEEE Boundary Scan (Standard 1149). There are four breakpoint pins for the debug registers. These can be used for a breakpoint match.

## Signal Functions

Figure 3.8 shows a block diagram of the Pentium processor, which is a 32-bit microprocessor with 32-bit addressing and a 64-bit data bus. A 273-pin grid array package is used with the following signals.

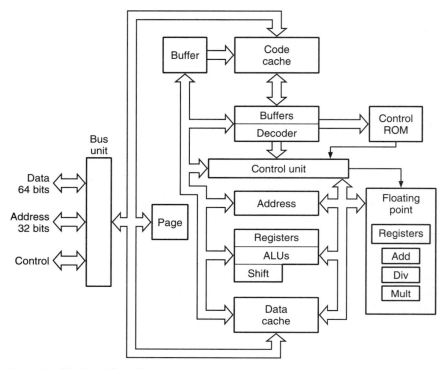

**Figure 3.8** Pentium block diagram.

**A20M.** The Address 20 Mask used to emulate the 1-Mbyte address wraparound on the 8086. When this asynchronous input is low, the Pentium processor masks physical address bit 20 (A20) before performing a lookup to the internal caches or driving a memory cycle on the bus.

**A31-A3.** The address lines which define the physical area of memory or I/O accessed. When used as outputs, the address lines along with the byte-enable signals (BE7-BE0) make up the address bus and define the physical area of memory or I/O accessed. The Pentium can address 4 gigabytes of physical memory space and 64 Kbytes of I/O address space. When they are used as inputs, the address bus lines drive addresses back into the processor to perform inquire cycles.

**ADS.** The address strobe. When it goes low, it shows that a new valid bus cycle is being driven by the Pentium processor. The following pins are driven to their valid level when ADS is used: A31-A3, AP, BE7-0, LOCK, M/IO, W/R, D/C, SCYC, PWT, and PCD.

**AHOLD.** The Address Hold. It floats the address bus so an inquire cycle can be driven to the processor. AHOLD allows another bus master to drive the processor address bus with the address for an inquire cycle.

*AP.* The bidirectional address parity pin for the address lines of processor. There is one address parity pin for address lines A31-A5. A4 and A3 are not used in the parity determination.

*APCHK.* The address parity check. The status of the address parity check appears on the APCHK low output. This will appear two clocks after EADS is sampled when the processor detects a parity error on the A31-A5 during inquire cycles.

*BE7-BE0.* The Byte Enables. When they go low, they help to define the physical area of memory or I/O accessed. The byte-enable outputs are used with the address lines to provide the physical memory and I/O port addresses. The byte enables tell what bytes of data must be written to external memory, or what bytes were requested by the CPU for the current cycle.

*BOFF.* The backoff input. A low forces the processor off the bus in the next clock. The processor will abort any outstanding bus cycles that have not been completed and float the processor bus in the next clock.

*BP/PM.* Pins that are used for breakpoint and performance monitoring. The breakpoint pins (BP3-BP0) correspond to debug registers DR3-DR0. These pins indicate a breakpoint match of a debug register. BP1 and BP0 can also be configured for performance monitoring.

*BRDY.* Burst Ready, which indicates when a transfer is complete. When it goes low, it shows there is valid data on the data pins in response to a read request, or that the external system has accepted the processor data in response to a write request.

*BREQ.* Bus request, which indicates that a bus cycle is pending. The processor uses the BREQ output in the first clock of a bus cycle with ADS.

*BT3-BT0.* The branch trace pins. They provide bits 0 through 2 of the branch target linear address and the default operand size during a branch trace cycle.

*BUSCHK.* Used as a bus check. It indicates an unsuccessful completion of a bus cycle. When this pin is low, the processor will latch the address and control signals of the failing cycle in the machine check registers.

*Cache.* Used for cacheability. It indicates cacheability of the cycle (if a read), and indicates a burst writeback (if a write). CACHE is used for cycles coming from the cache (writebacks) and for cycles that will go into the cache if KEN# is asserted (linefills). CACHE is active low for cacheable reads, cacheable code fetches, and writebacks.

*CLK.* Clock, which provides the basic timing for the processor. Its frequency is the internal operating frequency of the processor.

*D/C.*  Data/Code, the output which distinguishes a data access (high) from a code access (low). This is one of the primary bus cycle definition pins.

*D63-D0.*  The data lines for the 64-bit data bus. Lines D7-D0 define the least significant byte of the data bus and lines D63-D56 define the most significant byte of the data bus.

*DP7-DP0.*  Used for data parity. There is one parity pin for each byte of the data bus. DP7 applies to D63-D56 and DP0 applies to D7-D0.

*EADS.*  The external address strobe. It signals the processor to run an inquire cycle with the address on the bus. The address sent to the processor when EADS is low will be checked with the current cache contents.

*EWBE.*  The external write buffer empty input. When it is inactive (high), it indicates that a write-through cycle is pending. When the processor generates a write to memory or I/O, and EWBE is inactive, the processor will not issue any more writes until all write-through cycles have been completed.

*FERR.*  Indicates a floating-point error. It is active low when an unmasked floating-point error occurs. FERR is similar to the ERROR pin on the 387 math coprocessor.

*FLUSH.*  A cache flush. When it is low, it forces the processor to write-back all modified lines in the data cache and invalidate both internal caches. A Flush Acknowledge cycle is then generated by the processor to indicate completion of the invalidation and writeback.

*FRMC.*  Functional redundancy checking master/checker configuration. Indicates if the processor is configured as a master or checker. When it is configured as a master (high), the processor drives its output pins as required by the bus. When it is used as a checker (low), the processor tristates all outputs (except IERR and TDO) and samples the output pins that would normally be driven. The processor may then use IERR to indicate an error.

*HIT.*  Used as an inquire cycle hit/miss indication. It tells when an inquire cycle results in a hit or miss. When it is low (a hit), the inquire address on the address bus is valid in an internal cache.

*HITM.*  A hit/miss to a modified line. It indicates if an inquire cycle hit a modified line in the data cache. When it is low, the inquire address on the address bus is in the modified state in the data cache.

*HLDA.*  A bus hold acknowledge. It indicates that the processor has given the bus to another bus master and is initiated by HOLD. The internal instruction execution will continue from the internal caches during the bus HOLD/HLDA.

*HOLD.* A bus hold. It allows another bus master to take control of the processor bus. After completing any outstanding bus cycles the processor will float most of its output and input/output pins and send a HLDA.

*BT.* Instruction branch taken. It indicates that a branch was taken. The instruction branch taken output will be driven high for one clock.

*IERR.* An internal parity or functional redundancy check error. When it is low, it alerts the system of these errors.

*IGNNE.* An ignore numeric exception. When it is low, a numeric exception is ignored by the processor.

*INT.* Used for initialization. This input forces the processor to begin execution in a known state without flushing the caches or affecting floating-point state. The processor state after INIT is the same as the state after RESET except that the internal caches, write buffers, model specific registers, and floating-point registers retain the values they had prior to INIT.

*INTR.* Used for an external interrupt. This input indicates that an external interrupt has been generated. The processor will generate two locked interrupt acknowledge bus cycles in response to the INTR pin going active.

*INV.* An invalidation request. It determines the final state of a cache line as a result of an inquire hit. If the inquire cycle is a miss in the cache, the INV input has no effect.

*IU.* Means the u-pipeline instruction is complete. This output is driven high for one clock.

*IV.* Means the v-pipeline instruction is complete. This output is driven high for one clock.

*KEN.* Used for cache enable. When it is low, the current cycle is cacheable.

*LOCK.* The bus lock. It indicates to the system that the current sequence of bus cycles should not be interrupted. The bus lock output is low when the processor is running a read-modify-write cycle where the external bus cannot be relinquished between the read and write cycles.

*M/IO.* The Memory/Input-Output. It indicates a memory access (high) or an I/O access (low). This is one of the primary bus cycle definition pins.

*NA.* Used for the next address. A low indicates that external memory is prepared for a pipelined cycle. The external memory is ready to accept a new bus cycle although all data transfers for the current cycle may not yet be completed. This is called *bus cycle pipelining.*

*NMI.* A nonmaskable interrupt. It indicates that an external non-maskable interrupt has been generated. External interrupt acknowledge cycles are not generated.

*PCD.* The page cacheability disable. It indicates the state of the cache disable paging attribute bit for the current cycle.

*PCHK.* A data parity check. A low indicates the result of a parity check on a data read. Data parity is checked during code reads, memory reads, and I/O reads. Data parity is not checked during the first Interrupt Acknowledge cycle. PCHK indicates the parity status only for the bytes on which valid data is expected.

*PEN.* The parity enable. A low indicates to the processor that the correct data parity is being returned by the system. It is used to determine if a machine check exception should be taken if a data parity error is detected.

*PM/BP.* Performance monitoring and breakpoint outputs. BP1 and BP0 are multiplexed with the Performance Monitoring pins (PM1 and PM0). The PB1 and PB0 bits in the Debug Mode Control Register determine if the pins are configured as breakpoint or performance-monitoring pins. The pins come out of the reset mode configured for performance monitoring.

*PRDY.* Used with the debug port. It indicates that the processor has stopped normal execution in response to the R/S pin-going active, or the Probe Mode being entered.

*PWT.* The page write-through. It indicates the state of the cache write-through paging attribute bit for the current cycle. When paging is disabled, the processor drives PWT low.

*R/S.* Used with the debug port. A low stops the normal execution of the processor and places it in an idle state, so it acts as an interrupt. While in this state, the processor will not recognize any external interrupts. These interrupts are serviced when the processor resumes normal operation.

*RESET.* Forces the processor to begin execution at a known state. All internal caches and translation lookaside buffers as well as the branch target buffer and segment descriptor cache are invalidated upon the RESET. Modified lines in the data cache are not written back. When RESET is used, the processor aborts all bus activity and starts the RESET sequence.

*SCYC.* The split cycle indication. It indicates that a misaligned locked transfer is on the bus. It is used when more than two cycles will be locked together. This signal is not defined for cycles which are not locked.

*SMI.* The system management interrupt. A low latches a system management interrupt request.

*SMIACT.* The system management interrupt active output. A low indicates that the processor is operating in System Management Mode (SMM).

*TCK.* The test clock input. This is a test input that provides the clocking function for the processor boundary scan. It is used to clock state information and data into and out during the boundary scan or probe mode operation.

*TDI.* The test data input for receiving serial test data and instructions for the Boundary Scan and Probe Mode test logic.

*TDO.* The test data output for serial test data and instructions for the Boundary Scan and Probe Mode test logic.

*TMS.* The test mode select for Boundary Scan test logic control input.

*TRST.* A test reset for the Boundary Scan test logic reset or initialization pin. When in the low state, the test logic is disabled so that normal operation of the device can continue unhindered.

*W/R.* A Write/Read output. It distinguishes a read cycle (low) from a write cycle (high) and is one of the primary bus cycle definition pins.

*WB/WT.* The Write-back/Write-through pin. It allows a cache line to be defined as write-back (high) or write-through (low) on a line-by-line basis.

## Bus Cycles

The Pentium supports a number of different bus cycles. The simplest type of bus cycle is a single-transfer, noncacheable 64-bit cycle, with or without wait states. The processor starts a cycle by placing the address status signal (ADS) in the first clock in the bus cycle. A low ADS output indicates that a valid bus cycle definition and address is available on the cycle definition pins and the address bus. The CACHE output is switched high to indicate that the cycle will be a single transfer cycle.

For a zero wait-state transfer, BRDY is used in the second clock of the bus cycle. A low BRDY indicates that the external system has valid data on the data pins in response to a read or that the external system has accepted data in response to a write. The processor samples the BRDY input in the second and subsequent clocks of a bus cycle.

## Bus Differences Between 486 and Pentium

The Pentium bus is similar to the 486 bus. Enhancements have been made to achieve more performance and support for multiprocessing.

There are the following differences between the Pentium and the 486 CPU buses:

1. The Pentium has a 64-bit data bus, while the 486 supports a 32-bit data bus. The Pentium has more byte enables (BE7-BE0) and more data parity pins (DP7-0) than the 486 to support the larger data bus.

2. The Pentium has the capability of driving two cycles concurrently to the bus. It samples the cacheability input KEN only once while the 486 samples KEN twice. Burst length information is driven in the Pentium with the CACHE pin along with the address. The 486 controls burst length with the BLAST pin.

3. The Pentium processor generates 8-byte writes as one bus cycle, and does not use the PLOCK pin. It does not change lower-order bits of address and byte enables during the burst.

4. The Pentium requires write-backs and line fills to be run as burst cycles, and the burst cannot be terminated in the middle since there are no RDY or BLAST pins. Noncacheable burst cycles and nonburst cacheable cycles are not supported on Pentium.

5. The Pentium processor supports a write-back cache protocol using the following new pins: CACHE, HIT, HITM, INV, and WB/WT. It does not support the dynamic bus sizing implemented with BS8 and BS16 or allow invalidations on every clock, or invalidations when the Pentium is driving the address bus.

6. The Pentium provides an idle clock between consecutive LOCKED cycles and the SCYC pin to indicate a split cycle during locked operations. Noncacheable code prefetches are 8 bytes for the Pentium processor, not 16 bytes.

7. The Pentium processor uses an INIT pin in the reset function and holds the states of the internal caches and the floating point unit. The Pentium supports strong store ordering between the processor and the external system along with internal parity error checking, enhanced data parity checking, and address parity error checking. The following new pins implement these features: APCK, BUSCHK, PEN, IERR, and AP. The Pentium implements boundary scan testing with the following pins: TDI, TDO, TMS, TRST and TCK. This allows a test of the board connections.

8. The Pentium processor has IU, IV, and IBT pins and a branch trace message cycle for execution tracing. The Pentium supports Functional Redundancy Checking (FRC) with the FRCMC and IERR pins and performance monitoring and external breakpoints with the following pins: BP3, BP2, PM1/BP1, and PMO/BPO. The Pentium has a system management mode using SMI and SMIACT.

# 4

# Microcomputer Buses

Most microcomputer systems are not confined to a single circuit board, so a set of connectors is needed for the different boards. A backplane technique is often used for the interconnections. The backplane refers to a circuit board with connectors.

Other boards which have their own functions, including memory and I/O, plug into the backplane. The backplane furnishes a path for communications between the different circuit boards as well as power to them. Figure 4.1 shows a typical backplane arrangement with circuit boards plugged into it.

A backplane or system board is used to electrically interconnect a group of circuit boards (expansion boards) while providing the mechanical support for those boards. Most backplanes are constructed using a multilayer printed-circuit board, sometimes with a metal support layer.

The electrical interconnection between the expansion boards is made using the circuit traces in the system board. A wide range of connector types are used for connecting the boards to the backplane. The differences in the backplane interconnections are the contact spacing, number of contact rows, and spacing between boards.

## Board Mounting

In most cases the boards are mounted perpendicularly to the backplane or system board. The expansion boards are inserted into a rack, or cage, and plugged into the system board. This method is widely used since it is flexible and can be used for many bus configurations.

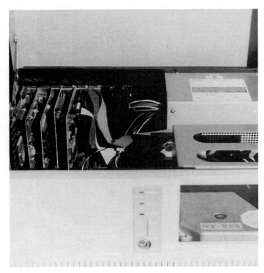

**Figure 4.1**  Personal computer with backplane for
circuit board.

Split backplanes have the boards mounted between two system
boards. This increases the number of allowable interconnections, but is
more costly and requires complete disassembly unless special ZIF connectors are used.

## Edge-Card Connectors

This type of backplane interconnection has been in use for many years
and accounts for the majority of backplane connectors. The connection
techniques used with edge-card backplane systems are similar to those
used for edge-card board-to-board connections. Most edge-card backplane connectors use a 100-mil (0.100-inch) pitch.

Two-piece connectors are also used for backplane connections. These
typically use a 25-mil square pin with socket. Either the socket housing or the pin housing can be mounted on the system board.

The advantages of this technique for backplanes are lower two-piece
insertion force and multiple-contact-row capability, which allows a connectors greater contact density compared to edge-card types. Backplane
connectors with up to five rows of contacts at 100-mil pitch are available.

Other interconnection techniques have been developed. One technique requires forming contacts of specific geometry. Another uses
alternating layers of ground, dielectric, and signal contacts. These are
arranged in a row and clamped to the system board.

Flexible circuits that are held in place by a metal spring are also used in backplane connectors. The advantages of using a flexible circuit include soldering to the system or expansion board. These circuits are used in laptops where small size and flexibility are needed.

## Parallel Mounting

Mounting the expansion boards perpendicularly to the system board limits the number of boards that can be used because of the limited size of the system board. It also restricts the number of connectors that will fit on the system board and the total number of I/O connections. The signal paths can be long, which creates electrical problems as signal speeds increase.

Stacking the connectors so the boards are connected in series solves these problems and eliminates the backplane. Boards can easily be added, but complete disassembly is required to replace a board.

The backplane must provide a set of signals that is called the *backplane bus*. These signals will depend on the type of processor used in the system.

The backplane must also provide the power supply voltages to power the circuit boards connected to the backplane. These voltages usually include a source of 5 volts since most digital integrated circuits require this voltage for power. Other power-supply voltages that may be used are ±12 volts and ±15 volts. The 12-volt supplies are often used for RS-232 serial-communication circuits. The 15-volt supplies are typically used by analog-to-digital and digital-to-analog circuits.

The connectors used to plug the circuit boards into the backplane are usually edge-type connectors. The circuit board has metallic pads which insert into these edge connectors.

The type of computer used defines the size and shape of the circuit boards which can be plugged in. There is usually a special area designed for installing the circuit boards along with some type of mechanical support for the circuit cards. The size of this cage is determined by the size and the number of boards which are allowed.

Smaller specialized boards provide a more modular computer system, but it increases the number of boards required to meet the requirements of the system. The use of small boards keeps the board complexity low along with the cost. Small, low cost boards mean easy replacement for repairs and upgrading.

As 16- and then 32-bit processors were introduced, more and more functions were designed into the main computer board. This tends to reduce the number of boards needed for a computer system. Most of the newer personal computers use larger, denser circuit boards with more functions defined on the main circuit board.

Since more boards mean more connectors in the computer system, the denser computer boards result in less expensive systems for these 16- and 32-bit computers. Connectors are more expensive than integrated circuits, and the connectors represent potential reliability problems. So, these more complex systems use fewer, larger circuit boards.

The IBM personal computer bus represents one of the most popular computer buses in use. Although there are a great many different computer buses with varying philosophies, there are many similarities in each of these just as there are in microprocessor buses.

## IBM PC Bus

In 1981 IBM introduced its personal computer based on the Intel 8088 microprocessor. This was a first for IBM, since the company had not been in the popular and rapidly growing microcomputer market in the late 1970s and early 1980s.

IBM controlled the minicomputer, medium-sized, and large-mainframe markets. This product introduction placed IBM's approval on the personal microcomputer for many business users and opened the market for both suppliers and users.

IBM also validated the Intel series of microprocessors along with operating-system software from Microsoft. The IBM PC was also introduced as an open system, since IBM published the specifications of its PC bus for all the world to use.

The first IBM PC-XT used the Intel 8088 microprocessor running at a clock rate of 4.77 MHz. The bus had the following characteristics:

1. A set of eight bidirectional data lines

2. A set of 20 address lines

3. Six interrupt lines

4. Three sets of Direct-Memory-Access control lines

5. A group of lines for data control and status

6. Power supply and ground lines

The 62 pins that make up the bus are divided into two rows (A1-A31 and B1-B31) for the edge connectors. These connectors, which are sometimes called *expansion connectors,* are located on the main circuit board of the computer. The microprocessor along with some of the I/O circuits and memory are also on this board.

In the IBM PC-XT, there are five edge connectors for the expansion boards. Data moves over the bus on the data lines A2-A9. Addresses for data transfers are specified on the 20 address lines A12-A31.

The use of the 8-bit version of the Intel 8086 16-bit processor in the PC and XT reduced the number of bus lines needed and resulted in a smaller bus and lower hardware costs.

### IBM PC Bus Pins

Table 4.1 is a list of the 62 pins which make up the IBM PC bus. The IBM PC is a single-board computer. The processor and some of the computer I/O circuitry and memory are on a large board called the *system board* or the *motherboard*. Also on this board are the five edge connectors that form the IBM PC bus.

The six interrupt pins B21-B25 and B4 are connected to an interrupt controller on the system board. This controller generates the addresses needed for interrupt servicing.

**TABLE 4.1    IBM PC Bus Signals**

| Connector Pin | Signal | Connector Pin | Signal |
|:---:|:---:|:---:|:---:|
| B1 | GND | A1 | I/O CH CK |
| B2 | RESET DRV | A2 | D7 |
| B3 | +5V | A3 | D6 |
| B4 | IRQ2 | A4 | D5 |
| B5 | –5V | A5 | D4 |
| B6 | DRQ2 | A6 | D3 |
| B7 | –12V | A7 | D2 |
| B8 | Reserved | A8 | D1 |
| B9 | +12V | A9 | D0 |
| B10 | GND | A10 | I/O CH RDY |
| B11 | MEMW | A11 | AEN |
| B12 | MEMR | A12 | A19 |
| B13 | IOW | A13 | A18 |
| B14 | IOR | A14 | A17 |
| B15 | DACK3 | A15 | A16 |
| B16 | DRQ3 | A16 | A15 |
| B17 | DACK1 | A17 | A14 |
| B18 | DRQ1 | A18 | A13 |
| B19 | DACK0 | A19 | A12 |
| B20 | CLK | A20 | A12 |
| B21 | IRQ7 | A21 | A10 |
| B22 | IRQ6 | A22 | A9 |
| B23 | IRQ5 | A23 | A8 |
| B24 | IRQ4 | A24 | A7 |
| B25 | IRQ3 | A25 | A6 |
| B26 | DACK2 | A26 | A5 |
| B27 | T/C | A27 | A4 |
| B28 | ALE | A28 | A3 |
| B29 | +5V | A29 | A2 |
| B30 | OSC | A30 | A1 |
| B31 | GND | A31 | A0 |

The DMA handshake lines include the DRQ1-3 lines (B-18, B-6 and B-16 pins). These lines are used for DMA requests. DACK1-3 (B17, B26 and B-15 pins) are used as acknowledge lines.

DACK0 (pin B-19) is used to refresh dynamic RAM boards which may be plugged into the bus. T/C (B-27) is used to indicate when the correct number of DMA bus cycles has occurred during a DMA transfer. OSC (B-30) is used for a 14.31818-MHz clock and CLK(B-20) is the 4.77-MHz clock which runs the processor. RESET DRV (B2) is a reset signal for all cards on the bus.

A bus handshake line, I/O CH RDY (A10), may be used to increase the current bus cycle. This line can be on for only a few microseconds so that the dynamic memory continues to be refreshed. RAM refresh in the PC is handled by one channel of the system DMA controller, which requires the bus.

There are six interrupt lines, IRQ2 through IRQ7. These are connected to an interrupt controller on the processor board which automatically generates vectors for the interrupt service routine. As a result, there is no explicit interrupt-acknowledge signal on the IBM PC bus. Interrupts are acknowledged by data transactions with the processor.

Also, there are three pairs of DMA handshake lines. DRQ1* through DRQ3 are the DMA request lines and DACK1* through DACK3* are the acknowledge lines. DACKO* is a special line used to refresh dynamic RAM boards which may be plugged into the bus. Another signal, T/C, is pulsed when the proper number of DMA bus cycles has occurred during a DMA transfer.

Other signal lines include OSC, a 14.31818-MHz master timing signal, and CLK, the 4.77-MHz clock which is used to run the processor. RESET DRV is a reset signal for all cards on the bus. Power available for plug-in circuit boards includes +5 volts, −5 volts, and positive and negative 12 volts. There are also three ground pins on the bus.

## Bus Timing

In the original IBM PC bus, a bus cycle takes four clock cycles, (840 ns) and a DMA cycle takes five clock cycles (1.05 microseconds). The bus cycles are controlled by the 8288 bus controller running at 4.77 MHz.

## Bus Control

Since the PC-XT used the 8088 processor in what is known as the maximum mode, an Intel 8288 bus controller was required. The maximum mode allows the 8088 to be used with another processor including a coprocessor.

The bus controller can also be used to drive a system bus shared by several 8088 processors, each with its own 8288 bus controller. Systems with shared system buses and private I/O buses can also be put together, as well as systems with shared I/O buses.

The S0, S1, and S2 pins from the 8088 processor are connected to the 8288 status decoder. CLK, which is the 8088 clock signal, is also sent to the 8288 to synchronize the bus controller with the processor.

This is done because the S0, S1, and S2 pins provide status only at certain times in the machine cycle. The 8288 needs to know when these pins have valid information on them. When the following states occur, the processor is telling the 8288 bus controller that a new machine cycle is about to start:

$$S0 = 0$$

$$S1 = 1$$

$$S2 = 0$$

This provides the needed synchronization between the processor and the bus controller.

When synchronized with the processor, the bus controller generates the signals needed to run a multiprocessor system. These signals are produced by circuitry known as the *command-* and *control-signal* generators in the bus controller.

The AEN input to the bus controller determines if the outputs of the command-signal generator are active. If AEN is high, the command outputs are disabled and will not drive the bus. When AEN goes low, the command output signals are enabled.

AEN is used in systems where more than one processor may control the bus. Some type of arbitration logic is needed in these systems. When a processor needs to drive the system bus, the arbitration logic decides if that processor can take over the bus. If the bus is available, the arbitration logic drives the AEN input of the particular bus controller low and this allows that processor to drive the bus command lines.

MRDC and MWTC are Memory Read and Write control signals. MRDC is low when the processor needs to do a read operation from memory and not I/O space. MWTC is low for a memory write operation.

AMWC is the Advanced-Memory-Write control signal. It goes low to provide an early indication that a write is taking place. IORC and IOWC are I/O Read and Write control signals. IORC is low when the processor is doing a read operation from I/O space. IOWC goes low for I/O write operations.

AMWC is the Advanced I/O Write control signal and goes low for I/O write operations like AMWC does for memory write operations. INTA is the same interrupt-acknowledge signal generated by the 8088 processor. The difference is that the 8288 bus controller now generates this negative-true signal for the 8088.

Three other signals from the control-signal generator are also the same. DT/R, DEN, and ALE can be generated by the 8088, but these signals are generated by the 8288.

The DEN signal is high-true from the 8288 while it was low-true when generated by the 8088. The other output provided by the control-signal generator has dual functions—MCE/PDEN. The function performed is determined by the 8288 control input IOB.

If there are separate data buses for I/O and memory, then the IOB pin on the 8288 is held high. This enables the PDEN function. PDEN is the Peripheral-Data-ENable pin. It goes low and enables the I/O data bus buffers when an I/O bus transaction is taking place. PDEN is used for the I/O data bus in a similar way as DEN is used for the processor data bus.

When the 8288 is in the mode of operation called the *I/O Bus* mode, the I/O command lines IORC, IOWC, AIOWC, and INTA are enabled (low) and the I/O bus is committed to a single processor. A separate I/O data bus allows transactions on this bus to take place while other transactions are taking place on the system data bus. This type of parallel operation improves system performance since twice the number of bus transactions can occur in a given time.

The 8288-generated control signals are brought out to the PC bus. The two signals ALE (Address Latch Enable) and AEN (Address ENable) are on pins B28 and A11. ALE indicates when a valid address is on the bus address lines and AEN signals if the processor or the DMA controller is driving the bus during a DMA transaction. Other 8288 signals that can also be found on the bus include:

| | |
|---|---|
| I/O Read (IOR) | B14 |
| MEMory Read (MEMR)* | B12 |
| I/O Write (IOW) | B13 |
| MEMory Write (MENW)* | B11 |

Power supplies available to the bus cards includes +5 volts (B-3), −5 volts (B-5), +12 volts (B-9), and −12 volts (B-7). There are three ground pins (B-1, B-10, and B-31).

Bus cycles use four clock cycles, or 840 ns, while DNA cycles take five clock cycles, or 1.05 microseconds. The cycles are controlled by the 8288 bus controller running at 4.77 MHz.

Although it never evolved into an actual industry standard, the IBM PC bus became the most popular microprocessor backplane bus ever introduced. Thousands of boards from hundreds of companies have been designed to plug into the PC bus.

## IBM PC Bus Physical Characteristics

Although there are no standard-size IBM PC bus cards, they must fit into the physical area designed for them as well as the expansion connectors. Each bus card has a metal plate attached to one end. This plate functions as a shield, a card guide for the back of the card, and a support for any I/O connectors which may be attached to the card. The I/O connector on the board approach eliminates any more cables inside the computer.

Many different types of boards are available from hundreds of companies. These boards are designed to plug into the original IBM PC bus and extended versions for 16- and 32-bit Intel microprocessors.

## PC-AT Bus

A few years after introducing its PC, IBM introduced its AT, which is a full 16-bit computer based on the Intel 80286 microprocessor. The 80286 uses a 16-bit data bus and the AT expansion bus has a wider data path, more interrupt lines, and more DMA signals. Like the PC bus, the AT bus signals resemble the microprocessor signals on which the computer is based.

In order to maintain compatibility with expansion boards designed for the PC, the original 62-pin connector and pin definitions remained the same. A second connector with 36 pins was added to carry the additional signals. The second connector is in front of the 62-pin connector.

Some older boards designed for the IBM PC will physically interfere with the AT expansion connector. Since there was never an actual standard board size and shape for the PC expansion boards, some manufacturers made use of the available space by dropping the bottom edge of the board just in front of the PC's edge connector.

## PC-AT Bus Signals

Many signals on the PC-AT bus have the same names they had on the PC's bus. Some signals were given new names, but the functions are similar.

DACKO in the PC was a negative-true signal that became REFRESH in the AT bus. B-8 in the PC bus was reserved and became OWS (zero wait state) in the AT bus. This signal allows an expansion board to stop the processor from inserting wait states into the bus cycle.

MEM CS16 (D-1) and I/O CS16 (D-2) go low to allow an expansion board to signal when it can accept a 16-bit, 1-wait-state transfer. These signals are on the 36-pin connector.

BHE (byte high enable) was added for 16-bit transfers. DMA channels 5 to 7 were added to the AT bus while channel 4 is now reserved for the system board.

Some of the address lines (C-2 through C-8) on the 36-pin connector partially duplicate the addresses on the 62-pin connector. Unlike the PC's original address lines, the AT's 36-pin address lines are not latched on the computer's motherboard. Expansion boards that use these lines must latch the address values with the falling edge of the ALE signal.

Since the introduction of the original AT, the clock speeds of compatible computers have increased as Intel and other microprocessor vendors have improved their manufacturing processes. The manufacturers of compatible computers adopted the AT bus for their 80286-based machines. Chip manufacturers such as Chips and Technologies and Western Digital developed ICs that reduced the motherboard size. In addition to machines based on the 80286 microprocessor, some 80386-based machines also use the AT bus, adding extensions for 32-bit memory boards. However, vendors of 80386-based computers may use different techniques for extending the AT bus to 32 bits so memory boards for these computers are not compatible.

With the EISA (Enhanced Industry Standard Architecture) machines, full 32-bit microcomputer buses are used. These high-end machines use an extended version of the older ISA (Industry Standard Architecture) expansion bus which is used in the 16-bit AT class of computers.

EISA offers about the same capabilities as IBM's MCA, including 32-bit expansion slots, faster data transfers between expansion cards and memory, automatic board configuration (no need to set DIP switches), and support for bus mastering (in which microprocessors built into the expansion cards access memory without needing help from the main processor). EISA is also compatible with existing expansion cards for the PC and AT-style computers, allowing EISA machines to work with all ISA expansion cards without modification.

Some vendors offer their own extensions to the AT bus. AST Research offers an AT bus extension called *Smartslot* which adds an additional eight pins to the bus. These pins allow multiple processors on several expansion cards to share the bus using an arbitration scheme. A central arbiter for all Smartslot cards grants the bus to one of the requesting cards.

The IEEE created the P996 Bus committee to study the feasibility of standardizing the AT bus, but before the committee could produce a standard, IBM introduced its PS/2 line of personal computers that use a completely different and incompatible bus.

## PS/2 Micro Channel Bus

In 1987, IBM introduced the PS/2 computer line and the Micro Channel bus. IBM patented several aspects of the PS/2's bus, so manufacturers need a license to use the Micro Channel. There are similarities and differences between the older PC and newer PS/2 buses.

The Micro Channel assigns more power and ground pins than the earlier PC and AT buses. These additional power and ground pins allow expansion cards to draw more power from the computer since the extra pins provide a lower impedance path to the computer's power supply. The ground and power pins also provide a lower impedance path to ac ground for radio frequency interference (RFI). This tends to reduce potential interference emissions and improve the general data integrity by reducing noise.

The Micro Channel supports three types of cards: 16-bit, 16-bit with a video extension, and 32-bit. The 16-bit version uses 116 pins and the extension adds another 20 pins. The Micro Channel bus is designed to support multiple bus masters. The processor or DMA controller on the PS/2 motherboard usually controls the bus, but the Micro Channel has a set of signals to allow expansion cards to take over as bus masters. The Micro Channel allows up to 15 masters to share the bus with the mainboard.

The 32-bit address bus width supports 4 Gbytes of memory or memory-mapped I/O addressing. The 24-bit subset of the bus permits the addressing of up to 16 Mbytes of memory or memory-mapped I/O. The 32-bit address bus and its 24-bit subset also act as a 16-bit I/O address bus. When used as a 16-bit I/O address bus, 64-kbyte I/O addresses can be accessed.

The data bus can also be used as a 24-bit data bus, 16-bit data bus, or an 8-bit data bus. Data can be transferred to system memory or system memory-mapped I/O devices using the matched-memory signals and the matched-memory procedure. This allows devices to be tuned to the transfer characteristics.

The 4-bit arbitration bus can support up to 16 total bus masters. Each bus master is assigned a unique priority level. Each system must have at least one bus master. At least one bus master must be assigned the lowest priority level. This bus master is called the *default bus master*. It is given control of the bus when no other bus master owns the bus or channel or during an exceptional condition.

The procedure for bus masters to gain control of the bus is controlled by a logic unit called the *system arbitration control point* (SCP).

An audio subsystem feature is provided in the Micro Channel architecture. An analog audio signal and analog ground signal are specified. The bandwidth of the audio signal is 50 Hz to 10 kHz. The subsystem provides high-quality audio capability between devices and output over the system speaker. This subsystem eliminates the need for duplicate audio circuitry on devices added to a system. The Micro Channel bus uses the AUDIO (B-2) and AUDIO GND (B-1) signals. This allows expansion cards to use the PS/2's audio amplifier and speaker. In a similar fashion, the video expansion connector allows an expansion card to override the video circuits on the PS/2 motherboard. The pin assignments for the 16-bit card are shown in Table 4.2. The pin assignments for the video extension to the 16-bit card are listed in Table 4.3 and the pin assignments for the 32-bit card are listed in Table 4.4. The 32-bit signal functions are summarized in Table 4.5.

A minus sign is usually placed in front of the signal name to indicate when a signal is low-true. An asterisk is used here to avoid confusion with other buses.

The data bus is made up of signals D0 through D15 on the 16-bit Micro Channel version and D0 through D31 is used in the 32-channel version. A0 through A23 make up the address bus for the 16-bit Micro Channel bus. The 32-bit bus includes A24 through A31.

Some of the signals on the Micro Channel bus are the same or similar as used in the original PC bus. These signals include:

| | |
|---|---|
| REFRESH* | Memory refresh |
| OSC | Oscillator |
| SBHE* | Byte high enable |
| CD CHRDY | Channel-ready |
| CD DS 16 | Card data-size 16 bits (combination of the PC/AT's MEM CS16 and IO CS16 identification signals) |
| CHRESET | Channel reset |
| TC | Indicates the last bus cycle of a DMA transfer |

The Micro Channel does not use the PC/AT's memory and I/O read and write control lines. There are three negative true lines; M/IO, S0, and S1, that work like those in the 82288 bus controller. The state of these lines is used to indicate the type of bus transfers:

| M/IO | S0 | S1 | |
|---|---|---|---|
| 0 | 0 | 1 | I/O Read |
| 0 | 1 | 0 | I/O Write |
| 1 | 0 | 1 | Memory read |
| 1 | 1 | 0 | Memory write |

## Micro Channel Setup

The Micro Channel bus does not use addressing and option-configuration switches on the expansion cards. This feature is called the Programmable Option Select (POS). When power is turned on, the system board addresses each expansion card with an individual CD SETUP line. This line is not common across the PS/2 backplane. Each expan-

**TABLE 4.2   16-bit Micro Channel Signals**

| PIN | Signal | PIN | Signal |
|-----|--------|-----|--------|
| B1 | Audio GND | A1 | CD SETUP* |
| B2 | Audio | A2 | MADE 24 |
| B3 | GND | A3 | GND |
| B4 | OSC | A4 | A11 |
| B5 | GND | A5 | A10 |
| B6 | A23 | A6 | A9 |
| B7 | A22 | A7 | +5V |
| B8 | A21 | A8 | A8 |
| B9 | GND | A9 | A7 |
| B10 | A20 | A10 | A6 |
| B11 | A19 | A11 | +5V |
| B12 | A18 | A12 | A5 |
| B13 | GND | A13 | A4 |
| B14 | A17 | A14 | A3 |
| B15 | A16 | A15 | +5V |
| B16 | A15 | A16 | A2 |
| B17 | GND | A17 | A1 |
| B18 | A14 | A18 | A0 |
| B19 | A13 | A19 | +12V |
| B20 | A12 | A20 | ADL* |
| B21 | GND | A21 | PREEMPT |
| B22 | IRQ2* | A22 | Burst |
| B23 | IRQ3* | A23 | +12V |
| B24 | IRQ4* | A24 | ARB0 |
| B25 | GND | A25 | ARB1 |
| B26 | IRQ5* | A26 | ARB2 |
| B27 | IRQ6* | A27 | +12V |
| B28 | IRQ7* | A28 | ARB3 |
| B29 | GND | A29 | ARB/–GNT |
| B30 | Reserved | A30 | TC |
| B31 | Reserved | A31 | +5V |
| B32 | CHCK* | A32 | S0* |
| B33 | GND | A33 | S1* |
| B34 | CMD* | A34 | M/IO* |
| B35 | CHRDYRTN | A35 | +12V |
| B36 | CD SFDBK* | A36 | CD CHRDY |
| B37 | GND | A37 | DO |
| B38 | D1 | A38 | D2 |
| B39 | D3 | A39 | +5V |
| B40 | D4 | A40 | D5 |
| B41 | GND | A41 | D6 |
| B42 | CHRESET | A42 | D7 |
| B43 | Reserved | A43 | GND |
| B44 | Reserved | A44 | DS 16 RTN* |
| B45 | GND | A45 | Refresh |
|  | Positioning key |  |  |
| B48 | D8 | A48 | +5V |
| B49 | D9 | A49 | D10 |
| B50 | GND | A50 | D11 |
| B51 | D12 | A51 | D13 |
| B52 | D14 | A52 | +12V |
| B53 | D15 | A53 | Reserved |
| B54 | GND | A54 | SBHE* |
| B55 | IRQ10* | A55 | CD DB 18 |
| B56 | IRQ11* | A56 | +5V |
| B57 | IRQ12* | A57 | IRQ14* |
| B58 | GND | A58 | IRQ15 |

TABLE 4.3    Video Extension Signals

| Pin | Signal | Pin | Signal |
|-----|--------|-----|--------|
| BV10 | ESYNC | AV10 | VSYNC |
| BV9 | GND | AV9 | HSYNC |
| BV8 | P5 | AV8 | BLANK |
| BV7 | P4 | AV7 | GND |
| BV6 | P3 | AV6 | P6 |
| BV5 | GND | AV5 | EDCLK |
| BV4 | P2 | AV4 | DCLK |
| BV3 | P1 | AV3 | GND |
| BV2 | P0 | AV2 | P7 |
| BV1 | GND | AV1 | EVIDEO |
| | Positioning key | | |
| | 16-bit microchannel slot | | |

sion slot has its own negative logic CD SETUP line. When a card is signaled by its CD SETUP line, it issues a code. The processor reads this code from the expansion card. The codes are used to define the following conditions:

Device not ready

Bus master

DMA device

Direct program control and Memory-mapped I/O

Memory storage

Video adapter

No device present

The processor matches the code with the configuration data stored in the computer's nonvolatile memory and loads that data into the expansion card. Configuration data can include the card's bus-master arbitration level, the range of any on-board I/O ROM, and the I/O address range for the card. Since each type of card from different manufacturers must have a unique POS code, this scheme allows IBM to control the types of cards available for PS/2 computers.

A Micro Channel card is 11.5 inches long and 3.475 inches high, including the edge connector. These cards use a smaller edge connector. The PC and AT cards use edge connectors with pads spaced 0.100 inches apart. The Micro Channel cards use pads that are spaced 0.050 inches apart. Positioning keys are used to align the cards. These fit into notches in the edge connectors.

A full-length Micro Channel card is about one-third smaller than a full-length PC/AT card. The smaller cards use denser ICs which require less room.

**TABLE 4.4   32-Bit Micro Channel Signals**

| PIN | Signal | PIN | Signal |
|-----|--------|-----|--------|
| BM4 | GND | AM4 | Reserved |
| BM3 | Reserved | AM3 | MMC CMD* |
| BM2 | MMCR* | AM2 | GND |
| BM1 | Reserved | AM1 | MMC* |
| B1 | Audio GND | A1 | CD SETUP* |
| B2 | Audio | A2 | MADE 24 |
| B3 | GND | A3 | GND |
| B4 | OSC | A4 | A11 |
| B5 | GND | A5 | A10 |
| B6 | A23 | A6 | A9 |
| B7 | A22 | A7 | +5V |
| B8 | A21 | A8 | A8 |
| B9 | GND | A9 | A7 |
| B10 | A20 | A10 | A6 |
| B11 | A19 | A11 | +5V |
| B12 | A18 | A12 | A5 |
| B13 | GND | A13 | A4 |
| B14 | A17 | A14 | A3 |
| B15 | A16 | A15 | +5V |
| B16 | A15 | A16 | A2 |
| B17 | GND | A17 | A1 |
| B18 | A14 | A18 | A0 |
| B19 | A13 | A19 | +12V |
| B20 | A12 | A20 | ADL* |
| B21 | GND | A21 | PREEMPT |
| B22 | IRQ2* | A22 | BURST |
| B23 | IRQ3* | A23 | +12V |
| B24 | IRQ4* | A24 | ARB0 |
| B25 | GND | A25 | ARB1 |
| B26 | IRQ5* | A26 | ARB2 |
| B27 | IRQ68 | A27 | +12V |
| B28 | IRQ7* | A28 | ARB3 |
| B29 | GND | A29 | ARB/GNT* |
| B30 | Reserved | A30 | TC |
| B31 | Reserved | A31 | +5V |
| B32 | CHCK* | A32 | S0* |
| B33 | GND | A33 | S1* |
| B34 | CMD* | A34 | M/IO* |
| B35 | CHRDYRTN | A35 | +12V |
| B36 | CD SFDBK* | A36 | CD CHRDY |
| B37 | GND | A37 | D0 |
| B38 | D1 | A38 | D2 |
| B39 | D3 | A39 | +5V |
| B40 | D4 | A40 | D5 |
| B41 | GND | A41 | D6 |
| B42 | CHRESET | A42 | D7 |
| B43 | Reserved | A43 | GND |
| B44 | Reserved | A44 | DS 16 RTN* |
| B45 | GND | A45 | Refresh |
|  | Positioning key |  |  |
| B48 | D8 | A48 | +5V |
| B49 | D9 | A49 | D10 |

**TABLE 4.4** *(Continued)*

| PIN | Signal | PIN | Signal |
|-----|--------|-----|--------|
| B50 | GND | A50 | D11 |
| B51 | D12 | A51 | D13 |
| B52 | D14 | A52 | +12V |
| B53 | D15 | A53 | Reserved |
| B54 | GND | A54 | SBHE* |
| B55 | IRQ10* | A55 | CD DB 18 |
| B56 | IRQ11* | A56 | +5V |
| B57 | IRQ12* | A57 | IRQ14* |
| B58 | GND | A58 | IRQ15* |
| B59 | Reserved | A59 | Reserved |
| B60 | Reserved | A60 | Reserved |
| B61 | Reserved | A61 | GND |
| B62 | Reserved | A62 | Reserved |
| B63 | GND | A63 | Reserved |
| B64 | D16 | A64 | Reserved |
| B65 | D17 | A65 | +12V |
| B66 | D18 | A66 | D19 |
| B67 | GND | A67 | D20 |
| B68 | D22 | A68 | D21 |
| B69 | D23 | A69 | +5V |
| B70 | Reserved | A70 | D24 |
| B71 | GND | A71 | D25 |
| B72 | D27 | A72 | D26 |
| B73 | D28 | A73 | +5V |
| B74 | D29 | A74 | D30 |
| B75 | GND | A75 | D31 |
| B76 | BE0* | A76 | Reserved |
| B77 | BE1* | A77 | +12V |
| B78 | BE2* | A78 | BE3* |
| B79 | GND | A79 | DS 32 RTN* |
| B80 | TR 32 | A80 | CD DS 32 |
| B81 | A24 | A81 | +12V |
| B82 | A25 | A82 | A26 |
| B83 | GND | A83 | A27 |
| B84 | A29 | A84 | A28 |
| B85 | A30 | A85 | +5V |
| B86 | A31 | A86 | Reserved |
| B87 | GND | A87 | Reserved |
| B88 | Reserved | A88 | Reserved |
| B89 | Reserved | A89 | GND |

The MADE 24 and TR32 signals change the use of the address lines. MADE 24 indicates when the address bus carries a 24-bit address. TR32 indicates a 32-bit-wide memory data transfer.

To start a bus cycle, ADL (address decode latch) is forced low. The expansion card that recognizes the address on the bus then forces either CD DS 16 or CD DS 32 low to indicate if it is a 16- or 32-bit card. Then CD SFDBK goes low to acknowledge the cycle. The PS/2 system

**TABLE 4.5    32-Bit Microchannel Signal Functions**

*Address signals*

| | |
|---|---|
| A0-A23 | 32-bit or 24-bit memory bus subset, 16-bit I/O address bus |
| A24-A31 | 32-bit address bus extension |
| M/IO* | Indicates memory or I/O address when low |
| MADE 24 | Indicates the memory address exceeds 16 Mbytes when high |

*Data signals*

| | |
|---|---|
| D0-D15 | Used as part of the 32-bit data bus and as the 16-bit data bus subset. |
| D16-D31 | Used with D0-D15 as the 32-bit data bus. |
| BE0*-BE3* | A low identifies which of the 4 data bytes on the 32-bit data bus contains valid data. |
| SBHE* | Enables transfer of bits D8-D15 when low. |

*Control signal group*

| | |
|---|---|
| ADL* | A low state provides two gating edges early in the bus/channel cycles for address latching. |
| CD DS 16* | A low is used by I/O and memory slaves to indicate that their data port size is at least 16 bits. |
| CD DS 32* | A low is used by I/O and memory slaves with CD DS 16 to indicate that their data port size is 32 bits. |
| DS 16 RTN* | A low is used by bus masters to determine the data port size of I/O and memory slaves. |
| DS 32 RTN* | A low is used by bus masters with DS 16 RTN to determine the data port size of I/O and memory slaves. |
| S0* or S1* | Used to indicate that the bus or channel cycle is a read (S0 low) or a write (S1 low) cycle. |
| CMD* | A low indicates when to execute a transfer. |
| CD SFDBK* | A low is used by I/O and memory slaves to acknowledge that they have been selected by a bus master. |
| CH CHRDY | A high is used by I/O and memory slaves to indicate that they can execute a 200-ns cycle. |
| CHRDYRTN | A high is used by bus masters to determine that the selected slave can execute a 200-ns cycle. |
| IRQ3*-IRQ7* | A low state indicates an interrupt service request. |
| IRQ8*-IRQ12* | A low state indicates an interrupt service request. |
| IRQ14*-IRQ15* | A low state indicates an interrupt service request. |
| CS SETUP* | A low indicates that the bus or channel cycle is a POS setup cycle. |
| OSC | Oscillator signal. |
| CHRESET | Bus, channel or system reset. |
| Refresh* | A low indicates that memory refresh cycles are being executed. |
| TR 32 | Indicates that a 32-bit bus master is controlling the bus or channel. |

*Arbitration signals*

| | |
|---|---|
| ARB0-ARB3 | Indicates the arbitration level of potential or current bus masters. |
| PREEMPT* | Indicates that a bus master wants control of the bus. |
| ARB/GNT* | Indicates that an arbitration cycle is taking place. |
| Burst* | Indicates that the bus master is executing multiple cycles. |
| TC* | Indicates that the terminal count of the current third-party DMA has been exceeded. |

*Audio signals*

| | |
|---|---|
| Audio | This is an analog audio summing node. This signal is used to communicate audio signals between devices on the bus to the system speaker circuits. |
| AUDIO GND | The analog audio ground return signal. |

*Matched-memory signals*

| | |
|---|---|
| MMC* | Allows bus masters to indicate that they can execute a matched-memory cycle. |
| MMCR* | Allows memory or memory-mapped I/O slaves to request a matched-memory cycle. |
| MMC CMD* | Used by bus masters instead of CMD during a matched-memory cycle. |

board generates either a DS 16 RTN or DS 32 RTN low to acknowledge the width of the transfer.

After a card acknowledges the address, the bus master can start the data transfer. If this is a write cycle, the master places data on the bus and forces CMD low. If the cycle is a read, the master just forces CMD low, which tells the addressed card to place data on the bus. The master must also negate ADL to end the bus cycle. The addressed expansion card can negate CD CHRDY to stretch out the bus cycle until it has completed the bus transaction.

The system board will generate a signal to respond to CD CHRDY. This is called CHRDYRTN (channel ready return) which is sent to all the expansion slots.

A faster 32-bit bus transfer called a *matched memory cycle* is available. Here, a 32-bit memory card that can perform such cycles forces MMCR (matched memory cycle request) low when addressed. The bus master responds by switching MMC (matched memory cycle) low and using the CMD (matched memory cycle command) to start the data transfer. The matched-memory signals are on a special extension of the 32-bit version of the bus (pins AM1-4 and BM1-4).

An expansion card can use the CHCK (channel check) to indicate an error. This includes parity errors and time-outs. Switching CHCK low causes an interrupt. There are 11 conventional interrupts numbered IRQ3-7, IRQ9-12, IRQ-14, and IRQ-15.

**Bus Arbitration**

Arbitration uses seven signals. ARB0-3 make up a 4-bit arbitration address bus that indicates the current bus master. Eight of these 16 addresses are used for the DMA controller on the system board. The ARB/GNT is forced low to show when bus masters may contend for control of the bus. A bus master must request an arbitration cycle by switching PREEMPT low. If no bus transfers are taking place, a bus arbiter on the system board called the Central Arbitration Control Point (CACP), forces ARB/GNT high to allow bus masters to contend for the bus. The bus masters will send their addresses onto the ARB0-3 lines. Contenders also need to monitor the state of these lines. If a higher-priority address (lower numeric value) appears on the arbitration address bus, the lower-priority cards will stop driving the ARB0-3 lines. As the cards drop out, the bus arbiter will switch ARB/GNT low and the address left on the ARB0-3 lines at that time takes over control of the bus.

**Apple Macintosh II NuBus**

The Macintosh II uses the NuBus. The basic Macintosh II has a system board and a video controller board. Six NuBus slots are provided by the system board (Fig. 4.2). The video card is installed in one NuBus slot, leaving five slots for other option cards.

The system board consists of a Motorola 68020 processor; memory management unit; floating point coprocessor; sockets for up to 8 Mbytes of local memory; floppy and hard drive controllers; two serial ports; and two ports to connect the keyboard, mouse, or other user-interface devices. The system board provides the connections for six NuBus cards. The internal hard-disk and external mass storage devices are connected using the small computer system interface (SCSI) standard.

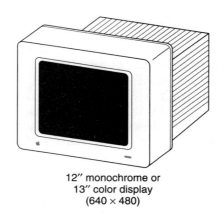

12″ monochrome or
13″ color display
(640 × 480)

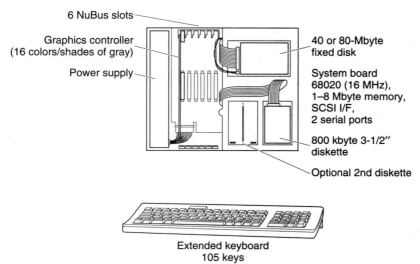

6 NuBus slots

Graphics controller
(16 colors/shades of gray)

Power supply

40 or 80-Mbyte
fixed disk

System board
68020 (16 MHz),
1–8 Mbyte memory,
SCSI I/F,
2 serial ports

800 kbyte 3-1/2″
diskette

Optional 2nd diskette

Extended keyboard
105 keys

**Figure 4.2**   Typical Macintosh system configuration.

The system board is slot 0 on the NuBus and cards on the NuBus can address the memory of the system board using any of the NuBus transactions except for blocks. The system board does not support block transfers, but some cards may use block transactions between other cards.

The system board supports the nonmaster request (NMRQ) signal on the NuBus with a signal from each NuBus connector. The processor determines the slot that is requesting service by reading the register from a priority encoder.

## Macintosh Cards

Six NuBus connectors are provided for option cards. These are designated as NuBus slots 9 through E. A video card is required and there are several types available from Apple and other vendors that range from medium resolution (640 × 480 pixels) black and white to high-resolution color. Other types of cards are available for network control, data acquisition, and coprocessors.

The processor accesses the card address space in two different modes. This is determined by the memory management unit (MMU) that converts the logical addresses to physical address. The MMU is normally in the 24-bit mode for compatibility with the older software. In the 24-bit mode, the processor can only access a 1-Mbyte area in each of the six NuBus slots. This 1-Mbyte area is located in the first megabyte of the 16-Mbyte slot space of each NuBus slot.

The MMU can be placed in the 32-bit mode by a system utility call. When in the 32-bit mode, the processor can access all of the 16-Mbytes of each NuBus slot.

Cards can also use the 256-Mbyte superslot space that is also assigned to each of the NuBus slots. This is accessible only in the 32-bit mode and used in the Macintosh for dividing up the 4-Gbyte NuBus address space.

## System Configuration

Each board has a ROM that identifies the type of board and provides an initialization code for the board. This ROM is called the declaration ROM. When the system is turned on, the processor accesses the declaration ROMs on each board using software called the slot manager. The slot manager determines the type of board in each slot, initializes and tests the board and loads a driver for the board.

The system is normally booted from a disk drive but the declaration ROM can change the boot to other resources. Once all of the boards have been initialized, drivers loaded, and operating system software installed, control of the system is turned over to the operating system.

## NuBus Characteristics

The NuBus is a 32-bit system bus that is based upon simplicity as the most effective way to optimize the system design. The bus requires only 51 signals, which is only 19 more than the 32 needed for multiplexing address and data. The synchronous nature of the NuBus improves reliability and testability.

The NuBus is optimized for 32-bit transfers, but 8-bit and 16-bit nonjustified transfers are also supported. Reads and writes are the only operations and I/O and interrupts are memory mapped. The NuBus has been adopted by the Institute of Electrical and Electronic Engineers (IEEE) as a recognized standard (IEEE 1196).

## Basic NuBus Operation

The NuBus is a synchronous bus in that all signal transitions and samplings are synchronized to a central system clock. However, transactions may be a variable number of clock periods long. This combines the flexibility of an asynchronous bus with the design simplicity of a synchronous bus.

Only read and write operations in a single large address space are supported. The modules attached to the NuBus are peers; no card or slot position is the master. Each slot has an ID code wired into the backplane. Thus, cards in these slots can differentiate themselves without jumpers or switches.

A bus transfer requires arbitration for access to the bus and transfer of the address, data, and status information. Transfers may be 8-, 16-, or 32-bit transactions. All of the NuBus transfers are unjustified.

Interrupts are implemented as write transactions. Any module on the bus can interrupt a processor module by performing a write operation. The interrupt space can be any address that the processor can monitor.

The NuBus provides a linear address space of 4 Gbytes. The upper $\frac{1}{16}$ (256 Mbytes) of this address space is called the slot space. This area is divided into sixteen 16-Mbyte pieces, which are mapped to the 16 card slots. The remaining $\frac{15}{16}$ of the address space is allocated as required.

## Cycles and Transactions

All NuBus signals are active when low and are usually indicated by a (∗) notation. An ACK (Transfer Acknowledge) cycle is the last cycle of a transaction (one clock period long) during which a negative true ACK is applied. An address cycle is the first cycle of a transaction (one clock period long) during which a negative true START is applied. This is also called a START cycle.

The cycle is a phase of a NuBus transaction. Address cycles are one clock period long and hold address and command information. Data cycles are also one period long and hold data and acknowledgment information. A data cycle is any cycle in which data is known to be valid and acknowledged. It includes ACK cycles as well as intermediate data cycles within a block transfer.

A transaction is a complete NuBus operation such as read, write, block read, or block write. It is made up of one address cycle and one or more data cycles.

## Utility Signals

The eight utility signals provide the following functions. These are not associated with any particular bus transaction. The Clock (CLK) is driven from a single source and it synchronizes bus arbitration and data transfers between system modules.

Reset (RESET) is an open-collector line that returns all cards to the initial power-up state. This signal may be used asynchronously to the Clock. The power fail warning (PFW) is an open-collector line that indicates that system power is about to fail. This signal can also be used asynchronously to the clock.

The Identification Signals (IDO-ID3) are binary coded to specify the physical location of each module. The highest-numbered slot (15) has the four signals wired low. The lowest-numbered slot (0) has all ID signals open. The arbitration logic uses the ID numbers to identify cards. The ID signals are also used to allocate a portion of the address space to each card.

The Nonmaster Request (NMRQ) is a negative true open-collector signal that is used to indicate when a board needs attention from another board in the system.

## Bus Transfer Signals

The bus transfer signals including control, address/data and bus parity. These are all three-state signals. The control signals include the Transfer Start (START) which is driven for one clock period by the current bus master at the beginning of a transaction. It indicates that the address and data signals are using a valid address. Transfer Acknowledge (ACK) is used for one clock period to indicate the completion of a transaction.

The Transfer Modes 0 and 1 (TM0, TM1) are used by the bus master during a START cycle to indicate the type of bus operation being initiated. They are also used by bus slaves during ACK cycles to indicate the acknowledgment status (normal or error conditions).

The multiplexed Address and Data (AD0-AD31) signals are used to carry a 32-bit byte address at the beginning of each transaction and 1, 2, or 4 bytes of data later in the transaction.

A System Parity (SP) line sends parity information between cards that have parity checking. System Parity Valid (SPV) indicates that the SP bit is used. Cards that do not check parity ignore SP and SPV.

The Arbitration Signals (ARB0-ARB3) are open-collector binary-coded lines used as contenders for the bus. They are used with the arbitration logic. Bus request (RQST) is an open-collector line that is driven low by contenders for the bus.

The system clock, bus time-out function, and signal line termination are provided by the backplane. The reset and power fail warning signals are usually driven by the power supply module. A bus time-out is used to prevent the system from hanging up if a transaction is attempted to an address that does not exist. If a transaction is started, but not completed within the allocated time, an ACK cycle is provided to complete the transaction.

## Board Size

Two different board sizes are used in NuBus systems; triple height and desktop. A triple-height has the dimensions for a triple-height and triple-depth Eurocard and is approximately 11 by 14.4 inches with three 96-pin DIN connectors. One connector is used for the NuBus and the other two are used for I/O connections.

The desktop card, used in the Macintosh, is 4 by 12.875 inches. It uses one 96-pin DIN connector on the bottom edge. The I/O connections are on the back edge.

## Transactions

The NuBus is optimized for transactions of 32-bit words and blocks of words, but it also supports byte and halfword transactions. A transaction consists of a request made by a master and a response made by the addressed slave. Before a master can initiate a transaction, it must take over the bus using arbitration.

Transactions consist of single or multiple data cycle read or write operations. The multiple operations are known as block transfers. All operations on the NuBus are accomplished using these two types of transactions.

Single data cycle transactions are the simplest transactions on the NuBus. They convey one data item and consist of a START cycle and an ACK cycle. The transactions are either reads or writes of bytes, halfwords, or words.

All transactions are started by a bus master that drives START active low while using TMX, AD0, and AD1 to define the cycle type. The other ADx lines are used for the address. The transaction is complete when the slave drives ACK active low while placing status information on the TMx lines. For write transactions, the master switches the ADx lines to data information in the second clock period and holds this data until acknowledged. In read cycles, the slave drives the data simultaneously with the acknowledge in the last period.

During ACK cycles the addressed slave drives the TMx lines while it drives ACK. The TMx lines provide the status information to the current bus master. There are four status conditions. A bus transfer complete response indicates the normal valid completion of a bus transaction. An error response indicates that during a read or write operation, an error such as an uncorrectable error during a memory read occurred. These errors are detected with error checking and correction ECC or parity checking. A bus time-out occurs if an unimplemented address location is found. A try-again-later condition occurs when a slave cannot respond to a transfer request. This is not treated as an error indication.

## Block Transfers

Block transfers consist of a START cycle, multiple-data cycles using sequential address locations, and an ACK cycle. The number of data cycles is controlled by the master. Block transfers are 2, 4, 8, and 16 words. During block transfers, each data cycle is acknowledged by the slave.

## Interrupts

Interrupts are implemented as write transactions, which are events. Any module can drive the nonmaster request (NMRQ) line to indicate that service is needed. Connectors on the system board allow the NuBus cards to be plugged into the system. An individual NMRQ signal is sent through each NuBus connector to a priority encoder on the system board.

## Arbitration

Arbitration is used to determine the next owner of the bus. This can be viewed as a token that is passed from module to module. The bus owner is the only module that can initiate bus transactions.

The NuBus uses a distributed arbitration mechanism that differs from a strict priority arbitration. It provides a more equal access to the system bus than buses that use priority-based arbitration. Low-priority boards may have a difficult time in obtaining access to the bus before a buffer overflows or a timer times out. Rearranging the position of the cards in the system can often cause the problem to go away, but it may not be eliminated. The NuBus guarantees a maximum arbitration time for every card in the system. So as long as adequate buffers are designed into the cards each one has a chance to take over the bus.

During arbitration, one or more modules may contend for control of the bus. Modules that desire ownership of the bus must use the RQST line and place their ID codes on the (ARB) arbitration signal lines. The arbitration logic that is distributed among the modules determines which of the modules has ownership. After two clock periods, the module with the highest ID code has bus ownership and can initiate a transaction.

If the module does not wish to lock the bus, it removes RQST and releases START to allow any other modules that originally requested the bus a chance to gain it. These modules are granted ownership from the highest ID number to the lowest ID number. Other modules are not included until all the original requesters have been served.

A set of logic equations determines the arbitration logic for the modules. According to these equations, after a short delay for the arbitration period, the arbitration signal lines (ARB) will hold the ID code of the highest priority module.

### Bus Locks

A module may need to lock the bus in a multiprocessor environment. This is done to implement semaphores, or signal bits. These are used to control the allocation of resources that may be shared by the different processors in the system. Bus locking is accomplished when a master continues to request the bus. Since it has the highest ID code, it keeps the bus.

Some boards have private buses that allow a processor to communicate with local memory on that board. In order to lock the internal bus of a module, such as a board with a processor and memory, a resource lock mechanism is used. A one-cycle transaction, which is called an attention-resource-lock cycle, is sent to all bus modules by a master that wishes to lock the bus.

At the end of the locked sequence, another one-cycle transaction, called an attention-null cycle, is sent to all bus modules to indicate that the locked sequence is completed. These special cycles, called *attention cycles,* are single bus cycles where both the START and ACK signals are switched low by the bus owner in the same clock period. The two TM signals are used to indicate the type of attention cycle.

A bus master that uses RQST parks on the bus and can use it at any time until another module uses RQST. Then the parked bus master completes its current transaction and gives up the bus. Bus parking reduces the average time period needed to acquire the bus in systems with a small number of contenders.

## ISA and EISA Systems

The ISA bus refers to the bus used in Industry-Standard-Architecture-compatible computers. This is the same as the IBM AT 16-bit bus. In an EISA system, which is the extended version of ISA with a 32-bit bus, it refers to the ISA subset of the EISA bus.

The EISA bus is a superset of the ISA bus. It has all of the ISA bus features, along with extensions to enhance performance and capabilities. The host CPU is the main system processor with its separate host bus.

An EISA master is a 16-bit or 32-bit bus master that uses the EISA signal set to generate memory or I/O cycles. A bus controller is used to convert the EISA control signals to ISA signals. An ISA master is a 16-bit bus master that uses the ISA subset of the EISA bus to generate memory or I/O cycles. This master must communicate with 8-bit or 16-bit ISA slaves, and route data to the proper paths. It is not used to handle any of the signals associated with the extended section of the EISA bus.

The EISA slaves can be 8-, 16-, or 32-bit memory or I/O slave devices that use the extended signal set of the EISA bus to accept cycles from the different masters. They handle information on the type and width of data using both extended and ISA signals.

The ISA slaves are 8- or 16-bit slave devices that use the ISA subset of the EISA bus to accept cycles from the different masters. They use ISA signals to indicate the type and width of data. A DMA slave is an I/O device that uses DMA signals like DREQ or DACK* to perform a direct memory access.

Assembly and disassembly are needed when the master/slave data bus size are mismatched. Multiple cycles are used to route bytes to the proper byte paths. When a 32-bit CPU accesses an 8-bit slave, four cycles will be used to route the bytes.

A cycle translation is performed when the master and slave are on different buses. The master protocol is translated to the slave protocol.

## EISA Systems

The Extended Industry Standard Architecture (EISA) is a 32-bit architecture based upon the Industry Standard Architecture (ISA) for the PC-AT. EISA's capabilities and 32-bit architecture are needed to get the maximum performance out of the 386 and 486 CPUs. The EISA consortium defined the EISA bus as a 32-bit high-performance ISA-compatible system. This open industry standard allows industrywide compatibility.

EISA provides 32-bit memory addressing and data transfers for CPU, DMA, and bus masters. It allows a 33 Mbyte/second transfer rate for DMA and bus masters on the EISA bus. EISA provides automatic configuration of add-in cards that eliminates the need for jumpers and switches. Interrupts are both shareable and programmable. Figure 4.3 shows the types of buses used in an EISA system. The bus-arbitration scheme allows intelligent bus master add-in cards.

Since the EISA system is compatible with the ISA 8- and 16-bit expansion boards and software, ISA cards can be plugged into the EISA connector slots. The EISA slots are defined as ISA or EISA for compatibility during configuration. The EISA connector set is a super-set of the ISA connector set so there is full compatibility with ISA expansion cards and software. The simultaneous use of EISA and ISA add-in boards is allowed with the automatic system and expansion board configuration scheme.

## EISA Chips

The Intel 82350 EISA chip set is an EISA/ISA-compatible chip set. It supports the 386 or 486 CPU, 82385 cache controller, and 80387 numerics coprocessor. The 82350 chip set is designed for PCs and PC-compatible workstations. The chip set also supports a buffered configuration for extended architectures with SCSI and LAN functions on the system board. The chip set includes the 82352 EISA Bus Buffers (EBB), 82357 Integrated System Peripheral (ISP) and 82358 EISA Bus Controller (EBC).

The EBB supports three buses when used in an EISA system. These are called the A, B, and S buses in the EBB and correspond to the host system bus and the LA and SA buses in the EISA system.

The ISP handles the DMA functions of the system. It has seven 32-bit DMA channels, five 16-bit timer/counters, two eight-channel interrupt controllers, and provides the NMI control and generation. It also provides refresh address generation and keeps track of the refresh requests when the bus is not available. The ISP support multiple EISA bus masters using a system arbitration scheme which grants the bus on a rotating basis.

The EBC acts as the EISA engine, since it works as an intelligent bus controller for the 8, 16, and 32-bit bus masters and slaves. It provides the state machine interface to host ISA/EISA buses and the other ICs in the chip set.

It provides the interface to the 386/486 CPUs and the EISA bus. The EBC acts as a bridge between the EISA and ISA devices. The

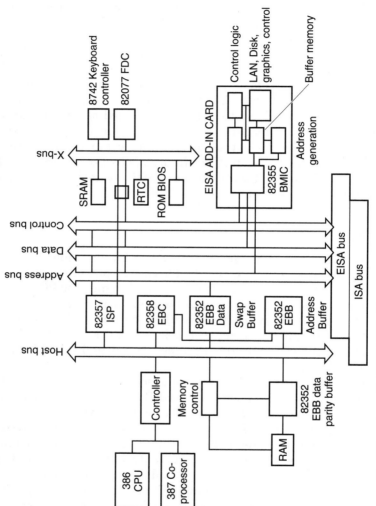

**Figure 4.3**   386 system with 82350 EISA chip set.

data bus size differences are handled by the EBC, including byte assembly and disassembly. The 82355 Bus Master Interface Chip (BMIC) is a device for add-in cards that makes use of the EISA bus master capabilities.

ICs like these support the EISA bus in 386 and 486 processors at various clock speeds. These chips use a CPU to memory protocol which allows the memory subsection to operate independently of the CPU clock. The CPU protocol is translated to this CPU speed independent of the protocol.

## System Components

A typical EISA system consists of the following components. The CPU will be either 386 or 486. A 386 system will use an external cache, usually a 82385 or 82395. The 486 CPU can be used by itself or with a second-level cache, usually a 485 turbocache. Both serial (two-bus) and parallel (single bus) write-through cache configurations are supported.

The 82359 DRAM controller provides the system address path and memory configuration registers, and drives the EISA bus without any additional components. It also provides the snoop address path.

The 82353 Advanced Data Path (ADP) chip provides the system data path and also drives EISA bus directly. The data path is critical to system performance. Each 82353 provides a 16-bit slice and two 82353s are used in 32-bit systems.

The Programmable State Tracker (PST) is contained in two programmable logic devices. It monitors the CPU bus cycles and starts the memory read/write cycles when needed. The 82359 DRAM controller tells the PST how many wait states are needed and the PST generates a READY signal at the end of the cycle. This scheme does not result in synchronization overhead on memory accesses. Different PLDs are used for the different CPU/cache combinations.

The 82351 EISA local IO (LIOE) chip provides a bidirectional parallel port, chip selects, reset, and other logic. The 82358 EISA bus controller (EBC) translates the 82359, EISA, and ISA protocols. It controls data steering in the 82353 and the address latches in the 82359.

The 82357 Integrated System Peripheral (ISP) provides EISA input/output functions such as DMA, timers, and interrupt controllers. The 82352 EISA bus buffer (EBB) buffers and latches the DMA address. An 82077 floppy disk controller provides a single chip implementation of the floppy disk interface. It uses a FIFO to make up any differences in bus latencies and includes tape drive support. An 8742 keyboard controller provides both keyboard and mouse support.

## Bus Architecture

Three buses are used: a host bus, the EISA bus, and a peripheral bus called the *X-bus*. The host bus connects the CPU or host master to the memory system. The EISA bus interfaces the system board resources to expansion bus resources. The peripheral bus supports the system board IO.

## Host Bus

The host bus provides the connection between the CPU and memory system. Zero-wait-state burst cycles are implemented using a 64/128-bit interleaved memory interface. There are zero-wait-state posted writes with the posted write buffer of the 82353.

CPU frequency independence is due to the 82359's delay line and the programmable state tracker function. The programmable delay line allows the DRAM cycle sequence to be tuned to DRAM parameters. The PST converts the CPU's clock-dependent handshake into a clockless memory interface handshake. Even though the interface handshake is clockless, it is synchronous, since the CPU wait state counts match those needed by the DRAM access.

## EISA Bus

The EISA bus connects the masters to memory and acts as a path for CPU accesses to system resources. The interface of EISA masters to memory is optimized for the full memory bandwidth defined by the EISA specifications. This is done with the synchronous tracking of the EISA master cycles by the 82359. The 82359 is always synchronous to the EISA master talking to it.

When the CPU accesses the system, the EBC converts the 82359 handshake into the EISA protocol. The EBC performs any required cycle control for byte assembly/disassembly, and controls the latches and transceivers of the 82359 DRAM controller and the 82353 data path chip. The EBC runs back-to-back read cycles to support CPU to system bursts and coordinates posted system writes.

## Peripheral Bus (X-Bus)

This is an 8-bit bus that supports the system board IO functions such as the keyboard, floppy, and the LIOE chip which contains a parallel port, and supports external real-time clock and serial ports. The peripheral bus is a buffered version of the 8-bit ISA bus.

## Memory Control

Main memory is a critical resource in the system. It is used by CPU and bus masters, which do not want to wait for memory to become available. The memory system needs to be optimized for this type of competitive environment. It should be responsive to the different characteristics of CPU, cache, and EISA bus masters.

The 82359 DRAM controller is used with two 82353 advanced data path ICs and DRAM for a complete memory subsystem for 386 and 486 processors. The 82359 DRAM controller has over 100 programmable registers. These registers control memory mapping, cacheability, timing generation, and memory arbitration.

The memory system controls the DRAM address and row/column signal generation. It also controls the DRAM data routing. A dual-ported scheme is used so these components provide a CPU-only path to DRAM and a system-bus-only path to DRAM. The memory implementation is based on a 128-bit-wide memory data path, although smaller memory widths may be implemented.

The 82359 supports 386 or 486 systems from 20 to 50 MHz. The memory width can be 32, 64, or 128 bits, with a capacity of 1 to 256 MB. The memory can be 64K, 256K, 1M, or 4M DRAMs. Typically four or eight 36-bit SIMM slots are used with single or double density. The cache line size is programmable from 4 to 64 bytes. Snooping is done with a snoop filter that eliminates repeated snoops to the same cache line.

## Dual Ports

The dual port memory architecture differs from previous implementations, since the CPU has its own port to memory which is separate from the EISA port. When the CPU requires access to main memory, it can do so independently of EISA bus activity.

If the main memory is servicing the EISA bus at the time of the CPU memory request, the memory controller will start EISA arbitration on behalf of the CPU. Without dual porting, the CPU would have to go into EISA arbitration, which could cause an 8-microsecond wait until memory is available.

The dual port architecture improves CPU performance when the EISA bus is heavily used. In a single port system, memory ownership is arbitrated along with EISA bus ownership. This produces a long latency of 8 microseconds from the time the CPU indicates that it needs memory until the EISA master actually releases the bus.

The dual-port architecture reduces this time by using separate paths to memory for EISA and for the CPU. The 82359 DRAM controller arbitrates the paths and allows the CPU to access memory while an EISA master still has the EISA bus. This reduces the CPU access time.

Another advantage of the dual port architecture is that EISA masters which talk to EISA memory do not affect the CPU. The CPU can access main memory concurrently with an EISA master accessing EISA resources, reducing memory latency even further.

Each memory cycle generated by the address controller chip causes 128 bits of memory data to be latched in two 82353 chips. Then, with the data latched, the 82353 chips multiplex the four words to the proper destination in a zero wait state. Because of the dual port architecture, EISA bus activities can occur independent of CPU-to-memory activity.

Most high-performance systems use a memory burst access scheme. This includes the 486 CPU, the 386 with 82395, and the 486 with 82485. The usual burst is 128 bits wide, and a bus with the same width allows reading the whole burst in one memory cycle. This results in a zero-wait-state burst. Using 1MB technology (256k × 4 DRAMs), a 128-bit memory bus requires a minimum of 4 megabytes of memory in the system. If the memory array is only partially filled, the 82359 generates multiple memory cycles until the burst is completed.

The memory controller integrates the state tracking function, accepts the CPU ADS* input, and generates a READY output. As frequency increases, this interface becomes a key part of system performance.

## Programmable State Tracker

The state tracking function is implemented in programmable logic. It is called the Programmable State Tracker (PST). Typically, 2 or 3 programmable logic devices are used for the PST functions.

The Programmable State Tracker is like a personality module. The 82359/82353 are part of the motherboard and are separate from the type of CPU/cache system that is used. The PST translates the processor cycles into a form recognized by the 82359. The PST function does not introduce any performance penalties including any synchronization delays. The PST provides only a partitioning; it does not change the way the memory controller works.

## Arbitration

The host bus is arbitrated by an external host arbiter which divides the bus ownership among the different host masters. In a single CPU system, this arbiter is not needed since the CPU has the host bus. This host arbitration is usually transparent to the memory system. This is not strictly true for the 82359's snoop arbiter. This arbiter does not actually arbitrate for the host bus in order to allow the memory system to become the bus master. It arbitrates for the host address bus so it can drive cache invalidation addresses to snooping host masters.

The memory is arbitrated by the 82359's internal memory arbiter, which arbitrates memory ownership between host and system masters and between internal requirements such as refresh. The system bus is arbitrated by an external system arbiter. The system arbiter divides the system bus ownership between the host CPU, EISA bus masters, and DMA channels.

## Throttles

The 82359 uses three programmable throttle mechanisms that control the arbitration of system bus and memory ownership. There is a host memory throttle, system memory throttle, and host system throttle.

The host memory and system memory throttles are part of the memory arbiter. They control the sharing of memory between host and system masters. The host system throttle is part of the slave system arbiter. It ensures that the host CPU gets an adequate part of the system bus bandwidth for accessing the memory resources.

These throttles allow resources to be optimally shared between the masters and they allow the host CPU's bandwidth requirements to be met in a busy system environment. The throttles also prevent resource thrashing. Instead of switching resource ownership on a cycle-by-cycle basis, the throttles set minimum time windows for master ownership. This minimizes the overhead associated with resource ownership transitions.

The memory and system throttles have two programmed variables. One defines the minimum time window during which the CPU has exclusive ownership of the resource. The second variable defines a time window in which the CPU must use the resource to preserve its ownership. If the CPU fails to use the resource during this window, the first window is overridden and the resource taken away from the host.

When the system master activity increases beyond a certain threshold, the system and memory throttles are activated. The system threshold occurs when the external system arbiter releases the system bus, but requests it again before the throttle times out. The threshold for the memory throttle occurs when the system master tries to maintain memory ownership beyond the interval specified by the system memory throttle.

If the system master does not voluntarily turn over the memory ownership, and the system memory throttle interval is up with an active host request, the 82359 takes the memory away from the system and gives it to the host. Then, after the interval specified by the host memory throttle is up, the memory is returned to the system.

If both sides want 100 percent of the memory bandwidth, the host and system memory windows adjust to the actual percent of time allotted to each port.

## Resource Monitoring

The 82359 uses read-only register/counter resource monitors that count resource management parameters. This includes throttle timeouts and the time allotted for host and system memory ownership. This allows software to monitor how the resources are used in an application. This allows dynamic tuning as a function of varying system load.

Host and system masters differ in their behavior and this affects the operation of the 82359's throttles. A system master operates on demand so when it arbitrates for and wins a resource, it uses it and then releases it. If the system master is given the resource for a specified time, the master will use the resource and then return if the time has not expired. The system master will not typically hold a resource if it is not using it.

A host CPU can arbitrate for memory just to meet a single cache miss. When ownership is granted, there is a set amount of time to use the resource as controlled by the throttle settings. After the service is complete, the CPU may not need the resource but it will not actively surrender it.

In order to serve the host accesses, any resources that are not being used are defaulted to host ownership. When the system bus is not very busy, this becomes the major mode of operation and the host does not have to actively arbitrate for resources. Its requirements are met because the system master activity is light. In this mode, the host memory and host system throttles are not needed and not used.

When a system master arbitrates for memory, the memory is taken from the host after the pending host cycle ends and is released to the system. If the system master returns the memory before the end of the time defined by the system memory throttle, the memory is returned to the host. The host memory throttle in this case has no effect.

## Concurrency Switch

The 82359 has a concurrency on/off switch. When the concurrency is off, the system bus and main memory are treated as a single arbitrated resource, so a system master cannot own the system bus independently of owning the memory. In this mode, the memory arbiter and its throttles are not used.

## Floppy Disk Controller

The 82077 floppy disk controller has all of the logic required for floppy disk control. It is used with a 24-MHz crystal and a resistor. It supports both tape drives and 4-Mb floppy drives at data rates through 1 Mbps. The chip supports 500/300/250 Kbps data rates for high- and low-density floppy drives, and is fabricated with Intel's CHMOS III technology in a 68-lead PLCC (plastic) package.

There are integrated drive and data bus buffers along with an integrated analog data separator and a high-speed processor interface. Perpendicular recording is supported and the chip includes 12-mA host interface drivers, 40-mA disk drivers, decoded drive select and motor signals. It uses programmable write precompensation delays, and addresses 256 tracks directly.

## Micro Channel Chips

A compatible Micro Channel system meets all of Micro Channel signal timings and electrical characteristics. Micro Channel computers have increased the system functions on the mainboard. In the older PC/AT systems, these functions required the addition of peripheral cards. The added functions on the system board include the serial port, parallel port, and video graphics.

The Micro Channel bus supports an open architecture with multimaster capability, multidevice arbitration and simple configuration of the system using the Programmable Option Select (POS). In order to provide multimaster capability, each master device is responsible for driving the address, data, arbitration, and control signals. The Micro Channel has four modes of memory and I/O bus cycles: (1) the default cycle, (2) synchronous extended cycle, (3) asynchronous extended cycle, and (4) matched memory cycle. Each of these bus cycles must be supported.

A typical system board will contain the 82303 or 82304 local I/O support chip, 82307 DMA/CACP controller, 82308 bus controller, 82309 address bus controller, and 82077 floppy disk controller. These chips are frequency-dependent, so a 20-MHz system requires –20 chips.

In a minimum configuration Micro Channel-compatible system board, each of the seven system components listed are needed in addition to the following components: 386 DX or SX microprocessor, TTL buffers for the different buses in the system, 8742 keyboard controller with firmware for 101 and 102 keyboard interface, battery-backup real-time clock with CMOS RAM, serial port, memory-ROM BIOS, DRAMs for main memory and VGA, system clock source, and connectors for cables and expansion boards.

## I/O Support Chips

The two I/O support chips, (82303, 82304) and the 82077 floppy disk controller replace 50 ICs. They support the I/O peripherals like the keyboard/mouse controller, serial/parallel ports, configuration RAM, and real-time clock. They integrate two 8259 PICs and the associated logic. There are three programmable timer counters. The chip uses low-power CHMOS technology in a 132-Pin PQFP package.

The 82304 Local Channel Support Chip, along with its companion chip (the 82303) and the 82077 floppy disk controller, significantly reduce system cost, design effort, and form factor constraints by replacing 50 IC devices in an equivalent IBM system.

The 82304 also contains the logic to support the VGA controller. The two 8259 programmable interrupt controllers along with the system status/control ports also have logic required to make the device microchannel-compatible.

## Bus Interface

A bus interface and control block interfaces the 82304 to the microchannel and peripheral buses. It inputs the unlatched microchannel address, latches it for internal use, and makes the latched address available for peripherals. It also provides signals to control an external latching data transceiver that goes between the microchannel and peripheral data buses. The bus interface unit also uses functions such as cycle extensions for slower peripherals and support of the microchannel system feedback function.

The 82304 uses the timers for the following functions:

| | |
|---|---|
| Interrupts | Timer 0 |
| Audio tone generation | Timer 2 |
| Watch-dog functions | Timer 3 |

The 82304 provides the decode signal for the 82077 floppy disk controller and uses the 82077's DMA acknowledge to support the system feedback function.

The 82304 supports VGA setup and enable/disable functions and contains the logic needed to support an external battery backed-up real-time clock chip and static RAM. The 82304 also has the logic needed for the microchannel's password security function. Writes to a specific port (70H) are monitored. If a write tries to access offsets (38-3FH) in the real-time clock chip's onboard RAM, and if a security bit (92H) indicates that these offsets are outside the limits, then no address latch signal is generated for the real-time clock chip.

The 82304 provides functions to support an external serial port chip (1655A) as well as the parallel port on the chip. The 82304 provides decoded read/writes strobes for the serial port chip and converts serial port interrupts into either IRQ3# or IRQ4#, depending on the serial port configuration (COMM1 or COMM2).

The 82304 generates a parallel port chip select for LPT1, LPT2, or LPT3. A signal is generated to indicate if the parallel port operates in a normal output-only mode, or the extended bidirectional mode. The 82307 DMA controller responds to software commands and sends a signal to reset the 80387 or 80387SX numeric coprocessor. The 82304 takes this pulse and stretches it so the 80387 reset input pulse is long enough. The 80387 reset pulse out of the 82304 is externally synchronized to the 80387 clock so the system phase to the 80387 is correct. The 82304 also uses CHRDY to extend the bus cycle that starts the reset which holds up the CPU until the 80387's reset and initialization are complete.

The 82304 provides a chip select for the 8742 keyboard controller. The 82304 also contains the logic needed to latch and clear the keyboard and mouse interrupts.

# Serial Interfaces

## Types of Peripheral Interfaces

The three major types of peripheral interfaces are parallel, serial, and analog. Each type also has a number of different variations. Parallel interfaces are like microprocessor buses. These are often used to interface personal computers to printers. Data is transferred over a set of wires called data lines, like the microprocessor data bus. There are variations in parallel interfaces among the number of data lines used and the amount of signals used for handshaking. Handshaking is a technique used to control the rate at which information moves from one device to another.

Serial interfaces use a single line to transmit one bit at a time. The two types of serial interface are asynchronous and synchronous. The asynchronous interface is more common in microcomputers. The serial interface is often used to interface a mouse or keyboard to a personal computer.

Analog interfaces are different from both serial and parallel interfaces since they do not use digital signals (zero or one). Microprocessor buses use digital signals and serial and parallel interfaces use digital signals to communicate with peripherals. Analog interfaces must convert digital signals into signals that vary continuously or convert continuous signals into digital signals.

Continuous signals include physical variables like temperature, pressure, gas and liquid flow, velocity, voltage, and current. Analog interfaces allow computers to interact with these physical variables.

A typical computer interface could be connected as shown in Fig. 5.1. A microprocessor bus has two interfaces connected to it. One interface is

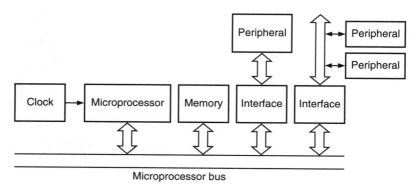

Microprocessor bus

**Figure 5.1**   Microprocessor, bus, memory, and peripherals.

connected to a peripheral device using a cable. Another interface is connected to two peripherals using a cable which is called an interface bus.

The interface bus allows a single interface to communicate with several peripherals, one at a time. A common interface bus is the General Purpose Interface Bus (GPIB). This is also called the IEEE-488 or simply the 488 bus after the standard, IEEE-488-1979, and Hewlett-Packard Interface Bus (HPIB) after the company that developed it. This is a parallel digital interface.

## Serial Interface Basics

When your computer writes to a communication port, the system usually addresses a communication controller chip. There are different addresses to handle the ports. If a character is to be sent over the serial port, it is first written to an address in the controller chip.

The controller circuitry assembles the character into the proper format while inserting control bits. Then one bit is sent at a time (serially) over the transmit data pin which is often labeled Tx. As bits are received serially (at the other end) on the receive data pin (Rx), the receiver strips away any control bits and converts the serial data bits into a parallel word.

When the received character or message is complete, the receiver may send an interrupt signal to the microprocessor. This interrupt causes the microprocessor to read the completed word or message.

There are other serial signals such as RTS, DTR, CTS, DSR, and DCD. These are used as handshaking signals to coordinate the data transfer. Not all of the handshaking signals may be used in all serial applications.

Line drivers are often used in the serial communication lines. These are the line control ICs. Serial communication does not use TTL voltage levels. Instead, bipolar signals are transmitted between computers and serial peripherals. A line driver converts TTL logic levels from a communication controller chip into positive or negative voltage bipolar signals for the serial lines. A line receiver translates these bipolar signals into TTL signal levels.

A typical serial data word is illustrated in Fig. 5.2. The serial data is made up of equal bit times in two logic states. A mark is a logical "1" (one) that is represented by a negative voltage in negative true polarity, and represented by a (*) after the signal name or a bar over it. In positive true polarity, the mark or "1" is represented by a positive voltage. A space is a logical "0" (zero) that is represented by a positive voltage in negative true polarity and a negative voltage in positive true polarity.

The serial word is generally made up of four parts: start bit, the data bits, parity bit, and stop bits. Each bit is needed in serial operations and the peripheral and computer must use the same parameters. When a serial line is idle, it sits in the mark state. The first bit received must be a start bit. Start bits are always the first space (logic 0) to be received. The bits following the start bit are the data bits. These can be either marks or spaces as required. A parity bit may follow the last data bit.

Parity is a simple technique for checking a serial data stream for single-bit errors. At the transmitter a parity bit is added to the data to make the sum of all bits either odd or even. At the receiver the sum of the bits is checked with the value of the received parity bit.

At the end of the word, the stop bits are added. The stop bits are always marks (logical 1s). The communication controller adds start, parity, and stop bits to the data bits, and removes those extra bits from received data words.

The serial bits must be sent at a constant rate, called the *baud rate*. The serial parameters can be set using DOS, or the applications software. Figure 5.3 shows the pinout for a standard serial port.

### Serial Interface Standards

A common serial interface standard is RS-232. The main RS-232 signal lines are those used to transmit and receive data (BA and BB). These lines are used to send the serial information between the two communicating systems. The following bit rates are common: 19,200, 9,600, 4,800 and 2,400. Other rates have also been used in the past.

Start bit          Stop bit

0  1  0  1  1  0  0  1

**Figure 5.2**  Serial word, positive true polarity.

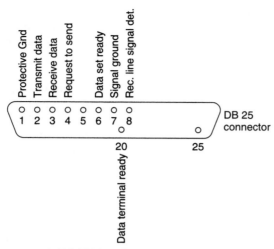

**Figure 5.3**   RS-232 interface connector.

When serial data is transmitted over telephone voice-grade lines, the data must first be modulated so that it can be transmitted. This is generally done with a modem (modulator-demodulator). The three major modulation methods are amplitude modulation, frequency modulation, and phase modulation. The basic technique consists of switching between different amplitudes, frequencies, or phases as the 1s and 0s are modulated. This is generally referred to as *shift keying*. The processes of amplitude-shift keying (ASK), frequency-shift keying (FSK) and phase-shift keying (PSK) are all used.

For bit rates of less than 300, the method of modulation used is FSK: frequency-shift-keying. The mark or logic 1 condition is represented by a tone of given frequency, and the space or logic 0 condition is represented by a second, different frequency. Bit rates above 300 use phase-modulation techniques, due to the lack of available bandwidth. Voice-grade lines are too noisy for high-rate communications and more expensive data-grade lines must be used.

The other signals of RS-232 are used to indicate the status of the modulator-demodulator (modem) communications link. Signals such as request-to-send, clear-to-send, data-set-ready, and data-terminal-ready are used to control the modem link. The signals between the modem (communications equipment) and the computer (or terminal) implement a handshake similar to that used in other buses.

The difference in RS-232, is that the handshake is used only at the beginning and end of a block of serial data. RS-232 has been popular in larger computers and this popularity has migrated to PC peripheral communications.

Another common bus standard is current loop. This was first used in mechanical teletypewriters. Interface converters are available to convert loop devices to RS-232. These are known as loop-to-EIA converters. A loop-to-EIA converter circuit is shown in Fig. 5.4. The current loop standard is used by many mechanical devices and transducers.

A useful variation of RS-232 is an auto loop back, shown in Fig. 5.5. This is used when the computer, terminal, or modem does not have the full complement of RS-232 connections. The jumpers allow the devices to believe that all conditions are in place for data to pass.

RS-232 transmits signals as single-ended voltages. The mark or space condition is represented by the voltage between two wires. One wire is the common ground. The transmit path will use the transmit

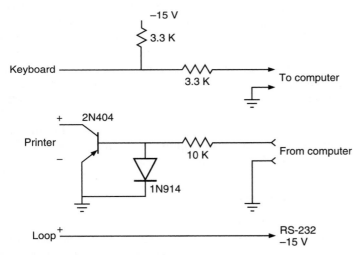

**Figure 5.4** Loop to EIA converter.

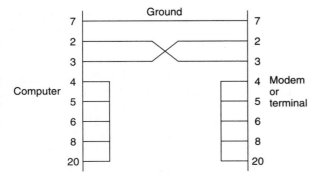

**Figure 5.5** Auto loop back connection.

TABLE 5.1    Serial Interface Standards—RS323C, RS422, & RS423

| Characteristic | RS-232 | RS-422 | RS-423 |
|---|---|---|---|
| Maximum line length | 100 ft | 5000 ft | 5000 ft |
| Maximum bits/sec | $2 \times 10^4$ | $10^6$ | $10^5$ |
| Data "1' = Mark | −1.5 to −36 V | Va > Vb | Va = − |
| Data "0' = Space | +1.5 to +36 V | Va < Vb | Vb = + |
| Receiver input, | 1.5 V | 100 mV | 100 mV |
| minimum | Single-ended | Differential | Differential |

wire and this ground. The receive path will use the receive wire and this ground. If, instead of a single-ended connection, a differential connection is used, the path may be physically longer between devices, due to the noise immunity of a differential channel. The data rate can also be higher, due to the reduced noise effects. This is shown in Table 5.1 which illustrates the differences between RS-232 and two similar standards, RS-422 and RS-423. Figure 5.6 shows the differences between the connections and the types of drivers and receivers used.

RS-422 and 423 are not as common since they are newer and there is a large existing base of RS-232 peripherals. The alternatives to RS-232 are used for higher data rates and longer line lengths.

The data that is sent over these standards can be formatted in many ways. This includes asynchronous and synchronous data transmission and the different standards for information exchange.

## Asynchronous Communications

When data streams are sent in bursts of equal duration, without the use of clock information, they are being sent asynchronously, and are not clocked. When data streams are sent with synchronizing bits along with the data, they are being sent synchronously and are said to be clocked.

The most common asynchronous data structure consists of a 10- or 11-bit data stream. The start bit, eight data bits and one or two stop bits make up a character. The most popular standards for character coding are the ASCII and EBCDIC codes. ASCII is the American Standard Code for Information Exchange and is discussed in Chap. 1. It uses seven bits to encode 128 possible characters. An eighth bit may be used for parity.

The EBCDIC code serves the same function except that the character and other codes are encoded differently. Code-conversion software or ROMs can be used to convert ASCII to EBCDIC or EBCDIC to ASCII. The ROM will use eight inputs: seven address lines for the data input, and one address line to specify the conversion mode (ASCII to EBCDIC or EBCDIC to ASCII). There are seven outputs for the converted character. The size of the ROM needed is 256 bytes by 7 bits per byte.

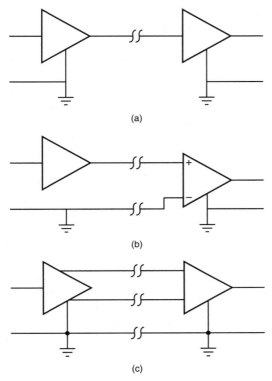

(a)

(b)

(c)

**Figure 5.6**   RS-232, 422, 423 drivers: (*a*) RS-232 single-ended connection; (*b*) RS-422 unbalanced differential connection; (*c*) RS-423 balanced differential connection.

## Serial and Parallel Ports

PC communications depend heavily on serial and parallel ports. The serial and parallel ports are the connectors (plug-ins) on the back of the computer. The parallel and serial ports are an important part of interfacing. They allow the computer to talk to the outside world. A port is simply a connection, or plug-in, that gives access to the computer. The computer peripherals, which are the devices that extend the usefulness of the computer, such as printers, mouse, and modems, all talk to the computer through the communications ports.

When you connect peripherals and communications ports, first you must determine the type of communications that the device uses, either parallel or serial. Then, you make the physical connection; this requires the proper port(s) on your computer, and the right cable(s). The next step is to inform the software of the connections that were made.

The connectors on the computer are referred to as ports. These can be thought of as the passageway through which the signals are sent and received. Sending signals from the computer is referred to as *output* and receiving signals is referred to as *input.* A printer and a modem are output devices and a keyboard and a mouse are input devices.

The two basic methods that PCs use to communicate with the outside world are the serial and parallel communications techniques. The main difference between parallel and serial is the way they transmit signals over their cables. Internally, the computer recognizes each character as an 8-bit code. In serial communications the signals are sent one at a time, over a single wire or a pair of wires.

In parallel transmission, the signals are sent over eight different wires. Parallel communications are like an eight-lane express way with automobiles next to each other in the lanes. Serial communications, on the other hand, are more like railroad cars traveling down a single track.

Parallel ports are like an expressway since they can handle larger volumes of traffic. But, just as vehicles in adjacent lanes can interfere with each other, so can the wires in parallel transmission. The longer the distance becomes, the greater is the chance of interference. Because of this potential for interference in parallel communications, it is normally used only to communicate short distance. Parallel cables are usually no longer than 15 feet. Serial communications are more like a train of cars connected together and riding on rails; it does not have the same potential for interference between the signals. This allows serial cables to be used for distances up to 50 feet. Serial communications cannot transmit the same volume as parallel communications because of the number of signal paths used. Another difference between serial and parallel communications is the ease of use. Parallel communications are more straightforward to the user. All that is needed is to plug them in; there are no transmission parameters to configure and match between the sender and the user.

Parallel communications always occur in the same way. If a printer has a parallel connector, it just needs to be plugged in to a parallel port. Serial communications are more flexible since they allow a variety of settings. This increases the potential uses but requires the proper settings for transmission.

One setting is the speed; effective communication is not possible if the sender uses one speed and the receiver a different speed. The speed of serial communications is called the *baud rate,* and common speeds are 300, 1200, 2400, 4800, and 9600 baud.

Because of their ease of use, parallel communications have become the method of choice for the majority of IBM-compatible printers. Parallel communications ports are easier to hook up and ready to be used after the connection is made. Serial printers are used when the distance to the printer is greater than 15 feet.

## Port Characteristics

Most PCs include one or more parallel ports, which are also called *printer ports*. These two terms are interchangeable. Serial ports are normally used for a mouse. Interface cards for both are available on expansion boards that can be installed in the expansion slots inside the computer. These cards are usually inexpensive and can be installed easily. Up to four parallel ports can be installed in a PC. These ports are designated LPT1 to LPT4. Serial ports are numbered COM1 to COM4. If you already have two serial ports in use, be sure any serial cards you add can be configured for COM3 (Communications Port #3) or COM4 (communications port #4). Many serial ports are not designed to work as COM3 and COM4. The serial ports in these cards can only serve as either COM1 or COM2.

Serial ports are RS-232 ports. This terminology is more common in larger computers. The RS means *recommended standard* and the 232 is the identification number for the standard that the Electronic Industries Association (EIA) uses. So if someone refers to a RS-232 port they are talking about a serial port or a COM port. The serial ports on the computer are either 9- or 25-pin male connectors. The parallel ports are always 25-pin female connectors.

## Identifying the Ports

In the back of your IBM personal computer or compatible, there are several different connectors. The parallel ports are the 25-pin female connectors. These are called *DB-25 connectors*. On many video cards, the parallel printer port is usually under the smaller 9-pin video output port.

Serial ports have the pins reversed to keep you from plugging a cable into the wrong plug. On most newer computers (from the 286 on) the serial ports have a 9-pin male connector (with the pins showing). This type of connector is known as a DB-9 connector. On most XT computers, the serial port is a male 25-pin (DB-25) connector. The newer computers use the 9-pin serial ports to save space. The smaller ports allow two serial ports in the same amount of space. PC serial ports use only 8 pins, so the other 17 pins of the DB-25 connector are unused.

There are adapters if you want to install a device that has a 9-pin serial connector into a PC that has a 25-pin serial connector. This can occur when you try to hook up a serial mouse that needs to be connected to a serial port. These adapters that allow such a connection to be made have a 9-pin connector on one end and a 25-pin connector on the other. These adapters are often included with a mouse or they can be purchased separately.

The other connectors on the computer include a 9-pin video port connector that connects to the monitor. A larger game port connector may also be used to connect a joystick or game paddle.

When you add or change the devices that are hooked-up to the computer, you may need to change the software configurations. This is minimal if the device uses parallel communications to one of the LPT parallel ports. You may be asked to confirm LPT port that the computer selected for you. But, if you want to have a serial communications path for a printer or other device connected to one of the COM serial ports, you will need to set the variable communications parameters.

The communication parameters instruct the computer which serial port to use, how fast it is, and other parameters such as parity, data bits, and stop bits. These parameters can either be set by an application software package or by the DOS MODE command.

## Using the MODE Command

Serial communications require that several specific parameters, or settings, must exist on both ends of the connection. The MODE command, which is supplied with DOS, can be used to check or change these settings. MODE will first indicate the serial port you want to use: COM1 to COM4. You can then check or make the proper settings for that port. As an example of the usage of the MODE command and accompanying parameters, suppose you want to check a modem's settings on COM2 but you already have a mouse attached to COM1. You need to tell the computer to use COM2 and to match the settings of the modem so that it is able to communicate with your computer. The modem manual indicates that the correct settings are 9600 baud, 8 data bits, no parity, and one stop bit. The MODE command should look like the following:

```
MODE COM2:9600,8,n,1
```

You may also need to configure the modem software, so it knows that the modem will be using COM2. This is usually done using the software setup or installation program supplied with the modem or other device. It is usually not necessary to use the MODE command for modems, mice, or other serial devices which have their own communications software.

## RS-232 Networks

Several PCs with a modem, laser printer, or dot-matrix printer can be connected with RS232. These are called *RS-232* or *zero slot LANs* (local area networks). They do not require a separate network interface card in each PC like most other LANs.

Instead, cables are used to connect the networked PCs' serial ports, using the same type of asynchronous signaling that a PC does to send data to a modem. This simple connection can still provide many of the features of the more costly card-based LANs.

The more costly RS-232 LANs are usually connected in a star, where all transmissions go to a central hub. This is usually the PC which routes the transmission to the receiving device.

The network operating system has configuration menus for the network and allows you to share printers and transfer files. The RS-232 LAN software is generally much simpler and easier to install compared to other networks.

The less expensive RS-232 networks do not use a central hub and are connected in either a bus or a ring topology. The network operating system software is loaded into each PC and then the serial ports are connected with cables. These systems tend to be slower as well as less expensive than hub-based systems.

An RS-232 LAN can run as fast as 115,200 bits per second. Bus and ring-based networks are more like card-based LANs in the way they control their media access. Most use the CSMA/CD media access control method like Ethernet. Star-connected, hub-based RS-232 LANs work more like data PBXs in that they set up virtual circuits between two communicating computers.

In some simpler data exchange schemes, if two computers wish to communicate, one of these will send a port select code followed by the computer port number and a terminating character. If the requested computer is free, the two computers are connected for full duplex communication, and an *on-line* message is sent by the hub to the computer requesting communication.

If the requested computer is busy, the computer requesting connection receives a busy message from the hub. To disconnect, either device will send a port-select code followed by a terminating character. At disconnect, an *off-line* message is sent by the hub to the computer requesting disconnect. This is similar to a data PBX and it is not transparent.

These simple networks are an alternative for getting the intelligent data transfer capabilities of card-based LANs, but they do not have the costs or upkeep of these more complex systems.

## Mixing LANs

Many complex card-based LANs tend to be weak in printer support but strong in file sharing. RS-232 LANs are often strong in printer support and weak on file sharing.

The two types of LANs can be mixed—an RS-232 network hub can be attached to a group of PCs, printers, and modems in a local work cluster. A card-based LAN can be used for rapid data transfer and multiuser access to shared files, while still making use of the specialized printer-sharing abilities of an RS-232 LAN.

RS-232 LANs vary in how they transfer, manipulate, and protect files. Most support file transfers between two PCs. The main difference is in the transparency of the transfer. Some make the remote disk drive look like a local DOS device just as card-based LANs do, while others use special commands for file transfers.

## Security

File security on an RS-232 LAN means that a LAN administrator can restrict access to individual files. This may be done using passwords or granting different types of privileges such as read only, where a user can view a file's contents but not make any modifications, or read/write, where a user can do both.

File locking can be used for insuring data integrity. In file locking, only one user can work on a file at a time. Other users are given a message that the file is already being edited and that they will not be able to obtain access at this time. After the first user is done, the second user can work on the file. In these systems, you check out or lock a file from the network, work on it, and check it in to unlock the file when you are done.

Record locking allows two or more users to work on the same file at the same time. A record is a data item in a database. A record could be all the data pertaining to a item, while the database is a collection of these individual records. In record locking, access is limited to one record at a time for each user. Most RS-232 LANs use some version of file locking and a few support record locking.

## Performance

RS-232 LANs are slower since network interface cards in other LANs handle tasks like formatting the data for transmission, communicating with other devices, and moving data to and from the network to the central processing unit (CPU) of the PC. When there is no network card, most of those tasks must be performed by the CPU. Since the CPU is divided between handling the network tasks and performing its other duties, performance is going to be much slower.

Serial communications using RS-232 signals on the PC's serial port is also limited in speed. IBM PC XTs or compatibles used a maximum serial port transmission rate of 19.2 Kbits per second. ATs and compatibles use up to 56 Kbits per second, while 386- and 486-based machines can transmit as high as 115,200 bits per second.

Products are also available for RS-422-based ports that allow higher speeds. RS-422 signalling raises the file transfer speed to as much as 1.5 Mbits per second, which is similar to the speed of many card-based LANs.

Since RS-232 file transfers are slow, large files can be transferred in the background. This allows you to do something else while these large transfers are taking place. The designated recipient may not be aware of the transfer until it is completed.

## Serial I/O Chips

The basic types of integrated circuits used for serial interfaces include:

1. Level converters
2. Receiver/transmitters
3. Bit-rate generators

Level converters change the TTL signal levels to RS-232C, RS-422A, or RS-423A levels. The TTL signal levels that are used in microprocessor systems are not compatible with the voltage levels used by serial interface standards. Transistor circuits have been used for level conversion, but the introduction of specialized integrated circuit drivers and receivers has replaced them in most applications. The IC drivers take up less space and are less expensive to purchase and install.

Receiver/transmitters handle the parallel-to-serial conversion and serial-to-parallel conversion needed for serial bit streams. Shift registers have been used for this function in the past, but the receiver/transmitter chips provide more functions at the same or lower cost. These low-cost receiver/transmitter chips resulted in the popularity of serial interfacing as a major interfacing technique for microprocessor systems.

Bit-rate generators provide clocking signals to receiver/transmitter chips at fixed, standard frequencies. Usually a 16X bit-rate clock is needed. Some receiver/transmitters have an internal bit-rate generator built in. Figure 5.7 shows how level converters, receiver/transmitters, and bit-rate generators are used in a microprocessor system.

## RS-232 Level Converters

Among the most popular RS-232 level converter circuits are the Motorola 1488 line driver and 1489 line receiver. Table 5.2 illustrates the pin layout for the 1488 quad driver. Table 5.3 illustrates the layout for the 1489 quad receiver.

The 1488 quad line driver has three NAND gates and one inverter. The inputs of these gates are compatible with TTL logic levels while the outputs are compatible with RS-232C signal levels. The 1488 uses a positive power supply voltage that can be between 9 and 15 volts and a negative power supply voltage that can be between −9 and −15 volts. These levels are in accordance with the RS-232C signal level specifica-

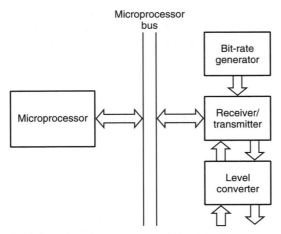

Microprocessor
bus

**Figure 5.7**   Serial interface to microprocessor.

tions. Although this part is TTL-compatible, no 5-volt power is needed. If it is important to meet the 30-volt-per-microsecond slew rate requirement of RS-232C, a 330 pF capacitor can be connected to the output of each gate of the 1488.

There are other applications for the 1488 besides converting TTL signals to RS-232C levels. It can also be used as a voltage level translator

**TABLE 5.2   1488 line driver interface showing IC pin number and layout with functions. Section A is a single input NAND (inverter) circuit while the other sections are dual input NAND circuits.**

| | |
|---|---|
| $V_{EE}$—1 | 14—$V_{CC}$ |
| Input A—2 | 13—Input D1 |
| Output A—3 | 12—Input D2 |
| Input B1—4 | 11—Output D |
| Input B2—5 | 10—Input C1 |
| Output B—6 | 9—Input C2 |
| Ground—7 | 8—Output C |

**TABLE 5.3   1489 line receiver interface shows pin layout and functions. Each section uses a single-ended NAND (inverter) that is enabled with the response control input.**

| | |
|---|---|
| Input A—1 | 14—$V_{cc}$ |
| Response Control A—2 | 13—Input D |
| Output A—3 | 12—Response Control D |
| Input B—4 | 11—Output D |
| Response Control B—5 | 10—Input C |
| Output B—6 | 9—Response Control C |
| Ground—7 | 8—Output C |

to obtain logic levels which are either higher than TTL 5-volt levels or have negative levels.

If the ground pin is not tied to ground, the inputs of the gates will rise to the level of the positive supply. This will usually damage the TTL circuits driving the 1488.

The 1489 chip has four gates which are inverters. The inputs are RS-232C compatible while the outputs supply TTL signal levels. A +5 volt power supply is required, even though up to + and −15 volt signals are being received.

Each gate has a response-control pin. It is usually left open for RS-232C operation. It is designed the be attached to an external voltage source to modify the input threshold. Connecting a capacitor from ground response-control pin will filter noise from the input signal.

The 1488 and 1489 interface drivers use bipolar IC technology and consume TTL levels of power. The 1488 driver also requires both +12 V and −12 V for operation. Most ICs in microcomputer systems operate with a +5 V power supply.

One solution that evolved for this problem was the incorporation of dc-dc converter circuits to raise the +5 V power supply to +12 V and then invert this voltage to provide −12 V. These dc-dc converters use transformers and are costly. In order to eliminate the transformer, a capacitor charge circuit was used. The capacitors are used to move a charge from one voltage level to another. This circuit works well for small currents. But, if a system has several RS-232C drivers, the interface voltage level is reduced.

The Maxim series of RS-232C drivers and receivers has the capacitor charge circuit built into the transceiver IC. Since each IC has its charge circuit, the voltage levels are stable. In the Maxim MAX230 series, most of the charge capacitors are 4.7 and 10 microfarads, so they are not part of the MAX230 ICs. Two devices in this series are hybrid circuits and contain the capacitors in the IC package.

Most of the MAX230 devices use a two-stage circuit. First the +5 V power is raised to +10 V and then it is inverted to −10 V. Others take +12 V power and convert it into −12 V power. Most microcomputer systems with floppy and hard disk drives already have a +12 V available. These systems need to invert this only for the −12 V.

The pins and signals available in the MAX230 and 231 are listed in Tables 5.4 and 5.5. Figures 5.8 and 5.9 show the layout of the driver and receiver circuits.

## RS-422 Devices

RS-422A line drivers include the Texas Instruments SN75172 and SN75174, Advanced Micro Devices AM26LS31C, and Motorola MC3487.

**TABLE 5.4   Pin Layout for the MAX230 RS232C Driver**

| | | |
|---|---|---|
| $T3_{OUT}$—1 | 20—$T4_{OUT}$ | |
| $T1_{OUT}$—2 | 19—$T5_{IN}$ | $T_1$ to $T_5$ are the line driver inverters. |
| $T2_{OUT}$—3 | 18—NC | |
| T2—4 | 17—Shutdown | |
| $T1_{IN}$—5 | 16—$T5_{OUT}$ | V– is the –10 volt output from the +10 to –10 volt |
| | | inverter. |
| GND—6 | 15—$T4_{IN}$ | |
| $V_{CC}$—7 | 14—$T3_{IN}$ | V+ is the +10 volt output from the voltage doubler. |
| C1+—8 | 13—V– | |
| V+—9 | 12—C2– | C1 and C2 are 4.7 microfarad capacitors. |
| C1-—10 | 11—C2+ | |

**TABLE 5.5   Pinout for the MAX231 RS-232C Transceiver**

| | | |
|---|---|---|
| C+—1 | 14—V+ | C is a 4.7 microfarad capacitor. |
| C-—2 | 13—$V_{cc}$ | V+ is the +12 volt input. |
| V-—3 | 12—GND | V– is the –12 volt output from the voltage convertor. |
| $T2_{OUT}$—4 | 11—$T1_{OUT}$ | |
| $R2_{IN}$—5 | 10—$R1_{IN}$ | $T_1$ and $T_2$ are TTL to RS-232 translators and $R_1$ and $R_2$ |
| | | are RS-232 to TTL translators. |
| $R2_{OUT}$—6 | 9—$R1_{OUT}$ | |
| $T2_{IN}$—7 | 8—$T1_{IN}$ | |

RS-422A line receivers include the Texas Instruments SN75173 and SN75175, Advanced Micro Devices AM26LS32A, and Motorola MC3486.

RS-423A line drivers include the Fairchild uA9637A, and most RS-422A line receivers can be used as RS-423A line receivers. All of these line drivers and receivers have four converter circuits in a single package.

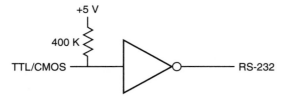

**Figure 5.8**   MAX 230 RS-232C driver circuit.

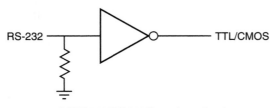

**Figure 5.9**   MAX 230 RS-232C receiver circuit.

## Receiver/Transmitter ICs

The early serial interfaces used integrated-circuit shift registers for the parallel-to-serial and serial-to-parallel conversions. Shift registers for synchronous transmission use a clock to indicate when the next data bit is to be shifted in or out. In asynchronous transmission the start and stop bits are loaded into the shift register and shifted out like the data bits. When shift registers are used for asynchronous reception, circuits are needed to synchronize the receiving shift register with the incoming bits.

Receiver/transmitter chips were introduced during the 1970s. These integrated circuits usually provide two channels of asynchronous and synchronous receivers and transmitters along with bit-rate generators, buffers and status, interrupt, and DMA control lines.

These receiver/transmitter integrated circuits include the General Instruments AY-3-1015D UART, Motorola 6850 ACIA, National Semiconductor 8250 ACE, and Intel 8251A USART. The following definitions are used for these receiver/transmitter chips:

| | |
|---|---|
| UART | Universal Asynchronous Receiver/Transmitter |
| ACIA | Asynchronous Communications Interface Adapter |
| ACE | Asynchronous Communications Element |
| USART | Universal/Synchronous/Asynchronous Receiver/Transmitter |

Each of these integrated circuits performs the same task, but there are different capabilities among these chips.

## UART Chips

One of the first receiver/transmitter integrated circuits to become popular was the Universal Asynchronous Receiver/Transmitter or UART (pronounced "you-art"). It combines the transmitter and receiver shift registers with other features to simplify serial interfacing. Figure 5.10a shows the basic structure of a UART and Fig. 5.10b shows how the serial transmission is made up of start, stop, and data bits.

The UART has separate receiver, transmitter and control sections. The transmitter and receiver sections operate independently but they share the control and status pins. The pinout for the UART is as follows:

| | |
|---|---|
| VCC(+5V)—1 | 40—TCP |
| VGG(–12V)—2 | 39—EPS |
| GND—3 | 38—NB1 |
| RDE*—4 | 37—NB2 |
| RDB—5 | 36—TSB |
| RD7—6 | 35—NP |

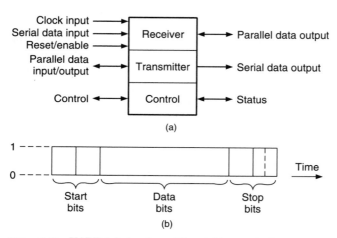

Figure 5.10   UART: (a) structure; (b) serial transmission.

| | |
|---|---|
| RD6—7 | 34—CS |
| RDS—8 | 33—DB8 |
| RD4—9 | 32—DB7 |
| RD3—10 | 31—DB6 |
| RD2—11 | 30—DB5 |
| RD1—12 | 29—DB4 |
| PE—13 | 28—DB3 |
| FE—14 | 27—DB2 |
| OR—15 | 28—DB1 |
| SWE*—16 | 25—SO |
| RCP—17 | 24—EOC |
| RDAV*—18 | 23—DS* |
| DAV—19 | 22—TBMT |
| SI—20 | 21—XR |

The UART is like four separate shift registers that have their own control signal line. The two write registers are a transmit-buffer register and a control register and the two read registers are a received-data buffer register and a status register. Each register has its own data lines and control signal line.

The transmit register is first loaded with a character to be transmitted by setting the digital on the TRANSMITTER DATA BIT lines. These are then clocked into the register by setting the DATA STROBE* negative true. Next, the END OF CHARACTER status line is set false until the character is transmitted, it is switched true until another character is written to the transmitter register. The following lines are set with the proper control information. These are clocked in with the CONTROL STROBE line. Parity selection, the number of stop bits, and the number of bits per character must be the same for both the receiver and transmitter. These parameters are set as follows:

NO PARITY: 1 = no parity bit, 0 = send and receive parity

NUMBER OF STOP BITS: 1 = 2 stop bits, 0 = 1 stop bit

ODD/EVEN PARITY SELECT: 1 = even parity, 0 = odd parity

NUMBER OF DATA BITS:

| NB2 | NB1 | Number of data bits |
|-----|-----|---------------------|
| 0 | 0 | 5 |
| 0 | 1 | 6 |
| 1 | 0 | 7 |
| 1 | 1 | 8 |

The status register is read by switching the STATUS-WORD ENABLE* line low. This dumps the contents of the status register on the following lines:

```
OVERRUN
FRAMING ERROR
PARITY ERROR
TRANSMITTER-BUFFER-EMPTY
DATA AVAILABLE
```

An overrun will occur if a character is received before the previously received character. The data-available bit in the status register must be set true for this condition to occur with the RESET DATA AVAIL-ABLE* line. A framing error occurs when the last character received has an invalid stop bit (not a 1).

A parity error will occur when the last received character has an incorrect parity bit and parity is enabled. Error bits in the status register must be cleared with the external reset pin.

When the microprocessor needs to transmit a character, it checks the TRANSMITTER-BUFFER-EMPTY bit. If there is already a character in the transmitter register, then the microprocessor must wait and check the bit until it changes before writing a character to the transmitter register. The microprocessor will also check the DATA AVAIL-ABLE bit and status line before reading a received character from the receiver register.

When a character is read from the received data buffer, the RECEIVED-DATA-ENABLE line is forced low. This places the contents of the received-data register on the RECEIVER DATA BITS lines. Then the DATA AVAILABLE bit is switched on and the microprocessor can read the character and then switch the RESET-DATA-AVAILABLE pin on the UART so it is ready for the next character.

If the STATUS-WORD-ENABLE* and RECEIVER-DATA-ENABLE* lines are negative true, their output lines are in a three-state condition. This allows them to be directly connected to the microprocessor bus with the enable pins driven by an address decoder. The control and transmitter-data register inputs can also be tied to the microprocessor data bus with the address decoder providing the strobe signals. This is illustrated in Fig. 5.11.

An address decoder for this type of circuit is shown in Fig. 5.12. A 74LS139 decoder is used—the two lowest address bits of the microprocessor address bus are combined with the read and write signals to generate the five control signals required. An inverter is used for the CONTROL STROBE since the 74LS139 generates low-true outputs. The microprocessor sees the UART as two read and three write registers as shown in the following:

| A1 | A0 | Read | Write |
|----|----|------|-------|
| 0 | 0 | Receive Data | Transmit Data |
| 0 | 1 | Status Register | Control Register |
| 1 | 0 | — | Reset Data Available |

The UART also has transmit ($16 \times T$ clock) and receive ($16 \times R$ clock) clock inputs. These use a clock signal running at 16 times the bit rate.

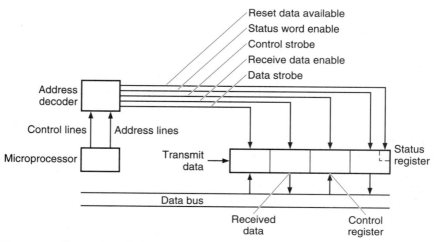

**Figure 5.11**   Connection of a UART to a microprocessor bus.

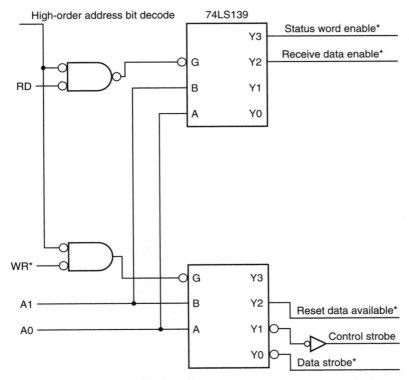

**Figure 5.12**   Address decoder for the UART-based serial interface.

The higher frequency allows the UART receiver to divide each bit time into 16 parts. The UART samples the incoming-data line near the center of the bit time which improves the UART sensitivity to frequency errors. Since there is an independent bit-rate clock input for both the receiver and transmitter, the UART can be run with different bit rates for transmission and reception.

### 6850 ACIA

The Motorola 6850 Asynchronous Communications Adapter (ACIA) is another serial I/O chip. Unlike a UART, the 6850 is designed to be attached to a microprocessor bus. The basic structure of the 6850 is shown in Fig. 5.13. On the left is the microprocessor bus interface and on the right are the serial communications lines. The following list shows the pinout for the 6850 ACIA:

$V_{SS}$—1            24—CTS*

Rx data—2         23—DCD*

Rx CLK—3          22—DO
Tx CLK—4          21—D1
RTS*—5            20—D2
Txdata—6          19—D3
IRQ*—7            18—D4
CSO—8             17—D5
CS2*—9            16—D6
CS1—10            15—D7
RS—11             14—E
$V_{CC}$—12       13—R/W

The 6850 was designed for the 6800 bus interface. There are three chip selects with one of these low-true: a read/write line, enable clock, and a register-select line. The 6850 has two read and two write registers. They are selected as shown in the following:

| Register select | Read/Write* | Register selected |
| --- | --- | --- |
| 0 | 0 | Control register |
| 0 | 1 | Status register |
| 1 | 0 | Transmit data |
| 1 | 1 | Receive data |

The transmit clock and receive clock lines determine the bit rate frequencies for the transmitter and receiver sections. The transmit and receive clocks can run at the desired bit-rate frequency, 16 times the bit rate, or 64 times the bit rate. If the receive clock is set at the bit-rate frequency, it must be externally synchronized with the incoming data.

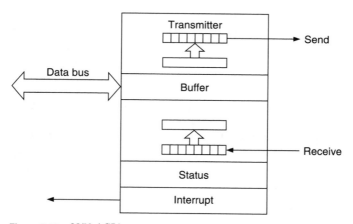

**Figure 5.13**    6850 ACIA.

The serial communications lines are the positive true transmit data and receive data pins. The request-to-send, clear-to-send and data carrier detect lines are all negative-true.

In order to use the ACIA, the microprocessor system must first initialize the chip by writing a byte to the control register. The following bit definitions are used:

7    Receive-Interrupt Enable

6    Transmit Control 2

5    Transmit Control 1

4    Word Select 3

3    Word Select 2

2    Word Select 1

1    Counter-Divide Select 2

0    Counter-Divide Select 1

The three control bit groups—transmit control, word select, and counter divide—are used to set up the ACIA. The receive-interrupt enable bit allows the use of the interrupt request line.

The two transmit-control bits determine the operation of the request-to-send* (RTS) line and determine when interrupts are allowed. These bits are also used to transmit a break, which is a constant zero. Normally, a serial line sits at one in the idle state. The bits are encoded as shown in the following:

| Transmit | Control | Function |
|---|---|---|
| Bit 2 | 1 | |
| 0 | 0 | Request-To-Send = Low, transmitter interrupt disabled |
| 0 | 1 | Request-To-Send = Low, transmitter interrupt enabled |
| 1 | 0 | Request-To-Send = High, transmitter interrupt disabled |
| 1 | 1 | Request-To-Send = Low, send break on transmit data, transmitter interrupt disabled |

The word-select bits are used to set up the following parameters:

1. The number of data bits per character

2. The number of stop bits

3. Parity or no parity

4. Parity type

The combinations allowed are shown as follows:

| Word-Select Bit | | | |
|---|---|---|---|
| 3 | 2 | 1 | |
| 0 | 0 | 0 | 7 bits/character, even parity, 2 stop bits |
| 0 | 0 | 1 | 7 bits/character, odd parity, 2 stop bits |
| 0 | 1 | 0 | 7 bits/character, even parity, 1 stop bit |
| 0 | 1 | 1 | 7 bits/character, odd parity, 1 stop bit |
| 1 | 0 | 0 | 8 bits/character, no parity, 2 stop bits |
| 1 | 0 | 1 | 8 bits/character, no parity, 1 stop bit |
| 1 | 1 | 0 | 8 bits/character, even parity, 1 stop bit |
| 1 | 1 | 1 | 8 bits/character, odd parity, 1 stop bit |

These combinations apply simultaneously to both the transmitter and receiver sections of the chip.

The counter-divide bits set up the transmit and receive clocks with the transmit and receive bit rates. These bits may also be used to set a software reset to the ACIA. The bit encodings which set the transmitter and receiver, are shown as follows:

| Word select 2 | Word select 1 | |
|---|---|---|
| 0 | 0 | Bit rate = Clock |
| 0 | 1 | Bit rate = $\frac{1}{16}$ Clock |
| 1 | 0 | Bit rate = $\frac{1}{64}$ Clock |
| 1 | 1 | Reset |

When the ACIA is set up by the control register, it can be used by checking the status register and then performing the required operations. The status register provides a report of the following conditions:

*Bit*

7    Interrupt Request

6    Parity Error

5    Receiver Overrun

4    Framing Error

3    Clear-to-Send

2    Data-Carrier Detect

1    Transmit Data Register Empty

0    Receive Data Register Full

The status of the interrupt request line can be checked if several devices are connected to the microprocessor's interrupt-request input. Then an interrupt-service routine can be used to determine the device requesting the interrupt. Parity error, receive overrun, and framing error indicate errors in the reception of a character. A parity error indicates that a character in the receiver register was received with bad parity. This bit is turned off when the problem character is read from the receive-data register.

The receiver overrun bit is on when a character is received and another character is already waiting to be read in the receive-data register. The ACIA has no place to put this new character so it is lost. This is indicated by the overrun-error bit which is cleared when a new character is read. A framing error is used when a character is received without a stop bit at the end. This can occur when the number-of-bits-per-character does not match what is actually being received. The bit rate must match at both ends of the communications link and the parity bit be set properly. The framing-error status bit is updated for each character that is received.

The transmit-data-register empty and receive-data-register full bits tell the microprocessor when the transmitter and receiver sections of the ACIA need service. If the transmit-data-register-empty bit is true, the microprocessor can place another character in the transmit-data register to be transmitted. If a character is placed in the transmit-data register when it is not empty, the character that is already in the transmit-data register will be overwritten and never transmitted. The receive-data-register-full bit tells the microprocessor when a character is ready in the receive-data register to be read.

The transmit-data and receive-data registers, are used to send and receive data through the ACIA. A character that is placed in the transmit-data register will be transmitted out the TX-data pin. Bits received on the RX-data pin are assembled into characters and placed in the receive-data register to be read. The basic operational flow of the ACIA is shown in Fig. 5.14.

## 8250 ACE

There are also asynchronous-only serial I/O chips like the National Semiconductor 8250 Asynchronous Communications Adapter (ACE). This chip does the serial-to-parallel and parallel-to-serial conversion for asynchronous communications. It also has a built-in bit-rate generator and a complex interrupt structure.

A block diagram of the 8250 is shown in Fig. 5.15. The pin list appears as follows:

(On the left of the block diagram is the microprocessor interface and on the right are the serial-communications pins.)

$D_0$—1             40—$V_{CC}$

$D_1$—2             39—RI*

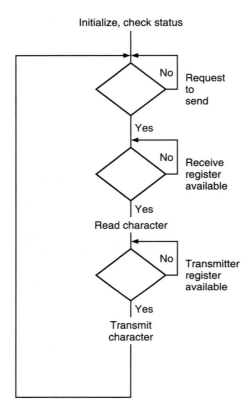

Initialize, check status

Request to send

Receive register available

Read character

Transmitter register available

Transmit character

**Figure 5.14** ACIA operational flow.

| | |
|---|---|
| $D_2$—3 | 38—RLSD* |
| $D_3$—4 | 37—DSR* |
| $D_4$—5 | 36—CTS* |
| $D_5$—6 | 35—MR |
| $D_6$—7 | 34—OUT1* |
| $D_7$—8 | 33—DTR* |
| RCLK—9 | 32—RTS* |
| SIN—10 | 31—OUT2* |
| SOUT—11 | 30—INTRPT |
| CS0—12 | 29—Not connected |
| CS1—13 | 28—$A_0$ |
| CS2—14 | 27—$A_1$ |
| BAUDOUT*—15 | 26—$A_2$ |
| XTAL1—16 | 25—ADS* |
| XTAL2—17 | 24—CSOUT |

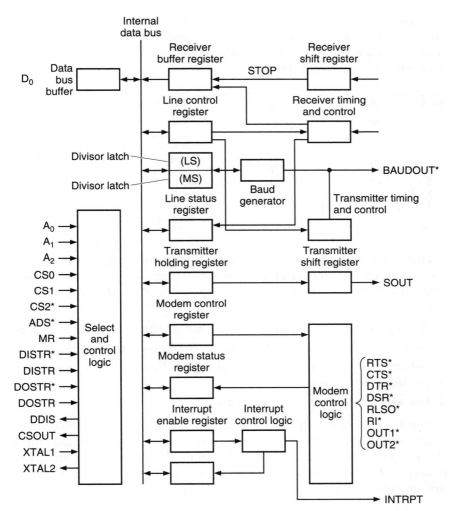

**Figure 5.15**    8250 asynchronous communications element (ACE).

| | |
|---|---|
| DOSTR*—18 | 23—DDIS |
| DOSTR—19 | 22—DISTR |
| $V_{SS}$—20 | 21—DISTR* |

The microprocessor interface is more complete than some others that may need extra gates to connect the chip to a microprocessor bus. The 8250 has eight data lines (D7–D0) and there are three chip selects—CS0, CS1 and CS2*. All of these must be on for bus access to the 8250. When the 8250 has all of the chip select pins on, it will switch on the CSOUT (chip-select out) output pin.

There are three register select lines—A0, A1, and A2—for the on-chip registers. All of the registers are selected by multiplexing the access to some of the registers as shown in the following with the indirect register pointer bit (DLAB).

| DLAB | A2 | A1 | A0 | Register selected |
|------|----|----|----|-------------------|
| 0 | 0 | 0 | 0 | Receive data (read) or transmit data (write) |
| 0 | 0 | 0 | 1 | Interrupt enable (read/write) |
| X | 0 | 1 | 0 | Interrupt identification (read only) |
| X | 0 | 1 | 1 | Line control |
| X | 1 | 0 | 0 | Modem control |
| X | 1 | 0 | 1 | Line status |
| X | 1 | 1 | 0 | Modem status |
| 1 | 0 | 0 | 1 | Bit rate divisor (low) |
| 1 | 0 | 0 | 1 | Bit rate divisor (high) |

DLAB is the most significant bit of the line-control register. It is set to 1 during initialization of the chip and for setting the bit rate divisor, and then cleared to zero and left there until a change in the bit rate is made.
Other configuration steps include:

1. Setting the bit-rate divisor in the high and low bit-rate divisor registers
2. Setting the communication format in the line-control register
3. Setting the levels of the serial-control-line outputs using the modem-control register
4. Loading the interrupt-enable register

The bit rate is set in the bit-rate-divisor registers with two bytes. These are combined to make a 16-bit number which divides the chip's clock input. The divisor is set to 16 times the required bit rate. For example, the following asynchronous bit rates are obtained with the divisors shown for a 3.072-MHz master clock:

| Bit rate | Divisor | High byte | Low byte |
|----------|---------|-----------|----------|
| 110 | 1745 | 6 | 209 |
| 150 | 1280 | 5 | 0 |
| 300 | 640 | 2 | 128 |
| 600 | 320 | 1 | 64 |
| 1200 | 160 | 0 | 160 |
| 1800 | 108 | 0 | 107 |
| 2000 | 96 | 0 | 96 |
| 2400 | 80 | 0 | 80 |
| 3600 | 53 | 0 | 53 |
| 4800 | 40 | 0 | 40 |
| 7200 | 27 | 0 | 27 |
| 9600 | 20 | 0 | 20 |
| 19200 | 10 | 0 | 10 |

Notice that the master-clock frequency is divided by an integer, so some bit rate frequencies like 110, 1800, 2000, 3600, and 7200 have a slight error. However, this is less than 1.5 percent, which is acceptable for asynchronous communications.

The asynchronous communications-bit format is configured using the line-control register. The bits in this register set the following parameters:

1. The number of bits per character

2. The number of stop bits

3. The parity

4. The break level

5. The register pointer (DLAB)

The bits in the line control register are used as shown in the following:

| Bit | Function |
|---|---|
| 7 | DLAB (indirect register pointer) |
| 6 | Send break |
| 5 | Stick parity |
| 4 | Odd/even parity |
| 3 | Parity enable |
| 2 | Number of stop bits |
| 1 | WLS1 (word-length select 1) |
| 0 | WLS0 (word-length select 0) |

The word-length-select bits set the number of data bits for the character to be transmitted and received. These are used with bit 2 to also obtain the stop bits as listed in the following:

| Bit 2 | WLS1 | WLS0 | Bits/Character | Number of STOP bits |
|---|---|---|---|---|
| 0 | 0 | 0 | 5 | 1 |
| 0 | 0 | 1 | 6 | 1 |
| 0 | 1 | 0 | 7 | 1 |
| 0 | 1 | 1 | 8 | 1 |
| 1 | 0 | 0 | 5 | 1.5 |
| 1 | 0 | 1 | 6 | 2 |
| 1 | 1 | 0 | 7 | 2 |
| 1 | 1 | 1 | 8 | 2 |

Bits 3, 4, and 5 are used to set up the parity. Bit 3 enables parity. If this bit is a 1, a parity bit is added to all transmitted characters and parity is tested on all incoming characters. If bit 4 is set to a 1, even parity is used. Odd parity is used if this bit is set to 0.

Bit 5 changes the definition of bit 4. If bit 5 (called the *stuck parity bit*) is set, the parity bit that is transmitted is always the same as bit 4. The ACE will also check for these stuck parity bits on incoming information. Using a stuck parity bit limits your error detection capabilities, but some hardware requires it.

Setting the send break, bit 6, forces the SOUT line low. This produces a break condition on the line which usually needs to be at least 200 milliseconds long. Bit 7 (DLAB) is set to gain access to all of the registers.

In the modem control register, bits 5, 6, and 7 are not used and are set to 0. The other bits in this register are used as follows:

*Bit*

| | |
|---|---|
| 4 | Local loopback |
| 3 | OUT2* |
| 2 | OUT1* |
| 1 | Request To send (RTS*) |
| 0 | Data terminal ready (DTR*) |

When the local loopback is set, SOUT goes high and the receiver is disconnected from SIN and connected to the transmitter. The four output-control lines and four input-status lines are connected to allow the microprocessor to test the receiver/transmitter section as well as the interrupt system.

In the interrupt enable register bits 4 to 7 are not used. The other bits are used as follows:

*Bit*

| | |
|---|---|
| 3 | Enables the modem status interrupts |
| 2 | Enables the receiver line status interrupts |
| 1 | Enables the transmitter holding register empty interrupts |
| 0 | Enables received data available interrupts |

If all bits in the interrupt enable register are set to 0, the INTRPT output line cannot be used. The received data available and transmitter-holding-register-empty interrupts are used for interrupt-initiated data transfers. The receiver line status includes error bits for overrun, parity, and framing errors along with a break detection indicator. If any of these bits goes true, they can cause an interrupt if bit 2 is on.

The modem-status register provides a status indication of the four status-input lines. A change of state in one of these lines can be used to generate an interrupt if bit 3 of the interrupt-enable register is set.

There are three status registers used during I/O operations. These are the line-status, modem-status, and interrupt-identification registers. The line-status register bit settings are as follows:

*Bit*

| | |
|---|---|
| 7 | Not used |
| 6 | Transmitter shift register empty |
| 5 | Transmitter holding register empty |
| 4 | Break interrupt |
| 3 | Framing error |
| 2 | Parity error |
| 1 | Overrun error |
| 0 | Data ready |

Bits 1 through 4 can be used to generate interrupts, or the microprocessor may check them after each received character without using interrupts. Reading the line-status register clears bits 1 through 4. Bit 0 tells you that a character has been received and should be read. This bit is cleared by reading the receive-buffer register or by writing a zero to bit 0 of the line-status register. If bit 5 is on, a character may be in the process of being transmitted but there is space in the transmitter-holding register for another character to be transmitted. Bit 6 is on when the transmitter is idle. This tells you that the transmitter has finished sending out all characters written to the ACE.

## Modem Status Register

The modem status register bit settings are as follows:

*Bit*

| | |
|---|---|
| 7 | Received Line Signal Detect (RLSD) |
| 6 | Ring Indicator (RI) |
| 5 | Data Set Ready (DSR) |
| 4 | Clear-to-Send (CTS) |
| 3 | Delta Received Line Signal Detect |
| 2 | Delta Ring Indicator |
| 1 | Delta Data Set Ready |
| 0 | Delta Clear to Send |

Bits 4 through 7 indicate the states of the input-status lines. If loop-back is active, these lines indicate the bit settings of the modem-control register for the control output lines.

If an input status line is on when a change occurs on one of the input status lines, the associated delta bit in the modem status register is switched on.

An address strobe (ADS)* is available to latch the three-register-select lines. This is used for microprocessor systems with multiplexed address/data buses. There are four read/write control lines. Two are used for reading registers and two are used for writing. One of the read lines is high-true, data-input strobe (DISTR) and the other is low true (DISTR*). The write control line is also available as a high-true data-output strobe (DOSTR) or a low-true (DOSTR*) signal. When a read operation is performed, one of the data-input-strobe control lines is used, while the chip is selected. The interrupt output (INTRPT) is used for errors in serial reception, data transfers, or when one the serial-status lines changes state. There is also a master reset (MR) to clear most of the registers except those used for the transmit and receive data and the bit-rate setting.

For serial communications, there is a transmit data (SOUT) and a receive data (SIN) pin. Four status inputs and four control output are used for controlling the serial interface. These status inputs are as follows:

1. Clear-To-Send (CTS*).

2. Data-Set Ready (DSR*).

3. Received-Line-Signal-Detect (RLSD*).

4. Ring Indicator (RI*).

The control outputs are as follows:

1. Data-Terminal-Ready (DTR*)

2. Request-To-Send (RTS*)

3. General Purpose Outputs OUT1* and OUT2*

Notice the similarity of the names of the inputs and outputs to RS-232C signals. These input and output pins are low-true so they match inverting RS-232C drivers and receivers.

The clock input may be either a crystal or an external clock frequency. If a crystal is used, it is connected between the XTAL1 and XTAL2 pins. If an external clock frequency is used, it is connected to XTAL1 and XTAL2 is not connected. The clock runs the internal operations and acts as a frequency reference for the internal bit-rate generator which divides the clock frequency by the bit-rate divisor.

There is a frequency output pin (BAUDOUT) which can be connected to the receiver-clock input. This input can also be connected to an external bit-rate source.

When loopback is used, the bits in the modem status register will mimic the states of the bits in the modem control register as shown in the following:

| Modem status register | Modem control register |
|---|---|
| CTS (Bit 4) | RTS (Bit 1) |
| DSR (Bit 5) | DTR (Bit 0) |
| RI (Bit 6) | OUT1 (Bit 2) |
| RLSD (Bit 7) | OUT2 (Bit 3) |

When a mimicked bit in the modem control register is set, it will also be set in the modem status register during loopback.

### Interrupt Identification Register

The interrupt identification register tells the microprocessor the cause of an interrupt. Bits 3 to 7 are not used. Bit 2 provides the most significant bit of the interrupt source and bit 1 gives the least significant bit. Bit 0 indicates that no interrupts are pending. If bit 0 is 1, then bits 1 and 2 will be 0.

Bits 1 and 2 indicate the code of the highest priority interrupting condition in the chip. These interrupt codes are shown as follows:

| Bit 2 | Bit 1 | Type | Source | Priority |
|---|---|---|---|---|
| 1 | 1 | Receiver line status | Overrun error<br>Framing error<br>Parity error<br>Break detect | Highest |
| 1 | 0 | Received data<br>Available receiver | | Second |
| 0 | 1 | Transmitter empty | Transmitter | Third |
| 0 | 0 | Modem status | Delta CTS<br>Delta DSR<br>Delta RI<br>Delta RLSD | Lowest |

The other registers are the transmitter-holding register and the receiver-buffer register. Data to be transmitted is written to the transmitter-holding register and incoming characters are read from the receiver-buffer register.

### Intel 8251A USART

Another receiver/transmitter integrated circuit is the Intel 8251A Universal Synchronous/Asynchronous Receiver/Transmitter (USART).

This part can perform serial-to-parallel and parallel-to-serial conversion for asynchronous communications and also output and input bit streams synchronously. A simplified diagram of the 8251A is shown in Fig. 5.16, and a more detailed diagram is shown in Fig. 5.17. The pinouts are listed as follows:

| | |
|---|---|
| $D_2$—1 | 28—$D_1$ |
| D—2 | 27—$D_3$ |
| RxD—3 | 26—$V_{CC}$ |
| GND—4 | 25—RxC* |
| $D_4$—5 | 24—DTR* |
| $D_5$—6 | 23—RTS* |
| $D_6$—7 | 22—DSR* |
| $D_7$—8 | 21—RESET |
| TxC*—9 | 20—CLK |
| WR*—10 | 19—TxD |
| CS*—11 | 18—TxEMPTY |
| C/D*—12 | 17—CTS* |
| RD*—13 | 16—SYNDET/BD |
| RxRDY—14 | 15—TxRDY |

The microprocessor interface is on the left of Fig. 5.17 and the serial communications lines are on the right.

The 8251A has a standard Intel interface. There is a single, low-true chip select, a read strobe (RD*), a write strobe (WR*), and eight data lines. C/D* is the control/data-select pin and is used for register selection. This pin is usually connected to the microprocessor's least-significant address line.

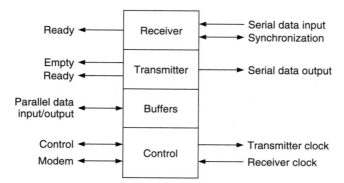

**Figure 5.16**   8251A USART functions.

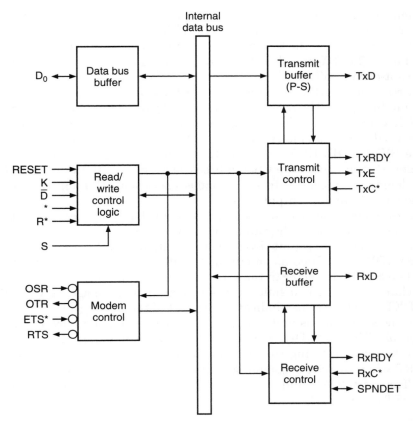

**Figure 5.17** 8251A universal synchronous/asynchronous receiver/transmitter (USAR)

The modem-control section has two inputs and two outputs for the serial-communications circuits. These are DTR* and RTS* and correspond to the Data-Terminal-Ready and Request-To-Send RS-232 signals, but they are actually general-purpose outputs which can be used for any function. The two inputs are DSR* and CTS*, which correspond to the Data-Set-Ready and Clear-To-Send RS-232 signals. DSR* is a general-purpose input, but CTS* is more specific. The USART cannot transmit unless CTS* is negative true.

The chip's serial transmitter sends the serial data out through the TxD line. The transmitter bit rate is set by the clock frequency that is applied to the transmitter clock input TxC*.

There are two output pins for the status of the transmitter section. TsRDY tells you when the transmitter is ready to accept another character from the microprocessor. There may still be a character in the transmitter shift register but if there is space in the transmitter data-input register, TsRDY will be true. TxEMPTY tells you that the transmitter has completed the transmission of any characters written to the transmitter. TxRDY and TxEMPTY may be used as interrupt pins for interrupt-driven software.

The receiver takes the serial data from the RxD input and assembles the bits into characters. The receiver bit rate is set by the clock that is applied to the RxC pin. When a character is received, RsRDY goes true. This pin can be used to drive an interrupt line for interrupt-driven software.

The SYNDET/BRKDET pin has three functions. In asynchronous systems, this pin goes true when a break lasting more than two character lengths is received. In synchronous operations, this pin can be defined as an input or output.

Synchronous transmissions use no start or stop bits, but a special start character is used at the beginning of each message which allows the receiver some time to get into byte synchronization with the transmitter.

If SYNDET is defined as an output, it will go true when the 8251A detects a SYNC character in the serial transmission. The SYNC is the first character to be transmitted in a synchronous message, so when SYNDET goes true it also indicates the start of the message.

In some synchronous protocols, internal SYNC detection may not be acceptable. Then SYNDET is defined as an input to external circuits that take over detecting the start of the message and signaling the USART when to start assembling characters from the incoming data bits. The first 8251s did not detect breaks. The A version added BRKDET to SYNDET.

## Configuration

The chip is configured by loading its registers with the desired parameters. The bytes are written to the control port. A pointer register determines what register is accessed when the control port is written to.

When the pointer register is reset, the mode register is accessed through the control port. The bit definitions in this register depend on whether synchronous or asynchronous operations are used. In the asynchronous mode the bits are used as follows:

| | |
|---|---|
| 7 | Number of stop bits—most significant bit |
| 6 | Number of stop bits—least significant bit |
| 5 | Even/odd parity |
| 4 | Parity enable |
| 3 | Character length—most significant bit |
| 2 | Character length—least significant bit |
| 1 | Bit-rate factor—most significant bit |
| 0 | Bit-rate factor—least significant bit |

The bit-rate factor is the relationship between the receive and transmit clocks and the actual receive and transmit bit rates. The following bit-rate factors are allowed:

| Bit 1 | Bit 0 | Bit-rate factor |
|-------|-------|-----------------|
| 0 | 0 | Synchronous USART operation |
| 0 | 1 | Bit rate = Clock rate |
| 1 | 0 | Bit rate = Clock rate/16 |
| 1 | 1 | Bit rate = Clock rate/64 |

In synchronous mode, the mode-register-bit assignments for bits 2 through 7 shown previously do not apply.

It is best to use a high bit-rate factor since the higher bit-rate clocks allow the USART to divide the bit time more fully and more accurately identify the center of the bit time. This provides the USART with more tolerance to timing differences between the transmitting device and the receiver.

However, a high bit-rate factor puts a lower limit on the maximum bit rate than the USART can run at. The transmit and receive clocks are limited to 615 kMz for the 64X bit-rate factor, which gives a bit rate of about 9600 bits per second. The USART is limited to transmit and receive clocks of 310 kHz for a bit-rate factor of 16X which gives a bit rate of about 19,200 bits per second. At the 1X bit-rate factor the USART can run at 64,000 bits per second, but the USART cannot find the center of a character without external circuitry.

This is needed to center the rising edge of the receive clock in the middle of the bit time. The receive clock must be connected to the clock of the transmitting device. This mode is sometimes called *isochronous serial communications.*

The character length in asynchronous operation is set with bits 2 and 3 of the mode register. The following settings are used:

| Bit 3 | Bit 2 | Bits per character |
|-------|-------|--------------------|
| 0 | 0 | 5 |
| 0 | 1 | 6 |
| 1 | 0 | 7 |
| 1 | 1 | 8 |

Parity is enabled with bit 4 of the mode register. The type of parity is set with bit 5 of the mode register. When bit 5 is 1, even parity is used, if bit 5 is 0, odd parity is used.

The number of stop bits is set with bits 6 and 7 of the mode register. The following stop bits are available.

| Bit 7 | Bit 6 | Number of stop bits |
|-------|-------|---------------------|
| 0     | 1     | 1                   |
| 1     | 0     | 1.5                 |
| 1     | 1     | 2                   |

Although the transmitter can be set to operate at 1.5 or 2 stop bits per character, the receiver only needs 1 stop bit to operate.

## Synchronous Mode

The mode register bits are used as follows for synchronous operations:

*Bit*

| | |
|---|---|
| 7 | One or two SYNC characters |
| 6 | Internal/external SYNC detection |
| 5 | Even/odd parity select |
| 4 | Parity enable |
| 3 | Character length, most significant bit |
| 2 | Character length, least significant bit |
| 1 | Set to 0 for synchronous operation |
| 0 | Set to 0 for synchronous operation |

The use of bits 0 through 5 are the same as the asynchronous mode register settings. Bits 0 and 1 of the bit-rate factor must be set to 0 for synchronous operation.

Bit 6 determines if the SYNDET pin is an input or an output. If bit 6 is set to one, SYNDET is an input, and external circuitry is needed to synchronize the chip with the incoming message. If bit 6 is 0, SYNDET is an output, and the chip will synchronize internally on the first SYNC character.

Bit 7 in the synchronous mode register sets the number of SYNC characters at the start of a message. Some synchronous protocols, like Bisync, use two SYNC characters at the beginning of each message. If bit 7 is set to 1, the chip will start making characters after receiving the first SYNC. If bit 7 is set to 0, the chip will expect two SYNC characters at the start of each message.

When the mode register has been initialized, the internal-register pointer will move to another register. If asynchronous operation is used, the command register will be loaded next. If synchronous operation has been selected, the SYNC character registers are loaded next.

The next byte the processor writes to the control port becomes the first SYNC character. If double SYNC operation is used, the pointer moves to the second SYNC character register for the next output to the control port. After the SYNC characters have been sent out, the pointer moves to the command register until a reset occurs. The following bits are used in the command register:

*Bit*

| | |
|---|---|
| 7 | Enter hunt mode (synchronous only) |
| 6 | Internal reset |
| 5 | Request to send |
| 4 | Error reset |
| 3 | Send break |
| 2 | Receive enable |
| 1 | Data terminal ready |
| 0 | Transmit enable |

Bit 0 allows the transmitter to operate. When it goes true and the CTS* pin is low the transmitter can send out characters. Bit 1 controls the DTR* output. If bit 1 is true, DTR can be switched on. Bit 2 is the receiver enable. It allows incoming bits to be converted to characters. Bit 3 controls the TxD pin. If this bit goes true for 200 milliseconds and is then switched off, a break is sent over the communications line.

Bit 4 resets the error-status bits in the status register. Bit 5 controls the RTS* output. If bit 5 is true, the RTS pin can be switched on.

Software can be used to reset the internal-pointer register. This is done by turning on bit 6 of the command register. In a reset all internal operations are idled and the pointer moves to the mode register.

Bit 7 is used for synchronous operation, it allows the USART to enter a hunt mode and search for a SYNC character. When the character is found, the chip can assemble characters from the incoming bit stream.

During power-up, the pointer register setting is not defined. The recommended procedure is to write three bytes of zero to the control port. This will push the pointer to the command register. Then, write a 64 to the command register to start a software reset which prepares the mode register, SYNC register, and command register for normal operations.

The status register is read by reading the control port. The bits are set the following way:

*Bit*

| | |
|---|---|
| 7 | Data set ready |
| 6 | SYNDET |
| 5 | Framing error |
| 4 | Overrun error |

| | |
|---|---|
| 3 | Parity error |
| 2 | TxEMPTY |
| 1 | RxRDY |
| 0 | TxRDY |

Bits 0, 1, 2, and 6 show the status of the pins with the same name. The three error bits are reset by turning on bit 4 of the command. The data-set ready bit allows the microprocessor to read the state of the DSR* input.

## Bit-Rate Generators

Some receiver/transmitters have on-board bit-rate generators while others require external generators. There are two types of bit-rate generator-integrated circuits. One type uses a master-clock frequency, usually from a crystal, and divides it into the bit-rate frequencies. The other type has an internal register which the microprocessor writes to. The value in the register sets the bit rate which is sent out on a frequency-output pin. This type of generator is used in programmable serial interfaces. The Western Digital BR1911 is an example of this type of part. Other parts like the Fairchild 4702 do not have a register. These are used with switches, or with an external latch.

## Tools for Serial Interfaces

A useful tool for dealing with serial interfaces is a null modem. This is actually a cable for connecting two devices which act like DTEs or DCEs together. Pin 2 of one connector and pin 3 of the other connector are tied together as shown in Fig. 5.18 for the data flow. Pin 20 of each connector is tied to pins 5 and 6 of the same connector. This takes care of the clear-to-send and data-set ready inputs and the data-terminal-ready output.

Another tool is a type of breakout box, with the RS-232 connectors wired to 25 switches. Each of the 25 RS-232 lines can be interrupted and the state of each side of the line can be determined. Light-emitting diodes (LEDs) are often used to indicate the state of the line. The breakout box can be used to identify the signals on an unknown RS-232 configuration.

Most current microcomputers have a serial port connector. This is usually a D-type, 9-pin male connector (DB-9M). If you attach a serial port breakout box between the port and cable, you can display the conditions of transmitted and received data, as well as the conditions of the handshaking signals.

Besides being a handy tool for providing an overview of serial port activity, most LED breakout boxes are designed to handle the wide

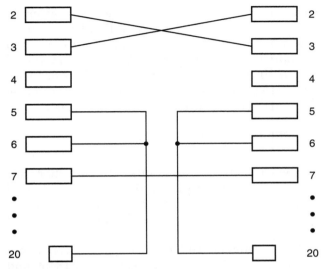

**Figure 5.18**   RS-232C null modem.

range of bipolar signal voltages found in serial ports. High bipolar voltages can damage most logic probes.

Now, initiate a data transfer over the serial port using any convenient software package. For example, you could drive a serial printer using a word processor. The serial port is typically COM1:, and the serial configuration must be set properly for the computer and peripheral device. If the communication parameters are not the same, the serial communication link will not work. During a normal data transfer, both the Tx and Rx LEDs should indicate some activity. There should also be some activity on the port's handshaking lines.

If the TX signal shows no activity, the port is not transmitting data. Check the TTL-level Tx signal entering the line driver IC. If the TTL Tx data enters the line driver but does not exit as a bipolar signal, the line driver IC is suspect and needs to be replaced. Check the TTL Rx data from the line receiver. If the Rx line is active but no TTL data is leaving the line receiver IC, then you may have a defective line receiver. If Rx shows no activity at the serial connector, you are not getting data from the peripheral device.

You can check the handshaking signals in the same way. Any bipolar signal activity on the LED breakout box should have a corresponding TTL activity at either the line driver or line receiver. If the handshaking signals are active as TTL levels at the line driver but do not appear as bipolar signals at the breakout box, you may have a defective line driver IC. If bipolar handshaking signals are received at the serial connector, but do not appear as TTL-level signals from the line receiver IC, the line receiver IC is probably defective. If outgoing TTL-level signals, such as Tx, are missing and incoming TTL-levels signals are active, you may have a bad serial communication controller IC or clock crystal.

The interrupt or control lines used can be checked in the same way. During a data transfer, those lines should each appear active as a pulse signal. If these lines are inactive, the serial controller is suspect.

## 82050 Asynchronous Communications Controller

This Intel chip allows asynchronous operation in a 5- to 8-bit character format. Odd-, even-, or no-parity generation and detection is allowed with a bit rate to 56 Kb/s. There is a programmable, 16-bit baud rate generator with an on-chip crystal oscillator. It is available in a 28 lead DIP PLCC package (see Fig. 5.19).

This CHMOS 82050 asynchronous communications controller is a low-cost alternative to the INS 16450. It emulates the INS 16450 and is compatible with IBM PC software. The 82050 is also used in modems when combined with modem chips like Intel's 89024.

### 82050 Signals

The three address pins (A2–A0) on pins 24–22 interface with the system address bus to select one of the internal registers for read or write

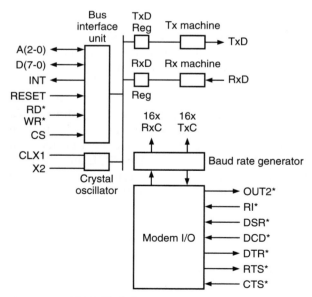

**Figure 5.19**    82050 block diagram.

operations. D7–D0 on pins 1–4 and 25–28 make up the bidirectional, three state, 8-bit data bus. It allows the transfer of bytes between the microprocessor and the 82050. A RESET input on pin 17 resets the 82050. CS* is the chip select on pin 18. A low on this input pin enables the 82050 and allows the following read or write operations:

1. RD* on pin 20 allows the microprocessor to read data or status from the chip.

2. WR* on pin 19 allows the microprocessor to write data or control bytes to the 82050.

INTERRUPT is on pin 5. A high on this output indicates an interrupt request to the microprocessor. The source and cause of the interrupt can be found by reading the status registers.

CLK/X1 on pin 9 is used for the internal system clock. In the CLK mode an externally generated clock is used. In the X1 mode the clock is generated by a crystal that is connected between the X1 and X2 pin.

OUT2*/X2 on pin 8 is another dual-function pin. OUT2* is a general-purpose output used by the CLK/X1 pin. It is driven by an externally generated clock. X2 is an output pin for the crystal oscillator. The configuration of this pin takes place during a hardware reset.

TXD on pin 6 is the TRANSMIT DATA pin. The serial data is transmitted on this output pin starting at the least significant bit. RXD on pin 13 is used as the RECEIVE DATA pin. The serial data is received on this pin starting at the least significant bit.

RI* on pin 10 is used as a ring indicator input. DTR* on pin 15 is the DATA TERMINAL READY output. During a hardware reset, this pin is an input used to set the system clock mode.

DSR* on pin 11 is the DATA SET READY input. RTS* on pin 16 is the REQUEST TO SEND output. During hardware reset, this pin is an input used to set the system clock mode.

CTS* on pin 14 is the CLEAR TO SEND input. DCD* on pin 12 is the DATA CARRIER DETECTED input. Pin 21 is the device power supply and pin 7 is ground.

## System Interface

The 82050 uses a demultiplexed bus interface made up of a bidirectional, three-state, 8-bit data bus and a 3-bit address bus. The Reset, Chip Select, Read, and Write pins, along with the Interrupt pin, are the other signals needed to interface to the microprocessor.

The system clock can be generated externally and sent to the CLK pin. The on-chip crystal oscillator is used by connecting a crystal to the X1 and X2 pins. The 82050 chip along with a transceiver, address decoder, and crystal, complete the interface to the IBM PC bus.

## Baud Rate Generation

The 82050 has a programmable 16-bit Baud Rate Generator (BRG). The baud rate is generated by dividing the source clock with the divisor count from the two BRG divisor registers (BAL, BAH). The BRG source clock is the 82050 system clock divided by five.

During a reset, all 82050 registers (except TXD and RSX) are returned to their default states. The clock mode of operation is also selected at this time by options on the RTS and DTR pins.

## Interrupts

The INT pin is enabled with the Interrupt Enable Register (IER). It goes high when one of the following conditions occurs:

1. Receive data available
2. Receive machine error or break condition
3. Transmit data register empty
4. Change in state of modem input pins

The INT pin is reset when the interrupt source is serviced. The Interrupt Identification Register (IIR) along with the Line Status Register (LSR) and the Modem Status Register (MSR) are used to identify the source requesting service. The IIR register identifies which one of the four conditions listed has occurred. The particular event or status which triggered the interrupt mechanism is identified by reading either the Line Status Register or the Modem Status Register.

If there are multiple interrupt sources, then the highest priority interrupt source is indicated in the IIR register when the interrupt pin goes active. After the highest-priority interrupt is serviced, then the next-highest-priority interrupt source is sent to the IIR register. The procedure is continued until there are no more pending interrupt sources.

## Transmitting and Receiving

In the 82050, the transmission mechanism involves a section in the chip called the TX machine along with the TXD register. The TX machine reads characters from the TXD register, serializes the bits, and transmits them over the TXD pin according to signals provided by the baud rate generator. It also generates the parity and break transmissions.

Receiving involves a section called the RX machine along with the RXD register. The RX machine assembles the incoming characters and loads them onto the RXD register. The RX machine also synchronizes the data, passes it through a digital filter to filter out spikes, and generates the bit polarity. The falling edge of the start bit triggers the RX machine, which then samples the RXD input. When a start bit is detected, the RX machine samples for data bits.

If the RXD input is low for an entire character time, then the RX machine sets Break Detect and Framing Error bits in the Line Status Register (LSR) and loads a NULL character into the RXD register. The RX machine then goes into an idle state until it senses a one and it resumes normal operation.

Like other I/O-based peripherals, the 82050 is programmed through its registers. The 82050 register set is the same as the 16450 register set to provide compatibility with previous software written for the IBM PC.

## Register Set

The 82050 register set occupies eight addresses and includes control status and data registers. The three address lines and the divisor latch access bit are used to select the 82050 registers.

**Transmit Data Register (TXD).** Holds the next data byte to be transmitted. When the transmit shift register becomes empty, the contents of the transmit data register are loaded into TXD and the transmit data register becomes empty.

**Receive Data Register (RXD).** Holds the last character received by the RX machine. Reading the register empties it and resets the Received Character Available condition.

**BRG Divisor Low Byte (BAL).** Register that holds the least significant byte of the baud rate generator's 16-bit divisor. This register is accessed when the DLAB bit is set in the LCR register. The other divisor register, BRG Divisor High Byte (BAH), holds the most significant byte of the baud rate generator divisor. This register is also accessed when the DLAB bit is set in the LCR register.

**Interrupt Enable Register (IER).** Enables the four types of interrupts available. Each of these interrupt types is disabled by also setting bits in the IER register. If all interrupts are disabled, then interrupt requests are inhibited from the IIR register and the INT pin. The other functions, including the status register and line status register bits, are not affected.

**Interrupt Identification Register (IIR).** Contains the highest-priority-enabled and active interrupt request. The source of the interrupt request is identified by reading bits 2 and 1. These two bits indicate the highest priority, enabled and pending interrupt request. An error condition is given the highest priority and a modem interrupt the lowest priority.

If the IPN (Interrupt Pending) bit is low, this indicates that there is an interrupt pending. The interrupt logic sets the INT pin true when this bit goes low. The IIR register is always updated, so a new interrupt with higher priority can enter IIR and replace the older interrupt.

**Line Control Register (LCR).** A read/write register that sets the basic configuration of the serial link. DLAB is the Divisor Latch Access Bit. It allows access to the Divisor Count Registers BAL and BAH. SBK (Set Break) forces the TXD pin low. PM2–PM0 are parity mode bits that select the different parity modes as shown in the following:

| PM0 | PM2 | PM1 | Parity mode |
|-----|-----|-----|-------------|
| 0 | X | X | No parity |
| 1 | 0 | 0 | Odd parity |
| 1 | 0 | 1 | Even parity |
| 1 | 1 | 0 | High parity |
| 1 | 1 | 1 | Low parity |

SBL is the Stop Bit Length which sets the stop bit lengths for transmitting. The RX machine uses the following stop bits:

| BL | Character length | Stop bits |
|----|------------------|-----------|
| 0 | X | 1 |
| 1 | 5 bits | 1½ |
| 1 | 6, 7 or 8-bits | 2 |

CL0–CL1 are the character length bits. They are used to set the character length used on the serial link as listed in the following:

| CL1 | CL0 | Character length |
|-----|-----|------------------|
| 0 | 0 | 5 bits |
| 0 | 1 | 6 bits |
| 1 | 0 | 7 bits |
| 1 | 1 | 8 bits |

**Line Status Register (LSR).** Contains the status of the serial link. The following bits in this register are set:

| | |
|---|---|
| RXDA (RX Data Available) | Indicates when the RXD register has data available for the CPU to read. |
| OE (Overrun Error) | Indicates when a received character was lost because the RXD register was not empty. |
| PE (Parity Error) | Is set when a received character has a parity error. |

| FE (Framing Error) | Is set when a received character has a framing error. |
| BKD (Break Detected) | Is set when a break condition is detected. |
| TXDE (TXD Empty) | Indicates that the 82050 is ready for a new character for transmission. This bit causes an interrupt request to be generated if the TXD Register Empty interrupt is enabled. |
| TXST (TX Machine Status) | Is set when both the TXD register and the TX Shift Register are empty. |

**Modem Control Register (MCR).** Controls the modem output pins. These outputs invert the data, so their output is the complement of the data written into this register.

### 82510 Asynchronous Serial Controller

This chip allows asynchronous operation in a 5- to 9-bit character format with error detection and multiple sampling windows. There are two 4-byte transmit and receive FIFOs with programmable thresholds and two 16-bit baud rate generators. These generators can also be configured as timers and used when the transmit and receive baud rates are different. There is also an on-chip crystal oscillator. The interrupts are maskable at two levels and there are autoecho and loopback modes. The chip comes in 28-lead DIP and PLCC packages (Fig. 5.20).

### 82510 Signals

The 82510 uses a demultiplexed bus interface, made up of a bidirectional, three-state, 8-bit data bus and a 3-bit address bus. The interrupt pin along with the Read, Write, and Chip Select are used to interface with the microprocessor. The three address lines and a bank pointer register are used to select the registers. Like other I/O-based peripherals, it is programmed through its registers.

A2–A0 on pins 24–22 are the *address pins*. These are used to select one of the internal registers. D7–D0 on pins 28–25 and 4–1 make up the bidirectional, three-state, 8-bit data bus. CS∗ on pin 18 is the *Chip Select*. A low on this input enables the 82510 and allows read or write operations.

RD∗ on pin 20 is the *Read* input. It allows the microprocessor to read data or status bytes from the 82510. WR∗ on pin 19 is the *Write* input. It allows the microprocessor to write data or control bytes to the 82510. INT on pin 5 signals an interrupt request to the microprocessor. The microprocessor can determine the source and cause of the interrupt by reading the 82510 status registers. The *reset* pin is 17. A high level on this input pin resets the chip to the default wake-up mode.

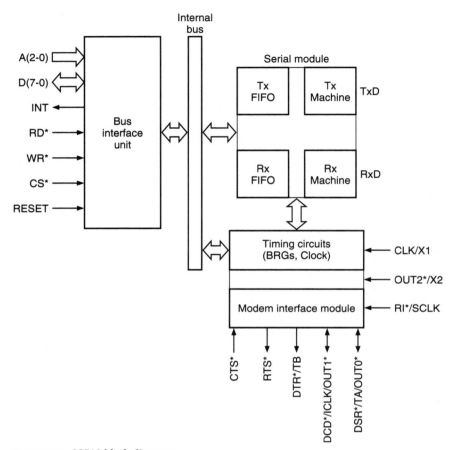

**Figure 5.20**    82510 block diagram.

CLK/X1 on pin 9 has two modes. It is a source for the internal system clock. In the CLK mode an externally generated, TTL-compatible clock is used to drive this input pin. In the X1 mode the clock is internally generated by an on-chip crystal oscillator. The crystal is connected between the X1 and X2 pins.

OUT2*/X2 on pin 8 is another dual function pin. OUT2* is a general-purpose output pin that is available when the CLK/X1 pin is driven by an externally generated clock. In the X2 mode, this pin acts as an output pin for the crystal oscillator. The configuration of this pin takes place during a hardware reset.

TXD on pin 6 is the *Transmit Data* output. Serial data is transmitted on this pin starting at the least significant bit. RXD on pin 3 is the *Receive Data* input. Serial data is received on this pin starting at the least significant bit.

RTS* on pin 16 is the REQUEST TO SEND output pin. In automatic transmission mode this pin, along with CTS*, is used to control the transmission of data. During a hardware reset this pin acts as an input to determine the system clock mode. CTS* on pin 14 is the CLEAR TO SEND input. In automatic transmission mode it is used to control the transmit machine. This pin is also used as a general-purpose input.

RI*/SCLK on pin 10 is a dual-function pin. It can be configured as a Ring Indicator input. This is a general-purpose input. In the SCLK mode it serves as a source for the internal serial clocks, RxClk and TxClk.

DTR*/TB on pin 15 is a dual-function pin which can be configured as a Data Terminal Ready output. This is a general-purpose output pin. In the TB mode this pin outputs the BRGB output signal if configured as a clock generator or a timer. If BRGB is configured as a timer, this pin outputs a timer-expired pulse. If BRGB is configured as a clock generator, it outputs the BRGB output clock.

DSR*/TA/OUT0* on pin 11 is a multifunction pin which can be configured to one of the following functions. DSR stands for *Data Set Ready*. This is a general-purpose input pin. The TA pin is similar to pin TB except it outputs the signals from BRGA instead of BRGB. OUT0 is a general-purpose output pin controlled by the microprocessor.

DCD*/ICLK/OUT1* on pin 12 has three functions. It may be configured as a Data Carrier Detected input. ICLK is the output of the internal system clock. OUT1* is a general-purpose output pin. Pin 21 is the device power supply and pin 7 is ground.

## 82510 Functional Blocks

The 82510 can be functionally divided into seven major blocks:

1. Bus interface unit
2. Timing unit
3. Modem
4. Tx FIFO
5. Rx FIFO
6. Tx machine
7. Rx machine

All of these units, except the bus interface unit, can generate block interrupts. Three of these blocks can generate second-level interrupts for errors or status: the receive machine, the timing unit, and the modem.

The bus interface unit provides the interface for the 82510 with the rest of the system. It controls access to the device registers and generates interrupts to the external circuitry.

The FIFOs are used to buffer the microprocessor from the serial machine. They also reduce the interrupt overhead needed for serial operations. The timing unit controls operation of the system clock using either the on-chip crystal oscillator or an externally generated clock. It also has two baud rate generator/timers to support serial communications.

## Register Banks

There are 35 registers which are divided into four banks. Only one bank is accessible at any one time. The bank switching is done by changing the contents of a bank pointer. The banks are grouped as follows:

1. 8250A/16450 compatible bank (this is the default bank upon power-up)
2. General work bank
3. General configuration
4. Modem configuration

During power-up or reset, the 82510 comes up in a default wakeup mode. The 8250/16450-compatible bank is the accessible bank and the other registers are configured in default values to support this mode.

## Interrupt Scheme

There are two levels of interrupt/status reports. The first level consists of the block level interrupts for the Rx FIFO, Tx FIFO, Rx machine, Tx machine, timing unit, and modem. The status of these blocks appears in the general status and general interrupt registers. The second level includes the sources in each block. Only three of the blocks can generate second-level interrupts: the Rx Machine, the timing unit, and modem.

Interrupt requests are maskable at the block level and at the individual source level. If more than one unmasked block requests interrupt service, an on-chip interrupt controller is used to resolve contention on a priority basis. Each block is given a fixed priority.

An interrupt request from a particular block is activated when one of the unmasked status bits in the status register for the block is set. A microprocessor service operation, like reading a status register, resets the status bits.

The interrupt logic sets the INT pin when an interrupt is loaded into the general interrupt register. The INT pin goes low on acknowledgment. There are two modes of interrupt acknowledgment. In manual acknowledgment, the microprocessor issues an explicit interrupt acknowledge command using the interrupt acknowledge bit of the internal command register. The INT pin will go low for two clocks and is then updated. In automatic acknowledgment, an interrupt service operation is considered as an automatic acknowledgment. Then the INT pin goes low for two clock cycles and the INT pin is updated. If there is still an active nonmasked interrupt request, the INT pin goes high.

A service operation is performed by the microprocessor and this causes the source of the interrupt to reset the status bit causing the interrupt. An interrupt request is not reset until the interrupt source has been serviced.

A source can be serviced in several ways. One way is to disable the status bit causing the interrupt using the block enable register. Setting a bit in the enable register to zero will mask off the corresponding bit in the status register. Another method is to mask off the particular block interrupt request using the general enable register. A method which can be applied to all sources is to issue the status-clear command from the internal command register.

### Clock Generation

There are two modes of clock operation. An externally generated clock can be used or a crystal can be used to internally generate the system clock. The 82510 has an on-chip oscillator to generate its system clock. The crystal is attached to the X1 and X2 pins.

### Transmission

The main blocks used for transmission are the transmit FIFO and the transmit machine. The Tx FIFO acts as a buffer between the microprocessor and the Tx machine. When a data character is written to the transmit data register, it is loaded into the Tx FIFO. The Tx FIFO will hold up to four 11-bit characters, 9 bits of data, parity bit, and address flag.

There are separate read and write mechanisms. The read and write pointers are incremented after each operation to allow the data transfer to occur in a first-in first-out manner. The Tx FIFO generate a maskable interrupt when the level in the FIFO is below a programmable threshold. If the threshold is equal to two, and the number of characters in the Tx FIFO drops from three to two, the FIFO generates an interrupt.

The Tx machine reads characters from the Tx FIFO, serializes the bits, and transmits them over the TXD pin. It can also generate parity, transmit breaks, and control the modem handshaking signals, CTS* and RTS*.

The Tx machine is controlled with the transmit command register or CTS. If the transmitter is disabled during a character transmission, the transmission continues until the end of the character.

There are two modes for transmission clocking, 1X and 16X. In 1X clocking the transmitted data is synchronous to the clock on the SCLK pin. In 16X clocking the data is not required to be synchronous to the clock.

## Handshaking

The transmitter has three modes for handshaking. In manual mode, the CTS and RTS pins are not used by the Tx machine. The transmission is started regardless of the state of CTS. They can control the handshake, using CTS and RTS along with the Modem Control and Modem Status registers. In semiautomatic mode, the RTS pin is set when the transmitter is enabled and CTS controls the transmission. The automatic mode is similar to the semiautomatic mode, except that RTS is set when the transmitter is enabled and there are more characters to transmit.

## Receive Operations

Reception involves the Rx machine and the Rx FIFO. The Rx machine assembles the incoming character and loads them to the Rx FIFO. The top of the FIFO is read by the receive data register and the receive flags register. The receive operation can take place in two modes. In the normal mode the characters are received in standard asynchronous format and only the control characters are recognized. In the ulan mode, the 9-bit protocol of MCS-51 is used. The ulan address characters are recognized instead of the control characters.

The Rx FIFO operates like the Tx FIFO. It generates a maskable interrupt when the FIFO level is above a threshold. The Rx FIFO can also be used as a 1-byte buffer. This is used for 8250-compatible software drivers.

An overrun occurs when the FIFO is full and the Rx machine has a new character for the FIFO. The oldest character is dropped and the new character is loaded from the Rx machine. An overrun error bit is set in the RECEIVE STATUS and LINE STATUS registers.

In automatic mode, the Rx machine opens the FIFO when there is an address match. It locks the FIFO if there is an address mismatch. In semiautomatic mode, the Rx machine opens the FIFO when an address character is received. It will not lock the FIFO if the address does not match. In manual mode, the Rx machine does not control the FIFO automatically. The FIFO is controlled with the Receive Command register.

The Rx machine has two modes of clocking the incoming data, 16X or 1X. In the 16X mode, synchronization is done internally. In the 1X mode, the data has to be synchronous to the SCLK input. The Rx machine synchronizes the data, passes it through a digital filter to filter out spikes, and then uses a voting counter to generate the data bits.

Bit polarity is determined from majority voting. If the majority of the samples are one, this results in a "1" bit. If the samples do not agree, then the bit is reported as a noisy bit in the Receive Flags register. The Rx machine will generate a parity and address marker as well as framing error. If the input is low for a character frame, the Rx machine sets a break detected as well as a framing error in the Receive Status and Line Status registers.

## 82350 Serial Communications Controller

The 82350 SCC is a two-channel, multiprotocol data communications peripheral chip (Fig. 5.21). It functions as a serial-to-parallel, parallel-to-serial converter/controller. This device contains on-chip baud rate

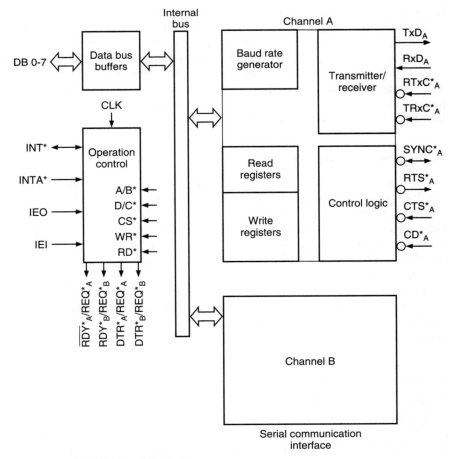

**Figure 5.21** 82350 internal block diagram.

generators and digital phase locked loops, and operates with several data encoding and decoding schemes. The SCC operates with asynchronous formats and synchronous byte-oriented protocols such as IBM Bisync as well as synchronous bit-oriented protocols such as HDLC and IBM SDLC.

There are also diagnostic capabilities like automatic echo and local loopback that can detect and isolate a failure in the network. The 82530 can generate and check CRC codes in synchronous mode and can be programmed to check data integrity.

## Internal Structure

The 82530 has two full-duplex channels, two baud rate generators, control and interrupt logic, and a bus interface for nonmultiplexed buses. Each channel has its own read and write registers for mode control and status information, as well as the logic to interface modems or other devices. Both channels provide formatting, synchronization, and validation techniques for data transferred in and out of the channel interface.

As a data communications device, the chip transmits and receives data using different communications protocols. As a microprocessor peripheral, it interacts with the microprocessor and provides vectored interrupts and handshaking signals.

## Asynchronous Operation

In asynchronous mode, transmission and reception take place independently on each channel with 5 to 8 bits per character, plus parity. The transmitter can supply 1, 1½ or 2 stop bits per character and provide breaks. The receiver break-detection logic interrupts the microprocessor at the start and end of a break. There is a transient spike rejection mechanism that checks the signal after a low is detected on the receive input ($RxD_A$ or ($RxD_B$).

The transmitter and receiver can handle data at a rate of 1, $\frac{1}{16}$, $\frac{1}{32}$, or $\frac{1}{64}$ of the clock rate. In asynchronous mode, a data rate that is equal to the clock rate (1x mode) requires external synchronization. In asynchronous mode, the SYNC pin can be used for functions like ring indication.

## Synchronous Operation

Synchronous-byte-oriented protocols use character synchronization with a 6- or 8-bit synchronous character (monosync), a 12- or 16-bit synchronous pattern (Bisync), or with an external synchronous signal. Leading synchronous characters are removed without interrupting the microprocessor. The 5- or 7-bit synchronous characters are detected with 8- or 16-bit patterns by overlapping the larger pattern across several incoming synchronous characters.

When the SCC supports synchronous bit-oriented protocols, like SDLC and HDLC, it performs automatic flag sending, zero insertion, and CRC generation. CRC checks in the synchronous byte-oriented mode are delayed by one character time so the microprocessor can disable CRC checking on certain characters. This allows the implementation of protocols like IBM bisync. Both CRC-16 and CCITT error checking polynomials are supported. When there is no data or CRC to send in synchronous modes, the transmitter inserts 6-, 8-, or 16-bit synchronous characters.

At the end of a message, the SCC automatically transmits the CRC and trailing flag if the transmitter underruns. The transmitter can also send an idle line consisting of continuous flag characters or marks. The receiver automatically acquires synchronization on the leading flag of a frame in SDLC or HDLC mode and provides a synchronization signal on the SYNC pin.

When a transmit underrun occurs in the middle of a message, an external status interrupt warns the microprocessor so an abort can be issued. The SCC can also send an abort by itself.

The receiver automatically deletes all zeros inserted by the transmitter during character assembly. CRC is also calculated and is automatically checked to validate frame transmission. At the end of transmission, the status of the received frame is available in the status registers. NRZ, NRZI, or FM coding can be used in any 1x mode.

## Data Encoding

The SCC can encode and decode the serial data in four different ways. In NRZ encoding, a "1" is represented by a high level and a "0" is represented by a low level. In NRZI encoding, a "1" is represented by no change in level and a "0" is represented by a change in level. In $FM_1$ encoding (biphase mark) a transition occurs at the beginning of each bit cell. A "1" is represented by an additional transition at the center of the bit cell and a "0" is represented by no additional transition at the center of the bit cell. In FM (biphase space), a transition occurs at the start of each bit cell. A "0" is represented by an additional transition at the center of the bit cell, and a "1" is represented by no additional transition at the center of the bit cell.

The SCC can also be used to decode Manchester (biphase level) data using the phase locked loop in the FM mode and setting up the receiver for NRZ data. Manchester coding always produces a transition at the center of the bit cell. When the transition goes from "0" to "1" the bit is a "0". When the transition goes from "1" to "0" the bit is a "1".

## Baud Rate Generation

Each channel in the SCC chip has its own programmable baud rate generator. Each generator uses two 8-bit time-constant registers to form a 16-bit time constant. There is also a 16-bit down counter with a flip-flop on the output to produce a square wave.

During power-up, the flip-flop on the output is set to high and the value in the time-constant register is loaded into the counter. The counter starts counting down and upon reaching zero, the value in the time-constant register is loaded into the counter and the process continues. The time constant may change at any time but the new value does not take effect until the next load of the counter.

## Phase Locked Loop

The SCC uses a digital phase locked loop to recover clock information from a data stream with NRZI or FM encoding. This circuit is driven by a clock that is 32 (NRZI) or 16 (FM) times the data rate. This clock is used with the data stream to construct a clock for the reception and transmission of data.

In NRZI, the loop counts the 32X clock to create nominal bit times. As the 32X clock is counted, the loop searches the incoming data stream for either 1/0 or 0/1 changes. Then the loop makes a count adjustment during the next counting cycle. This provides a count closer to the center of the bit cell.

In FM encoding, the loop also counts from 1 to 31, but uses a cycle of 2-bit times. The loop locks between counts 15 and 16 and counts 31 and 0.

## Register Set

The register set for each channel includes 10 control (write) registers, two synchronous character (write) registers, and four status (read) registers. Each baud rate generator has two (read/write) registers for the time constant used to set the baud rate. There is also a write register for the interrupt vector in either channel, a write-only Master Interrupt Control register, and three read registers. One holds the vector with status information for Channel B. Another contains the vector without status for A and another holds the interrupt bits pending for A.

Each channel has fifteen write registers that are programmed from the system bus to configure each channel. Each channel also has eight read registers that the system uses to read status, baud rate, or interrupt information.

Writing to or reading from any register except RR0, WR0, and the Data Registers involves two operations. First, a write into WR0, then a write or read of the register.

There are nine read registers counting the receive buffer. Four of these are read to obtain status information—RR0, RR1, RR10, and RR15. Two of the registers (RR12 and RR13) can be read to determine the baud rate generator time constant. RR3 holds the interrupt pending bits (Channel A).

There are 16 write registers including WR8, the transmit buffer, in each channel. These registers are programmed to configure the functions of the channels. Two registers, WR2 and WR9, are shared by the channels. WR2 holds the interrupt vector for both channels and WR9 contains the interrupt control bits.

## Data Flow

The transmit and receive data path is the same for both channels. The receiver has three 8-bit buffer registers arranged like a FIFO and there is an 8-bit receive shift register. This allows additional time for the microprocessor to service an interrupt.

The incoming data is sent through as data or CRC depending on the mode selected. The character length in asynchronous operation also determines the data path.

The transmitter has an 8-bit transmit data buffer register loaded from the internal data bus and a 20-bit transmit shift register that is loaded either from the sync-character registers or from the transmit data register.

Depending on the mode, outgoing data is sent through one of four main paths prior to transmission from the Transmit Data output (TxD).

Channel A/Channel B selection is made by the A/B input; High = A, Low = B. The program first issues a set of commands to initialize the basic mode of operation. This is followed by other commands to set conditions for the selected mode. The asynchronous mode, character length, clock rate, number of stop bits, and even or odd parity would be set first; then the interrupt mode, followed by the receiver or transmitter enable.

## Interrupts

The chip can use polling, interrupts, and block transfers to move data, status, and control information to and from the microprocessor. Block transfers can take place under microprocessor or DMA control. Figure 5.22 shows a daisy-chained configuration.

In polling, all interrupts are disabled and three of the status registers are automatically updated when any function takes place. The microprocessor periodically checks the status registers until the register contents show the need for data to be transferred. Depending on its contents, the microprocessor either writes data, reads data, or does

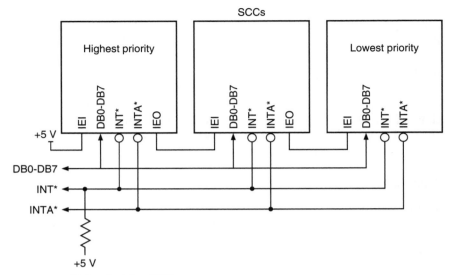

**Figure 5.22**  Daisy chaining SCCs.

nothing. There can also be a poll of the interrupt-pending register to determine the source of an interrupt.

There are three types of interrupts: transmit, receive, and external/status. Each type is enabled under program control with Channel A having a higher priority than Channel B. The receiver, transmit, and external/status interrupts are prioritized in this order.

When the transmit interrupt is enabled, the microprocessor is interrupted when the transmit buffer becomes empty. When the receiver is enabled, it can interrupt the CPU in several ways. An interrupt can occur on the first or all receiver characters, or on a special receiver condition.

Combinations of these are typically used in the block transfer mode. A special receive condition includes receiver overrun, framing error in asynchronous mode, end-of-frame in SDLC mode, or a parity error.

A block transfer uses the READY/REQUEST output along with the READY/REQUEST bit in register WR1. To a DMA controller, a negative true REQUEST output indicates that the SCC is ready to transfer data to or from memory. To the microprocessor, the READY line is used to indicate that the SCC is not ready to transfer data and it asks the microprocessor to extend the I/O cycle. The DTR*/REQUEST* line allows full-duplex operation under DMA control.

### DMA Control

The SCC can be used under DMA control for high-speed reception or transmission. The SCC would interrupt the microprocessor when the first character of a message is received. The microprocessor then allows the DMA to transfer the message to memory. The SCC chip then sends an end-of-frame interrupt and the microprocessor can check the status of the received message. This allows the microprocessor to be free for other operations while the message is being received.

The microprocessor can also enable the DMA first and have the SCC interrupt only at the end of the frame. This allows all data to be transferred with DMA.

## Loop Mode

There is an SDLC Loop Mode in addition to normal SDLC. In a loop system a primary controller station manages the message traffic flow for any number of secondary stations. In the loop mode, the SCC operates as a secondary station while another SCC runs in the normal SDLC mode and acts as the controller. A secondary station in the SDLC Loop listens to the messages being sent around the loop and passes these messages to the rest of the loop by retransmitting them with a 1-bit time delay. The secondary station can place a message on the loop only at specific time slots.

The controller allows secondary stations to transmit messages by sending a special character, called an EOP (End of Pool), around the loop. The EOP character uses the bit pattern 11111110. Because of the zero insertion during messages, this bit pattern is unique.

When a secondary station has a message to transmit and sees an EOP on the line, it changes the last "1" of the EOP to a "0" before transmission. This changes the EOP into a flag sequence. Then the secondary station places its message on the loop and terminates the message with an EOP.

Secondary stations on down the loop with messages to transmit can append their messages to the message of the first secondary station using the same process. Secondary stations without messages to send echo the incoming messages and cannot place messages on the loop except when they recognize an EOP.

## Echo and Loopback

The chip can provide an automatic echo of bits it receives. This is used mainly in asynchronous modes, but it can be used in synchronous and SDLC modes. In the automatic echo mode TxD is RxD. Local loopback is also provided where TxD is RxD and the internal transmit data is tied to the internal receive data. RxD is not used, except for being echoed out as TxD. CTS and CD are not used as transmit and receive enables, but transitions on these lines can still cause interrupts. Local loopback is used in asynchronous, synchronous, and SDLC modes with NRZ, NRZI or FM coding of the data stream.

# 6

# Parallel Interfaces

## Parallel Interfacing Techniques

Microcomputer interfaces are designed to link microprocessor buses with peripheral devices. They can take the form of a board plugged into the microprocessor bus or they can be built into the main circuit board. Built into the interface board or the main circuit board is a connector to link the interface to the peripheral. The interface depends on the signals that are passed through this cable and the circuits on the interface board or main board that generate these signals.

A simple parallel interface can be built with a single TTL integrated circuit. Other parallel interfacing techniques, such as IEEE-488 or SCSI, require complex circuitry.

Parallel interfaces have two major distinguishing features. There is the data path or width, which is the number of bits transferred in parallel by the interface. In addition to the data path, there is the type of handshake used to coordinate the movement of these bits between the computer and the peripheral.

The data width can range from a single bit to 128 bits or wider. The most common size for microcomputers is an 8-bit data path. This allows the microprocessor to transfer an 8-bit data word over the interface during each transfer. The 8-bit parallel interface is also used by 16- and 32-bit microprocessors. This is because of the large number of 8-bit peripherals available. These devices, such as printers, were originally designed for 8-bit computers. Another reason is that ASCII, the most common character code, requires at least a 7-bit interface. Larger data words are also transferred where higher speeds are required.

## Handshaking

The type of handshake used to move information over the data line can be classified by the number of wires dedicated to the handshaking operation. This results in zero-wire handshakes, one-wire handshakes, two-wire handshakes and three-wire handshakes. Within these classifications there are variations on how the wires are actually used for the handshake. This includes how they are pulsed or interlocked.

The zero-wire handshake is the most simple of these interfaces. It uses an 8-bit latch to store the state of the processor's data bus. On the rising edge of a write signal, the latch takes the states of the data bus lines and stores them in the latch. The states are reproduced on the output lines of the latch after a read signal occurs. A 16-bit interface can be built by adding a second 8-bit latch.

This type of zero-wire handshake, parallel-output interface, can be used to drive simple outputs for lights or relays. Devices such as these do not have handshaking requirements. Each of the output lines from the interface can be used to drive a light or relay.

The single wire handshake requires adding another wire to indicate when data is valid on the data lines. This signal has the effect of stretching the write pulse from the microprocessor. This allows slower devices to respond to the write pulse and provide some settling time.

A two-wire handshake adds another line so the receiving device can indicate when it is ready for data. This provides a true handshake using this acknowledge line, and full interlocking is possible. The two-wire handshake is adequate for interfacing a single peripheral, but some interfaces use a third wire to create a protocol that allows several peripherals to use the interface. An example of this is the IEEE-488 bus.

## Zero-Wire Handshake

In this relatively simple interface, an 8-bit latch stores the signals from the microprocessor's data bus. An address circuit is also used to interface to the microprocessor. This can take the form of a NAND gate, as shown in Fig. 6.1. The gate has two inputs. The address valid input goes true when the address of the circuit appears on the microprocessor address bus. The generation of this address may require a comparison of the states of address and control lines in the microprocessor. This is usually done with exclusive-OR gates.

The write input may be generated by the microprocessor or it may be decoded from the microprocessor address and control-line states. When both the write and address valid signals are high, the output of the NAND gate is low. When the write input goes low, the output of the NAND gate goes high, which is the idle state.

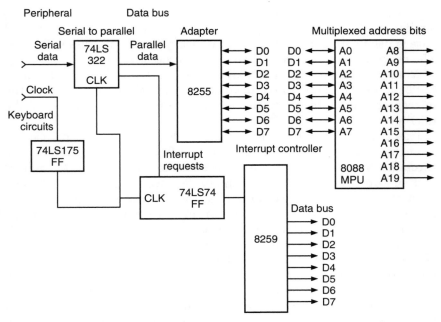

**Figure 6.1**  Typical keyboard processing.

When the write input switches to low and the NAND gate output goes high, the latch stores the states of the microprocessor data bus lines. These states are then available on the output lines of the latch. The latch works like memory since it remembers the state of the microprocessor data bus at a certain point in time. This time occurs when the microprocessor is sending data to the parallel interface. This value stays on the output lines of the latch until another value is sent to the parallel interface or the power is turned off. Wider interfaces can be built by adding additional latches.

The zero-wire-handshake parallel-output interface is used to drive simple peripherals such as lights or relays. Each of the output lines from the interface is used to drive a relay, incandescent lamp, or light-emitting diode (LEDs). If the light or relay is connected between the latch outputs and a +5 volt power supply, then the lamp or relay will be on when that bit in the latch is a zero. Most TTL circuits use this approach since the TTL outputs are a better sink for current than a source for current.

A resistor is usually connected in series with the LED. This is done to limit the current to safe values. An LED has a voltage drop of about 2 volts, so the rest of the voltage appears across the current-limiting resistor. Typically the resistors in 5-volt circuits range from 220 to 330 ohms.

A zero-wire-handshake parallel-input interface can also be used. It is similar to the zero-wire handshake output interface, since a NAND gate is used with one of the inputs connected to the address valid line. The other input is connected to a microprocessor read line.

When both inputs to the NAND gate are true, then the latch or buffer is enabled and the data at the buffer inputs is placed on the microprocessor data bus. This occurs during the read cycle of the microprocessor.

This type of zero-wire-handshake parallel interface can be used to read the status of a bank of switches. Each of the buffer inputs goes through a switch and a resistor. These resistors act as current limiters and pull-up resistors. They pull the buffer inputs up closer to +5 volts when the switch is open. The buffer has some resistance to ground so the resistor is used to swamp this resistance. These resistors also limit the current when the switch is closed since the +5 volts would be grounded.

A read to the desired address by the microprocessor allows the states of the input lines on the buffer to be placed on the microprocessor data bus so that the processor may read them. The input lines are controlled by the states of the switches.

The IBM PC and clones use an encoded keyboard which is connected to the system unit with a 5-pin input-output plug. Two of the pins provide the power (+5 volts and ground). The other three are left to provide the interface between the keyboard and the system board. This is done with serial transmission through the keyboard cable.

In the keyboard, a key depression causes the encoded circuits to generate the ASCII code for the key. The keyboard feeds its ASCII output to the system unit. Most keyboards use a keyboard processor, like an 8048 microprocessor. The 8048 has an 8-bit microprocessor and 2 Kbytes of ROM. The ROM is preloaded with a character code known as a scan code.

The microprocessor uses a row-scanning technique to monitor the keyboard matrix. Each key makes a connection at one of the row-column intersections when depressed. The 8048 processor scans the rows for keystrikes by sending a high-level logic signal to each of the columns, one at a time. The scan of the matrix is repeated every 5 milliseconds. The 8048 receives a high-level logic signal from each row if a key in that row has not been pressed. These signals are stored in the scanning buffer resister in the 8048.

When a key is pressed, then the intersection connection is made and a low is received. The 8048 matches the column which is being scanned with the row that changed state. This sets the intersection point. The 8048 then looks up the character for this key in its character ROM. The coded bit pattern for the character is then sent out through the keyboard cable to the system board.

Inside the keyboard is a circuit board with the row-column matrix along with the electronic components needed (see Fig. 6.2).

The 8048 processor has internal clock circuits with their own clock crystal, which generates the timing for the processor. This signal is also sent to the system board. The clock output syncs the keyboard timing with the system board.

The matrix is divided into rows and columns. The rows are held in the high state by +5 volts through a pull-up resistor. The columns use inverter amplifiers to couple the outputs to the 8048 buffer register. The rows are constantly scanned by the 8048 internal circuits. If a key is not pressed, the column outputs are all high. The set of bits leaves the 8048 and is input to the main board in a serial form.

The data output line and the clock output line are sent to a NOT gate before going to the main board. The gate inverts the output and also amplifies it so it can drive the system board circuits.

A BUSY line goes from the system board to the keyboard. It also uses an inverter. The BUSY signal tells the 8048 when it can send data since the system board may be busy and not able to accept data at that time.

## Debouncing

The mechanical contact that occurs when you strike a key can generate oscillations. When a key is pressed and makes the metallic connection, there is a short period of oscillation until the connection is completed. This usually lasts for a few milliseconds. During this time the keyswitch voltage is not stable and it oscillates between the two switching voltages. The same type of oscillations occur when the key is released.

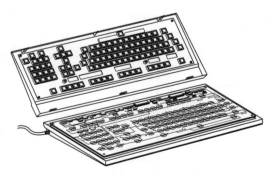

**Figure 6.2**   Keyboard circuit board with row-column matrix and electronic components.

In nonencoded keyboards a resistor and capacitor can be used as a filter to reduce these oscillations. In the encoded keyboards used in the IBM PCs and clones, a delay of a few milliseconds is used before the keystrike is encoded. The delay is usually made with a programmed loop that inserts the delay. This inhibiting of the key action during the switch bouncing is called *debouncing*. The 8048 microprocessor performs this debouncing by generating an interrupt during the time the keyboard voltage is bouncing.

### Keyboard to System Board Interface

The encoded keyboard signals are sent to the system board as shown in Fig. 6.3. The keyboard output is a serial data signal that is sent to the system board circuits. A busy signal is used to control when the keyboard can send characters to the system board. The keyboard bits are sent in a serial format with the least significant bit sent first and the most significant bit of the data byte sent last. The serial data in older PCs may be sent to a serial-to-parallel 74LS322 register which changes the serial format to parallel. The 74LS322 is also connected to a dual-D flip-flop, the 74LS74. The latched clock signal from the keyboard is

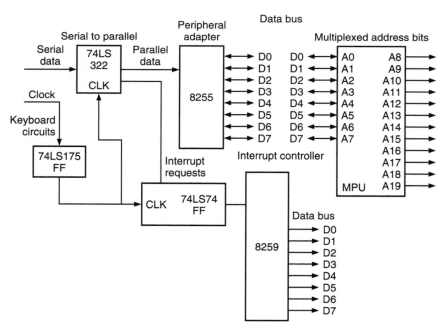

**Figure 6.3**  System board–keyboard processing.

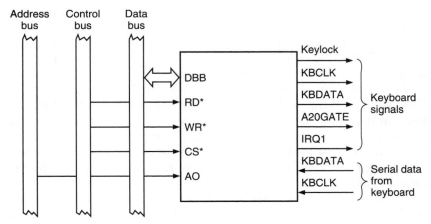

**Figure 6.4**   82C42 keyboard controller.

sent from the 74LS175 to the serial/parallel register and the 74LS74 to sync these chips with the keyboard.

The 74LS74 flip-flop is used to generate an interrupt request to the 8259 programmable interrupt controller. This chip generates an output signal which interrupts the microprocessor.

The 74LS322 shift register sends its parallel bits to one of the ports of the 8255 I/O chip. The parallel bits are then sent to the system data bus.

These bits that hold the keyboard characters are then read by the microprocessor and stored in the video RAM section of memory. They can then be used by the video display system and sent to the monitor or to the printer for hardcopy output.

In newer PCs, a chip like the Intel 82C42 may be used. This is available as a preprogrammed keyboard controller. The interface is shown in Fig. 6.4.

## Keyboard Scanners

A switch interface built from these types of output and input interfaces can be used as a keyboard scanner. A grid of wires is used to connect to the keyboard switches. Each key switch is connected between the row and column wires that meet at each grid intersection. The rows and columns are not connected except at the switch connections. A resistor is used on each row wire to +5 volts for current limiting and pull-up purposes as discussed above.

First, the microprocessor initializes the circuit by forcing all the column wires in the output interface high. If a switch in the matrix is closed, it will drive the attached row wire high also. The microprocessor then causes one column of the output interface to go low.

If any of the switches attached to this column are closed, the row or rows attached to the closed switch or switches are also driven low. The microprocessor now reads the input interface to find the closed switches. It does this by looking for zeroes in the interface.

The switches in the keyboard matrix are uniquely identified by a row and column address. Each switch can force only one row low only when the corresponding column is driven low. The microprocessor scans the columns by going through the interface in sequence. It uses numbers which have a single zero bit. This walking zero corresponds to the column to be driven.

In between each output, the microprocessor reads the input interface. It looks at the individual bits to determine which switch or switches are closed.

Parallel input interfaces can be used to read signals which change slowly. The zero-wire parallel input interface is not very useful for looking at signals which frequently change state. This is because there is no time information supplied by the interface, so there is no way of knowing when a signal changed state, only that it was in one state the last time the interface was read and it may be different or it may be the same.

Parallel interfaces with no handshake wires are undirectional since there are no signals to indicate the direction for the data path. If the data direction through the interface is controlled, then there must also be some timing information for the data transfer over the interface. Additional lines must be added for the handshake.

## One-Wire Handshake

Most peripheral devices like printers have timing requirements for the various operations. A single-handshake wire can be used to indicate when information is valid on the data lines.

The one-wire handshake is the next step up from the zero-wire handshake. In the zero-wire handshake interface the output latch or input buffer were controlled by a single wire tied to the clock input on the latch or the enable input on the buffer.

A one-wire parallel-output interface can be built from a zero-wire parallel-output interface. A new signal for the peripheral-write-pulse handshake signal can be generated with flip-flops. This circuit is shown in Fig. 6.5.

When the microprocessor write signal ends, this is used to toggle the first D flip-flop. The D input to this flip-flop is always high, so the flip-flop is set when a positive going signal appears at its clock input. This flip-flop indicates that an output operation has been started.

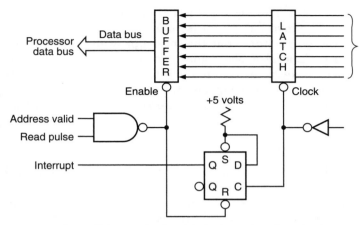

**Figure 6.5** A parallel, one-wire-handshake input-interface circuit.

The next clock signal will set the second flip-flop. This provides a delay between the time the microprocessor places data in the latch and the time a signal is sent to the peripheral device. This delay allows the data lines to the peripheral some time to settle after being switched. This time is a function of the length of the cable between the micropro-cessor and the peripheral device and the current capability of the latch. The delay is usually between one and two clock cycles.

On the next clock, the next flip-flop is set. This flip-flop generates the peripheral write output which lasts for one clock cycle. The next clock clears this flip-flop. The delay flip-flop was cleared at the start of the write output. The circuit reverts back to a stable state and nothing happens until the processor writes another byte to the latch.

The major characteristic of the one-wire parallel-output interface is this stretching out of the write signal from the microprocessor. This is done to provide some cable-settling time and to allow the device being interfaced to respond to the write output.

A one-wire-handshake parallel-input interface can also be from a zero-wire-handshake input interface. The peripheral needs to send the microprocessor some information at a particular time, so it places the information on the peripheral data lines and then sends the peripheral strobe. This allows the latch to hold the information on the peripheral data lines and sets the interrupt flip-flop.

The interrupt takes the microprocessor into an interrupt service rou-tine, which forces the processor to read the input interface. The read operation places the contents of the latch on the data bus and resets the interrupt flip-flop.

The peripheral output is directly connected to the clock input of the interrupt flip-flop. The inverted output is not used. This would produce an interrupt at the proper time, but the interrupt would occur at the beginning of the peripheral-strobe signal instead of at the end. This allows the microprocessor to respond to the interrupt before the peripheral strobe output goes off. If this happens, the interrupt could remain on since the flip-flop is not reset and a second interrupt service could occur.

## Two-Wire Handshake

The single-handshake interface does not indicate if the peripheral device is ready for a data transfer. The single handshake presents the message and it assumes the peripheral is ready to accept the data. Multiple-wire handshakes are usually implemented with integrated circuit designed for the interface instead of using latches, buffers, flip-flops, and gates. These ICs are discussed later in this chapter.

One type of two-wire handshake interface for parallel output ports uses a pulsed handshake. The interface places the data to be output on the data lines and then a strobe pulse is sent. This is the same as a one-wire handshake. The additional line is used by the peripheral as an acknowledge signal. It indicates that the peripheral has accepted the information. It is also used to signal that the peripheral is ready for another data transfer. Both of these are signaled by the falling edge of the acknowledge pulse.

A disadvantage of pulsed handshakes is that the state of the interface cannot be determined at all times. In Fig. 6.6 the initial and final state of both the strobe and acknowledge lines is low, but this same state occurs in the middle of the transfer cycle.

An interlocked handshake with unique state conditions is needed. If the strobe and acknowledge are overlapped as shown in Fig. 6.7, then the two-handshake lines are interlocked. The strobe and acknowledge timings start with data being placed on the data bus and then the strobe is turned on, starting the transfer. The strobe is held on while acknowledge is switched on. Then strobe is turned off, followed by acknowledge, to end the cycle.

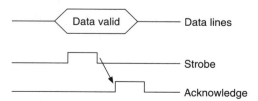

**Figure 6.6**  Pulsed two-wire handshake.

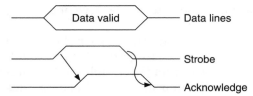

**Figure 6.7**    Interlocked two-wire handshake.

This interlocked handshake allows the state of the transfer to be determined at any time. Either strobe or acknowledge must be on or no transfer is taking place. If strobe is on and acknowledge is not, the transfer is just starting. If both strobe and acknowledge are on, the transfer is almost complete. Note that each signal is on until acknowledged by the other signal.

There are four signal transitions in the interlocked handshake: turn-on of strobe, turn-on of acknowledge, turn-off of strobe, and turn-off of acknowledge. Each of these adds some delay to the handshake. For high-speed data transfers, the number of transitions in the handshake can be halved by Non-Return-to-Zero (NRZ) coding.

In an interlocked, NRZ handshake, two data transfers can take place for the four on and off transitions of strobe and acknowledge. When both strobe and acknowledge are at the same logic level, the transfer cycle ends. A transfer starts when data is placed on the data bus and the strobe changes state. Then, when the peripheral responds and changes the state of acknowledge, both strobe and acknowledge are at the same state, completing the transfer.

The idle states occur when

$$\text{strobe} = 0 \qquad \text{acknowledge} = 0$$

and when

$$\text{strobe} = 1 \qquad \text{acknowledge} = 1$$

The transfer in progress states occur when

$$\text{strobe} = 1 \qquad \text{acknowledge} = 0$$

and when

$$\text{strobe} = 0 \qquad \text{acknowledge} = 1$$

An exclusive-OR gate connected to the two lines can be used to detect the status of the transfer. When the inputs to the gate are the same, the output of gate will be zero, indicating the idle state. When the inputs are not the same, the output of the gate will be zero, indicating a transfer in progress.

The two-wire-handshake parallel-input interface is similar to the two-wire-output interface. In a pulsed two-wire parallel input handshake, the interface asks for information from the peripheral by sending the strobe. The peripheral places the information on the data lines and sends acknowledge. The interface will use a data latch to hold the data during the acknowledge pulse.

In an interlocked, two-wire-input handshake, the interface asks for information from the peripheral by sending the strobe. The strobe remains on and overlaps the acknowledge which is turned on when the peripheral places the information on the data lines. These lines remain valid until strobe is turned off. This allows the microprocessor enough time to read the data lines, so no latch is needed. When the data is accepted by the processor, the strobe is turned off. The microprocessor then turns off acknowledge and completes the transfer.

In an NRZ, interlocked, input handshake, the idle state occurs when both strobe and acknowledge are at the same states. When strobe is initiated, the transfer starts. The peripheral places the requested information on the data bus. Then the peripheral sends acknowledge to finish the cycle. The next cycle starts when strobe is turned off.

In the two handshake interface, the microprocessor starts the transfer with the strobe and the peripheral ends it with the acknowledge. Adding a data-direction line to the interface allows bidirectional data flow. This requires bidirectional hardware on the data lines.

### Centronics Parallel Printer Interface

The Centronics printer interface is an 8-bit parallel connection that uses a three-wire handshake. This interface does not support device addresses, so only one device can be connected to the output port. The following signals are used in this interface.

| Signal | Function |
| --- | --- |
| STROBE | Starts the reading of data, initiated by the computer |
| ACK | Indicates that the printer has received data and it is ready to accept the next data |
| BUSY | Indicates that the printer cannot receive data |
| PE | Indicates that the printer is out of paper |
| SELECT | Indicates that the printer is online |
| DEMAND | Inverse of the BUSY signal |
| INPUT PRINT | A pulse from the computer that initializes the printer |
| FAULT | Indicates that the printer is in the error mode |

Table 6.1 lists the pins for the Centronics Parallel Interface. The timing chart shown in Fig. 6.8 illustrates the timing relationships of the handshake signals. This serves as the communications protocol for printers operating with this type of interface.

## Basic Operation

During a typical operation, when the printer is ready, the BUSY signal is low. Then the computer places the data on the data bus and sends a pulse to the STROBE line. The BUSY signal goes high and the computer reads in the latched data, places the data in the print queue, and outputs an ACK pulse.

The BUSY signal goes low after the ACK pulse. The DEMAND signal is the inverse of the BUSY signal. The printer will activate the FAULT line if the printer senses a print head or print wheel restore error and is in a check condition.

## Normal Handshake

In a normal handshake, the computer indicates to the printer that the data lines have valid information on them. The data needs to be valid

**TABLE 6.1    Pinout for the Centronics Parallel Interface**

| Signal | Signal pin number | Associated ground wire pin number |
|---|---|---|
| Data strobe* | 1 | 19 |
| Data 1 | 2 | 20 |
| Data 2 | 3 | 21 |
| Data 3 | 4 | 22 |
| Data 4 | 5 | 23 |
| Data 5 | 6 | 24 |
| Data 6 | 7 | 25 |
| Data 7 | 8 | 26 |
| Data 8 | 9 | 27 |
| Acknowledge* | 10 | 28 |
| Busy | 11 | 29 |
| Paper out | 12 | None |
| Select printer | 13 | None |
| Signal ground | 14 | None |
| OSCXT (OSCILLATOR output) | 15 | None |
| Signal ground | 16 | None |
| Chassis ground | 17 | None |
| +5 volt supply | 18 | None |
| Input prime* (printer reset) | 31 | 30 |
| Fault* | 32 | None |
| Line count   Negative | 34 | 35 |

* Indicates a negative true signal.

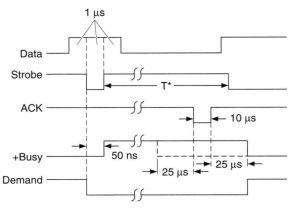

* Depends on program loop time.

**Figure 6.8**  Centronics timing.

at least one microsecond before the STROBE goes negative-true and the data must stay valid for at least one microsecond after the STROBE goes negative. The STROBE may be true from 1 to 500 microseconds.

The falling edge of STROBE causes the printer to send an ACK signal. The delay between the STROBE going true and the ACK signal ranges from 2 to 10 microseconds.

These times apply for a normal data transfer handshake. The handshaking sequence is also called Normal-Data-Input Timing. Figure 6.9 illustrates this timing. A normal transfer occurs when the printer is loading an internal line buffer and is not printing or performing some other operation. If any of these operations is being performed, a BUSY condition exists and the timing is different.

## Busy Condition Handshake

The printer is in a BUSY condition when it has a command to print the line in the print buffer (carriage return), or when a vertical tab, form feed, line feed, delete, bell, select, or deselect character is sent to it. When the printer receives one of these special characters for some mechanical operation, it takes much more time than a few microseconds and the handshake timing changes to the BUSY condition to reflect this.

The handshake mechanism for a BUSY condition is different in the following way. After the STROBE goes true, BUSY is used instead of ACKNOWLEDGE. The BUSY signal indicates that the printer is involved in an operation and cannot complete the handshake until it is done. The printer may be busy for a duration of 2 to 300 milliseconds.

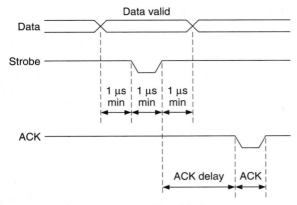

**Figure 6.9** Centronics normal handshake.

When BUSY turns off, the printer uses the ACKNOWLEDGE line for a few microseconds. The busy condition handshake ends when it turns off. The ending is the same as the normal handshake. Figure 6.10 illustrates the busy condition handshake.

Some printers do not use the BUSY line at all since the endings are the same for both normal and busy handshake. This makes the handshake two wire instead of three. Other printers use a switch to implement the BUSY line. The switch allows either a two- or three-wire handshake to be used.

Some printers which use the Centronics interface do not use the original Centronics delay times. For example, they might require the data to be valid for 0.5 microsecond before STROBE is turned on and 0.5 microsecond after STROBE is turned off. The STROBE is only on for

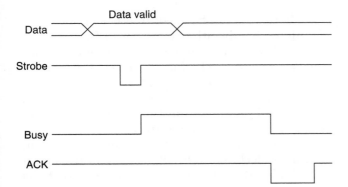

**Figure 6.10** Busy condition handshake.

0.5 microsecond. These times are all half of the original Centronics specification.

BUSY may also switch on with the falling edge of STROBE instead of the rising edge, and turn off after ACK goes off. The original Centronics specification requires that ACK not be used until BUSY is over.

### Input/Output Control Techniques

The addition of an input-output device to the microcomputer system usually requires an interface. The device may also require a device-controller and the proper use of a device connected to the microcomputer system will normally require some form of scheduling strategy to be utilized. The required interface can range from a few simple latches or registers to several larger chips in some systems. To simplify the interfacing, general-purpose interface chips are often used. Some of these will be described in this chapter.

The actual interfacing techniques used for most common input-output devices depend on the application. The more complex controllers are usually required for memory or I/O devices having complex time-dependent operations. Some controllers incorporate an internal microprocessor which receives instructions from the main processor and executes them. These controllers implement the control sequence required by the memory or I/O device. In some cases, it might advance the read-write head for a disk drive using a stepping motor. These controllers are available in LSI form for the more common I/O applications.

A common input device in microcomputer systems is the keyboard. This type of data input/output is, in general, low-speed and bit-oriented. Besides keyboards which must be scanned and read, other examples include relays which are turned off and on and transducers which must be sensed. This places a heavy emphasis on bit I/O which is dominated by simple BCD arithmetic and logical operations based on binary inputs and/or data comparisons. Thus, a simple I/O format for single-bit or four-bit characters can be used. In other applications, microcomputers need a higher bandwidth byte or word I/O.

The techniques in use for dealing with simple microcomputer I/O use bus or port I/O and bit I/O schemes. The bus or port I/O techniques divide the I/O pins into 8-bit groups, which are called a port.

A few bits in the instruction address of these ports can provide a coarse addressability. Fine addressing within the bits may be accomplished by a logical operation with a mask and the port.

Many variations of the bus or port architecture can exist. For example, memory locations can be declared to be I/O ports and the bits in these ports are then manipulated with moves and logical instructions.

One advantage is that no additional specific I/O instructions are required. The same instructions which address memory perform the I/O functions. This I/O architecture is called "memory-mapped I/O." It generally requires more bits in the instruction than the bit technique, but the CPU control is simpler.

A memory-mapped I/O system uses memory-type instructions to access the I/O devices. Thus, the processor can use the same instructions for memory transfers as it does for input-output transfers. The I/O ports are treated as memory locations.

These earlier computers normally had many more memory instructions than I/O instructions. In the memory-mapped I/O system, operations are performed directly on an input or output port or register without having to transfer the data in and out of intermediate registers.

When higher-bandwidth, byte-wide I/O is used, the microcomputer may transfer data to or from the data memory and a port using a program loop to move the data through the accumulator or other registers.

A bit I/O architecture has specific features and instructions for addressing bits or individual output pins. Each of the output pins is addressed, with an implied address, using an instruction like Set Bit and Reset Bit. This technique is used for output devices like fixed displays using light-emitting diodes (LEDs) or liquid-crystal displays (LCDs). These seven-segment displays allow the display of digits and some provide letters. These display devices are used in low-cost applications. Other bit-oriented output devices that the microprocessor system might be connected to include mechanisms such as relays or stepper-motors.

A disadvantage of an I/O-mapped system is that for each I/O port used there is one fewer location available for memory. However, instructions that operate on the memory tend to require several bytes to address the location but I/O instructions may need only 1 byte to specify a port. So, in applications that are I/O-dependent, memory-mapped I/O instructions can also take longer to execute than I/O instructions because of the extra bytes. This can be minimized by using shorter addressing modes. Figure 6.11 shows the typical interface in a memory-mapped system.

In an I/O-mapped input-output system, the processor uses control signals to indicate when the cycle is for input or output and not for memory. An advantage in I/O-mapped input-output is that the separate I/O instructions are easily distinguished from memory-reference instructions during programming. The shorter addresses require less hardware for decoding and the instructions are usually faster. The control pins are dedicated for the I/O read and I/O write. This technique is used in many microprocessors.

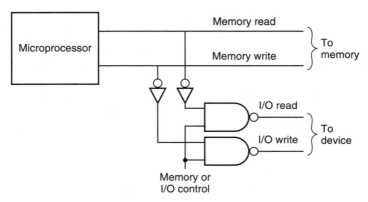

**Figure 6.11**   Memory-mapped system.

## The Basic Interface

The basic parallel interface uses latches and bus drivers. The latches hold the signals sent from the microprocessor until the external device requires them. There must also be a selection mechanism and read/write control for the I/O registers or ports. Figure 6.12 shows the basic requirements of an I/O port. An input latch must hold the external information until the system can read it and an output latch must hold the data sent by the system until required. Bus buffers or drivers are needed to receive and drive the data bus. A status register is also required to indicate when data is to be read or if data from the processor can be sent to the device.

These ports can be built up using separate devices, but many components for input/output are available to perform functions like the following for handshaking and other control functions: (1) address decoding, (2) data input/output buffering, (3) multiplexing, (4) serial parallel conversion, and (5) status.

## Chip Selection

The selection of the input/output interface chips for addressing purposes is done using the same techniques for memory which have already been described. The selection of registers within the chips is accomplished using the address bus, in the same way as addressing a memory location. Chips with up to eight internal registers will use three pins for internal register selection. The signals on these pins are internally decoded to select one of the registers. These pins will typically be connected to the address bus. The internal registers are read

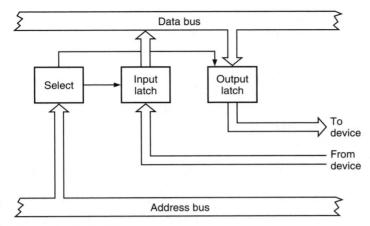

**Figure 6.12**   Basic I/O port.

or written into and may consist of input or output latches, direction registers, and status registers.

## Types of Parallel Interfaces

The nonprogrammable parallel interface is used for the simplest applications. It performs the basic bus-interface functions and although it can include some interrupt-request control logic, it operates as a simple parallel I/O port.

A hardware-programmable interface includes decoding logic, addressable parallel I/O ports, and interrupt-control logic. External wiring or switches are used to determine the address, data direction, and width of each port, and to control the operations of the interface.

The type of general-purpose parallel interface that is most popular is software-programmable. Here the computer software will determine how the interface is structured. The interface is controlled from the contents of a control register which is loaded and updated by the software program. This type of interface can also include another control register called the data-direction register. It allows the input or output function of individual I/O lines to be selected by the program.

These programmable input/output interface chips are not based on an industry standard. Since no standards have been established for these devices, the component manufacturers use various names for them. PIO is sometimes used to designate this general class of programmable I/O devices. The various differences are found in the manufacturers' literature.

These PIO programmable interface devices provide the basic input and output functions for a parallel data interface. In order to connect an input or output device to a microprocessor data bus, the minimum connection requires latches for the inputs and outputs. An input latch must hold the data long enough for the microprocessor to read the data and it also isolates the signals from the bus.

The output latches must hold the output data long enough for the output device to make use of it. The data on a typical microprocessor bus may be valid for a time period that is too fast for many input/output devices to react and make use of it.

The status of these latches or registers must also be available to allow handshaking communication between the microprocessor and I/O. Before reading the contents of an input buffer or register, the microprocessor needs to know if the contents are valid. Thus, status bits can be supplied, or an interrupt is sent as a signal to the microprocessor. For example, this can signal that an output register is full or empty so the microprocessor can determine if it should output the next word. This status signal can also be used by an output device to determine if it can use the contents of the register.

This basic type of general-purpose parallel I/O interface thus requires at least one input register, one output register, status bits, and some interrupt control. There are least 16 or 24 I/O lines in these general-purpose interface chips to provide a number of channels. These channels, which are also called ports, usually provide an 8-bit signal-byte connection which is configured as some combination of inputs or outputs. One or more command registers may be used to specify the configuration of the ports and the operation of the control logic.

The use of a data-direction register allows you to define these ports as each bit is configured as an input or output in the combination desired. Each bit of the data-direction register specifies if a corresponding bit of the PIO port will be an input or an output. The use of a 0 in the data-direction register may specify an input, while a 1 specifies an output.

The typical PIO multiplexes its connections to the microprocessor data bus into two or more of the 8-bit ports. The maximum is three, because of the control and address lines for the I/O devices, using a 40-pin package for the PIO. A typical PIO configuration is shown in Fig. 6.13. The device has two ports and each has its own buffer and function or direction register. A status or mode register is used to indicate the status of each 8-bit port.

The main difference between the PIO chips and a built-up hardware interface is that the PIO is programmable and is available on a single chip. Since the control logic is programmable for each port, the soft-

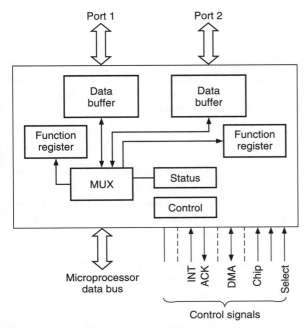

**Figure 6.13** Typical PIO configuration.

ware can specify which line will be used for handshaking as well as the function and direction in which it will be used.

The control logic can also specify when a device's signal will trigger interrupts to the microprocessor. The fact that each data line or group of data lines for a port is programmable allows the PIO to be a general-purpose interface device which can be used in many interface situations. Since it is possible to connect combinations of input and output lines to the same PIO or group of PIOs, an interface using PIOs will fit many applications.

In this type of interface the data registers accumulate the data for the inputs or outputs on each of the I/O lines. The direction registers which configure the lines as an input or an output normally use "0" for an input and "1" for an output. This is done for safety reasons, since when the system is initialized, the contents of all registers are normally reset to "0". As the system starts up spurious signals can be generated. If any of these signals is present on the I/O lines, these lines are configured as inputs to the microprocessor rather than as outputs to devices which could cause safety problems.

An output to a latching relay driver circuit could present a safety problem in a control system application, but an erroneous input to the microprocessor is more likely to cause the system to assume a nonoperative safe state.

The control register stores the command bits issued by the microprocessor for controlling the port. For each port, the microprocessor will specify if interrupts are to be generated and which control signals will be used by the port. When a data buffer becomes full or empty, a status bit in the control register is set or reset.

## Using the PIO

In order to use a PIO, the microprocessor must execute the following operations: (1) lead the control registers to specify the mode in which the control signals operate and (2) load the direction registers to specify the direction which the lines (which make up the ports) will use.

These operations must be done for every port in the interface. The data which is to be loaded in the various registers is placed on the data bus and then a register select is performed. This is done by providing the correct address on the address bus. At least 1 bit is used to select the chip. The microprocessor selects one of the internal registers with the appropriate pattern on the address bus and then supplies the 8 data bits to be transferred into one of these registers using the data bus. The multiplexer in the chip will gate the 8-bit data to the register.

The microprocessor must also generate the read or write signal on the control bus. To read the status from the chip, the contents of the status register are read. After the chip has been configured with its control and direction registers loaded, no additional changes are normally necessary and the microprocessor will communicate with the data buffers using a single instruction.

The trend in interfaces has been toward more programmed functions. Higher levels of integration result in more functions per chip. This trend has been occurring in most of the newer microprocessor chips.

## Programmable Interfaces

A programmable interface to connect three L.E.D. display digits would use three I/O ports, one for each digit. A scanned multiplex system could also be used which would use two ports but more software. There are a number of chips that can be used for this simple application and, depending which type is used, it will tend to have certain characteristics that may differ from other chips. The chip designed for the 6800 microprocessor family is the 6820 peripheral interface adapter (PIA). Each 6820 is a double port device with two sets of eight output lines.

In an application like this requiring three digits, one-and-a-half PIA chips are needed to service the display. Each chip has two data registers which are called peripheral registers in the PIA. One of these registers is used for each set of input/output lines. There are also two other types of registers used with each peripheral register. This gives a total of six registers in each chip. One of these is the data direction register which controls the directions of the input/output lines. Each data direction register has eight bits, one for each input/output line.

The control register format for the A side is shown in Table 6.2. Bit 7 indicates the state of the CA1 input to the register. It is used as an interrupt bit or flag. Bit 6 monitors the CA2 input to the register. Bits 5, 4, and 3 are used to set the eight right different modes of the device and the function of the CA2 pin. Bit 2 indicates if the direction register or data register is to be selected. Bits 1 and 0 are used as interrupt enable/disable control bits.

Since the PIA has six registers and only two register select (RS) pins, the data and data direction registers in each port share the same address. They differ by the value of bit 2 of the control register. Table 6.3 indicates how the registers are selected using the RS1 and RS0 pins and the state of the internal bit 2 of the control register.

Since the PIA cannot drive a heavily loaded data bus with many connections, it is sometimes required to buffer the data bus to this chip using a tristate buffer.

Most microprocessors have their own family of peripheral control chips. Eight-bit compatible chips are often used. If 6800 peripheral chips are connected to one of the 68000 series of microprocessors used in the Macintosh, then the least significant bit is located at an odd address and the most significant bit is always located at an even address. The data direction and control registers are configured in a similar manner as discussed for the 6820.

The use of timer chips provides a programmable controller that can be used for many real-time control applications. Using these timers, a signal can be generated when the desired period of time has elapsed for scheduling purposes. The independent counters can operate in binary or BCD with several programmable modes of operation. In some microcomputer applications, it may be necessary to measure the elapsed

**TABLE 6.2  6820 Register Selection**

| RS1 | RS0 | CRA Bit 2 | CRB Bit 2 | Register |
|-----|-----|-----------|-----------|----------|
| 0 | 0 | 0 | - | Data direction A |
| 0 | 0 | 1 | - | Data buffer A |
| 0 | 1 | - | - | Control A |
| 1 | 0 | - | 0 | Data direction B |
| 1 | 0 | - | 1 | Data buffer B |
| 1 | 1 | - | - | Control B |

**TABLE 6.3  6820 Control Register Bits**

| 7 | 6 | 5 | 4 | 3 | 2 | 1 | 0 |
|---|---|---|---|---|---|---|---|
| IRQA1 | IRQA2 | CA2 Control mode | | | D.D.R. Select | CA1 control Interrupt mode | |

time for input or output scheduling. Since using looping techniques is time-consuming, the availability of programmable timers frees the microprocessor for other tasks.

Many components are available which are a combination of PIA, a UART for serial interfacing, and other components such as programmable interval timers. One typical chip has a PIO with two 8-bit ports plus an asynchronous serial line, interrupts, and programmable interval timers. It interfaces in a similar manner to the chips that we have discussed.

## 8255 Programmable Peripheral Interface (PIA)

This is a parallel I/O chip with four registers. The interface to the microprocessor is made up of a chip-select pin (CS), two address pins (A0 and A1), three control pins [READ (RD), WRITE (WR), and RESET] and eight bidirectional data pins (D0 through D7). The I/O pins are grouped into four ports: Port A, Port B, Port C Upper, and Port C Lower. Ports A and B are 8 bits wide, while ports C Upper and C Lower have 4 bits each. This provides a total of 24 I/O pins.

Control of the registers depends on the state of the inputs shown as follows:

| AO | A1 | RD* | WR* | CS* | |
|----|----|----|----|----|----|
| 0 | 0 | 0 | 1 | 0 | Read Port A |
| 0 | 1 | 0 | 1 | 0 | Read Port B |
| 1 | 0 | 0 | 1 | 0 | Read Port C |
| 0 | 0 | 1 | 0 | 0 | Write to Port A |
| 0 | 1 | 1 | 0 | 0 | Write to Port B |
| 1 | 0 | 1 | 0 | 0 | Write to Port C |
| 1 | 1 | 1 | 0 | 0 | Write to Control Register |
| X | X | X | X | 1 | Not recognized |
| 1 | 1 | 0 | 1 | 0 | Illegal |
| X | X | 1 | 1 | 0 | Not recognized |

X indicates that the pin may assume either level.

There are three modes of operation:

Mode 0    The basic input and output mode for all 24 I/O pins, also called the bit I/O mode

Mode 1    Provides a strobed input/output (Port C is used for control and status)

Mode 2    The bidirectional data bus mode (five bits on Port C are used for handshaking)

Ports A and B can be set to the various modes as needed, but Port C Upper depends on how Port A is set and Port C Lower depends on how Port B is set. Programming takes place by sending a control word from the microprocessor through the 8255 data bus.

In the mode definition control word, the bits are used as follows. Bit 7 is set to "1" to trip the mode-active flag. Bits 5 and 6 are used to set the Port A mode. Bit 4 is the Port A data-direction bit, it determines if the Port A pins are inputs or outputs. Bit 3 determines the direction of the Port C Upper pins.

Bit 2 is the mode-select bit for Port B. Port B cannot be used in mode 2, which is the bidirectional-bus mode. Bit 1 determines the direction of the Port B pins and Bit 0 determines the direction of the Port C Lower pins.

Along with this control word, a bit set/reset control word is used. This allows the Port C pins to be set or reset for status and control for Ports A and B. Bit 7 is set to "0" for the bit control. It is "1" for mode-select operations. Bits 4, 5 and 6 are not used in the bit control word. Bits 1 through 3 specify which Port C bit is to be used and bit 0 sets the state of the bit.

## Mode 0

This is the simplest mode, where the 8255 operates in a bit I/O configuration. The pins are set as outputs or inputs by the microprocessor. The outputs are latched and single-buffered. The inputs are not latched.

All of the bits in Port A must be set as either inputs or outputs. This is also true for the pins of Port B, C Upper, and C Lower. The data direction must be the same for all signal lines in a given port. The A or B ports cannot be set as a mixture of inputs and outputs. Since, Port C is split it can be set as eight outputs, eight inputs, or four inputs and four outputs. Mode 0 is like a zero-wire handshake since no timing information is passed between the microprocessor and peripheral.

## Mode 1

This is a strobed I/O mode, where the data ports are A and B, and the C ports are used as control and status for the strobed handshake. Port A uses Port C bits 3, 4, and 5 for handshaking, and Port B uses Port C bits 0, 1, and 2. The remaining Port C, bits 6 and 7 are available for bit I/O.

### Input Handshake

Three lines are used for the input handshake. These are the Strobe (STB*), Input Buffer Full (IBF), and Interrupt Request (INTR). For Port A, STB*, IBF, and INTR correspond to Port C bits 4, 5, and 3, and for Port B they correspond to Port C bits 2, 1, and 0.

A device can place a byte of data into the input latch of the data port by setting STB* low. This causes the data on the data lines to be latched and IBF to be set.

STB is low-true while IBF is high-true. STB is switched off by raising it to a high logic level, while INTR is raised to a high logic level to signal the acquisition of a data byte. INTR is switched off at the start of a read cycle by the microprocessor to the port input latch. IBF is turned off at the end of this read cycle.

The above handshake can be used to provide a full interlocked handshake with a peripheral. The peripheral must wait for IBF to be in a false state. Then it can place data on the data lines and set STB*. After the 8255 accepts the data and sets IBF, the peripheral will turn off STB* and wait for IBF to go off for the next transfer. The input handshake is depicted as follows:

```
STB* High____                   _____
            t1_____t3
                                               ____t8
IBF   Low_____t2              _____
                        _____t6
INTR Low_____t4        _____
RD* High_____    t5 _____
                        ____t7
```

### Output Handshake

For the output handshake, the microprocessor places a data byte on the output-data pins. This sets the Output Buffer Full (OBF*). The peripheral then sends an Acknowledge (ACK*) to indicate that the data has been accepted.

An Interrupt-Request (INTR) is used to show that the peripheral has accepted the data by setting ACK*. This sequence is started by a WR* (write) control signal which causes INTR to switch off. When the write switches off, OBF* is set. This signals the peripheral that a byte of data is ready. Next the peripheral accepts the data by setting ACK* and the 8255 turns off OBF. When the peripheral turns off ACK, the 8255 sets INTR, which requests another data byte.

## Polling

The INTR line for both input and output operations does not have to be used as an interrupt request. If the two INTR lines are buffered so the microprocessor can read the state of the lines, the 8255 can be operated as a polled device. The microprocessor can then periodically check the status of the INTR lines to determine if one of the data ports is requesting service. The interrupt-enable A (INTE A) is controlled with Port C, bit 6, and interrupt enable B (INTE B) is controlled with Port C, bit 2.

Mode 1 operation is like a two-wire handshake. The peripheral device places data on the data lines where it is strobed into the input latch with the STB* signal. The 8255 indicates that it is ready for another transfer using the IBF line.

In a one-wire handshake, the peripheral would ignore the IBF signal, but the peripheral cannot transfer information faster than the computer can accept it. This suggests an implicit return handshake. Another scheme lets the 8255 handshake with itself; tying OBF* to ACK* forces ACK* on the 8255 as soon as it sets OBF*.

## Mode 2

This is the most complex of the 8255 modes and only Port A may be operated in mode 2. Port A is used as a bidirectional data port and in Port C, 5 bits become the handshake lines.

Port B may be operated in either mode 0 or mode 1 while Port A is operating in mode 2. The remainder of the Port-C bits can be used either for bit I/O or as handshake lines for Port B.

The Interrupt Request (INTR) acts as a handshake line for both input and output operations in mode 2. INTR is used to indicate when the data port needs service. The other output handshake lines are Output Buffer Full (OBF*) and Acknowledge (ACK*).

The input handshake lines are Strobe (STB*), and Input Buffer Full (IBF). INTR uses Port C, bit 3, while OBF* and ACK* use bits 4 and 5 of this port. The handshake in mode 2 is like a mode 1 transfer. The difference is that data flows in both directions on the Port A data pins.

The 8255 does not move the data in the output latch to the Port A data lines until ACK* is set by the peripheral. This provides some control over the data direction. The peripheral sets ACK* and when the 8255 receives the ACK*, it sends the contents of the output latch to the Port A data lines within 300 nanoseconds.

The interrupt-request line can be enabled for both input or output transfers. INTE 1 enables the INTR line for output transfers, and INTE 2 enables the INTR line for input transfers.

When an interrupt occurs, the microprocessor must determine the cause of the request. The input latch could be full or the output latch could be empty, or both conditions may occur. The type of request is determined by reading Port C to determine the status of the IBF* and OBF* lines. A high IBF* indicates there is data in the input register. A high OBF* indicates that the output data latch is empty. Since the mode 2 handshakes are similar to the mode 1 handshakes, the same types of variations for one- and two-wire protocols are possible.

## Digital I/O Boards

There are digital I/O expansion boards for the personal computer that contain 8255 programmable peripheral interface chips. These provide programmable I/O lines on several ports. The I/O lines are usually organized like the 8255 ports. Typically, three ports are used—an 8-bit PA port, an 8-bit PB port, and an 8-bit PC port. The PC port can also be used as two half ports of 4 bits, PC upper and PC lower.

Each of the ports and half ports is configured as an input or an output by software that sets the contents of a write-only control register. The PA, PB, and PC ports can be read as well as written to. Possible configurations include unidirectional and bidirectional strobed I/O where the PC ports are used to control data transfers and interrupts.

The interrupts are under the control of the interrupt controller in the computer which is set by the BIOS system initialization. The user must program the interrupts so they respond to their requirements. The actual interrupt handling on the board is done using a tristate driver with a separate enable. The interrupt enables are activated by switches or jumpers on the board.

The 8255 uses four I/O address locations in the I/O address space of the PC. The base address is often set by a DIP switch on the board and the address can be placed anywhere in I/O address space. Base addresses below FF hex (255 decimal) are not used since this address range is used by the internal I/O of the computer.

Programming is usually done with assembly language or BASIC. The 8255 is configured in the initialization section of the program by writing to the control register. During a power-up or reset, all ports are configured as inputs.

The configuration is set by writing the appropriate control code. The operating modes are based on the 8255. The PA/PC4-7 and PB/PCO-3 groups can be in different modes at the same time. Mode 0 is the basic I/O mode with all ports used as I/O ports. Mode 1 is the strobed I/O where part of the PC port controls the data transfers. Mode 2 is the bidirectional I/O for PA only, where part of PC controls the data transfers.

The following control bytes (hexidecimal) are typical:

PA, PB, and PC are inputs—80

PA, PB, PC-upper outputs, PC-lower input—81

PA and PC outputs, PB input—82

PA output, PB and PC inputs—8B

PA, PB, and PC all inputs—9B

Once the configuration has been set in the initialization, the 8255 will stay in that configuration until a write occurs to the control register. In the 8255 all port registers are cleared by a write to the control register. Repeated changes of configuration require some provision for restoring data to cleared ports.

The outputs and inputs are usually TTL/DTL-compatible. Outputs will usually drive one standard TTL load (74 series) or a 4 LSTTL (74LS) load. CMOS compatibility can be obtained by connecting a 10K ohm pull-up resistor from the input or output to +5 V. Power consumption is typically less than 170 watts at +5 volts.

The parallel digital I/O interface boards that make use of parallel I/O chips like the 8255 have many applications in data acquisition and control. A parallel digital I/O card can provide TTL/DTL-compatible digital I/O lines, interrupt input and enable lines, and external connections to the PC's bus power supplies. It is a useful interface for parallel input/output devices such as encoders, displays, and user-constructed systems and equipment. Absolute position encoders and similar devices can be interfaced to the PC using these expansion boards.

## IEEE-488 Bus

The 488 bus allows connection to devices that can have the following functions:

1. Control other units, acting as a controller

2. Take information from the controlling unit, acting as a listener

3. Provide information to the controlling unit as a talker

The bus consists of eight bidirectional data lines, three byte-transfer control lines, and five general control lines. The eight data lines carry device commands of 7 bits and address and data words of 8 bits. The transfer-control lines are used to implement the handshaking required between the sending devices and the receiving devices.

The five management lines are concerned with the general conditions of the system. These are discussed as follows:

1. The *attention* line, when false, indicates that the data lines contain data from 1 to 8 bits. When the attention line is true, the data bus holds a 7-bit command or 7-bit address.
2. The *interface clear* line places the system in a known state. It is like a system-reset.
3. The *service request,* when set true, flags the controlling unit to indicate a device needs attention.
4. The *remote enable* line sets the mode of each device to operate remotely or locally.
5. The *end-or-identify* is used to flag the controlling unit, to indicate the end of a data transfer.

The handshaking function is used when devices must wait for information to become available.

One line starts the dialogue and says, "Ready for data."

Another line replies, "OK, I have something."

The returning reply is: "Send it to me, I am ready."

This continues with, "OK, here it comes."

In the 488 standard, three lines are used for handshaking:

1. DAV Data valid on data lines
2. NRFD Not-ready-for-data
3. NDAC Not-data-accepted

The timing of the handshake is complex and all listening devices must accept the transfer of data before the next transfer is initiated. In order to initiate a talk, the controller sends the address and command-to-talk to the talker. Upon recognizing its address, and the command, the talker will then send information to a listener, via the data bus, using the handshake signals. When the transfer is finished, the end-line can be used to indicate the end of the block.

A listen works in a similar way. The controller sends the address via the data bus. The next command is for the device to listen to a talker. The transfer of data is done, byte by byte, using the data bus and handshake signals. The endline then indicates that the transfer is complete.

The IEEE-488 bus provided an advancement in intelligent data-acquisition systems, and as more manufacturers produced compatible equipment, the standard became more widespread.

## 9914 GPIBA Adapter Chip

The Texas Instruments 9914 General-Purpose Interface-Bus Adapter (GPIBA) implements the three parts of the IEEE-488 bus: talker, listener, and controller. This chip allows an IEEE-488 interface to be built into a microcomputer system.

There is an eight-bit data bus, three register-select lines, and a chip enable. The read and write control lines are DBIN and WR*, and the DMA handshake pins ACCRQ* and ACCGR*. The 9914 uses a negative-true write strobe (WR*) and a positive-true read (DBIN).

The two DMA handshake pins are used with a DMA controller for a faster data-transfer rate. ACCRQ* (Access Request) is the DMA request signal. It indicates when the 9914 is due to transfer another byte in the current transfer path. ACCGR* (Access Grant) is the acknowledge signal sent from the DMA controller. It indicates when the next DMA transfer is about to take place.

The interface to the IEEE-488 bus is made up of the eight GPIB data lines, the three data-byte-transfer control lines, and the five interface-management lines.

## Registers

There are three register select lines and six read and seven write registers. The register-select lines are used to access the different registers on the chip. The microprocessor reads and writes these registers to control the 9914 chip.

Among the read registers are two interrupt status registers, an address-status register, a bus-status register, a command-pass-through register, and a data-input register. The 9914 does not have an address-switch register. This register is implemented with switches and three-state buffers.

The data-input register is used by the microprocessor to read information from the 488 bus. The bus-status register provides the current state of the data-transfer control and interface management lines. The following bits in this register are used, starting with the most significant:

*Bit*

7    ATN (attention)

6    DAV (data valid)

5    NDAC (not data accepted)

4    NRFD (not ready for data)

3    EOI (end of identify)

2    SRQ (service request)

1    IFC (interface clear)

0    REN (remote enable)

## Address-Status Register

The address-status register indicates the current state of the 9914 to the microprocessor. The following bits are used in this register, starting with the most significant bits:

*Bit*

7    REM (remote state)

6    LLO (local lockout, front panel disabled)

5    ATN (attention, command on the way)

4    LPAS (listener primary addressed state)

3    TPAS (talker primary addressed state)

2    LADS (listener addressed device selected, 9914 addressed to listen)

1    TADS (talker addressed device selected, 9914 addressed to talk)

0    ULPA (upper, lower primary address)

All but the last of these definitions correspond to states in the 488 standard. UPLA provides a dual primary addressing mode. Here, the 9914 ignores the least-significant bit of the addresses on the bus. This means that the 9914 recognizes two addresses which differ only in their least significant bit. The microprocessor uses the ULPA bit in the address status register to determine which of these two addresses is currently active.

The command-pass-through register is used for 488 commands that the 9914 does not recognize. It is also used in systems with secondary addressing.

Secondary addressing allows other devices under a primary address to be individually accessed. The 9914 cannot recognize these devices so the secondary addresses are sent to the microprocessor for additional processing.

## Interrupt Conditions

The other read registers are used for interrupt-status. These two 8-bit registers provide sixteen conditions which allow the 9914 to request interrupts.

Bits 7 and 6 of interrupt status register 0 tell you which of the two interrupt-status registers holds the condition causing the current interrupt. Bit 5 of this register indicates that a byte from 488 bus has been received by the 9914. Bit 4 tells you that the 9914 is ready to accept another byte from the microprocessor for the 488 bus. These bits are used for interrupt-driven data transfers.

Bit 3 indicates that the EOI line is on during data transfers. This bit can be used to show the transfer of the last byte of a data set.

Bit 2 of the interrupt-status register 0 is set when a serial poll occurs. This can be used to get the microprocessor to send a status byte to the bus. Bit 1 is a remote local command (RLC) and it used to switch between remote and local status. Bit 0 sets an interrupt if the bus address of the 9914 is changed.

In interrupt register 1, bit 7 is called the GET bit, for *group-execute-trigger* command. This command is used to start a number of 488 devices after they have been configured. Bit 6 (ERR) indicates that an incomplete handshake has occurred on the 488 bus.

Bit 5 (UCG) is used to signal that an unidentified command has occurred. The command-pass-through register can then be used to allow the microprocessor to read and interpret the command. Bit 4 (APT) indicates that a secondary address exists which the microprocessor must also process. Bit 3 (DCS) indicates a device clear. Bit 2 (MA) is on when the 9914 is addressed to either talk or listen. Bit 1 (SRQ) is used to indicate that a service request on the bus has occurred. Bit 0 (IFC) is used for an interface clear.

All of the interrupt conditions require interrupt-service routines. The 9914 handles the handshaking, major-command recognition, and primary-address recognition.

The bits in the two interrupt-mask registers (write) correspond to the bits in the interrupt-status registers. If a bit in the interrupt-mask register is set to 1, the corresponding condition will generate an interrupt when it occurs. If the GET, ERR, UCG, APT, DCAS, or MA interrupt conditions should occur, the 9914 will stop the bus handshake and let the microprocessor take over.

The data-out register is used by the microprocessor to send information to the 488 bus. It will use this for commands when acting as a controller and for supplying information as a talker.

## Addresses

The address register is used by the microprocessor for the 9914 addresses. The address may come from the off-chip address-switch register, or it may be software-generated.

The five least-significant bits of the address register are used to determine the 9914 bus address. Bit 5 is used to disable the 9914 talk functions. Bit 6 is used to disable the listen functions. These bits are also used to tell the 9914 that a connected device is a talk-only or listen-only device.

The most significant bit of the address register enables the dual primary-addressing function of the 9914 that was discussed earlier.

The parallel and serial-poll registers are loaded by the microprocessor with the values needed for these polls. Then, when the 9914 is polled by another controller, it will supply the proper byte.

## Auxiliary Commands

The auxiliary-command register is a write register used for controlling the 9914. Using this register, the microprocessor is able to send some 24 different commands to the 9914. A command number is sent to the auxiliary-command register using the five least-significant bits.

Some of these commands have a clear/set* select bit which uses the most significant bit. When this bit is negative true 1, when the command is sent, the function that is selected will be activated. If this bit is false, the function is not enabled. The following auxiliary commands are used.

| | |
|---|---|
| dacr | This releases ACDS holdoff. This command allows a 488 bus handshake to be completed for unrecognized commands and secondary addresses. If these are sent to the 9914 by another 488 bus controller, the 9914A will not accept the command or address until the dacr command is stored in the auxiliary-command register. The clear/set* bit must be negative true for unrecognized commands, and for secondary addresses, it should be true if the address is valid and false if the address is not. |
| dai | This will *disable all interrupts*. It will disable the 9914 INT interrupt line when the clear/set* bit is negative true and enables the INT line when this bit is false. |
| feoi | This is a *force end of identify*. It causes the EOI line to switch on with the next outgoing data byte. |
| fget | This is a *force group-execute trigger*. It is used with the 9914 trigger signal. When the clear/set* bit is false, the trigger will be on for five clock cycles if gfet is used. If this bit is negative true, the trigger will stay on until the fget command is used again with the clear/set* bit false. The trigger is normally used to synchronize other circuits or subsystems in the microprocessor system. |
| gts | This is a *go to standby*. It is used when the 9914 is the system controller and sends commands to configure the bus. The ATN line goes negative with this command, which allows the addressed talker to take control of the bus-control lines. |
| hdfa | This is a *holdoff on all data*. It causes each byte handshake to be held off by the 9914A until an rhdf command is written to the auxiliary command register. The command must be written with the clear/set* bit negative true and turned off with this bit off. |
| hdfe | This is a *holdoff on end*. The 9914 complete all bus handshakes unless the EOI signal is on. Then, an rhdf auxiliary command is used to release the holdoff. |
| lon | This is used for *listen only*. If the clear/set* bit is negative true, the 9914 becomes an active listener. If this bit is false, the listener state is turned off. |
| nbaf | This is used to set a *new byte available false*. It allows a byte sent to the 9914 data output register to be discarded. |

pts   The microprocessor sends the 9914 this command. The next byte received can also be passed through to be used by the microprocessor to configure the parallel-poll byte.

rhdf  This is a *release ready for data holdoff*. It is caused by the hdfa or hdfe auxiliary commands.

rlc   This will *release control*. The active controller can pass bus control to some other controller using this command to the 9914 which will disable ATN and release control to the bus.

rpp   This *requests* a *parallel poll*. If it is used and the clear/set* bit is negative true, the 9914 will request a parallel poll on the bus, if it is the active system controller. The poll byte is read in the command-pass-through register. This command is also used with this bit false to withdraw the poll request on the bus.

rqc   This is a *request for control*. If the microprocessor receives the 488 take control (TCT) command as an unrecognized command through the 9914A command-pass-through register, it will send the rqc command to the 9914A. Then, if ATN is disabled by the system controller, the 9914 becomes the active controller.

rtl   This is a *return to local*. It resets the remote/local status bit of the address-status register and generates an interrupt to the microprocessor.

shdw  This is a *shadow* handshake. If the clear/set* bit is on, the 9914 will monitor the bus handshake even if it is not performing data transfers. This allows a 9914 acting as a controller, but not as a listener, to synchronize with the handshaking on the bus. The lon (listen only) command must also be sent to the 9914 along the shdw command.

sic   This is a *send interface clear*. The IFC bus line is on when this command is used with the clear/set* bit negative true. The IFC line should be on for more than 100 microseconds. This command is used with the clear/set* bit off to disable IFC.

sre   This is a *send remote enable*. The REN bus line will be switched on if the clear/set* bit is negative true and turned off if this bit is false.

stdl  This sets the T1 delay. It controls the T1 delay in the talker handshake. The T1 delay is the bus settling time between the switching on of the data lines and the switching on of data valid. During power on, this delay is 10 clock cycles. When the stdl command is sent with the clear/set* bit on, the delay is changed to 6 clock cycles. The delay changes to 10 cycles when this bit is off.

swrst  This is a *software reset* that forces the 9914 to an idle state. The parallel and serial poll registers are not changed but all bus operations are stopped. This command must be used with the clear/set* bit at negative true.

tca   This allows the 9914 to *take control asynchronously* of the bus. The 9914 will take control of the bus by turning on the ATN line. If a data transfer is taking place, the data will probably be corrupted.

tcs    This is used to *take control synchronously* of the bus. It tells the 9914 to take control of the bus at the end of the current byte transfer. If the 9914 is in the active listener mode, a shdw (shadow handshake) auxiliary command is used so the 9914 becomes synchronized with the handshake lines.

ton    This is used for *talk only.* If the clear/set* bit is negative true, the 9914 becomes an active talker. If this bit is false, the talker state is turned off.

vstdl    This is a *very short talk delay.* It reduces the T1 delay to three clock cycles if the clear/set* bit is on. If this bit is off, this command acts like stdl.

## 488 Buffers

Texas Instruments produces the 75160 series of buffers for the 9914, which does not have built-in bus drivers. Buffering is required to drive the IEEE-488 bus. The 75160 is designed to buffer the eight data lines. The 75161 and 75162 chips are designed to buffer the data-transfer-control and interface-management lines.

In a single-controller system, where the 9914 always controls the bus, the 75161 is used. The 75162 is needed for multiple-controller systems where the current active controller has control over the control lines. The pins on one side of these chips are connected to the 9914 while the pins on the other side are connected to the 488 bus. Figure 6.14 shows how these chips are connected.

The 9914 is a complex I/O controller since it implements the state diagrams of the IEEE-488 specification and it does this much faster than can be done with software. The 9914 frees the processor from many tasks and improves performance.

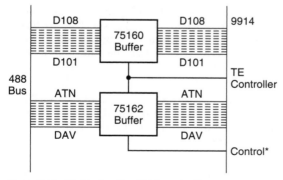

**Figure 6.14**   Buffering the 9914 controller.

## IEEE-488 Interface Expansion Boards

GPIB/IEEE-488 interface boards are also available that plug into a standard expansion slot in a PC or compatible. A standard IEEE-488 connector is used at the rear of the PC to connect to a standard IEEE-488/GPIB cable. The 488 bus can handle up to 14 other Talker/Listener devices. The controller may be the PC or any of the 14 devices on the bus. The board hardware handles all the system timing for talking, listening, and controlling the bus.

The software driver/interpreter for the 488 board is usually provided on floppy disks. The driver takes care of the initialization procedures and the protocol conversions needed to access the functions in the -488 specification. The driver allows the user to interface to the bus using high-level -488 commands such as

```
REMOTE
LOCAL
ENTER
OUTPUT
```

Sometimes the software is designed to be used as a DOS resident driver to simplify the user interface to upper-level languages. This software will include routines which allow the driver to be run from BASIC, FORTRAN, TURBO-PASCAL or other high-level languages.

Control information is passed to the software driver in the form of an ASCII command string. Other parameters must also be passed to the driver. Typical parameter names and data transfer requirements are described as follows:

COMMAND     These are device addresses, secondary commands, and image terminators. They are usually a string, which is decoded by the command line interpreter. Separation of the commands from the operands (devices) may be done with spaces. Other separators include a comma, period, or brackets. The command line interpreter will check the syntax and will send back an error code to isolate the error. An image specifier allows the user to specify the variable field operations at the beginning and end of the data transfer variable. The variable can be a variable name, array identifier, numeric data value, or a string.

VAR     This represents the data variable OUTPUT/INPUT to be transferred to or from some locations. Data is transferred as specified by the image specifier. If an image specifier is not used, the data is treated as an integer. The data may be in the form of a string or integer.

FLAG     This is used for the transfer status of a call statement. If an error occurs, FLAG will hold a hex number representing the error condition. A set of error and transfer message codes will be generated at the completion of each call.

BASADR    This is the address of the interface expansion board being used.

User commands include the following:

ABORT    This command terminates the current selected device and command. If no device is given, the bus is cleared and set to the state given in the last CONFIG command. The PC must be the active controller or an error message will be generated.

CLEAR    This command clears or resets selected or all of the devices. If no device is given, the bus is cleared and set to the state given in the last CONFIG command. The PC must be the active controller or an error message will be generated. *Example:*

```
COMMAND="CLEAR 10, 11, 12"
(CLEARS DEVICES 10, 11, and 12)
```

CONFIG    This command configures the bus to the user demands. The bus will remain in this state until reconfigured. The variable is not changed with this command. *Example:*

```
COMMAND="CONFIG TALK=6, LISTEN=12, 13, MLA"
(DEVICE #6 IS TALKER; DEVICES 12, 13, AND PC ARE
LISTENERS)
```

ENTER    This command inputs the bus data from a selected talker to a string array. A variable array must be previously dimensioned. The FLAG will contain error codes if an error occurs. The PC must have been previously pro-grammed as a listener. *Example:*

```
COMMAND="ENTER 12 [0, 28]"
(ENTER FROM ADDRESS 12, ARRAY ELEMENT 0 TO 28)
```

EOI    This end-of-input command sends a data byte on the selected device with EOI asserted. The bus must have been programmed to talk before the command is executed. The variable contains the data to be transferred. The user must ensure that the data and type match. *Example:*

```
COMMAND="EOI 12"
(ISSUE AN EOI WITH LAST BYTE OF THE STRING TO
LISTENER 12)
```

LOCAL    This sets the selected devices to the local state. If no devices are specified, then all devices on the bus are set to local. The PC must be the active controller or an error message will be issued. *Example:*

```
COMMAND="LOCAL 10, 15"
(SETS DEVICES 10 AND 15 TO LOCAL STATE)
```

LOCKOUT      Performs a local lockout of the specified device. If no devices are specified, all devices on the bus will be set to local lockout. The PC must be the active controller or an error message will be generated. *Example:*

```
COMMAND="LOCKOUT 4, 9"
(LOCKOUT OF DEVICES 4 AND 9)
```

OUTPUT      This command outputs a selected string to a selected listener on the bus. The variable will contain the data to be transferred. The image specifier will contain the data type and terminators. The FLAG will contain the error codes if an error occurs. The PC must have been previously programmed as a talker. Devices may be separated by commas and secondary commands by a period. *Example:*

```
COMMAND="OUTPUT 10, 12 [E]"
(OUTPUTS AN EVEN PARITY STRING TO LISTENER
DEVICES 10 AND 12)
```

PASCTL      (Pass Control) The active control of the bus is passed to the specified device address and the PC becomes the listener/talker. The PC must be the active controller or an error will occur. The command can be reissued to allow the PC to be the controller. If listen or talk are not specified, the PC is set to the listen mode. *Example:*

```
COMMAND="PASCTL 4"
(DEVICE 4 HAS CONTROL OF THE BUS)
```

PPCONF      (Parallel Poll Configure) This command sets up the desired parallel poll bus configuration for the user. The PC must be the active controller or an error will occur. *Example:*

```
COMMAND="PPCONF 12"
(PARALLEL POLL FOR DEVICE 12)
```

PPUNCF      (Parallel Poll UnConfigure) This command resets the parallel poll bus configuration of the selected device. The PC must be the active controller or an error will occur. *Example:*

```
COMMAND="PPUNCF 12"
(REMOVE PARALLEL POLL FROM DEVICE 12)
```

PARPOL      (Parallel Poll) This command will read the status bit messages for the devices on the bus which have been set for a parallel poll configuration. The PC must be the active controller or an error will occur. *Example:*

```
COMMAND="PARPOL"
```

REMOTE      This command sets the selected device on the bus to the remote position. The PC must be the active controller or an error will occur. If an error occurs, the FLAG will contain the error code. *Example:*

```
COMMAND="REMOTE 10, 11, 12"
(SET DEVICES 10, 11, AND 12 TO REMOTE)
```

REQUEST    This command requests service from the active controller on the bus. It is used when the PC is not the active controller. An error will occur if the PC is already the active controller. *Example:*

```
COMMAND="REQUEST"
(PC IS IN CONTROL)
```

STATUS    This command allows a serial polled device status byte to be read into the selected variable. The PC must be the active controller or an error will occur. Only one device is allowed with one secondary address. If no device is specified, an error will occur. *Example:*

```
COMMAND="STATUS 12"
```

SYSCON    This command provides system configuration and initialization of the bus. This command must be used before using the bus. If this is not done, an error is generated.

RXCTL    (Receive Control) of the Bus. *Example:*

```
COMMAND="RXCTL"
```

TIMEOUT    This command sets the time and duration when transferring data to and from the device. *Example:*

```
COMMAND="TIMEOUT"
```

TRIGGER    This command sends a trigger message to the selected device or a group of devices. The PC must be the active controller or an error will occur. *Example:*

```
COMMAND="TRIGGER 11, 14"
(DEVICES 11 AND 14 ARE TRIGGERED AT THE SAME TIME)
```

The mating cable is a CGIB-01 with a total bus length of about 20 meters. This cannot be more than 2 times the number of instruments connected.

The typical data transfer rate is 2 Kbyte/sec with a DMA data transfer rate of 450 Kbyte/sec. There can be only one talker at any one time for the 15 listeners for a board. The hardware handles all of the system timing for talking, listening, and controlling the 488 bus.

The input power is usually +5 V at about 0.5 amp. The typical operating temperature range is 0 to 50°C.

Some 488 boards have a built-in ROM interpreter to handle initialization and protocol functions so disk files with driver routines are not needed. The interpreter allows the use of commands in high-level

IEEE-488 command syntax such as REMOTE or ENTER. The interpreter can be a relocatable block of code which is entered using a BASIC CALL statement or DOS interrupt command using assembly language. Some interpreters also include a group of subroutines which can be used to condition the data before data transfer when using assembly language programs.

An IEEE-488 board will take one slot in the PC as well as address locations in the I/O space. Some of the I/O address locations will be used by internal I/O or other peripheral cards. In order to avoid conflicts with other devices a DIP switch is usually provided to set the I/O addresses on the proper boundary in the PC-decoded I/O space. This will also allow the use of a second 488 interface board in the same computer. The user may transfer data to or from the two groups of devices connected to the boards. The maximum number of devices for the two boards can be up to 30.

The interpreter will require a free block of memory for its on-board ROM and RAM. The addressing DIP switch is used to select the block of memory on the proper boundary. The setting of the switches corresponds to the absolute address location.

A 16-Kbyte interpreter with 12 Kbytes of ROM and 4 Kbytes of RAM is distributed as shown in the following map:

```
Hex Address    IEEE-488 16 KBYTE INTERPRETER MAP

0000
                    (12K ROM INTERPRETER)
0ADB      ASSEMBLY LANGUAGE LINK ROUTINE ADDRESS
0BB8        ASSEMBLY LANGUAGE UTILITY ROUTINES
3000          _____ RAM BUFFER BEGINS _____
            INTERNAL RAM BUFFERS FOR INTERPRETER
                        2 Kbytes
3800                _____
              USER RAM AREA FOR SCRATCH PAD
                      2048 bytes
                NOT USED BY INTERPRETER
3FFF         _____ END OF RAM BUFFERS _____
```

The following IEEE-488 function classifications are allowed:

Basic talker, serial poll, no extended talker

Basic listener, no extended listener function

Source and acceptor handshake capability

Service request capability

Parallel poll remote configuration capability

Remote/local capability

Device clear and device trigger capability

## Disk Drives

Most disk drives are thought of as parallel interfaces, actually the floppy disk drive has a parallel interface for the control signals, but the data is transferred in serial mode. Hard disk drives are a true parallel interface since both the control and data signals use individual connections. We will examine these interfaces in detail.

## Magnetic Disks

In a floppy or hard drive mechanism, the magnetic recording media actually holds the information. The drive is used for accessing the media. The floppy drive media is a disk of plastic, which is usually mylar. It is coated on both sides with a thin layer of magnetic oxide. The 3.5-in coated disks are mounted in a hard plastic jacket to protect the disk. The 5.25-in disks are protected with a soft plastic jacket and stored in a thin cardboard or paper envelope.

A metal enclosure shields the disk when it is in the floppy drive. When the disk is inserted in the floppy drive, a mechanical linkage clamps the disk to the metal spindle. This allows the read/write heads access to the disk. The disk is rotated using the metal spindle during a read or write operation.

A hard drive operates using similar principles. The main difference is the speed of rotation, which is 3600 rpm, or ten or more times than floppy drives. This requires that the disk be made of a rigid material. Aluminum, glass, and ceramic are used for the hard disk, which is enclosed in a sealed container. The heads actually operate on an air cushion, so they do not touch the disk. A synchronized dc motor is used to turn the disk and moving coil motors are used to position the heads in current designs. The moving coil motor provides the faster head actuator positioning which in needed in higher-density drives.

## Floppy Disk Drives

In a floppy disk drive there is circuit board that handles the drive's mechanical operations and interprets inputs from the drive's sensors (Fig. 6.15). Signals to and from the computer's main board take place over a single, 34-pin ribbon cable. The 34-pin configuration is standard for IBM PCs and compatibles. A separate four-conductor cable supplies power to the drive.

**Figure 6.15** Bottom view of floppy disk drive showing circuit board and ribbon cable connector.

The floppy drive needs to control three main mechanisms: the R/W heads, stepping motor, and spindle motor. This is done with a disk controller IC which handles the communications with the motherboard as well as with the drive's sensors. Older drives use several ICs for these operations but newer drives use more integrated devices that combine most or all of the functions into a single IC chip.

The floppy drive uses four sensors: index sensor, disk-in-place sensor, write protect sensor and track 00 sensor. The index sensor is an optical sensor that monitors the diskette's rotation. An index wheel spins along with the disk and causes a pulsed signal to be sent to the controller chip. If the pulses indicate that the disk speed is not correct, the controller changes the spindle motor speed to hold the speed at 300 or 360 rpm.

The disk-in-place sensor provides a signal to indicate that a disk is in the drive. This keeps the drive from operating without a disk. The write protect sensor checks the write-protect notch. When this notch is uncovered, the drive does not allow any write operations to take place; the disk can only be read. The track 00 sensor is used to generate a signal when the R/W heads are in the track 00 position. This is done to initialize the heads to a fixed starting location.

The transfer of information in or out of a drive involves the interaction of the microprocessor and the floppy drive controller. The overall operation of the drive is handled by the floppy drive controller which may plug into or be a part of the system board. The microprocessor does not interact directly with the floppy drive. It directs the controller to start the data transfer in or out of the floppy drive. The instructions or routines needed to operate the floppy drive are fetched by the microprocessor from the BIOS ROM on the system board.

Data being loaded into a floppy drive is taken one byte at a time from system RAM by the floppy disk controller and converted into serial form. They are sent as serial data over the drive cable. Other control signals are needed to handle the drive's motors and sensors. When the data bits arrive at the floppy drive, they are converted into magnetic recording signals so they can be written to the disk.

When data is read from the floppy disk, the process involves finding the desired program or file. The floppy disk controller must seek the track and sector with the recorded data. After the starting location is found, the disk's read-write head produces signals from the recorded data. These low-level signals are amplified and then converted into standard digital logic levels. The digital data is sent in serial format over the cable to the floppy disk controller. The controller converts the serial data into parallel words while deleting the housekeeping information, and sends the data to RAM.

## Drive Interface

The connections between the floppy disk controller and the floppy drive unit is the drive interface. This a standard set of connections used by most floppy drives and controllers. The standard interface allows any floppy drive to operate in the computer as long as it uses the standard interface.

The interface is made up of two cables, power and signal. The signal cable pinout is shown in Table 6.4. The power connector is a 4-pin, mate-n-lock–type connector. The digital signals use +5.0 Vdc (pin 4, pin 3 return) in most desktop systems although +3.3 or +3.0 Vdc are used in some portable computers. The motors normally operate on +12 Vdc (pin 1, pin 2 return). A return or ground lead is provided for each supply in the connector. In the 34-pin signal connector, the odd-numbered pins are ground lines, while even-numbered pins are used for the signals.

Up to four drive-selection inputs, DRIVE SELECT 0* through DRIVE SELECT 3*, are used to determine which drive in the system is active. Smaller computers will not use all of these lines. A MOTOR ON* signal is used to start the drive spindle motor turning. This signal must be negative true before a read or write operation can take place.

The head direction is controlled by a DIRECTION SELECT* signal that tells the head stepping motor to move in toward the center of the

TABLE 6.4     Pinlist for IBM PC Floppy Drive Interface

| Pin | Function | Pin | Function |
|-----|----------|-----|----------|
| 2  | Normal/high density* | 1  | Ground |
| 4  | In use/head load*    | 3  | Ground |
| 6  | Drive select 3       | 5  | Ground |
| 8  | Index                | 7  | Ground |
| 10 | Drive select 0*      | 9  | Ground |
| 12 | Drive select 1*      | 11 | Ground |
| 14 | Drive select 2*      | 13 | Ground |
| 16 | Motor ON*            | 15 | Ground |
| 18 | Direction*           | 17 | Ground |
| 20 | Step                 | 19 | Ground |
| 22 | Write data           | 21 | Ground |
| 24 | Write gate*          | 23 | Ground |
| 26 | Track 00*            | 25 | Ground |
| 28 | Write protect*       | 27 | Ground |
| 30 | Read data            | 29 | Ground |
| 32 | Side select*         | 32 | Ground |
| 34 | Disk change/ready*   | 33 | Ground |

disk or out toward the edge of the disk. A STEP* pulse controls the number of steps that the head stepping motor must take. Both STEP* and DIRECTION* position the R/W heads on the disk.

A WRITE DATA line records information on the disk, and a WRITE GATE* signal is used to enable the drive to accept data on the WRITE DATA line. The IN USE/HEAD LOAD* signal indicates that the read/write head is busy. The WRITE PROTECT* output prevents writing to the disk if the write protection notch is covered. When a read takes place, the data is sent on the READ DATA line. The DISK CHANGE/READY signal tells when the disk is ready for a read or write operation. The SIDE SELECT* input determines which side of the disk is written or read to.

The output signals include a NORMAL/HIGH-DENSITY* signal that tells the floppy drive controller IC what type of media is currently in use.

The INDEX* signal is actually a stream of negative indexing pulses. These are sent to the floppy drive controller to regulate the spindle speed at the proper value. The TRACK 00* signal indicates that the head is at track 00 on the disk.

## Floppy Disk Controllers

The Intel 82077 is a single-chip floppy disk, and tape drive controller for the PC-AT and PS/2 buses. The 82077 needs only a 24-MHz crystal, resistor array, and chip select circuits to implement the floppy-disk controller. The drive control signals are decoded and buffered. There is an analog data separator for motor speed control and a 16-byte FIFO (First-In-First-Out) register. All command parameters and data transfers go through the FIFO.

### Controller Interface

The following signals make up the controller interface. CS* on pin 6 is used to decode the base address range. A0, A1, and A2 on pins 7, 8, and 10 are used to select one of the chip's registers as shown in the following:

| A2 | A1 | A0 | Read/Write | Select Register |
|----|----|----|------------|-----------------|
| 0 | 0 | 0 | Read | Status Register A |
| 0 | 0 | 1 | Read | Status Register B |
| 0 | 1 | 0 | Read/Write | Digital Output Register |
| 0 | 1 | 1 | Read/Write | Tape Drive Register |
| 1 | 0 | 0 | Read | Main Status Register |
| 1 | 0 | 0 | Write | Data Rate Select Register |
| 1 | 0 | 1 | Read/Write | Data (FIFO) |
| 1 | 1 | 0 | Reserved | |
| 1 | 1 | 1 | Read | Digital Input Register |
| 1 | 1 | 1 | Write | Configuration Control Register |

The following pins are used for the data bus:

DB0—11

DB1—13

DB2—14

DB3—15

DB4—17

DB5—19

DB6—20

DB7—22

RD* on pin 4 is the READ control input and WR* on pin 5 is the WRITE control input. RDDATA on pin 41 is the READ DATA input. It provides serial data from the disk. INVERT affects the polarity of this signal. WP on pin 1 is the WRITE PROTECT input. It indicates if the disk drive is write-protected. DSKCHG in pin 31 indicates a DISK CHANGE has occurred. This means that the disk is now ready for a read or write.

DRQ on pin 24 is the DMA REQUEST signal, which is sent out to request service from a DMA controller. DACK* on pin 3 is the DMA ACKNOWLEDGE control input used in DMA cycles.

TC on pin 25 is the TERMINAL COUNT control signal sent from a DMA controller to end the disk transfer, DACK* must be active to use this signal. INT on pin 23 is the INTERRUPT output. It signals a data transfer in the non-DMA mode.

DENSEL on pin 49 is used as the DENSITY SELECT. It indicates if a low (250/300 Kbps) or high (500 Kbps/1 Mbps) data rate is selected. The polarity of the DENSEL pin is controlled with the IDENT pin, after a hardware reset.

In 5.25-in drives a high on DENSEL tells the drive that either the 500 Kbps or 1 Mbps data rate is selected. In some 3.5-in drives the polarity of DENSEL changes to a low for high data rates. These two types of drives have different electrical interface characteristics. The 5.25-in drives typically use open collector drivers and the 3.5-in drives use totem-pole drivers. The output buffers on the chip do not switch between open collector or totem-pole, they are totem-pole.

DRV2 on pin 30 indicates if a second drive is installed and its state is reflected in Status Register A. DRATE0 and DRATE1 on pins 28 and 29 indicate the contents of bits 0 and 1 of the Data Rate Register.

INDX on pin 26 is the INDEX input. It indicates the beginning of the track. TRK0 on pin 2 stands for the TRACK0 control line. It indicates that the head is on track 0.

HIFIL (HIGH FILTER) on pin 38 is the analog reference signal used for internal data separator compensation. LOFIL (LOW FILTER) on pin 37 is the low noise ground return for the reference filter capacitor which is also connected to HIFIL.

PLLO on pin 39 is an input used to optimize the data separator in the chip, for either floppy disks or tape drives. A "1" selects the floppy mode and a "0" selects the tape mode.

X1 and X2 on pins 33 and 34 are the CRYSTAL connections for a 24 MHz crystal. If X1 is driven with an external, then X2 is left unconnected.

MFM on pin 48 is used on hardware RESET, in configuring the chip. After the reset this pin becomes an output and indicates the current data encoding/decoding mode.

The RESET on pin 32 places the chip in a known idle state. All of the registers are cleared except those set by the specify command.

The INVERT* pin is used to select between using the internal buffers in the chip or external inverting buffers. When this pin is high, the internal buffers are disabled. A low enables the buffers. Most PCs use the internal buffers.

The chip runs on +5 volts on pins 18, 40, 60, and 68. The ground pins are 9, 12, 16, 21, 36, 50, 54, 59, and 65. AVCC on pin 46 is used for the analog supply and AVCC on pin 45 is used for the analog ground.

### Data Separator

The function of the data separator is to lock onto the incoming serial read data. When a lock is achieved, the chip's clock is synchronized to the read data. This synchronized clock is called the *Data Window* and is used to sample the serial data.

One state of the Data Window is used to sample the data portion of the bit cell, and the other state samples the clock portion. Serial-to-parallel conversion logic separates the read data into clock and data bytes.

For reliable disk/tape reads the data separator tracks changes in the read data frequency. These frequency errors may be caused by motor rotation speed variations and frequency shifts from bit jitter.

The data separator is made up of two analog phase lock loops (PLLs). These are called the reference PLL and the data PLL. The reference PLL is also called the master PLL since it is used to bias the data PLL. The reference PLL adjusts the data PLL's operating point as a function of the process, junction temperature, and supply voltage. This eliminates the need for external trimming.

## Write Precompensation

The write precompensation circuits are used to minimize bit shifts in the RDDATA stream from the disk drive. This shifting of bits is due to material changes in the magnetic media.

The 82077 monitors the bit stream that is being sent to the drive. The data patterns that require precompensation are adjusted relative to the surrounding bits.

A 13-bit shift register is used with three multiplexers. In the first stage the output from the shift registers is sent into two multiplexers, one for additional shifting. A final stage of multiplexing combines the data paths with two internal control signals into the WRDATA output.

## Read/Write Operations

A read or write operation takes several steps to complete. The motor is turned on, head positioned to the correct cylinder, DMA controller initialized, the read or write command initiated, and error recovery implemented.

Before data can be transferred to or from the diskette, the disk drive motor must be at full speed. In most 3½-in disk drives, this spin-up takes 300 ms, while the 5¼-in drive usually requires about 500 ms due to the increased inertia from the larger disk.

One method for minimizing the motor spin-up delay for a read involves starting the read operation right after the motor is turned on. If the motor is not up to speed, the internal data separator will not lock onto the incoming data stream and it reports the problem in the status registers. The read operation is repeated until a successful status report is obtained. If locking to the data stream takes place when the motor speed variation is significant, errors in reading the disk by some disk controllers can result.

After the motor is turned on, the data rate for the media in the drive is programmed to the chip from the Configuration Control Register (CCR). The disk drive head is positioned over the correct cylinder by executing a SEEK command. After the seek is complete, there is a head-settling time before the read or write operation can begin. For most drives, this delay is more than 15 ms. If the head is already positioned over the correct cylinder, the head-settling time does not exist.

Then, the DMA controller is initialized for the data transfer and the read or write command is executed. The DMA controller will start a Terminal Count when the data transfer is complete. The 82077 will finish the data transfer and send the INT signal indicating it has entered the result phase.

The result phase is also entered by the 82077 if an error is found or if the sector number reaches the End of Track (EOT). If an error is found after reading the result bytes, two more retries are performed by reinitializing the DMA controller.

## Hard Drives

Hard drives usually require a read/write controller, a head actuator/driver, a spindle motor controller, and a disk interface controller. Data enters and leaves the hard drive through the disk interface controller. This controller is designed for the drive's interface. Most early drives used the Seagate ST-506 for drives which were under 40 Mb. The ESDI (Enhanced Small Device Interface) doubled the transfer rate to 10 MB per second which allowed more data on the hard disk. Both of these use a 34-pin cable for the drive control signals, similar to a floppy drive, and a 20-pin cable for the parallel data transfers. The IDE and SCSI interfaces are later standards used in most current hard drives. The disk interface controller also controls the head actuator driver circuit and spindle motor driver.

The read/write controller works with the head preamplifier and drive circuits to convert the analog waveforms from the read heads into standard logic levels. The read/write controller separates the clock and synchronization signals from the actual binary data. When data is written to the disks, the read/write controller generates the write signals that are amplified by the write drive circuits.

Built into the hard drive circuitry is a small microprocessor that coordinates the drive's operations by synchronizing the disk interface controller and the read/write controller. This microprocessor is also used for disk spinup and spindown, as well as other safety control features that the drive might have. Some drives use a custom version of a microprocessor called a *microcontroller.* Other hard drives use a standard microprocessor. For the small drives, such as the 1.3-in units in small portable computers, these circuits are integrated onto one or two complex surface-mount ICs.

A data transfer starts when the main board microprocessor initiates a command to the hard drive controller. In many systems a system controller chip actually drives the hard drive controller. Any parameters that are needed to control the hard drive are taken by the microprocessor from the BIOS ROM.

The hard drive controller interfaces the system buses (control, address, and data) to the drive's interface. Data and commands from the drive are converted into computer bus signals by the hard drive controller. The control circuits on the hard drive are used to operate the drive's mechanical functions and to convert the digital information from the interface into magnetic flux patterns that are recorded on the disk. This process of recording and data transfer is reversed for write operation, where the flux patterns are amplified and interpreted for the microprocessor.

## IDE Drives

IDE, which stands for Intelligent Drive Electronics or Integrated Drive Electronics, is a popular interface in personal computers for connecting hard drives, especially the newer, smaller drives. The circuits needed to operate an IDE drive is on a circuit board which is part of the hard drive assembly. The software routines needed to communicate with the IDE drive are stored in the BIOS ROM on the system board.

The IDE interface connects the hard drive to the system board with a 40-pin connector. The signal cable typically uses a 40-pin insulation displacement connector (IDC). All signals on the IDE interface are TTL-compatible, a logic zero is 0.0 to +0.8 Vdc, and a logic one is +2.0 to $V_{CC}$.

There is also a 4-pin power cable in addition to the 40-pin signal cable. The signal cable pinouts are shown in Table 6.5. The power connector is a 4-pin mate-n-lock–type connector. IDE hard drives normally use +5 Vdc (pin 4) and +12 Vdc (pin 1). In some low-voltage systems, +3.0 or +3.3 Vdc is used instead of +5.0 Vdc. The return lines for each supply are also part of the power connector (+5 V return, pin 3, +12 V return, pin 2).

## Interface Signals

Addressing is done with the Drive Address bus lines (DA0 to DA2) which are used with the chip select inputs (CS1FX* and CS3FX*). A negative true signal on the Drive I/O Read (DIOR*) line, starts a read cycle, while a negative true on the drive I/O write (DIOW*) line begins a write cycle.

TABLE 6.5    Pinlist for IDE Hard Drive Interface

| Pin | Function | Pin | Function |
|-----|----------|-----|----------|
| 2 | Ground | 1 | Reset* |
| 4 | DD8 | 3 | DD7 |
| 6 | DD9 | 5 | DD6 |
| 8 | DD10 | 7 | DD5 |
| 10 | DD11 | 9 | DD4 |
| 12 | DD12 | 11 | DD3 |
| 14 | DD13 | 13 | DD2 |
| 16 | DD14 | 15 | DD1 |
| 18 | DD15 | 17 | DD0 |
| 20 | Connector key | 19 | Ground |
| 22 | Ground | 21 | DMARQ |
| 24 | Ground | 23 | DIOW* |
| 26 | Ground | 25 | DIOR* |
| 28 | Reserved | 27 | IORDY |
| 30 | Ground | 29 | DMACK* |
| 32 | IOCS16* | 31 | INTQ |
| 34 | PDIAG* | 33 | DA1 |
| 36 | DA2 | 35 | DA0 |
| 38 | CS3FX* | 37 | CS1FX* |
| 40 | Ground | 39 | DASP* |

The IDE interface provides sixteen bidirectional data lines (DD0 to DD15) to move data bits in and out of the drive. IORDY (I/O Ready) is used to indicate to the drive that a data transfer is needed. The direction of the data transfer is set with DIOR* and DIOW*. IOCS16 is the 16-bit I/O control signal. It tells the microprocessor that the drive is ready to send or receive data.

The outputs to the system board include a Direct Memory Access Request (DMARQ), which is used to start the transfer of data to or from the drive. When a data transfer is finished, a DMA ACKNOWL-EDGE (DMACK*) is sent to the drive from the hard disk controller. A Drive Interrupt Request (INTQ) is used by the drive when there is an interrupt pending. A Drive Active (DASP*) signal is used when the hard drive is busy.

A Passed Diagnostic (PDIAG) pin indicates the results of a diagnostic command or reset. If PDIAG* is negative true, the microprocessor knows that the drive is okay to use.

A negative true signal on the RESET* line forces the drive to its initial condition during power-on or reboot.

## SCSI Drives

The Small Computer Systems Interface (SCSI, pronounced "scuzzy") was developed as a hard disk drive interface. It differs from other disk interfaces in that it is intelligent. Rather than using a hard drive controller that controls the drive, SCSI drives use a host adapter that allows the computer to send commands to the drive. A SCSI drive has an instruction set of commands, and up to eight SCSI devices can be connected on a single computer.

SCSI is a computer bus which uses its own protocol (sequence of events) to communicate between devices. The system microprocessor is not required for the particular conditions of the drive; the hard drive system has enough intelligence to complete each task.

The original specification for SCSI appeared in 1986. Other enhanced versions, SCSI-2 and SCSI-3, were released after this. It is a complex parallel interface. The Small Computer System Interface, or SCSI, has its roots in a disk-drive interface developed by Shugart Associates. The Shugart interface was called the SASI (pronounced "sassy") bus for Shugart Associates System Interface. It was intended primarily for disk drives.

In both SASI and SCSI systems, a controller board moves data transfers over the SASI or SCSI bus. Like the IDE interface, a SCSI drive needs only to be connected to a system board using a standard cable. The SCSI bus uses a 50-pin connector even though it is an 8-bit interface.

The SCSI standard defines the way peripherals are connected to the computer system and how they communicate with the system. It is often grouped together with other hard disk interfaces, but it is more than a hard disk interface.

SCSI provides a common bus for many types of peripherals, such as CD-ROMs, optical memory devices, modems, and printers. The common bus allows the connection of up to seven other peripherals to one port on the back of the PC.

A SCSI hard disk drive system gives you high performance and automatic error correction. You also get an external port which allows daisy chaining of up to seven peripherals. SCSI drives for the PC cost more to install due to the additional cost of the SCSI interface. In the 30- to 60-MB range, the lowest-cost solution is usually MFM or RLL ST-506 technology in a drive kit or a drive with an integrated controller. The Apple Macintosh is an exception, being completely SCSI due to the built-in SCSI interfaces on Macintosh computers. SCSI offers the easiest plug-in installation when executed properly.

Usually when you connect peripherals to your system you need controller boards for each device. A CD-ROM drive, a modem, and a printer might require three controller boards and three expansion slots for any functions not provided on the system board.

You would also have to be sure that each of these devices is compatible with your system, and compatible with each other. Whenever there are multiple controller boards in the system, there are possible conflicts. SCSI does not use one board for one device. With a SCSI interface, you use one board called a *host adapter* from which you can connect the SCSI bus to the system bus. The peripherals attached to the SCSI must also be SCSI peripherals.

SCSI hard drives provide several advantages. The media defects are mapped out of the usable disk space and, when the disk is installed in a system, the defects are recorded so the disk does not use this area. Most hard disks use this feature, but SCSI disk drives can also handle media defects that occur under operating conditions. When the disk develops a bad sector, the drive will prevent data from being written to that sector and redirect the data to another location of the disk.

SCSI hard drives are a little different from other interfaces like the ESDI hard drive interface (Enhanced Small Device Interface). ESDI is only for hard disk drives. It does not allow the use of different types of peripheral devices connected to a common controller board. ESDI does allow two hard disks to run from the same controller. With a SCSI hard drive, bad sectors on the disk are skipped automatically. In ESDI, the drive manufacturer identifies the bad sector locations and the user runs a software program, which is compatible with the ESDI controller, to manage the bad sectors.

Most of the larger capacity drives are SCSI devices which attach using an SCSI cable supplied with the drive to the PCs SCSI connector. The other SCSI connector on the drive allows you to make a chain of SCSI devices. You can also use other SCSI peripherals, such as scanners and CD ROM drives.

## Daisy Chaining

SCSI devices that are connected in a chain require termination and SCSI ID numbers. Termination requires that a special resistor, called a *terminator*, be at both the beginning and the end of a SCSI chain. In many drives this resistor is built into the electronics. These drives are said to be internally terminated.

In some drives, a separate termination plug is used which you attach to one of the drive's SCSI connectors. Other drives allow you to turn the internal termination on and off with a switch.

If there are two or more SCSI peripherals connected to a PC, an internally terminated drive can be attached only at the beginning or end of the chain. If your PC has an internal hard drive, an internally terminated drive can be attached only at the end of the chain. External and switchable termination are more flexible and a switch is a little more convenient, since there is no terminator plug to lose.

In addition to proper termination, every peripheral on a SCSI chain must have an ID number and no two peripherals can have the same number. You can set the SCSI ID number with a thumb switch or a rotary dial, a DIP switch, jumpers (usually metal prongs that are covered with a plastic sleeve), or through software. Switches are the most convenient, and they are found on most large-capacity drives. You can usually override the SCSI ID setting with the utility software provided with some drives.

## Command Sets

In the past SCSI command sets have been given different interpretations and implementations, causing one manufacturer's device not to be recognized by another's interface card. Both IBM and Compaq started producing SCSI equipment after many of these different implementations were in use. There are differences among the host adapters. The driver software must be able to support both the host adapter and the target device. Different SCSI commands may be required for each target device even if they are the same types of products, like two hard drives manufactured by different vendors.

Some manufacturers do not provide SCSI host adapters with their devices and not all host adapters may work with the device. Other manufacturers provide host adapters with the SCSI devices they sell, which eliminates any compatibility problems.

The problem of different target devices requiring different SCSI commands is the job of the device driver. It should be able to use the proper SCSI commands to operate the target device.

Outside of these potential configuration problems, the user generally experiences only the benefits of SCSI devices such as higher performance and reliability. The complexity of the interface is handled by the device driver, which may need to be installed as part of the set-up procedure or it may reside on the host adapter.

The main difference with SCSI is that the code necessary to control a device is moved out of the host and an interface is established that is not hardware-specific. Before SCSI, most devices required a separate dedicated host controller. It was possible to find a controller that could be used with more than one device of the same type, but communications between a tape and a disk with only one host adapter was difficult or impossible. The device drivers in the host had to be able to coordinate their activity in such a way so that they did not conflict with each other. This was usually possible only when the hardware and software for the devices came from the same vendor.

SCSI makes it possible to have devices connected to the same adapter card that are not only of different types but are also from different vendors. A standard or convention is needed so that the tape and disk software can coordinate their activity to allow them to use the adapter concurrently. Otherwise, we could have a situation where a disk that is connected to the same adapter as the tape cannot be backed up on that tape because the tape and the disk software cannot be active at the same time.

## Host Adapters

Several conventions are provided by makers of the host adapters. Adaptec uses a software product that works with their cards. It is called ASPI (Advanced SCSI Programming Interface). Columbia Data Products developed software for cards made by Western Digital called SDLP (Standard Device Level Protocol). These products were developed to resolve the conflict of more than one program needing to have access to the same card concurrently. When using ASPI or SDLP, the drivers for the disk or tape do not access the hardware directly. They communicate with an ASPI or SDLP driver which coordinates requests and resolves any conflicts.

A more universal standard is provided by the Common Access Method (CAM). This specification allows the same independence and flexibility as ASPI and SDLP, but it does it as an industrywide standard.

A typical adapter supports the Common Command Set (CCS). Dual 128-byte buffers are used to allow concurrent data transfers on the host bus and the SCSI bus. An on-board BIOS supports bootable devices and automatically configures the system upon power-up. This eliminates the need to run a configuration program or add a driver each time an additional SCSI device is attached to the host adapter. Support is provided for up to seven SCSI devices and up to four 5¼- and 3½-in floppy disk drives. It can coreside with hard disk controllers and supports removable fixed disk drives. The board size is 3.8 × 6.0 in and uses 50-pin Centronics connectors. The current at +5 dc is typically 0.58 amps.

There are other adapters that provide a connection between the AT bus and SCSI bus. A typical kit includes AT-to-SCSI host adapter with floppy controller and DOS software support for up to 7 SCSI devices. The data transfer rate is 2 MBytes/sec asynchronous on the SCSI bus and 5 to 10 MBytes/sec on the AT bus.

Other kits are available from manufacturers such as Toshiba, Storage Dimensions, and Micropolis for Novell networks. These kits include the hard disk drive, controller and driver software for installation. Many of these kits are drives packaged with a SCSI hard drive controller. These controllers come with the software drivers to install almost any SCSI drive.

## The SCSI Bus

The SCSI bus allows modular additions of peripherals using a single SCSI interface board. The SCSI standard is ANSI X3T9 for a peripheral bus and command set. It also functions as a high-performance peripheral interface-permitting data to be distributed among peripherals independently of the CPU. This frees the CPU for more user-oriented activities.

The SCSI bus has 50 pins and 18 signals. Nine are used for an 8-bit data bus with parity and nine are used to coordinate device data transfers (see Tables 6.6 and 6.7).

Using a special I/O bus for a peripheral interface is one of the newer features in PCs. Most peripheral interfaces prior to SCSI normally connected only two devices, as in the serial interface RS-232C, which allows only one sender and one receiver to be connected. The SCSI bus is more like a computer bus in terms of signal organization, multiple-master capability, and operational phases.

The typical power connector is often the 4-pin mate-n-lock connector. SCSI hard drives use +5.0 Vdc and +12 Vdc. Some low-voltage systems use +3.0 or +3.3 Vdc instead of +5.0 Vdc. The return (ground) for each supply is also provided on the connector.

The signal cable is usually a 50-pin insulation displacement connector (IDC) cable. All of the odd-numbered lines are ground lines. SCSI signals are carried over the even-numbered lines. Every signal in the SCSI interface is TTL-compatible.

The communications protocol that takes place between a SCSI hard drive and motherboard is different from other hard drive interfaces including an IDE system.

## SCSI Single Drive Protocol

When an SCSI system needs to access the hard drive, it drives the SELECT (SEL*) signal to a negative true state. The drive can also use

**TABLE 6.6    SCSI Bus Signals**

| Signal | Pin | Signal | Pin |
|--------|-----|--------|-----|
| DB0 Data Bus 0 | 2 | Ground | 30 |
| DB1 Data Bus 1 | 4 | ATN Attention | 32 |
| DB2 Data Bus 2 | 6 | Ground | 34 |
| DB3 Data Bus 3 | 8 | BSY Busy | 36 |
| DB4 Data Bus 4 | 10 | ACK Acknowledge | 38 |
| DB5 Data Bus 5 | 12 | RST Reset | 40 |
| DB6 Data Bus 6 | 14 | MSG Message | 42 |
| DB7 Data Bus 7 | 16 | SEL Select | 44 |
| DBP Bus Parity | 18 | CD CMD Data | 46 |
| Ground | 20 | REQ Request | 48 |
| Ground | 22 | I/O I/O | 50 |
| Ground | 24 | | |
| Term Pwr | 26 | Reserved for optional terminator power (plus 5 volts) | |

**TABLE 6.7   SCSI Signal Definitions**

| | | |
|---|---|---|
| ATN | Attention | Indicates initiator has message to send to target |
| BSY | Busy | Acknowledges bus is busy |
| ACK | Acknowledge | Used with Request to provide complete asynchronous handshake for data bus transfers |
| RST | Reset | Clears all activity on bus |
| MSG | Message | Indicates bus is in message-transfer phase |
| SEL | Select | Used during device selection phase |
| CD | Command/Data | Defines type of information on bus—command/status or data |
| REQ | Request | Used with ACK to complete asynchronous handshake for data bus transfers |
| I/O | Input/Output | Indicates data-flow direction on bus |

the SEL∗ line to start a data transfer, but this is generally not done. Next, the ATTENTION (ATN∗) pin goes true and the drive forces the REQUEST (REQ∗) line true.

Then an 8-bit message can be placed on the bidirectional data bus (DB0 to DB7), and the MESSAGE (MSG∗) signal goes true. The DATA BIT PARITY (DBP) signal is used with the data to provide data error checking.

The CONTROL/DATA (C/D∗) is operated by the hard drive. A "false" on this line indicates that the drive has placed a control byte on the data lines, while a "true" shows that data is being placed on the bus. The direction of data transfer is determined by the INPUT/OUTPUT (I/O∗) pin. A false will input data from the hard drive, while a true outputs data to the hard drive. After a data transfer takes place, the system microprocessor switches the ACKNOWLEDGE (ACK∗) line to a true state to show that data has been transmitted or received.

While the SCSI bus is being used, the BUSY (BSY∗) signal is true. During power-up or a reboot, the RESERT (RST) pulse initializes the drive.

## Expansion

The SCSI bus allows users to expand when they reach the maximum capability of their initial system configuration. The SCSI bus is both cost-effective and easily implemented. Only one card slot is used and the SCSI bus standard includes generic commands for specific peripheral devices. The intelligent SCSI controller allows peripheral-to-peripheral transfers without operating system involvement.

In many PC applications, four or five card slots may be occupied, allowing only one for expansion (Fig. 6.16). After using the system as purchased over a period of time, users may determine that their database exceeds the use of the connected hard disks, and if another hard disk subsystem is added, it will require use of the last remaining expansion slot.

The SCSI bus and intelligent peripherals approach allows the user to add another mass-storage subsystem using a SCSI bus controller in that expansion slot. However, this does not limit system expansion but opens up new paths for future growth. Installation of the SCSI bus controller and initial disk drive allows future expansion through 2 ports located at the rear of the drive. One port is used for the SCSI-IN cable and the other for the SCSI-OUT cable. Any peripheral device compatible with the SCSI bus/controller may then be added with daisy-chained cables. Each master device provides connection for up to a total of 8 slave devices.

A typical IBM PC will have at least one floppy and hard disk drive, monitor, printer, and modem. Several of the backplane slots may be occupied with this configuration. When the user outgrows this basic configuration and decides to expand using the SCSI bus and intelligent peripherals approach, the SCSI bus controller is installed in a remaining card slot. The bus controller is used as the controller for additional mass storage.

Although SCSI and the PC backplane (internal bus) are both computer buses, their objectives differ. Backplane buses provide for transfers between different expansion module types with many functions and varying levels of intelligence. The SCSI bus is designed for bulk

**Figure 6.16**   Five card slots are used in this PC.

data transfers between peripherals and hosts. Since all SCSI bus devices are similar, the SCSI specification allows the use of different devices using an independent command set.

When using the SCSI bus, only one connection is needed to the internal PC bus to handle all the system's peripheral devices. The SCSI bus controller takes up a single card slot in the PC for the SCSI bus controller card. The bus can be used to connect a number of components, such as hard disk drives, tape subsystems, printers, additional peripheral devices, and host PCs. The SCSI bus controller provides all the hardware and the software in ROM that is needed to configure these components.

## SCSI Operation with Multiple Devices

Two different definitions for SCSI allow for single-ended (ground-referenced) and differential transmissions. Table 6.8 lists the pin assignments for the single-ended SCSI cable and Table 6.9 lists the differential pin assignments. A single-ended SCSI cable can be as long as 6 meters and a differential SCSI cable can stretch 25 meters.

**TABLE 6.8    Single-ended SCSI Signals**

| Pin number | Signal | Pin number | Signal |
|---|---|---|---|
| 1 | GND | 2 | DB(0)* |
| 3 | GND | 4 | DB(1)* |
| 5 | GND | 6 | DB(2)* |
| 7 | GND | 8 | DB(3)* |
| 9 | GND | 10 | DB(4)* |
| 11 | GND | 12 | DB(5)* |
| 13 | GND | 14 | DB(6)* |
| 15 | GND | 16 | DB(7)* |
| 17 | GND | 18 | DB(PARITY)* |
| 19 | GND | 20 | GND |
| 21 | GND | 22 | GND |
| 23 | GND | 24 | GND |
| 25 | NOT CONNECTED | 26 | TERMINATION POWER |
| 27 | GND | 28 | GND |
| 29 | GND | 30 | GND |
| 31 | GND | 32 | ATN* |
| 33 | GND | 34 | GND |
| 35 | GND | 36 | BSY* |
| 37 | GND | 38 | ACK* |
| 39 | GND | 40 | RST* |
| 41 | GND | 42 | MSG* |
| 43 | GND | 44 | SEL* |
| 45 | GND | 46 | C/D* |
| 47 | GND | 48 | REQ* |
| 49 | GND | 50 | I/O* |

* Signifies a low-true signal.

TABLE 6.9   Differential SCSI Signals

| Pin number | Signal | Pin number | Signal |
|:---:|:---|:---:|:---|
| 1 | Shield GND | 2 | GND |
| 3 | +DB(0) | 4 | −DB(0) |
| 5 | +DB(1) | 6 | −DB(1) |
| 7 | +DB(2) | 8 | −DB(2) |
| 9 | +DB(3) | 10 | −DB(3) |
| 11 | +DB(4) | 12 | −DB(4) |
| 13 | +DB(5) | 14 | −DB(5) |
| 15 | +DB(6) | 16 | −DB(6) |
| 17 | +DB(7) | 18 | −DB(7) |
| 19 | +DB(Parity) | 20 | −DB (Parity) |
| 21 | DIFFSENS | 22 | GND |
| 23 | GND | 24 | GND |
| 25 | Termination Power | 26 | Termination Power |
| 27 | GND | 28 | GND |
| 29 | +ATN | 30 | −ATN |
| 31 | GND | 32 | GND |
| 33 | +BSY | 34 | −BSY |
| 35 | +ACK | 36 | −ACK |
| 37 | +RST | 38 | −RST |
| 39 | +MSG | 40 | −MSG |
| 41 | +SEL | 42 | −SEL |
| 43 | +C/D | 44 | −C/D |
| 45 | +REQ | 46 | −REQ |
| 47 | +I/O | 48 | I/O |
| 49 | GND | 50 | GND |

NOTE: A (−) prefix signifies a low-true signal and a (+) prefix signifies a high-true signal in a differential pair.

SCSI supports as many as eight devices, numbered 0 through 7. Thus, one SCSI bus can connect several computers and peripherals together. In a SCSI system, the device that starts a data transfer is called the *initiator,* and the data is sent to another device called the *target.* The SCSI bus supports multiple initiators, but only one initiator can control the bus at a given time.

### Data Transfers

In order to start a data transfer, an initiator needs to obtain control of the SCSI bus through arbitration. Before arbitration can start, the SCSI bus must be inactive. This is called the *bus-free phase.* This is signaled by turning off the BSY (busy) and SEL (Select) control lines. When the bus has been in the bus-free phase for 800 nanoseconds, an initiator can start arbitration by switching BSY on and using the SCSI data bits DB(0) through DB(7) for its ID code.

More than one initiator can try to take over the SCSI bus during arbitration. If there are several initiators waiting for ownership of the bus, the last data transaction of the previous transfer must end before the bus enters the bus-free phase. After the SCSI bus has been in the bus-free phase for 800 nanoseconds, the initiators that wish the bus turn on BSY and place their ID codes on the bus data lines. After a few microseconds, the initiators check the data lines and determine which of the initiators has won control of the bus. The initiator with the highest priority (highest-numbered ID code) takes control of the bus and indicates that it has control by turning on SEL. This ends the bus arbitration phase and the other initiators stop driving the bus and wait for the next arbitration in another bus-free phase.

The bus controller uses a selection sequence to target a data transfer. This sequence is called the *SCSI selection phase*. While it continues to use BSY, SEL, and its ID bit, the controller turns on the ID bit for the target device. Then the initiator turns off BSY. This alerts other potential targets that a target ID is already on the data bus.

All of the targets check the ID codes until the selected target recognizes its ID and turns on BSY. When the controller senses the assertion of BSY by the target, it releases SEL and the data bus, completing the selection phase.

## Handshaking

The transfer of data over the SCSI bus uses a two-wire handshake on the REQ (request) and ACK (acknowledge) lines. The target must determine the type of transfer the initiator needs by obtaining a command. SCSI commands take several bytes and go from the initiator to the target. They specify the type of data transfer needed by the initiator.

There are eight command groups, 0 through 7. Groups 0, 1, and 5 are the most common commands that every SCSI device should support. Group 0 contains 6-byte commands, group 1 holds 10-byte commands, and group 5 holds 12-byte commands. Groups 2, 3, and 4 are reserved. Groups 6 and 7 are used for vendor or product-specific commands. The individual commands for command groups 0 and 1 are shown in Tables 6.10 and 6.11.

The target asks for the first command byte by switching the I/O* (input/output) control line high. This signals the initiator to output a byte. Then the target sets the C/D* (command/data) control line low asking for a command byte and turns on REQ, so that it is sure to get the first command byte.

The initiator will place the requested byte on the data lines and turn on ACK, so that the target can accept the byte. The target reads the byte and turns off REQ. The transfer is complete when the initiator turns off ACK. This sequence is repeated until all the bytes of the command are transferred.

**TABLE 6.10    SCSI Group 0 Commands**

---

TEST UNIT READY
REZERO UNIT
REQUEST SENSE
FORMAT UNIT
READ BLOCK LIMITS
REASSIGN BLOCKS
READ
WRITE OR PRINT
SEEK
READ REVERSE
WRITE FILE MARK (FLUSH BUFFER)
SPACE
INQUIRY
VERIFY
RECOVER BUFFERED DATA
MODE SELECT
RESERVE UNIT
RELEASE UNIT
COPY
ERASE
MODE SENSE
START/STOP (LOAD/UNLOAD)
RECEIVE DIAGNOSTIC
SEND DIAGNOSTIC
PREVENT/ALLOW MEDIA REMOVAL

---

Each command in a command group has a set number of bytes and all the command bytes must be transferred to the target so the command can be carried out.

Data transfers are similar to command transfers. The target receives a command from the initiator and uses the I/O* line to set up the data direction and C/D* to tell command and status bytes from data bytes. Then REQ is sent to start the handshake and the initiator sends back ACK to complete the handshake.

## Status Transfers

The transfer of commands and data over the bus use a group of transfer cycles called an *information-transfer phase*. The other types of transfers that can occur during this phase are status and message transfers. In a status transfer, the target transfers a number of status bytes. The target will force C/D* low, like a command transfer, but the bytes will actually be status bytes. The I/O* line will be switched low, since the data will go from the target to the initiator. Many SCSI commands ask the target to send status information back to the initiator.

TABLE 6.11    Group 1 Commands

READ CAPACITY
EXTENDED ADDRESS READ
EXTENDED ADDRESS WRITE
WRITE AND VERIFY
VERIFY
SEARCH DATA HIGH
SEARCH DATA EQUAL
SEARCH DATA LOW
SET LIMITS
COMPARE
COPY AND VERIFY

## Message Transfers

Messages are used as part of the interrupt scheme. An initiator may indicate to the target that an abnormal condition has occurred. The initiator starts to send the target a message by turning on the ATN (attention) control line. This can be done during the command, data-transfer, status-transfer, and selection phases, but not during the bus-free and arbitration phases. The initiator must use ATN during a REQ/ACK transfer cycle. It can then turn on ACK.

After the target gets the ATN request it sets up a message-out bus state with the following line settings:

```
MSG*  Low
C/D*  Low
I/O*  High
```

The target will then use REQ to ask for the first message byte. The initiator supplies the byte and turns on ACK. The initiator will continue to use ATN until the message is complete.

## Reselection

A reselection phase is used to allow a target to disconnect itself from the initiator. This will free up the SCSI bus and allow other bus traffic. The target will stay busy executing its command.

The target disconnects itself by releasing BSY and starting a bus-free phase on the bus. It must wait for another bus-free phase to reconnect. When a bus-free phase is available on the bus, the target arbitrates for the bus like an initiator. When the target has ownership of the bus, it selects an initiator the same way that the initiator uses to select a target.

The RST (reset) line can be used by any target or initiator. RST causes all devices to stop using the other bus signals. The state of these devices depends on how the reset is implemented. Devices that uses a hard reset clear any uncompleted commands and go to a power-up default state. Devices that use a soft reset try to complete any commands that are executed and stay at the present state. A soft reset allows an initiator to clear the bus without affecting the execution of commands sent by other initiators on the bus.

The SCSI protocols tend to be complex and the early SASI and SCSI interfaces used many ICs and required a lot of support from the processor. This, of course, affects the system performance, so several one-chip SCSI controllers were developed, including the NCR 5380.

## 5380 SCSI I/O Chip

This is a type of parallel I/O chip used for the SCSI interface. It is a 40-pin device (Table 6.12) with the handshaking circuits and bus drivers needed for SCSI bus transfers (Table 6.13). It also includes the interrupt and DMA (direct memory access) circuits needed to interface the chip to a microprocessor system. The 5380 can be either an initiator or target in the SCSI environment.

In the NCR 5380 the SCSI signals take up pins 1 through 20 while the microprocessor-bus signals use pins 21 through 40. The pins that connect the chip to a microprocessor are like other interfaces we have seen. Three pins are used for addressing A0, A1, and A2. These are

**TABLE 6.12   Pinout of the 5380 SCSI Adapter Chip**

| | | | |
|---|---|---|---|
| D0 | 1 | 40 | D1 |
| DB7* | 2 | 39 | D2 |
| DB6* | 3 | 38 | D3 |
| DB5* | 4 | 37 | D4 |
| DB4* | 5 | 36 | D5 |
| DB3* | 6 | 35 | D6 |
| DB2* | 7 | 34 | D7 |
| DB1* | 8 | 33 | A2 |
| DB0* | 9 | 32 | A1 |
| DBP* | 10 | 31 | $V_{DD}$ |
| GND | 11 | 30 | A0 |
| SEL* | 12 | 29 | IOW* |
| BSY | 13 | 28 | RESET* |
| ACK* | 14 | 27 | EOP* |
| ATN* | 15 | 26 | DACK* |
| RST* | 16 | 25 | READY |
| I/O* | 17 | 24 | IOR* |
| C/D* | 18 | 23 | IRQ |
| MSG* | 19 | 22 | DRQ |
| REQ* | 20 | 21 | C/S* |

**TABLE 6.13    Functional Signals of the 5380 SCSI Adapter Chip**

|  |  | SCSI Data bus |
|---|---|---|
| DMA | EOP* Input | Bidirectional |
|  | READY Output | DB0–7, DBP* |
| Control | DRQ Output | BSY* SCSI |
|  | DACK* Input | SEL* |
|  |  | RST* Controls |
| Register | CS* | ATN* |
|  | IOR* | ACK* |
|  |  | Bidirectional |
| Addressing | IOW* | REQ* |
|  | A0 | MSG* |
| Inputs |  |  |
|  | A1 | C/D* |
|  | A2 | I/O* |
| Data Bus | D0–D7 Bidirectional |  |
|  | RESET* Input |  |
|  | IRQ Output |  |

used with the I/O read (IOR*) and I/O write (IOW*) pins to allow the microprocessor to address the 16 registers used in the chip.

Switching the chip select (CS) signal low makes the chip ready for microprocessor bus communications. The RESET signal resets the chip by placing into a known, stable state. The data lines (D0 through D7) make up the data port.

The other microprocessor bus signal lines are used for interrupt and DMA operations. IRQ is the interrupt request line and it is used to signal an error or the completion of a command. DRQ is the DMA request line, it indicates that an internal data register should be read or written to for a SCSI data transfer. DACK is used by the DMA controller to signal that it has responded to a DMA request. DACK allows access to the data registers without using the address lines.

Other DMA signals include the EOP input which allows a DMA controller to tell the 5380 that the current transfer cycle on the microprocessor bus is the last data transfer of a block. READY allows the 5380 to control when the DMA controller moves data in and out. READY indicates when the 5380 is prepared to take another transfer, based on the activity on the SCSI bus. The READY signal is used with DRQ for block-mode DMA transfers. The DMA controller can be set to take control of the microprocessor bus for a specified number of transfers.

## Registers

There are 8 read and 8 write registers in the 5380. Register 0 is a read and write register for the current SCSI data. Register 6 is a read register for the SCSI input data. These registers are used to transfer SCSI commands, data status and messages between the microprocessor data bus and the SCSI data bus. Register 0 acts as a transparent input port and provides the current state of the SCSI data lines. This register is not latched so that the microprocessor can read the data lines at any instant.

The microprocessor will read register 0 when it wants to accept a data byte from the SCSI bus using a programmed I/O data transfer. It is also used to check ID codes during a SCSI arbitration.

A register 0 write takes place when the 5380 wants to place that byte on the SCSI bus. This register is used for programmed I/O data transfers, DMA transfers and to set ID bits on the SCSI data lines during arbitration. A register 6 read takes place for incoming data transfers using DMA.

### Initiator Command Register

Register 1 is used for reads and writes of the initiator commands. These commands are used in the following ways.

Bit 0 loads the data bus. This bit causes the 5380 to place the contents of register 0 on the SCSI data lines. The 5380 will also generate a parity bit from the data on the SCSI data lines and it places that bit on the data bus parity (DBP) pin.

Bits 1 through 4 assert four of the negative true signal lines on the SCSI bus. Reading the bit provides the current status of the SCSI line. The following lines are controlled:

Bit 1    ATN*

Bit 2    SEL*

Bit 3    BSY*

Bit 4    ACK*

A bit 5 write is used as a differential enable in the 5381 which is a differential version of the 5380. It is not used in the 5380.

A bit 5 read is used when the 5380 loses arbitration. The 5380 sets this bit when it senses a bus-free phase and arbitrates for ownership of the SCSI bus, but it loses the arbitration.

A bit 6 write is used for setting the test mode. This bit disables all of the 5380's SCSI output drives, which disconnects the device from the SCSI bus.

A bit 6 read indicates that an arbitration is in progress. This bit indicates that the 5380 is currently arbitrating for control of the SCSI bus.

Bit 7 causes the 5380 to set the RST line negative true on the SCSI bus. A read of this bit provides the current status of the SCSI RST* line.

## Mode Register

Register 2 is the mode register. It controls the overall operation of the 5380 including the following:

1. Is the 5380 in the target or initiator role?
2. Will data transfers use programmed I/O or DMA?
3. What conditions will generate an interrupt?

The bits are set up as follows:

Bit 0 is used for an arbitrate command. When it is set, this bit instructs the 5380 to arbitrate for ownership of the SCSI bus when it senses a bus-free phase. Before setting this bit, the microprocessor should be set to correct the ID bit in register 0. This will ensure that as the 5380 starts the arbitration. It will place the correct ID code on the SCSI data bus.

Bit 1 sets the DMA mode. When this bit is set, the 5380 will use the DMA pins for data transfers.

When bit 2 is set, the 5380 will check the BSY* line and generate an interrupt if this line is negative true. This interrupt may be used to indicate that a target has been disconnected from the bus.

Bit 3 enables the EOP (end of process) interrupt. This bit is used in DMA transfers. When this bit is set, the 5380 will generate an interrupt when the EOP pin goes true. The DMA controller normally uses this pin when it completes the transfer of a data block. The resulting interrupt allows the microprocessor to start another block transfer or forces the 5380 to release ownership of the SCSI bus.

Bit 4 enables the parity interrupt. When this bit is set, the 5380 will generate an interrupt if it senses a parity error during a SCSI bus data transfer. Bit 5 in this register will also need to be set to enable parity checking.

Bit 5 enables parity checking. When this bit is set, the 5380 internal parity checker goes on. Then, if a parity error occurs, the 5380 parity-error latch of bit 5 in Register 5 is set.

Bit 6 places the 5380 in the target mode. This means the 5380 will operate as a SCSI target device. When this bit is clear, the 5380 will operate as an initiator.

Bit 7 is used for a block mode DMA. It controls the type of handshake used for DMA transfers. When this bit is off, the 5380 uses the DRQ (data request) and DACK (data acknowledge) signals in an interlocked handshake. When this bit is on, the 5380 uses DRQ and IOW or IOR pins in an interlocked handshake. DACK is held on during the entire block transfer.

## Target Command Register

Register 3 is the target command register. It has four bits that allow the microprocessor to control the four data transfer control lines: Bit 0 I/O∗, Bit 1 C/D∗, Bit 2 MSG∗, and Bit 3 REQ∗. This allows the 5380 to perform the SCSI information-transfer phase data transfers. These phases are defined by the following control line states:

|             | I/O∗ | C/D∗ | MSG∗ |
|-------------|------|------|------|
| DATA OUT    | 0    | 0    | 0    |
| COMMAND     | 0    | 1    | 0    |
| MESSAGE OUT | 0    | 1    | 1    |
| DATA IN     | 1    | 0    | 0    |
| STATUS      | 1    | 1    | 1    |
| MESSAGE IN  | 1    | 1    | 1    |

Register 4 is used as a read register to provide the present state of the SCSI bus control lines. The following bits are used:

| | | | |
|---|---|---|---|
| Bit 0 | DSP∗ (data bus parity) | Bit 1 | SEL∗ (select) |
| Bit 2 | I/O∗ (input/output) | Bit 3 | C/D∗ (command/data) |
| Bit 4 | MSG∗ (message) | Bit 5 | REQ∗ (request) |
| Bit 6 | BSY∗ (busy) | Bit 7 | RST∗ (reset) |

This register can be used by the microprocessor to find the cause of an interrupt.

## Select Enable Register

Register 4 is used as a write register for select enable functions. It allows the 5380 to check the SCSI bus for specific ID codes during a SCSI selection phase. By setting a bit in this register, the microprocessor allows the 5380 to generate an interrupt when the correct ID code appears on the SCSI data lines and when SEL∗ is negative true and BSY∗ is false. This interrupt can be used to signal a SCSI target device when it is selected by an initiator during a selection phase.

## Bus and Status Register

Register 5 is used as a read register for bus and status information. It allows the microprocessor to check the SCSI bus lines not handled by the current SCSI bus status register (register 4, read) and determine the bus status. The following bits are used:

Bit 0 is used for the ACK (acknowledge) signal and bit 1 is used for the ATN* (attention) signal. Bit 2 is a busy error and is used by the 5380 when the BSY* line goes negative.

Bit 3 is used for a phase match. The MSG*, I/O*, and C/D* SCSI signals specify the bus transfer phase. When the states of these signal lines match the required bits in the 5380 target command register (register 3), the 5380 sets the phase match bit. The 5380 can then perform a data transfer.

Bit 4 is used to indicate that an interrupt request is active. This bit indicates the state of the 5380 interrupt pin. A system that does not use hardware interrupts or the interrupt output line can check this bit as a part of a polled-interrupt operation.

Bit 5 is used for a parity error. The 5380 sets this bit when it senses a parity error during a data transfer. Register 2, bit 5 must be set to enable parity checking.

Bit 6 is a DMA request. This bit indicates the state of the 5380 DMA request pin (DRQ). This pin will usually be connected to the DMA controller. The microprocessor can use this bit to check 5380 DMA activity.

Bit 7 indicates the end of a DMA transfer. The 5380 will use this bit when EPO, DACK, and either IOR or IOW are all on for a minimum of 100 nanoseconds. This means that the last byte transfer in a block transfer is occurring.

# Analog Interfaces

Analog interfaces are used in data acquisition systems. Analog or continuous signals are used by many devices as inputs or outputs to computer systems. An example of an input would be temperature measurement and an example of an output would be motor control. These signals generally use voltage or current variations, but frequency and pulse width are among the other techniques used. No matter what form the analog signal has, it must be converted to a digital representation to be used by the computer. Any digital control signals that are sent to analog control devices must be converted to the proper analog format. The devices for accomplishing this are analog-to-digital and digital-to-analog converters.

## Coding Techniques

Digital coding for characters has been discussed in Chap. 1. Analog interfaces use a different set of codes to represent numbers. The analog or continuous values in physical control and measurement applications can be represented by digital numbers. The presence or absence of fixed voltage levels characterize these numbers. These digital representations are binary since each bit or unit of information can have one of two possible states: *TRUE* or *FALSE, ON* or *OFF, ONE* or *ZERO, HIGH* or *LOW.*

A binary code is used to interpret the analog value. The different bits represent different portions or weights of the digital number. The bit with the most weight is the first bit in the leftmost position. This is called the *most significant bit* or MSB. The bit with the least weight is the last bit in the rightmost position and is called the *least significant bit* or LSB.

An analog-to-digital converter is used to change the analog values to their digital equivalents. The resolution of an analog-to-digital converter is determined by the number of bits. The coding used is the set of coefficients representing the fractional parts of full scale.

## Natural Binary Coding

This is the most basic digital code since it follows a natural binary progression. A natural binary code of $n$ bits has the following characteristics:

1. The MSB has a weight of $\frac{1}{2}$ ($2^{-1}$).
2. The second bit has a weight of $\frac{1}{4}$ ($2^{-2}$).
3. The third bit has a weight of $\frac{1}{8}$ ($2^{-3}$).
4. The LSB has a weight of $2^{-n}$.

The value of the binary number represented is found by adding the weights of the nonzero bits. A sample of values for a 4-bit code is listed as follows. The binary weights and the equivalent numbers are listed for decimal and binary fractions.

| | Natural Binary Code | | | | |
|---|---|---|---|---|---|
| Decimal fraction | Binary fraction | Msb ($\times\frac{1}{2}$) | Bit 2 ($\times\frac{1}{4}$) | Bit 3 ($\times\frac{1}{8}$) | Bit 4 ($\times\frac{1}{16}$) |
| 0 | 0.0000 | 0 | 0 | 0 | 0 |
| $\frac{1}{16}$ = (LSB) | 0.0001 | 0 | 0 | 0 | 1 |
| $\frac{2}{16} = \frac{1}{8}$ | 0.0010 | 0 | 0 | 1 | 0 |
| $\frac{3}{16} = \frac{1}{8} + \frac{1}{16}$ | 0.0011 | 0 | 0 | 1 | 1 |
| $\frac{4}{16} = \frac{1}{4}$ | 0.0100 | 0 | 1 | 0 | 0 |
| $\frac{5}{16} = \frac{1}{4} + \frac{1}{16}$ | 0.0101 | 0 | 1 | 0 | 1 |

The bit weights in binary for numbers up to 12 bits are shown as follows. This is the range for many data acquisition boards; to obtain the weights for larger numbers of bits, continue to divide by 2. The weight assigned to the LSB is the resolution.

| BIT | $\frac{1}{2}^n$ (fraction) | dB | $\frac{1}{2}^n$ (decimal) | % | ppm (parts per million) |
|---|---|---|---|---|---|
| 0(Full scale) | 1 | 0 | 1.0 | 100 | 1,000,000 |
| MSB | $\frac{1}{2}$ | −6 | 0.5 | 50 | 500,000 |
| 2 | $\frac{1}{4}$ | −12 | 0.25 | 25 | 250,000 |
| 3 | $\frac{1}{8}$ | −18.1 | 0.125 | 12.5 | 125,000 |
| 4 | $\frac{1}{16}$ | −24.1 | 0.0625 | 6.2 | 62,500 |
| 5 | $\frac{1}{32}$ | −30.1 | 0.03125 | 3.1 | 31,250 |
| 6 | $\frac{1}{64}$ | −36.1 | 0.025625 | 1.6 | 15,625 |
| 7 | $\frac{1}{128}$ | −42.1 | 0.007812 | 0.8 | 7,812 |
| 8 | $\frac{1}{256}$ | −48.2 | 0.003906 | 0.4 | 3,906 |
| 9 | $\frac{1}{512}$ | −54.2 | 0.001953 | 0.2 | 1,953 |
| 10 | $\frac{1}{1,024}$ | −60.2 | 0.0009766 | 0.1 | 977 |
| 11 | $\frac{1}{2,048}$ | −66.2 | 0.00048828 | 0.05 | 488 |
| 12 | $\frac{1}{4,096}$ | −72.2 | 0.00024414 | 0.024 | 244 |

The dB (decibel) value is the logarithm (base 10) of the ratio of the LSB value to unity multiplied by 20. Each successive power of 2 represents a change of 6.02 dB.

## Bipolar Codes

In some digital codes, the bits are represented by their complements. Unipolar converters use analog signals of one polarity while bipolar converters use an extra bit for the sign. The unipolar version of natural binary is sometimes called *unipolar straight binary* (USB).

When the sign digit doubles both the range and the number of levels, the LSB's ratio to full scale in either polarity is

$$2^{-(n-1)}$$

rather than

$$2^{-n}$$

The most popular binary codes for bipolar conversion are:

1. Sign-magnitude (magnitude plus sign)

2. Offset binary

3. Two's complement

4. One's complement

Each of these codes in 4 bits (3 bits plus sign) can be compared in Table 7.1.

**TABLE 7.1   Bipolar Codes**

| Decimal number | Decimal positive reference | Fraction negative reference | Sign magnitude | Twos complement | Offset binary | Ones complement |
|---|---|---|---|---|---|---|
| +7 | +7/8 | -7/8 | 0 1 1 1 | 0 1 1 1 | 1 1 1 1 | 0 1 1 1 |
| +6 | +6/8 | -6/8 | 0 1 1 0 | 0 1 1 0 | 1 1 1 0 | 0 1 1 0 |
| +5 | +5/8 | -5/8 | 0 1 0 1 | 0 1 0 1 | 1 1 0 1 | 0 1 0 1 |
| +4 | +4/8 | -4/8 | 0 1 0 0 | 0 1 0 0 | 1 1 0 0 | 0 1 0 0 |
| +3 | +3/8 | -3/8 | 0 0 1 1 | 0 0 1 1 | 1 0 1 1 | 0 0 1 1 |
| +2 | +2/8 | -2/8 | 0 0 1 0 | 0 0 1 0 | 1 0 1 0 | 0 0 1 0 |
| +1 | +1/8 | -1/8 | 0 0 0 1 | 0 0 0 1 | 1 0 0 1 | 0 0 0 1 |
| 0 | 0+ | 0- | 0 0 0 0 | 0 0 0 0 | 1 0 0 0 | 0 0 0 0 |
| 0 | 0- | 0+ | 1 0 0 0 | (0 0 0 0) | (1 0 0 0) | 1 1 1 1 |
| -1 | -1/8 | +1/8 | 1 0 0 1 | 1 1 1 1 | 0 1 1 1 | 1 1 1 0 |
| -2 | -2/8 | +2/8 | 1 0 1 0 | 1 1 1 0 | 0 1 1 0 | 1 1 0 1 |
| -3 | -3/8 | +3/8 | 1 0 1 1 | 1 1 0 1 | 0 1 0 1 | 1 1 0 0 |
| -4 | -4/8 | +4/8 | 1 1 0 0 | 1 1 0 0 | 0 1 0 0 | 1 0 1 1 |
| -5 | -5/8 | +5/8 | 1 1 0 1 | 1 0 1 1 | 0 0 1 1 | 1 0 1 0 |
| -6 | -6/8 | +6/8 | 1 1 1 0 | 1 0 1 0 | 0 0 1 0 | 1 0 0 1 |
| -7 | -7/8 | +7/8 | 1 1 1 1 | 1 0 0 1 | 0 0 0 1 | 1 0 0 0 |
| -8 | -8/8 | +8/8 | | (1 0 0 0) | (0 0 0 0) | |

## Polarity

The analog signal can be given a choice of polarity; then the relationship between the code and the polarity of the signal needs to be specified. If a positive reference is used, the analog signal increases positively as the digit number increases. If a negative reference is used, the analog signal decreases toward negative full scale as the digital number increases.

## Sign Magnitude

This is a technique for indicating signed analog quantities. A polarity bit is added to the code. This is most useful in converters that operate near zero. It provides a smoother transition from a small positive voltage to a small negative voltage. It is the only code where the 3 magnitude bits do not have to make a major transition such as all 0s to all 1s, at zero.

However, this advantage makes sign-magnitude more costly to implement than the other codes. The two codes for zero require some additional hardware or software and zero errors can be larger. In sign magnitude, the zero level is usually computed from the difference between the MSB (½ full scale) and a bias (½ full scale). These are usually two large numbers and any variations can produce errors.

## Two's Complement

This code uses a binary code for positive magnitudes with a 0 sign bit. The two's complement is formed by complementing the number and adding one LSB. The two's complement of ¾ (binary 0011) is the complement (1100) plus the LSB (0001), which gives 1101.

Two's complement is like a set of negative numbers. To subtract ¾ from ⅝, you add ⅝ to −¾ which is the same as adding 0100 to 1101. This results in 0001, neglecting the extra carry which is ⅛.

The bipolar version of two's complement is referred to as BTC and the bipolar version of offset binary is known as BOB. In the two's complement and the offset binary codes, the only difference is that the MSB is replaced by the complement of the other. An offset-binary-coded converter can be used for two's complement by complementing the MSB at the output of an A/D converter or at the output of a D/A converter's input register.

## Offset Binary

This is the easiest code to implement with a converter. This code for three bits plus a sign bit is the same as natural binary for four bits, except for the following:

1. The zero is at negative full scale.
2. The LSB is $\frac{1}{16}$ of the total bipolar range.
3. The MSB is on at zero.

An offset binary 3 bit with sign converter can be implemented from a 4-bit D/A converter with a 0- to 10-V full-scale range. The scale factor is doubled to 20 V and then offset the zero by half of the full range to $-10$ V. For an A/D converter, cut the input in half and then implement a bias of half the range.

The major disadvantage of offset binary is the bit transition which occurs at 0 when all bits can change (for example from 0111 to 1000). The differences in switching speeds from the electronic components turning on and off can produce spikes and linearity errors. These errors can occur at major transitions, since these transitions indicate the difference between two large numbers. Offset binary is more compatible with microcomputer inputs and outputs since it is easily changed to the more common two's complement by complementing the MSB. Two's complement has a single unambiguous code for zero, but it also has the same disadvantages as offset binary, since the conversion process is the same.

### One's Complement

This is a way of representing negative numbers. The one's complement is obtained by complementing all bits. The one's complement of $\frac{3}{8}$ (0011) is 1100. A number is subtracted by adding its one's complement. The extra carry that is dropped in the two's complement code causes one LSB to be added to the total in the end-around carry. Subtracting $\frac{3}{8}$ from $\frac{4}{8}$, we get $0100 + 1100 = 0001$ (or $\frac{1}{8}$).

The one's complement code is formed by complementing each positive value to obtain the corresponding negative value. Zero is represented by two codes, 0000 and 1111. Besides this ambiguous zero, another disadvantage is that it is not as easy to implement as two's complement in converter circuits.

In both sign-magnitude and one's complement converters, two methods are used to deal with the ambiguous zero. One of the codes is forbidden and not used, or the $\pm\frac{1}{2}$ LSB zero region is divided into two regions. One region goes from 0 to $+\frac{1}{2}$ LSB and the other from 0 to $-\frac{1}{2}$ LSB. Each of these can then have its own unique code.

### D/A Converters

The $R$-$2R$ ladder circuit is often used in digital-to-analog (D/A) conversion. The basic circuit is shown in Fig. 7.1$a$. Notice that it is used with an inverting operational amplifier. When all bits but the MSB are off, (grounded) the output equals $(-R/2R)V_{\text{ref}})$.

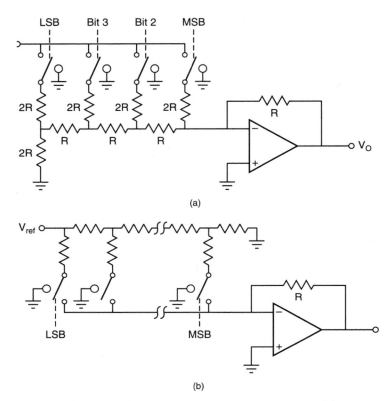

**Figure 7.1**   R-2R ladder circuits. (*a*) R-2R ladder network; (*b*) Inverted R-2R ladder.

When all bits except bit 2 are off, the output equals $\frac{1}{2}(-R/2R)V_{ref} = \frac{1}{4}$ $V_{ref}$. The lumped resistance of the LSB circuit to the left of bit 2 is $2R$. The equivalent circuit looking back from the MSB toward bit 2 is $V_{ref}/2$, and the series resistance is $2R$. The grounded MSB series resistance is also $2R$ but it has no effect since the amplifier is grounded. The output voltage is then $-V_{ref}/4$. This type of reasoning can be extended to show that the $n$th bit will provide an output equal to $2^{-n} V_{ref}$.

If a positive output voltage is desired, the circuit of Fig. 7.1*b* is used. Applying the same reasoning as above the MSB output is $\frac{1}{2} V_{ref}$. The entire circuit may be considered as a voltage generator with an output voltage $NV_{ref}$ (where $N$ is the fractional digital input) along with an internal resistance $R$.

A D/A converter with buffer storage can be used as a sample-hold with digital input and analog output and an infinite hold time. The register is under control of a strobe which causes the converter to update.

The rate at which the strobe may update is determined by the settling time of the converter and the response time of the logic.

If bipolar current-switching D/A conversion is used with offset binary or two's complement codes, an offset current equal and opposite to the MSB current is summed with the converter output. This is usually taken from a resistor divider network rather than a separate offset reference. This is done in order to minimize errors due to temperature changes.

If the gain of the output inverting amplifier is doubled, this increases the output range, from 0–10 V to ±10 V. When the amplifier is connected for sign inversion, the conversion is negative reference. In a noninverting application, the same values of offset voltage and resistance are used, but the value of the output voltage scale factor will depend on the load.

Some bipolar D/A converters with $R$-$2R$ ladder networks and offset binary or two's complement coding have switches that are normally grounded for unipolar operation. If the LSB node is grounded, the output will be symmetrical. For sign-magnitude conversion, the converter's current output can be inverted.

The analog output in a parallel-input D/A converter circuit will follow the state of the logic inputs. The converter may be preceded by a register, then the converter will respond only when the inputs are gated into it. This is done in some data distribution systems, where the data may be continually changing, but samples are needed on a periodic basis.

## DAC811

This is a single-chip integrated circuit microcomputer-compatible 12-bit digital-to-analog converter. The Burr-Brown DAC811 chip includes a precision voltage reference, interface logic, buffered latch, and a 12-bit D/A converter with a voltage output amplifier. Fast current switches and a laser-trimmed thin-film resistor network are used to provide an accurate and fast D/A converter. Laser trimming is done at the wafer level to maintain a ¼ LSB linearity error at 25°C and a ½ LSB error over the temperature range.

The DAC811 is available in a 28-pin plastic molded package, a 28-pin 0.6-inch-wide dual-in-line ceramic side-brazed package, and a 28-terminal 0.45-inch-square ceramic leadless chip carrier.

## Interface

The microprocessor interface uses a double-buffered latch which is divided into three 4-bit nybbles for interfacing to 4, 8, 12, or 16-bit

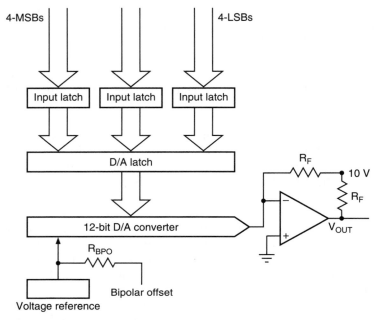

4-MSBs

4-LSBs

Input latch

Input latch

Input latch

D/A latch

$R_F$

10 V

$R_F$

$V_{OUT}$

12-bit D/A converter

$R_{BPO}$

Bipolar offset

Voltage reference

**Figure 7.2**   DAC 811 D/A converter.

buses and for handling right- or left-justified data (Fig. 7.2). The 12-bit data in the input latches is moved to the D/A latch which holds the output value. Loading the last nybble or byte of data can be done simultaneously with the transfer of data between latches. This avoids spurious analog output values and saves computer instructions.

The three 4-bit input latches hold the data while the 12-bit word is assembled before loading the D/A register. Each register is independently addressable. The input latches are controlled by Na*, Nb*, Nc*, and WR*. Na*, Nb*, and Nc* are NORed with WR*. This forces the input latches to transmit data when either Na*, Nb*, or Nc* and WR* are negative true. When either Na*, Nb*, Nc*, or WR* switch high, the input data is latched into the input registers and held until both Na* (or Nb*, Nc*) and WR* go negative true.

The D/A latch is controlled by LDAC* and WR*. LDAC* and WR* are NORed so that the latches transmit data to the D/A switches when both LDAC* and WR* are at logic zero. When either LDAC* or WR* are at logic one, the data is latched in the D/A latch and held until LDAC* and WR* switch to logic zero. The latches are level-triggered. The data that is present when the control signals are at logic zero will enter the latch. If any of the control signals switches to a logic one, the data is latched. The latches are controlled as shown in the following:

| WR* | Na* | Nb* | Nc* | LDAC* | |
|-----|-----|-----|-----|-------|---|
| 1 | X | X | X | X | No change |
| 0 | 0 | 1 | 1 | 1 | Enables input latch for 4 MSBs |
| 0 | 1 | 0 | 1 | 1 | Enables input latch for 4 middle bits |
| 0 | 1 | 1 | 0 | 1 | Enables input latch for 4 LSBs |
| 0 | 1 | 1 | 1 | 0 | Loads D/A latch from input latches |
| 0 | 0 | 0 | 0 | 0 | All latches are transparent |

The interface logic is designed for interfacing to microprocessor bus structures. The control signal WR* is derived from the external device select logic and the I/O or Memory Write signals.

The latch enable lines Na*, Nb*, Nc*, and LDAC may be used to enable several latches simultaneously. Data can be loaded into the input latches of several DAC811s and then strobed into the D/A latch of the D/A simultaneously to update the analog outputs.

Most interfaces require a base address decoder (Fig. 7.3), but if blocks of memory are not used, the base address decoder is simplified or not needed. For example, if half the memory space is not used, address line $A_{15}$ of the microprocessor may be used as the chip select control.

The control logic allows interfacing to right- or left-justified data format. When a 12-bit D/A converter is loaded from an 8-bit bus, 2 bytes of data are required. The base address is decoded from the high-order address bits and A and A are used to address the latches. Adjacent addresses are used.

## Offset and Gain

In unipolar configurations, the digital input code to produce zero voltage output is applied and the offset potentiometer is adjusted for zero output. In bipolar configurations, the digital input code to produce the maximum negative output voltage is applied and the offset potentiometer is adjusted for minus full-scale voltage. If the full scale range is 20 V, the maximum negative output voltage is −10 V.

In unipolar or bipolar configurations, the digital input to produce the maximum positive voltage output is applied and the gain potentiometer is adjusted for this positive full-scale voltage.

## Analog-to-Digital Converters

Most of the data acquisition boards for personal computers use successive approximation conversion. These A/D converters are built around a D/A converter and use a comparison technique. When a conversion command is applied, the D/A converter's MSB output (½ full scale) is compared with the input.

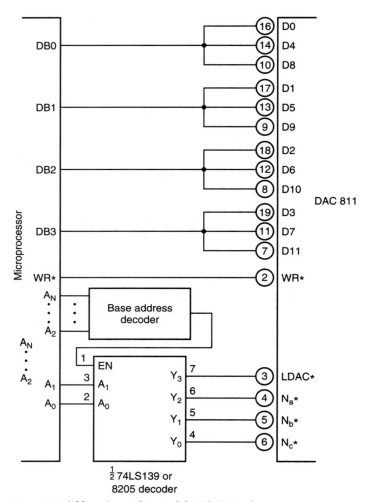

**Figure 7.3**   Addressing and control for 4-bit interface.

Then if the input is greater than the MSB, it remains on and the next bit is tested. But, if the input is less than the MSB, it is turned off, and the next bit is tested.

If the second bit does not have enough weight to exceed the input, it is left on and the third bit is tested. But, if the second bit exceeds the input, it is turned off. The bit testing continues until the last bit has been tested.

When the bit tests are complete, a status line indicates that a valid conversion has occurred. An output register is used to hold the digital code corresponding to the input signal.

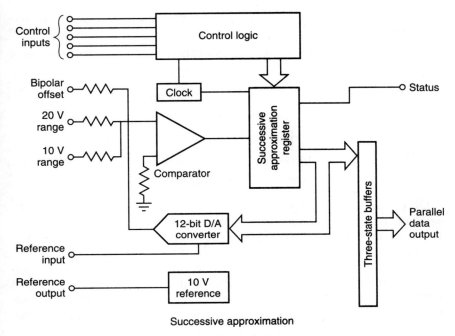

Successive approximation

**Figure 7.4** Successive approximation analog-to-digital converter.

Figure 7.4 is a block diagram of a successive approximation A/D converter. Internally, the converter operates as follows. When a true signal is applied to the command input, the D/A switches are set to their off state, except for the most significant bit, which is set to logic "1". This turns on the corresponding D/A switch to apply the analog equivalent of the MSB to the comparator. If the analog input voltage is less than the MSB weight, the MSB is switched off at the first edge of the clock pulse. If the analog input is greater than the MSB, the "1" remains in the register.

During the second pulse, the sum of the first result and the second bit is compared with the analog input voltage. The comparator is gated by the next clock pulse. It will cause the register to either accept or reject that bit. Successive clock pulses will cause all the bits, in order of decreasing significance, to be tested until the LSB is accepted or rejected.

## A/D Converter Considerations

The following considerations are important to A/D conversion:

1. The analog input range
2. Resolution required for the signal to be measured

3. The requirements for linearity error, relative accuracy, and stability of calibration

4. The changes in the various sources of error as temperature changes

5. Conditions for missed codes if allowable

6. The time allowed for a complete conversion

7. Stability of the system power supply

8. Errors due to power-supply variations

9. Character of the input signal: noisy, sampled, filtered, frequency

10. Types of preprocessing needed or desired

Other A/D conversion circuits may be more acceptable for the application instead of successive approximation. These include the integration and countercomparator types. The integrating types are generally better for converting noisy input signals at relatively slow rates.

Successive approximation is best suited for converting sampled or filtered inputs at rates up to the MHz range. Countercomparator types allow low cost, but can be both slow and noise-susceptible. They are useful for peak followers and sample-holds for digital storage applications.

## Converter Parameters

When the converter's full-scale range is adjusted, it will be set with respect to the reference voltage which can be traced to some recognized voltage standard. The absolute accuracy error is the tolerance of the full-scale point referred to this absolute voltage standard. Offset is measured for a zero input. It is the extent to which the output deviates from zero and it usually a function of time and temperature. Nonlinearity monotenicity is the ability to include all code numbers in actual operation. It is the amount by which the plot of output versus input deviates from a straight line. Settling time is the time required for the input to attain a final value within a specified fraction of full scale, usually ±½ LSB.

In the A/D conversion process, an error from the quantization uncertainty of ±½ LSB exists along with other conversion-processing errors. The way to reduce this quantization uncertainty error is to increase the number of bits.

Statistical interpolation can be used during processing or filtering after the conversion. This tends to fill in missing analog values for rapidly changing signals, but it will not reduce errors due to any variations within ±½ LSB.

It is usually easier to determine the location of a transition than to determine a midrange value, so errors and settings of A/D converters are normally defined in terms of the analog values when actual transitions occur in relation to the ideal transition values.

### ADC674 Analog-to-Digital Converter

This Burr-Brown chip is a complete 12-bit A/D converter with reference, clock and 8-, 12-, or 16-bit microprocessor bus interface. It has a 15-microsecond maximum conversion time and is specified for operation with no missing codes.

The chip contains a 12-bit successive approximation analog-to-digital converter. It has a self-contained +10 V reference, internal clock, digital interface for microprocessor control, and three-state outputs.

The reference circuit uses a buried zener and is laser-trimmed. The clock oscillator is current-controlled, and full-scale and offset errors may be externally trimmed. Internal scaling resistors are provided for selecting the following analog input signal ranges:

$$0 \text{ to } +10 \text{ V} \qquad 0 \text{ to } +20 \text{ V} \qquad + \text{ or } -5 \text{ V} \qquad + \text{ or } -10 \text{ V}$$

The converter can be externally programmed to provide 8- or 12-bit resolution. The output data is available in a parallel format from TTL-compatible three-state output buffers. The output data is coded in straight binary for unipolar input signals and bipolar offset binary for bipolar input signals. It is packaged in a 28-pin ceramic DIP.

### Calibration Techniques

Both digital-to-analog (D/A) and analog-to-digital (A/D) converters have offset errors since the first transition will not always occur at exactly ½ LSB. Scale-factor or gain errors can cause a difference between the values at which the first transition and the last transition occur since this is not always equal to ½ LSB. Linearity errors can exist since the differences between transition values are not all equal or uniform in changing. When the differential linearity error becomes too large, it is possible for codes to be missed.

Offset and full-scale errors are trimmed using external offset and full-scale trim potentiometers connected to the reference and offset terminals. If adjustments for unipolar offset and full scale are not required, a 50-ohm 1 percent metal film resistor is connected between pin 10 (Reference In) and pin 8 (Reference Out). Pin 12 (Bipolar Offset) is connected to pin 9 (Analog Common), grounding the offset adjustment.

If adjustment is required, one 100-ohm potentiometer is connected between pins 10 and 8, and another is connected between pins 8 and 12. Then the input is varied through the end-point transition voltage; 0 V + ½ LSB; +1.22 mV for the 10-V range, +2.44 mV for the 20-V range.

This causes the output code to be DB0 ON (high). Then the potentiometer between pins 12 and 8 until DB0 just switches off with all other bits off. Next, an input voltage of full-scale value minus 3/2 LSB is applied to cause all bits to be on. This value is +9.9963 V for the 10-V range and +19.9927 V for the 20-V range. The potentiometer between pins 8 and 10 is adjusted until bits DB1 and DB11 are on and DB0 is switching between on and off.

If external adjustments of full-scale and bipolar offset are not required, the potentiometers are replaced with 50-ohm metal film resistors. If adjustments are required, the calibration procedure is similar to that used for unipolar operation, except that the offset adjustment is performed with an input voltage which is ½ LSB above the minus full-scale value, −4.9988 V for the +5-V range, −9.9976 V for the +10-V range. Then the pot between pins 8 and 12 is adjusted for DB0 to switch between on and off with all other bits off.

To adjust full-scale, a DC input signal is used which is 3/2 LSB below the nominal plus the full-scale value. This is +4.9963 V for the +5-V range and +9.9927 V for the +10-V range. Then the pot between pins 8 and 10 is adjusted for DB0 to switch between on and off with all other bits on.

## Interfacing

The AD674 is designed to be interfaced to microprocessor systems and other digital systems. The microprocessor can have full control of the conversions, or the converter can operate in a stand-alone mode, controlled by the R/C* input. Full control involves the following:

1. Setting up an 8- or 12-bit conversion cycle
2. Initiating the conversion
3. Reading the output data

This can be done by reading the 12 bits all at once, or 8 bits followed by 4 bits in a left-justified format. There are five control inputs—12/8*, CS*, $A_0$, R/C*, and CE. These are all TTL/CMOS-compatible. The functions of the control inputs are shown in Table 7.2.

The stand-alone mode is used in systems with dedicated input ports. In stand-alone operation, control of the converter is done with a single control line connected to R/C*. In this mode CS* and $A_0$ are tied to digital common and CE and 12/8* are tied to +5 V. The output will be in 12-bit words.

The conversion is initiated by forcing R/C* to low. The three-state data output buffers are enabled when R/C* is high and STATUS is low. The conversion can be initiated with either positive or negative pulses. The R/C pulse must be low for at least 50 nanoseconds.

**TABLE 7.2    Control Signals**

| Signal | Function | |
| --- | --- | --- |
| CE, Pin 6 | Chip enable | Must be high to start a conversion or read the output data. The rising edge can be used to start a conversion. |
| CS*, Pin 3 | Chip select | Must be low to start a conversion or read the output data. The falling edge can be used to start a conversion. |
| R/C*, Pin 5 | Read/Convert | Must be low to start a conversion. The falling edge can be used to start a conversion. Must be high to read the output data. The rising edge can be used to start a read operation. |
| $A_0$, Pin 4 | Byte address | In the start-convert mode, a high selects 8-bit conversion and a low selects 12-bit conversion. When reading output data in two 8-bit bytes, a low accesses 8 MSBs (the high byte) and a high accesses 4 LSBs and trailing zeros (the low byte). |
| $12/8$*, Pin 2 | Data mode | When reading output data, a high enables all 12 output bits and a low enables the MSBs or LSBs as set $A_0$ (8 bits enabled). |

When conversion is initiated by an R/C pulse which goes low and returns to the high state during the conversion, the three-state outputs go to a high-impedance state. They are enabled after completion of the conversion.

When conversion is initiated by a positive R/C pulse, the output data from the previous conversion is enabled during the positive part of R/C*. A new conversion is started on the falling edge of R/C*, and the three-state outputs return to the high-impedance state until the next high R/C pulse.

In the fully controlled mode, the conversion length (8-bit or 12-bit) is determined by the state of the $A_0$ input, which is latched from a conversion start change. If $A_0$ is latched high, the conversion goes on for 8 bits. A full 12-bit conversion takes place if $A_0$ is low.

If all 12 bits are read following an 8-bit conversion, the 3LSBs (DB0–DB2) go low (logic 0) and DB3 goes high (logic 1). $A_0$ is latched since it is used in enabling the output buffers. No other control inputs are latched.

## Starting a Conversion

A conversion is started by a transition on any of the three inputs, CE, CS*, and R/C*. The conversion starts when the last of the three reaches the required state.

The STATUS output indicates the current state of the converter. It is held high during the conversion, and the three-state output buffers are in a high-impedance state, so data cannot be read during the conversion. During this time any additional transitions of the three digital inputs used to control conversion are ignored as long as $A_0$ does not change state.

## Read Operations

After conversion starts, the output data buffers are in a high-impedance state until the following conditions all exist:

| | |
|---|---|
| R/C* | High |
| STATUS | Low |
| CE | High |
| CS* | Low |

When this occurs, the data lines are enabled from the state of inputs 12/8* and $A_0$.

When 12/8* is high, all 12 output lines (DB0–DB11) are enabled for a full data word transfer to a 12- or 16-bit bus. In this mode, $A_0$ is ignored. When 12/8* is low, the data is present in the form of two 8-bit bytes. Byte selection is done with $A_0$ during the read cycle.

The interface to an 8-bit bus for left-justified data transfers is shown in Fig. 7.5. The $A_0$ input is usually driven by the least significant bit of the address bus, allowing the output word to be stored in two consecutive memory locations.

When $A_0$ is low, the byte addressed holds the 8 MSMs. When $A_0$ is high, the byte addressed holds the 4 LSBs from the conversion followed by four logic 0s that are formed by the control logic.

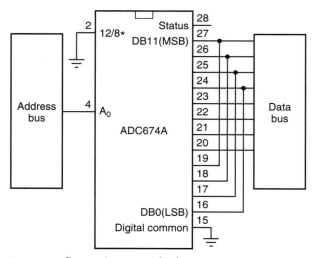

**Figure 7.5**  Connection to an 8-bit bus.

## Digital-Current Converters

The inputs to A/D converters are normally voltages. D/A converter outputs are usually voltages at low impedance from an operational amplifier. Many converters provide an output current instead of a voltage. The current output is linear and free from offsets. An operational amplifier may be used to convert the current to voltage.

The conversion relationship of D/I converters usually has a positive reference. As the current flowing out of the converter increases, the value represented by the digital code increases. It does not depend on the actual polarity of the converter's reference. If the current flowing into the converter increases as the number represented by the digital code increases, the relationship has a negative reference.

Converters that use current outputs or voltage outputs directly from resistive ladders can be considered as voltage generators with series resistance or current generators with parallel resistance. They can be used with operational amplifiers in either an inverting or noninverting mode. The inverting current-output connection gives a high internal impedance with a loop gain that is close to unity. The gain is almost independent of the feedback resistance, which minimizes amplifier errors, such as those due to voltage drift.

## Multiplexers

If more than one analog quantity has to be converted, it is necessary either to time-division multiplex the analog inputs to a single A/D converter, or to use an A/D converter for each input and then combine the converter outputs with digital multiplexing. Analog multiplexing is normally used because of its lower cost.

Multiplexer considerations include the following:

1. The number and type of input channels needed, single-ended or differential, high- or low-level, dynamic range

2. Settling time when switching from one channel to another, maximum switching rate

3. Allowable crosstalk error between channels, frequencies involved

4. Errors due to leakage

5. Multiplexer transfer errors due to the voltage divider formed by the on resistance of the multiplexer and the input resistance of the sample hold

6. Type of hierarchy used for a large amount of channels, addressing scheme

7. Channel-switching rate, fixed or flexible; continuous or interruptible; capable of stopping on one channel during test purposes

The number of channels controls the size of the multiplexer required along with the amount of wiring and interconnections that are needed. Analog multiplexing is used for handling up to 256 channels. Above this number of channels the analog errors are difficult to minimize.

High-speed conversion is expensive and analog time-division multiplexing requires a high-speed converter for the required sample rate. If there are wide dynamic ranges between channels, analog multiplexers may have crosstalk problems.

## MPC16C Analog Multiplexer

The Burr-Brown MPC16S is a single-ended monolithic 16-channel analog multiplexer. The MPC8D is the 8-channel version and the MPC4D is the 4-channel version. Both are constructed with failure protected CMOS devices. The digital and analog inputs are failure-protected from either overvoltages that exceed the power supplies or from the loss of power. Transfer accuracies of 0/01 percent can be obtained at sampling rates to 200 kHz with signal sources of up to ±10 volts. The devices are housed in 28-pin dual-in-line packages.

These are TTL/CMOS-compatible devices with binary channel address decoding. An ENABLE line allows an 8-channel group or a 4-channel group to be enabled for channel expansion in either single-layer or multitiered configurations.

The ENABLE input (pin 18) is used for channel expansion in a single-tier system as shown in Fig. 7.6. When the ENABLE line is at a logic 1, the channel is selected by the 3- or 4-bit Channel Select Address. When ENABLE is at logic 0, all channels are turned off, independent of the Channel Address Lines.

## Channel Expansion

Using the single-ended MPC16S, up to 64 channels, 4 multiplexers, can be connected to a single node. Up to 256 channels can be connected using 17 MPC16S multiplexers in a two-tiered structure. Using the differential MPC8D single or multitiered configurations can expand the multiplexer channel capacity up to 64 channels in a $64 \times 1$ or $8 \times 8$ configuration. The $64 \times 1$ configuration ties eight MPC8Ds to a single node. Programming is done with a 6-bit counter, using the 3 LSBs of the counter to control the Channel Address inputs $A_0$, $A_1$, and $A_2$. The 3 MSBs of the counter is used to drive an 8-of-1 decoder. The decoder is then used to drive the ENABLE inputs.

In an $8 \times 8$ two-tier expansion for 64 channels, the programming is simpler. The 6-bit counter output does not need an 8-of-1 decoder. The 3 LSBs of the counter drives the $A_0$, $A_1$, and $A_2$ inputs of the eight first-

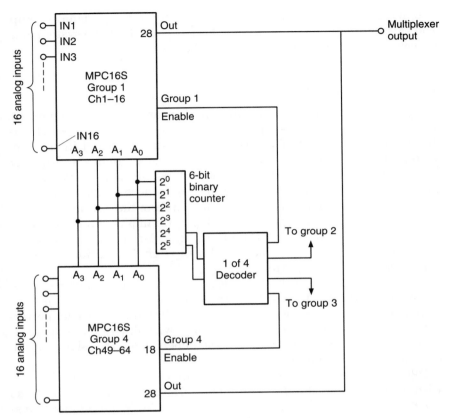

**Figure 7.6** 32- to 64-channel, single-tier expansion.

tier multiplexers. The 3 MSBs of the counter are sent to the $A_0$, $A_1$, and $A_2$ input of the second-tier multiplexer.

Along with reducing the programming, the two-tier configuration provides other advantages over the single-node expansion. This includes lower OFF channel current leakage, which reduces the Offset, improved CMR, and a more reliable connection if a channel should fail in the ON condition (short). If a channel fails ON in the single-node configuration, data cannot be taken from any channel, while only one channel group is out in the multitiered configuration.

For the best settling time, the input wiring and interconnections between multiplexer output and driven devices should be as short as possible. When driving the digital inputs from TTL, open collector output with pull-up resistors are recommended. To preserve common-mode rejection, twisted-shield pairs can be used for signal lines and intertier connections and the multiplexer output lines. This helps the common-mode capacitance balance and reduces stray signal pickup. The shields should be connected as close as possible to the system analog common or the common-mode guard driver.

## Multiplexer Application

In multiplexer systems the resolution of measurement is important. The cost of converters rises quickly as the resolution increases. This is due to the higher cost of precision components required in the converter. At the 8-bit level, the per-channel cost of an analog multiplexer is comparable to the cost of a converter. At resolutions above 12 bits, the reverse is true and analog multiplexing is more economical.

Signals less than 1 V usually require differential low-level analog multiplexing. This is expensive, and programmable-gain amplifiers may be needed as well after the multiplexer. An alternative is to use fixed-gain converters on each channel using signal-conditioning specifically designed for the channel.

Analog multiplexing is best for measurements at distances less than a few hundred feet (100 m) from the converter. The analog lines are sensitive to impedance losses, transmission-line reflections, and interference. The available cabling ranges from twisted wire-pairs to multiconductor shielded cable. The choice depends on the signal level, distance, and noise environment.

Digital multiplexing is suitable for distances to thousands of miles, with the proper transmission equipment. Digital transmission systems use noise-rejection schemes, which are needed for long-distance transmission.

The number of channels controls the size of the multiplexer required along with the amount of wiring and interconnections that are needed. Analog multiplexing is used for handling up to 256 channels. Above this number of channels the analog errors are difficult to minimize.

High-speed conversion is expensive and analog time-division multiplexing requires a high-speed converter for the required sample rate. If there are wide dynamic ranges between channels, analog multiplexers may have crosstalk problems.

Analog multiplexers should be used with sources that have enough overload capacity to afford good settling times after an overload. The switches used should offer a break-before-make action to prevent the possibility of shorting channels together. Not all multiplexers have this feature.

The channel-addressing lines are usually binary-coded, and it is also useful to have one or more inhibit or enable lines to turn all switches off regardless of the channel being addressed. This simplifies the external logic required to cascade multiplexers.

## Errors

A multiplexer must operate without introducing unacceptable errors at the sampling speed. In digital multiplexing, the speed is determined from the propagation-delay and the time needed for the output to settle on the data bus.

Analog multiplexer speed depends on the internal parameters of the switching devices and external parameters such as channel source impedance, stray capacitance, number of channels, and cable characteristics. Analog multiplexers introduce static and dynamic errors due to leakage through switches, coupling of control signals into the analog path, and the interaction of sources and amplifiers. Poor circuit layout and cabling adds to these effects and degrades performance.

Multiplexing introduces both static (dc) and dynamic errors into the signal. When these errors become large in relation to the measurement, they begin to change the measurement. Static errors can come from switch leakage and offsets in amplifiers. Gain errors may be due to switch on-resistance, source resistance, amplifier input resistance and amplifier-gain nonlinearities. Dynamic errors can occur from charge injection of the switch control voltage, settling times of the common bus and input sources due to circuit time constants, crosstalk between channels and output-amplifier settling characteristics. Leakage from cabling and wiring can be reduced with teflon-insulated cable.

The switch on-resistance is a function of the switch design. Solid-state switches have a resistance which ranges, for FET switches, from a few ohms to a few thousand ohms.

FET switches have a finite off-resistance and are affected by drain-to-source leakage currents. Junction FETs and Zener-diode-protected MOSFETs have leakage paths between gate and channel. Unprotected insulated-gate MOSFETs have negligible gate leakage, but are not used because they are vulnerable to transients. The leakage currents of the switches in a multiplexer return to ground via the input source resistance and the input resistance of the amplifier. Leakage on the input side of nonconducting channels does not affect the signal path. Leakage of the output sides of the channels and the conducting channel into the signal path will cause a voltage error.

## Leakage

Leakage is important when working with high-source impedances. In the multiplexer data sheet, this is called the *channel leakage*. In an 8-channel multiplexer with a channel leakage of 3 NA at 25°C with a source resistance of 50k ohm, the leakage error becomes a little more than 1 mV. For large multiplexers (256 channels), the leakage error can

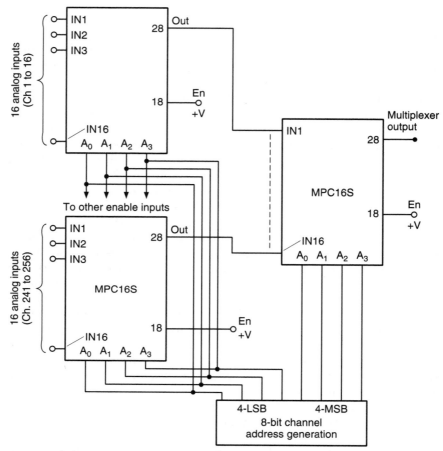

**Figure 7.7**   Channel expansion of up to 256 channels using $16 \times 16$ two-tiered system.

be decreased by cascading multiplexers and using submultiplexing as shown in Fig. 7.7. Multiplexing 256 channels by submultiplexing with 8-channel multiplexers can provide an order-of-magnitude improvement over a simple parallel connection.

The on-resistance of most types of multiplexer switches requires a high input impedance amplifier to buffer the output voltage. This amplifier may be part of the multiplexer or it may be included as part of the sample-hold or A/D converter following the multiplexer or it may need to be provided separately. Offset and bias-current drifts as well as common-mode effects of the amplifier can also introduce errors. The errors introduced by the buffer amplifier are generally less than errors from the multiplexer.

Voltage drift is less of a problem in high-level multiplexers operating with low-gain buffers. Current drift and offset are more important since the bias current flows through the multiplexer and source resistance.

Typically, using an operational amplifier following a multiplexer driven by a 10k ohm source can produce a static offset of 5 mV and a temperature variation of 1 mv due to the current drift. One technique involves grounding the input of one channel which is used as a reference.

Measurements of this channel are then subtracted from each of the other channels to provide corrected readings. This compensates for drift in the amplifier as well as A/D converter zero-drift and multiplexer leakage errors. It is most useful in measuring low-level signals.

## Settling Time

The output bus of a multiplexer will have a capacitance to ground and when switched to another channel, the output voltage will not change as fast as the source voltage. There are wide variations depending on construction. Large-area, low-on-resistance FETs have higher capacitances.

Stray capacitance depends to a large extent on the physical layout. It is typically about 15 pF. The input capacitance of the buffer amplifier is usually about 5 to 10 pF. For an 8-channel multiplexer, the bus capacitance is typically 35 to 65 pF. This provides a time constant of 18 to 34 ns with $R = 500$ ohms. The settling time to 0.01 percent full scale is 165 to 310 ms.

This time depends on the number of channels connected to the common bus. For a large numbers of channels, submultiplexing can be used since it will decrease the output bus capacitance and restrain the settling time.

The output buffer amplifier needs to be fast enough so it does not affect the settling time. Wideband amplifiers with fast settling times are used for high-speed multiplexing. When settling time is not important, a rough estimate can be made from the slew rate and bandwidth of the operational amplifier.

## Charge Coupling

Each time a channel is switched in a multiplexer, some of the switch-control signal is coupled inductively and capacitively into the analog signal path. In FET multiplexers, the coupling is due to the gate-drain and gate-source capacitance of the FET switches. Every time a switch is operated a quantity of charge is injected into the bus.

This charge is dissipated through the switch on-resistance and the source resistance. If the source resistance is low, the charge injection will produce a spike on the output bus each time a switch operates. At high sample rates, charge is pumped into the line capacitance more rapidly than it can leak away. This produces an offset voltage in series with the signal source. This pumpback limits the sampling rate in high-speed systems. For high sampling rates, low-capacitance, medium on-resistance switches will minimize pumpback errors.

## Crosstalk

This is a measure of the coupling between the off channels and the conducting channel of a multiplexer. It depends on the cable and circuit layout used for the multiplexer as well as the switch on/off impedance. Crosstalk is measured by applying a voltage of known magnitude and frequency at one or more of the off channels of a multiplexer and measuring the output voltage on the bus or at a source with an internal resistance, usually 1k ohm. Crosstalk can be measured at both dc and ac (usually 1 kHz) and depends on the source resistance.

In addition to analog settling delays, there are also propagation and risetime delays associated with the logic switching elements. Turn-on and turn-off times of switches are measured on each channel with full-scale input voltage. Turn-on time is the delay from application of channel address to 90 percent output voltage appearing on the bus, and turn-off time is the delay from removal of channel address to 10 percent output voltage on the bus.

## High Noise Techniques

When multiplexers are operated under conditions of high common-mode interference, guarded two-wire differential or flying-capacitor multiplexers may be used. Normal mode interference techniques include filtering, averaging, and integrating.

The use of low-pass filters on the channel inputs can be used to reduce normal-mode interference. The filters can increase settling time and pumpback effects, but these are usually small. It is possible to place the filter after the multiplexer, but this is not usually done, since each channel has to charge the filter and this greatly increases the settling time. In a differential system, the filters should have balanced impedances in both inputs or be connected differentially.

If passive filtering of each channel is not practical, an integrating A/D converter can be used to provide high normal-mode rejection. This works well at frequencies which have periods that are integral submultiples of the integration interval. The rejection occurs with a conversion time that is much shorter than the settling time of the filter that would be required to provide the same rejection. A rejection level of normal-mode interference of 40 to 70 dB can be achieved with an integrating converter. Many integrating converters use floating guarded input operation and provide both common and normal mode rejection.

If the storage in the PC system is used, the converter can be used to track the variations in input signal due to interference and software may be used to reduce the effects of interference. Multiple samples are collected on each channel and the results summed and averaged. The signal/noise ratio improves as the square-root of the number of samples, provided that sampling and interfering frequencies are uncorrelated.

## Sample-Holds

These devices have a signal input and output, along with a control input. Sample-holds usually have unit gain and are noninverting. The control inputs are logic levels. A logic 1 is usually the sample command and logic 0 the hold command. These are the two operating modes.

In the sample or tracking mode, the device acquires the input signal as rapidly as it can and tracks it until commanded to hold. Sample-holds are known as track-holds when they spend a larger portion of the time in the sample mode, tracking the input. In the hold mode, the device retains the last value of input signal that it had when the control signal initiated the hold mode.

In data-acquisition systems, sample-holds are used to freeze fast-changing signals. A typical application involves storing multiplexer outputs for conversion while the multiplexer is seeking the next signal to be converted. They are used in data reduction applications since they can determine peaks or lows and collect signals at different instants of time.

## Sample-Hold Elements

Two types of storage elements can be used in sample-holds. The conventional device uses a capacitor for storage. The other technique involves digital storage with an A/D converter, storage registers, and output through a D/A converter. This technique allows an essentially infinite hold time.

A basic circuit is the open-loop follower of Fig. 7.8a. In this circuit, the switch is closed and the capacitor charges exponentially to the input voltage. The amplifier's output closely follows the capacitor's voltage. When the switch is opened, the charge remains on the capacitor.

The acquisition time depends on the series resistance and the current available to charge the capacitance. After the charge is acquired to the desired accuracy, the switch can be opened (even though the amplifier has not yet settled) without affecting the final output value or the settling time. This can be done only when the amplifier's input stage draws negligible current.

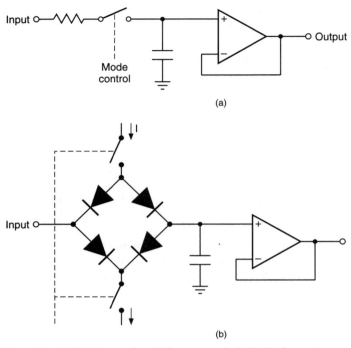

**Figure 7.8**  (a) Basic open-loop follower sample-hold; (b) Current source sample-hold.

The switch is usually a field effect transistor (FET) and the amplifier has an FET input. In this circuit, the capacitor loads the input source, which can cause oscillations and reduce the charging current.

An input follower can be added to isolate the source. Most commercial devices use this type of circuit. For faster charging, a diode bridge can be used as a current source as shown in Fig. 7.8b.

Sample-hold considerations include the following:

1. Input signal range
2. Slewing rate of the signal
3. Acquisition time
4. Accuracy, gain, linearity, and offset errors
5. Aperture delay, jitter
6. Amount of droop allowable in hold
7. Effects of time, temperature, and power supply variations
8. Offset errors due to the sample-hold's input bias current through the multiplex switch and sources

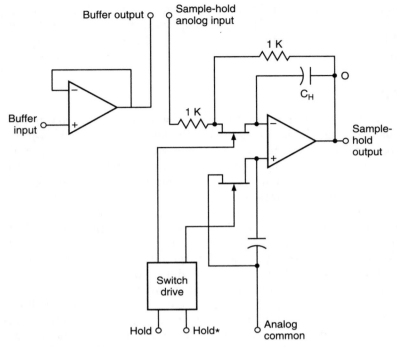

**Figure 7.9**    SHC803 sample-hold.

## SHC803 Sample-Hold

The Burr Brown SHC803 (Fig. 7.9) is a high-speed sample-hold ampli-fier designed for fast 12-bit data acquisition systems and signal process-ing systems. The device has a fast-settling unity-gain amplifier for buffering high impedance sources or for use with CMOS multiplexers. It can handle a 10-V signal change in less than 350 ns to ±½ LSB at 12 bits.

These sample holds can be used with Burr Brown's 12-bit analog-to-digital converter, the ADC803, for digitizing signals at sample rates up to 500k samples per second.

The digital inputs, HOLD and HOLD∗, are TTL-compatible. The device comes in a 24-pin dual-in-line package and is pin-compatible with other sample holds on the market with similar performance char-acteristics.

### Buffer Amplifier

The buffer amplifier built into the device provides the drive to the sam-ple hold amplifier. A 20- to 50-pF capacitor added to the output of the buffer amplifier can improve the charge offset performance.

The buffer amplifier is designed for fast settling with 10 $V_{p-p}$ signals. If input signals greater than 10V are used, a protection network should be used to prevent the buffer from overloads which result in long settling times.

## Control Signals

A TTL logic 0 at pin 11 or a logic 1 at pin 12 switches the device into the sample or tracking mode. In this mode, the device acts as a unity-gain inverting amplifier with the output following the inverse of the input. A logic one at pin 11 or a logic zero at pin 12 will switch the device into the hold mode. The output will be held constant at the value present when the hold command was issued. If pin 11 is used, pin 12 is connected to DCOM (pin 10). If pin 12 is used, pin 11 is tied to $V_{DD}$.

Use of the HOLD and HOLD∗ inputs for logic functions can affect the charge offset known as the pedestal. A digital signal with no ringing or overshoot at these inputs will charge offset errors. Pins 11 and 12 present about two LSTTL loads to the digital drive circuit.

If a sample hold has acquired an input signal and is tracking it, the sample hold can be commanded to hold at any instant. There is a short delay between the time the hold command takes place and the time the circuit actually holds. This delay is called *aperture delay*. The hold command signal can usually be advanced in time to cause the amplifier to hold earlier.

The throughput nonlinearity error is specified to be within ±½ LSB for 12-bit systems. There is a 25-psec maximum aperture uncertainty which allows sampling to 0.01 percent of full-scale range for signals with rates of change of up to 100 V/sec.

## Loading and Grounding

The output of the device is subject to possible oscillations. The maximum capacitive load to avoid oscillations is about 300 pF. Acquisition and sample-to-hold settling times are relatively unaffected by resistive loads down to 250 ohms in parallel with capacitive loads of up to 100 pF. Higher capacitances affect the acquisition and settling times.

There are four COMMON pins (10, 15, 21, and 23) which must be tied together and connected to the system analog common (V COM) as close to the package as possible. It is best to have a large ground plane surrounding the sample hold with the four common pins soldered directly to it. The metal case is internally connected to pin 23, so a ground loop can exist if the case is allowed to contact the ground plane.

Most of the digital return current passes through pin 10. Noise from the switch-drive circuit can get into the main op amp summing junction, which is a very noise-sensitive node. There should be little or no voltage differences between pin 10 and the other common pins. So pin 10 needs to be directly connected to the ground plane.

The logic supply also needs to be free of noise. The +V supply lines, pins 24 and 22, are internally bypassed to common with 0.01 microfarad capacitors. Additional external 0.1 to 1 microfarad tantalum bypass capacitors should be installed at each supply pin.

The output impedance of the signal source driving the device will affect the accuracy of the sample and hold operation both statically (DC) and dynamically. A small capacitor at the driving source can help to improve the charge offset errors that are affected by dynamic source impedance.

Digitizing errors result if the analog signal being digitized changes excessively during conversion. To ensure the accuracy of the output data, the analog input signal to the A/D converter should not change more than ½ LSB during the conversion. The maximum rate of change for ±10-volt sine wave inputs corresponds to a frequency of 26 Hz.

If a sample hold is used in front of the A/D converter, it freezes the converter's input signal when it is necessary to make a conversion and the rate-of-change limitation discussed above no longer exists.

## Errors

In the ideal sample hold, tracking is error-free, and the acquisition and release are instantaneous. The settling time is zero and the hold time is infinite since there is no leakage. Commercial units are rated in terms of the extent to which they differ from the ideal.

During the sample state an offset can be defined for a zero input as the extent to which the output deviates from zero. The nonlinearity is the amount by which a plot of output versus input deviates from a straight line. Scale factor error is the amount by which the output deviates from a specified gain, usually unity. Settling time is the time needed for the output to attain its final value. The aperture time is the time between the command to hold and the actual opening of the hold switch.

The sample-to-hold offset is a step error occurring at the start of the hold mode. It is due to the flow of charge into the storage capacitor from other circuit capacitance. Some of this comes from the capacitance of the switch.

During the hold period there is droop. This is a drifting of the output from the flow of current through the storage capacitor. Sample holds that use digital storage have no droop.

Feedthrough is that fraction of input signal that appears at the output in hold. Most of this is due to capacitance across the switch. There is also some error due to dielectric absorption. This is the tendency of charges in a capacitor to redistribute themselves over a period of time, resulting in a different voltage level. This change is less than 0.01 percent for polystyrene and teflon capacitors and can be as large as several percent for ceramic and mylar capacitors.

In the hold-to-sample state the acquisition time is the time duration that an input must be applied for sampling at the desired accuracy. There are transients or spikes that occur between the sample command and the final settling. These are not important for large changes, but become important when the spikes are large compared to the actual change. The acquisition time can include the settling time of the output amplifier. It is possible for the signal to be acquired and the circuit switched to hold before the output has settled.

## Error Sources

Errors may be due to the physical interconnections, grounding, power supplies, and protection circuitry. Many errors are due to the nonideal nature of the components and the interaction of these components. Errors due to the nonideal nature of the components can be determined from the specifications of the components. Interaction errors come from the parasitic interactions that are a function of the interconnections. These are affected by grounding and shielding methods and contact resistance.

Some offsets may be a result of series impedances in the signal path. These impedances might come from signal sources or multiplexer switch impedances.

If the system can tolerate a constant fractional error of 1 percent or less, logarithmic data compression may be useful. Medium accuracy in a fixed ratio is substituted for extreme accuracy over the complete full-scale range. This can be handled by using a PC for processing the data.

The wide use of modular interface boards for PC interfaces requires some consideration of their design. Many of these use jumpers, which allows the user to select one of several ranges by selecting the appropriate jumper connection. Many boards allow these modifications by connecting external resistors. The gain and offset temperature coefficients of these resistors can be a source of error.

## Common-Mode Errors

To reduce common-mode errors, a differential amplifier can be used to eliminate ground-potential differences. As discussed earlier, the signal source may be a remote transducer. The common-mode signal is the potential difference between the ground signal at the interface board and the ground signal at the transducer, plus any common-mode noise produced at the transducer and voltages developed by the unbalanced impedances of the two lines.

The amount of dc common-mode offset that is rejected depends on the CMRR of the amplifier. Bias currents flowing through the signal source leads may cause offsets if either the bias currents or the source impedances are unbalanced. CMRR specifications may include a specified amount of source unbalance.

The specifications may also indicate an upper frequency for which CMRR is valid. At higher frequencies with unbalanced conditions the series resistance, shunt capacitance, and the amplifier's internal unbalances reduce coefficients, and operating temperature range.

A relaxation of specifications of the first type can be achieved with the use of signal conditioning. The type of signal conditioning used depends on the input signals and the form of the information to be extracted from them. Unwanted signal components can be extracted from the input signals. A differential instrumentation amplifier may be used to reject common-mode signals, bias out dc offsets, and to scale the input.

A relaxation of time-dependent specifications can be achieved by adding a sample-hold amplifier to the system. The use of a sample-hold amplifier can increase the system throughput rate and increase the highest-frequency signal that can be encoded for the converter resolution. The system throughput rate, without the sample-hold, is determined mainly by the multiplexer's settling time and the A/D conversion time. Multiplexer settling time is the time required for the analog signal to settle to within its error budget, as measured at the input to the converter. In a 12-bit system, with a +10-V range, the multiplexer units typically settle within 1 µs.

A relaxation of the errors due to environment-related specifications can be achieved by allotting one multiplexer channel to carry a ground-level signal, and the other to carry a precision reference-voltage level that is close to full-scale. The data from these channels is used to correct gain and offset variations common to all the channels.

## The PC Interface

Many data acquisition boards are available as plug-ins for PCs. A key part of configuring the PC interface for a data acquisition application is to define the objectives as completely as possible. Consider all of the objectives and try to anticipate any unknowns. Try to include such factors as signal and noise levels, desired accuracy, throughput rate, characteristics of the interfaces, environmental conditions, size, and cost limitations.

Some of these may force performance compromises or the consideration of a different approach. Considering the different types of analog interface boards on the market and the complex manner in which some specifications may relate to a system application, selecting and properly utilizing the optimum board for an application is not an easy task.

It is essential to have an understanding of what the manufacturer means by the specifications. Product information must be interpreted in terms meaningful to the user's requirements, which requires a knowledge of how the terms are defined.

The analog interface involves the following questions:

1. What are the objectives of the system and how do they relate to the specifications?

2. How can the system may be adjusted or modified to relax the performance requirements?

3. How do the system components limit and degrade performance?

The major considerations for a control and measurement system may include the input and output signal ranges, data throughput rate, the error allowed for each functional block, environmental conditions, supply voltages, recalibration intervals, and other operational requirements. Special environmental conditions may also exist such as RF fields, shock, and vibration.

## A Typical Data-Acquisition Application

A data-acquisition system might be needed to process data from several strain gauges. Signal-conditioning hardware can usually be purchased with the gauges. The conditioned signals are ±10 V full-scale with a 10-ohm source impedance. It is desired that the signal channels be sequentially scanned in no more than 50 microseconds per channel. The maximum allowable error of the system is to be 0.1 percent of full scale. System logic levels are to be TTL and the output is needed in either binary or two's complement code in parallel format. The temperature range is +25 to +55°C.

A technique that usually works is to select each component to perform 10 times better than the overall desired performance. For a system that requires 0.1 percent performance, use a 0.01 percent converter (12 bits) with a compatible multiplexer and sample hold. An A/D Converter that completes a conversion in 35 to 45 microseconds is acceptable. Since the sample hold will probably add about 5 microseconds of settling time, the combination should be capable of meeting the 50 microsecond/channel scanning requirement.

Since the multiplexer will scan sequentially, its settling time is not critical. The multiplexer can be switched to the next address as soon as the sample hold goes into hold on data from the current address. It has 35 to 45 microseconds to settle before a measurement is called for.

An error analysis could consider the details of errors to determine if the worst-case situation is within the allowable 0.1 percent system error. In the multiplexer, if the switches are MOSFETs, with variable resistance channels, they will not be subject to voltage-offset errors. The errors will tend to be due to two factors. First, there is a leakage current into the on channel from the off channels. This can develop an offset voltage across the source impedance. There is also an error due to the voltage division between the MOSFET on resistance and input impedance of the sample hold.

An analysis can be used to prepare a system timing diagram and assign settling time allowances. But, if there is adequate settling time, a formal timing analysis is not needed.

For the A/D Converter the linearity error, which is the relative accuracy, is ½ LSB, or 0.0125 percent. This is also the quantizing uncertainty. It is a resolution limitation and is not usually considered as part of the error budget. If the temperature error is less than ½ LSB, the 12-bit monotonicity can be maintained with no missing codes.

The worse-case arithmetic sum of these errors can be calculated as well as the rms sum. If these values are less than 0.1 of the desired error of 0.1 percent, then the system is acceptable. The component specifications can be relaxed if hardware cost is an important factor.

Other sensors can be interfaced using the analog input channel of an I/O interface expansion board.

## Analog and Digital I/O Interface Boards

A typical analog/digital I/O expansion board plugs into an XT (8-bit) or AT (16-bit) expansion connector for data acquisition and control applications. It combines in a single board most of the features needed for data-acquisition systems. These include plotting and storing graphs in real time, analysis, transducer linearization, and graphical calibration and set-up procedures. A single BASIC CALL statement accesses all analog and digital I/O. Other features can include analog-input-switchable filters, switch-selectable-transducer interfaces, adjustable voltage references, and constant current sources.

Each port can usually be as an input or output. Electromechanical relay boards and solid-state I/O module boards can use these ports to monitor and control AC and DC loads. An external interrupt control allows the user to select any of the standard interrupt levels for programmed interrupt routines. This allows background data acquisition and interrupt control.

Some channels of the A/D converter may be equipped with instrumentation amplifiers by plugging them into sockets provided on the board and selecting the desired gains by switches. The instrumentation amplifiers can be used to provide gain scaling for resistance bridge transducers such as load cells and strain gauges. The input current is usually less than 10 nA with an average close to 2 nA at 25°C. The common mode range is usually from −3 V to +4 V. The common mode rejection can be greater than 90 dB.

If the input signals are noisy, additional attenuation at 60 Hz may be needed. This can be switched into each channel filter on some boards. This mechanism engages a single-pole RC filter. The filter time constant can introduce a settling time penalty of up to a second for a full-scale step input.

If an integrating dual-slope A/D converter is used, the resolution is usually 12 bits plus sign and the conversion rate will be at least 30 conversions/second. Digital I/O is often via the PB and PC ports of an 8255 programmable peripheral interface.

Some boards also contain a battery backed-up real time clock/calendar. The clock can also provide reference pulses of 1 second, 1 minute, or 1 hour intervals or output a frequency of 1024 Hz which can be used as a source for interrupts or external timing applications.

### Addressing

A typical board requires 16 consecutive address locations in I/O space. Some I/O address locations will be occupied by internal I/O and other peripheral cards. The I/O address may be set by a Base Address DIP switch. It can be anywhere in the PC decoded I/O space. A good choice is to put base address at Hexidecimal &H300, &H310, or &H320 (Decimal 768, 784, 800). Usually, the software will prompt you for the address in decimal or hex format. The program will round the address to the nearest 16-bit boundary and check for possible conflicts with installed I/O devices.

There are also utility programs for installation, graphics, and polynomial approximations that can be used to linearize transducers, graphic calibration, and set-up procedures. A graphics package allows the user plot predicted versus actual measured data from an experiment in real time and store the graph for retrieval at a later date.

The following modes of operation are typical using the 8255:

1. Free scan of all analog inputs

2. Conversion on one analog input, data transferred when finished

3. Conversion on all analog inputs, data transferred when finished

4. Conversion on all analog inputs, initiated by interrupt, data transferred when finished

5. Terminates interrupt processing, initiated by modes 3 and 5

6. Free Scan of all analog inputs, data collected on interrupt

7. Collect data after an interrupt using mode 3 or 5

8. Single-channel analog output

9. Output data to both analog output channels

10. Digital I/O on 8-bit PB output port and 4-bit PC port

11. Enable/disable clock output pulse

## Resistance Sensor Boards

There are also analog input boards for most variable resistance sensors. They can be used for the measurements of temperature sensors which are operated in a current excitation mode or in standard bridge configurations. Sensors accommodated include 2-, 3-, or 4-wire RTDs, thermistors, strain gauges, variable potentiometer devices, and others. Some are designed with cold-junction compensation for thermocouple measurements.

These boards can accept several input sensors and multiplex these into a single A/D board channel. The channel is usually selected by digital control lines which are provided as outputs from a host A/D board. Each input channel will have its own differential input amplifier with jumper-selectable input gains. Also included for each input channel is a precision current source for current excited measurements and a jumper-selectable precision reference voltage for voltage-excited sensors.

These boards often provide thermocouple cold-junction compensation (CJC) circuitry that measures the actual input terminal temperature, and allows the linearization software to subtract out the CJ error. When used for bridge measurements, the board allows the bridge completion resistors to be mounted on or off the board. Two user-installed resistors can be set to form one half the bridge. A relay and calibration resistor allow shunt calibration.

The following settling times are typical:

| Gain | Settling time | Gain temperature coefficient |
|------|---------------|------------------------------|
| 250  | 350 µs        | 20 ppm max.                  |
| 10   | 35 µs         | 15 ppm max.                  |
| 1    | 3.5 µs        | 10 ppm max.                  |

## Expansion Multiplexers

These boards allow the expansion of any analog input to 4 channels. They can supply cold-junction compensation for thermocouple inputs and shunt terminals are provided for current measurements.

An expansion multiplexer allows isolated inputs to be connected to an analog input board. The board will use digital output bits from the A/D converter board to select which board is to be monitored, and which channel is to be enabled. Each input is isolated from all other inputs and from the A/D converter board. Each input includes an instrumentation amplifier that can be set for input gains with a user-installed resistor.

The multiplexer is controlled by four digital output bits from the master A/D board. Each multiplexer has an address-selection switch. To allow expansion capability, the most significant 2 bits of the digital control lines are used as an enable control. This allows up to four boards to be connected to the same A/D input channel (one will be enabled while the other three will be disabled). The two least significant bits are used to control which channel is enabled.

A problem can occur when monitoring thermocouples. For accurate thermocouple measurement it is necessary to know the temperature of the connection of the thermocouple wire to the input terminal. This cold-junction temperature error is then compensated for with software. However, each cold-junction temperature measurement device requires an A/D input channel. If each MUX is also monitoring the cold-junction temperature, then some of the available input channels are taken, and the maximum number of thermocouples that can be monitored is reduced. If all boards are at approximately the same temperature, then the cold-junction monitoring device can be connected on one bank with only a slight loss of accuracy.

## Analog-to-Digital Board Specifications

The following factors are important in selecting the right A/D board for a particular application:

1. Number of input channels

2. Input scan rate in samples per second

3. Resolution or accuracy, usually referred to in bits of resolution

4. Input range specified in full-scale volts

5. Single-ended or differential inputs

6. Signal conditioning available

7. Other features such as D/A channels, digital I/O, and counter/timers

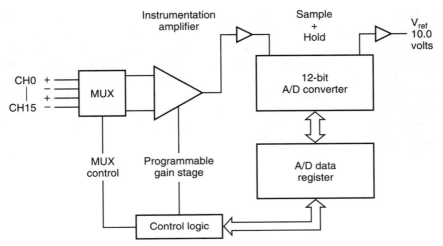

**Figure 7.10**  Typical A/D input stage for multichannel analog input board.

## A/D Sample Rate

Most suppliers specify the maximum sample rate as total board throughput. However, multichannel analog input boards typically use a single A/D converter and an input multiplexer. This circuit configuration is shown in Fig. 7.10.

When a single channel is being sampled, the maximum throughput applies. If more than one channel is being sampled, the maximum sample rate per channel can be found by dividing the maximum A/D board sample rate by the number of channels sampled.

The input resolution of a data acquisition system is usually specified in bits. The resolution is 2 raised to the number of bits used. So, a 12-bit A/D converter has a resolution of one part in $2^{12}$, or 4096. The input resolution in volts is equal to the full-scale input range divided by the number of parts of resolution. Thus, a 12-bit A/D converter, with a –5 to +5 volt input range has an input resolution of $10_{12}$ (Volts Full Scale)/$2^{12}$ = 0.00244 volts. This means that 2.44 mV is the smallest input voltage change that the system can detect.

Many A/D systems have a built-in input gain. To find the overall minimum detectable input voltage, divide the voltage resolution found above by the gain.

## 4–20 Milliamp Systems

A common current input signal is 4–20 mA. The 4–20-mA loop is often used in process monitoring because of its high noise immunity. A shunt resistor can be used to connect a 4–20-mA loop to a 0–5- or +5-volt input. The shunt resister in this case will be 5 V/20 mA or 250 ohms.

This means a 250-ohm shunt can be connected across the 4–20-mA input to convert it into a 1–5-volt input. Precision resistors should be used since the accuracy of the conversion is directly related to the resistance accuracy. Many terminal accessory boxes and system expansion multiplexers are designed for the installation of shunt resistors. Signal conditioning modules for monitoring 0–20- and 4–20-mA inputs are also available.

# 8

# Interface Scheduling Techniques

Interlocked with the design of the interface is the scheduling method of handling the input/output communications. Just as the input/output device is physically connected to the system using the interface, a communication procedure must be established between the device and the microprocessor.

The three basic scheduling techniques used for controlling the input/output devices and synchronizing the data transfers are as follows:

1. Polling or program-control

2. Interrupt-control

3. Direct-memory-access control

The one that is used in the microcomputer system depends on three factors: the rate that the data is to be transmitted, the time delays between the I/O device, and the actual data transfer and the feasibility of overlapping or interleaving I/O operations.

The polling or programmed I/O technique is the simplest to implement. The I/O devices are connected to the system bus with some connections to the control lines. The basic principle is to implement a procedure in hardware or software for determining which input/output device requires service. The polling technique is synchronous in nature as the microprocessor periodically questions each device if it requires service. Each device then answers with a yes or no. If a no is received, the microprocessor will advance to the next device and question it. In this way the microprocessor checks each I/O device successively to determine if service is required.

In practice, a status bit or flag is tested in the device or the interface. If the test is true, an action is initiated. This typically is the transfer of some data to or from the I/O device.

The actual polling procedure used may take the form of a polling loop. The process of checking the device and receiving an answer in return is a type of handshaking. It sets the communications protocol between one device and the next one in the link. In a typical polling loop, a status bit is checked to test if the device is ready to accept data. Before reading data from the device, a status bit is checked to see if the word is complete. Using program-controlled I/O, the input/output instructions are used to initiate and control the transfers of data.

The basic types of information transferred are the control data and the message data which are transmitted between the microprocessor and the I/O device. The control data synchronizes the I/O device before the message data is transmitted. The control data includes the device-status and the device commands. The status describes what the I/O device is doing. Each status bit can indicate a certain condition, such as:

1. Message data ready for transmission

2. Device busy

3. Transmission error

A command word can be used to control the device operation using command bits (for example, to stop an operation or change a transmission rate).

I/O program instructions can be organized in various ways. A unique instruction can be used for each type of I/O data transfer. This could result in four instructions:

```
READ THE INPUT MESSAGE.
WRITE THE OUTPUT MESSAGE.
SEND THE OUTPUT COMMAND.
ACCEPT THE INPUT STATUS.
```

The message and control data are usually sent or received through one of the registers. Some microprocessors use special registers for the control data while others use a status register. With the use of a status register, any conditional branch instructions may check the status register's individual bits directly.

The control data may synchronize the data transfer using the following steps:

1. Write the command word to the device.

2. Read the status word from the device.

3. Test the status bits. (This allows the message data to be transferred to the device.)

If the device is not ready for the transfers, the first two steps are repeated. Eventually the message data is ready or written, which resets the status of the device.

If the data transfer originates from the I/O device itself, the device signals its need to transfer data by setting the correct status bits.

In a basic polling program, the status check is repeated continuously until the device is ready. This loop tends to stall the program execution and take up processing time. To overcome this, the status check can be interleaved with other operations.

In a polling microcomputer the asynchronous inputs are detected by an instruction which checks if the input has occurred. The sequence of instructions in the polling loop tests the various input lines at a rate which will provide the desired system response time.

This poll of the inputs take place at a time which allows the processing task associated with the input to be accomplished. The polled input may use a latch or flip-flop for each input which will recognize and retain the presence of an input.

If an input latch is not used, the polling must be fast enough to detect the input change. The instructions will test the conditions of these latches or flip-flops, and if they are set, branch to the service program.

Another technique for detecting the presence of an asynchronous input uses an input bus of several bits which is tested by an instruction. The instruction looks at all of the input lines on the bus, and if any one of these lines is a logical one, a status bit is set to a one. Then, a second instruction detects the one and branches.

The major advantage of polling is the simplicity of the hardware and software needed. In applications where the response time is satisfactory, the possibility of programming errors is reduced since the input is serviced when the processor can attend to it.

In a microcomputer system that communicates with several I/O devices, the periodic status checks that must be made on each device can result in considerable time lags for some devices since they indicate when they are ready to transfer data and then they wait for the actual transfer.

In some microcomputer systems, the time spent checking the device status may be reduced with a common test line, which signals when a device needs attention. The microprocessor can periodically check the status of this line without having to poll the individual devices until one of them signals for service. Then, a polling loop is used to find which device requested service.

Polling takes minimal hardware since usually no special lines are required. It is also synchronous with the program execution, so it is easy to find when a device is being interrogated and how long it takes to service it. No events may occur, which tends to disrupt the scheduled polling sequence. In contrast, interrupts and DMA are asynchronous and cannot be predicted.

The major disadvantage of polling is the software overhead since each time the polling loop is entered, the devices must be checked (either with a common test line or individually). Most of the time they may not require service. To guarantee that each device is checked a certain time loop must be executed, even though it is not always required. This waste of processor time often leads to the use of one of the other techniques. In applications where this use of microprocessor time is not critical, polling is the simplest technique to implement. The knowledge of the order in which devices are polled can be a major advantage in programming some applications.

## Interrupts

In applications where the polling technique does not provide fast enough response—or uses too much microprocessor time—interrupts should be considered.

An interrupt line is connected to the microprocessor, and each of the devices is connected to this line. Each one of the devices which may need to get service has the option of using this line to request service. When a device requests service, it generates an interrupt pulse or level on this line. The microprocessor can then sense this change on the line. The microprocessor must accept the interrupt, identify it, and service it. Accepting the interrupt may be done with an internal mask bit called either an *interrupt mask, interrupt inhibit,* or *interrupt-enable.* This bit is normally stored in the flag or status register. After the interrupt is accepted, the microprocessor must then determine which device originated it.

Several devices may generate interrupts simultaneously. When multiple devices are connected to the same interrupt line, priorities must be assigned.

After the interrupt has been accepted and the device identified, the service requested by the device is performed. The microprocessor may suspend the program it was executing and branch to the interrupt routine. The required branching address will need to be available. The software that does this is called the *interrupt routine* or *interrupt.*

The execution of the interrupt routine handler is similar in some ways to that of a polling system. The termination of this routine allows the program which had been suspended by the interrupt to continue its execution. This may require several instructions.

## Interrupt Operation

When the interrupt-controlled I/O device is ready to transfer data, it may break into the main program. The simplest interrupt system uses a single I/O device connected to a single interrupt-request line. A change in the signal on this line causes the microprocessor to jump from the main program to the location in the program memory which holds an interrupt-trap address.

First, the current instruction must be executed, then the current contents of the program counter are stored so the program counter can be loaded with the proper program memory address. When only one I/O device can generate interrupts, its service routine can be loaded into the memory locations starting at an interrupt-trap address. At the completion of the routine, the previously stored contents of the program counter will provide the return address back to the main program. Interrupts are inhibited before the service routine starts, to prevent multiple interruptions by the same interrupt-request.

In some systems, the instruction for the jump back to the main program can also be used to reenable the interrupts. If the interrupts are inhibited by setting a mask bit in the microprocessor's status register, then it may be set or reset by the program. The mask bit can also be used to prevent the interruption of sections of program that are to be executed before the next input/output operations can occur.

Indirect addressing links can be used to allow the service program to be located at an arbitrary position in the program memory. Then, if the interrupt-trap address is in read/write memory, the program entry point may change while the main program is operating to vary the response of the system to the interrupt.

The service program can modify the main program execution if it uses and modifies any registers of the microprocessor. The service program must save and restore the contents of these registers so they will be the same after the interrupt; however, the more registers used this way, the longer the interrupt-response time. A more rapid interrupt response is possible when the microcomputer is designed to handle interrupts. With two sets of internal registers, the main program can use one set while the service program has the other set.

If locations in data memory are used to replace some of the internal registers, then a pointer register can define the memory locations. The system may store and modify the contents of the pointer before executing the service program, thus using a workspace that is separate from that used by the main program. When this service is complete, the pointer register is restored.

If the input/output operation is required to occur at a particular period within an interval, then the operation of the I/O device and the execution of the program controlling the data transfer must be synchronized in real time. To synchronize the I/O device with the program, a real-time clock is connected to the interrupt-request line. The interrupted can then occur periodically. An example of a real-time application, which is timer-driven, is an online data-acquisition system using a processor-controlled multichannel analog-to-digital converter.

A subroutine call such as an input poll is controlled by the program, but an interrupt can occur at any time. More information needs to be saved so that the complete state can be restored after the interrupt is serviced. This results in a higher level of status than that which is saved for a subroutine call or poll. The status which is saved for an interrupt consists of two classes of information. First, there are the results from the execution of the program and condition which are established by the program for use in the future. The first class includes the program counter value, overflow bit, and carry bits. In the second class, the conditions set by the program include interrupt enables, internal timer enable, internal counter enable, and internal flags.

## Multiple Interrupts

The details of the interrupt-servicing procedures discussed so far apply only when a single device is generating interrupts. Most microcomputer systems have more than one source and more than one type of interrupt. The types of interrupts fall into three general classes: external, internal, and simulated. External interrupts are generated from the peripheral devices. Internal interrupts are generated by the microcomputer system to indicate error conditions such as a power failure, system malfunction, or transmission break. Simulated interrupts are generated by the software for interrupt testing and debugging.

The different sources of interrupts can have different service requirements. Some may require immediate attention, while others can wait until the task underway is completed. The interrupt procedure must differentiate between the various sources and determine the order in which the interrupts are serviced when more than one occurs at the same time. Finally, the contents of registers must be saved and restored so the program can continue after the multiple interrupts.

If several interrupt-request lines are used, each can have its own interrupt-trap address. Then, with one source of interrupt assigned to each line, the system can distinguish between internal, external, and simulated interrupts. When several I/O devices use the same interrupt-request line, the interrupt may be recognized either by polling using software or by vectored interrupts using hardware. In the polling technique as we have discussed, the interrupt produces a jump to the service program using the interrupt trap address. The service program will check the status word of each I/O device to determine which one caused the interrupt. The interrupt status bit will indicate if a device has generated an interrupt request as it is checked for each device. The device status word is read into the status register of the microprocessor and if the bit is set, a jump is then made to the service program.

## Vectored Interrupts

A vectored interrupt system allows the microprocessor to recognize the interrupting device since each I/O device is assigned a unique interrupt address. This address then generates an interrupt trap address for the device. The trap addresses are normally located sequentially in the program memory in order to form the interrupt vector. Each location contains the starting address of a device-service program. The contents of the interrupt vector are loaded into the program counter and program control transferred to the correct device-service program.

Some vectored systems do not transmit an address. They use an I/O device to transmit an instruction to the microprocessor after the request has been acknowledged. Next, the system loads the instruction into an instruction register. Normal operation continues after this instruction is executed.

The vectoring is achieved by a jump instruction which derives the jump address from part of the instruction. A unique jump address is defined for each I/O device in the system.

In systems with several sources of interrupt, one or more interrupt request can occur during the servicing of an earlier request. In the simplest way to handle this, the interrupt mask bit is set when the first request is recognized. Then the following requests are placed in a queue, waiting until the service of the first interrupt is complete before they are recognized and serviced.

The order in which the queued interrupts are recognized will determine the individual delay before service. This order, or priority, is set either by software or by hardware using a priority scheme. After recognizing interrupt request, the service program can poll the devices in the desired order. The devices which are polled first will be serviced first.

In systems with hardware priority, the interrupt logic sends an external signal to the request logic in each of the I/O devices. This signal indicates the state of the interrupt mask bit and is passed to each device according to its priority. When the mask is set, the signal prevents any device from generating an interrupt request. If the mask is reset and the device has no interrupt request pending, the signal is passed on to the next device. The interrupt logic in the device will generate the interrupt request and prevent the signal from passing on. If more than one device requires interrupt service, the device receiving the control signal first will be serviced first.

Software and hardware priority schemes may be slow to respond to a high-priority interrupt if it occurs during the servicing of a low-priority interrupt. Individual interrupt mask bits for each interrupt-request line or each I/O device can then be used. By setting and resetting these individual mask bits under software control, the interrupt priorities are changed to fit the needs of the application.

Some microprocessors use one interrupt-request line that has software-controlled mask bits and another line that is permanently enabled. This nonmaskable interrupt request line has the higher priority and is used when service is required immediately.

Some vectored systems use the microprocessor to define and control the priorities. When an interrupt request occurs, it is transferred to the microprocessor and the vectored address is compared with an interrupt-enabling mask. When the vectored address is equal to or less than the mask, the request is recognized. The mask is then set to one less than this address and servicing starts. If the vectored address is greater than the mask, the request is simply queued.

Note that only interrupts issued from a device with an address lower than that of the device being serviced are recognized. The lower the address, the higher the priority.

## Interrupt Types

The types of interrupts include vectored, nonvectored, maskable, and nonmaskable. A maskable interrupt can be turned off by the processor and is used when a software operation cannot be interrupted. In these cases, the processor is instructed to disable the maskable interrupts. There is usually a disable-interrupt instruction in the processor's instruction set to do this. A nonmaskable interrupt cannot be turned off. This type of interrupt is designed for critical events such as a power failure.

When an interrupt occurs, the processor can branch to a location that contains the first instruction of the interrupt-service routine. Another approach is to use a location in memory for the starting address of the service routine. In most newer processors, a single interrupt service routine is not enough. These processors have several memory locations reserved for the addresses of the interrupt service routines.

The hardware selected interrupt scheme uses separate lines for each memory location and its service routine. This is called a *hardware-vectored interrupt*. The processor can use an interrupt acknowledge cycle where the hardware supplies additional information to the processor. This guides the processor to the proper service routine and is called a *software vectored interrupt*.

## 68000 Family Interrupts

A 16-bit processor, like the Motorola MC68000 family, has a more complex interrupt structure than an 8-bit processor. The MC68000 has three interrupt-input lines. These are not separate interrupt inputs; they use an encoded interrupt level. This supports seven active interrupt levels. When all of the interrupt inputs are high, there are no pending interrupt requests. This seven-level interrupt scheme is hardware-driven so it is hardware-vectored.

When a level is indicated on the interrupt lines, the 68000 compares it against the mask level in the status register. If the interrupt request is below the mask level, it is ignored. Interrupt-level 7 cannot be masked. The highest interrupt level is level 7. It has the highest priority. A lower-priority interrupt request cannot interrupt higher-level interrupt service routines. The mask level switches to the level of the interrupt being serviced. The mask is restored when the interrupt service routine returns to the main program using a return from exception (RTE) instruction. The interrupt acknowledge is signaled by a bus cycle with all of the function-code bits set true. Address bits A1–A3 indicate the level of interrupt being acknowledged.

The bus cycle is completed by placing an interrupt vector on the lower eight data bits and setting the data transfer acknowledge (DTACK*) line true. This allows 256 possible interrupt vectors and uses software-interrupt vectoring.

An alternative is to use the Valid Peripheral Address (VPA) input to request the microprocessor to use an autovector. There are seven autovectors in the microprocessor's vector table, one for each interrupt level. When an autovector request is made, the microprocessor selects the proper autovector for the interrupt level being acknowledged and branches to the correct location.

## Interrupt Routines

When an interrupt branch occurs for an I/O request for service, either data is waiting for input or output or there is a problem with the data transfer. The processor is much faster than the peripheral devices, so instead of waiting for the device to get ready for the transfer, interrupts are used.

Most I/O devices use buffers to hold the information to be transferred. When the output buffer becomes empty or the input buffer becomes full, the interrupt service routine signals that the data transfer is complete. The main program will create a buffer and then fill it if it is an output buffer. Next, the interrupts are enabled.

The interrupts may be enabled by the processor, if they are maskable interrupts, or they may be enabled by the I/O chip. In some cases hardware between the I/O chip and the processor may have an interrupt-enable facility.

## High-Level Interrupts

The low- or machine-level interrupts discussed previously are supported by the interrupt circuits built into the processor. When a microcomputer is executing a program written in a high-level language such as BASIC, thousands of machine instructions are being executed and the registers in the processor are changing frequently.

The Microsoft BASIC used in the IBM PC supports user interrupt servicing through its subroutines. The subroutines are invoked with the

GOSUB

(go subroutine) statement, and the main program is returned with

RETURN

The user interrupt service routines are a variation of the subroutine. After the interrupts are enabled, the subroutine is invoked when a peripheral causes an interrupt. The subroutine is written in the high-level language of the computer and is terminated with an interrupt return statement such as RETURN.

If the interface is not busy before interrupts are enabled, the interrupt is immediate. The interrupts must be reenabled in the interrupt service routine if the transfer is not done. This must be done when the enable is canceled as it is invoked. Otherwise, the interrupt service routine could be interrupted.

## Buffering

The high-level language program lines are slow compared to the hardware processing speeds. Only low data transfer rates can be supported using user-interrupt service routines. Buffer transfers are better for data transfers while the user routines can be used for special events.

The buffers are simply blocks of computer memory reserved for I/O. The data goes through the buffer before being sent to or out of the computer. The data transfer can be terminated using a counter or with a character match.

A buffered I/O routine is much simpler. First, a buffer is created. Then you fill the buffer with the contents of a data string and then send the data to the peripheral. The buffer holds the data until the data transfer to the peripheral is initiated. The program goes on to the next line in the program and when the interrupt occurs, the peripheral is given the data.

The interrupt in a high-level language program must occur at the end of a line. During the execution of a line in a high-level language, temporary locations are used and new addresses are calculated. Since the interrupt routine must be able to return to where the program was interrupted after the interrupt is serviced, the only safe place is the end of a line. Two types of interrupt buffers can be used: linear and circular. Linear buffers are good for output operations and circular buffers are best for input tasks. A linear buffer is a block of memory locations designated as a buffer. The processor fills the buffer using programmed I/O and starts the transfer. The interrupt service routine takes characters from the buffer until it is empty. Then the main program is signaled. The buffer may be refilled or the program may go on to another task. Figure 8.1a shows a linear output buffer.

A linear buffer can be used for input if a terminating condition for the input process can be defined. This can be a count or a character. A terminal count sets the number of characters to be received. After this number of characters is placed in the buffer, the input transfer ends and the main program is told that the buffer is full and needs to be read.

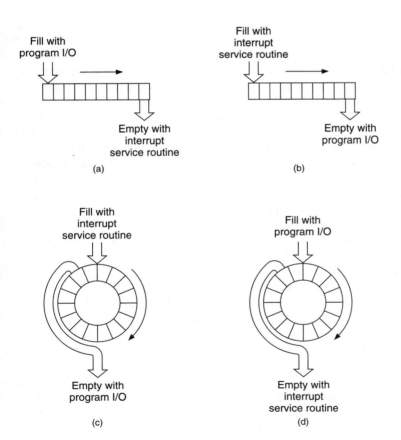

**Figure 8.1**  Types of interrupt buffering: (a) linear output buffering; (b) linear input buffering; (c) circular input buffering; (d) circular output buffering.

When a terminating character is used, the transfer ends on the receipt of that character into the input buffer. When the transfer ends, the buffer must be read before it can be reused. Figure 8.1b shows a linear input buffer.

Circular buffers are better for I/O processes which do not have a set terminating condition. An example is serial asynchronous communications used for a video display. The characters are in a continuous stream and are displayed on the screen as they are received. The process continues until the stream of characters ends. If the program is written in assembly language, interrupts may be used to handle the incoming characters on a character-by-character basis. The time needed to service an interrupt at this level is about 100 microseconds.

If the program has been written in a high-level language, and the interrupt service routines are also in a high-level language, the time required to service each interrupt can take milliseconds. This is because high-level languages that support interrupts allow the interrupt to occur only at the end of a line. This is the only safe way to have an orderly interruption of the program. Since the interrupt-service time is several milliseconds, only low bit rates would be allowed on the asynchronous communications port if the interrupt service routine handles one character at a time.

The use of a circular buffer allows the characters to be brought in with a small machine-level routine which fills the buffer at a fast rate. The high-level program can check with the buffer and handle all the characters in the buffer as a block, which also speeds up the process.

An output process can also use a circular buffer with similar advantages. Figure 8.1c shows a circular input buffer and Fig. 8.1d illustrates a circular output buffer. Circular buffers use the same block of RAM as used by a linear buffer. The difference is the way the programmed I/O and interrupt service routine keep track of their place in the buffer. In both cases, a software counter is used. In a linear buffer, the counter starts at the first address in the buffer and increments or decrements as each character is moved in or out. When the counter reaches the end of the buffer, the fill or empty is over.

The counter in a circular buffer starts at the address which acts as the start of the buffer, and increments or decrements. When the counter reaches the end of the buffer, the counter is reset to the beginning again. If this is to work, the process which empties the buffer must be faster than the process which fills it.

In a circular input buffer, the process used to fill the buffer is an interrupt service routine. An input device interrupts when it has a character ready to be placed in the buffer. This enables the interrupt service routine which takes the character and places it in the next available location in the buffer. The main program will periodically check the status of the buffer to see if it needs to be emptied.

As the characters are placed in the buffer by the interrupt service routine, it needs to be emptied by the main program. This prevents the circular buffer from filling to overflow. Data can be lost as older data in the buffer is replaced by newer data. If two counters are used, one can handle moving the data into the buffer and the other for getting the data out. The counter used for the fill is called a *fill pointer* and the counter used for the empty is called the *empty pointer.*

Circular buffers are often used for servicing keyboards. Other devices which have an unpredictable short-term I/O speed requirement but an average requirement that can always be serviced can use circular-interrupt buffering.

## 8259A Programmable Interrupt Controller

The Intel 8259A is an eight-level priority controller that is expandable to 64 levels. The programmable interrupt modes have an individual request-mask capability. The chip uses a single +5 V supply with no clocks and is available in a 28-pin DIP or 28-lead PLCC package.

The priority modes can be changed or reconfigured dynamically at any time during the main program. This allows the interrupt structure to be defined as required, based on the system environment. Figure 8.2 is a block diagram of this device and Fig. 8.3 shows the interface to the system bus.

## Interrupt Handling

The interrupts at the IR input lines are handled by two registers in cascade. These are called the Interrupt Request Register (IRR) and the In-Service (ISR). The IRR stores the interrupt levels which are requesting service, and the ISR stores the interrupt levels which are being serviced. The logic circuitry determines the priorities of the bits set in the IRR. The highest priority is selected and strobed into the corresponding bit of the ISR during the INTA* pulse. An Interrupt Mask Register (IMR) stores the bits used to mask the interrupt lines. The IMR operates on the IRR. An interrupt acknowledge (INTA*) will force the 8259A to release vectoring information to the data bus. The format of this data depends on the system mode.

A 3-state, bidirectional 8-bit buffer is used to interface the 8259A to the system data bus. Control words and status information are transferred through this buffer. Output commands from the CPU are sent to the Initialization Command Word (ICW) registers and Operation Command Word (OCW) registers hold the control formats for device operation.

A low on the chip select input (CS*) enables the 8259A. No reads or writes can occur unless the device is selected. The WR* (Write) input

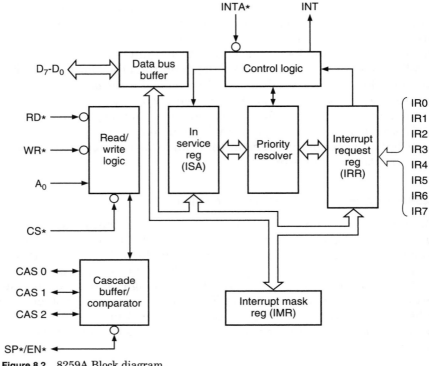

**Figure 8.2**    8259A Block diagram.

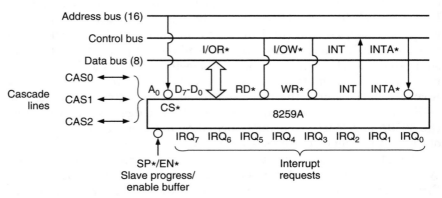

**Figure 8.3**    8259A Interface to system bus.

enables the CPU to write control words to the chip. A low on the RD∗ (read) input allows the 8259A to send the status of the Interrupt Request Register (IRR), In Service Register (ISR), Interrupt Mask Register (IMR), or the Interrupt level to the data bus. $A_0$ is used with the read and write signals to write commands into the command registers and read the status registers.

## Interrupt Sequence

The 8259A addressing capability allows direct or indirect jumps to the interrupt routine requested without polling the interrupting devices. The sequence of events during an interrupt follows:

1. One or more of the INTERRUPT REQUEST lines (IR7-0) go high, setting the corresponding IRR bit(s).

2. The 8259A checks the requests, and sends an INT to the CPU, if needed.

3. The CPU acknowledges the INT and sends an INTA pulse.

4. Upon receiving an INTA from the CPU, the highest-priority ISR bit is set and the corresponding IRR bit is reset. The 8259A does not drive the data bus during this cycle.

5. The microprocessor will initiate a second INTA pulse. During this pulse, the 8259A releases an 8-bit pointer to the data bus where it is read by the microprocessor.

6. This ends the interrupt cycle. In the automatic-end-of-interrupt (AEOI) mode the ISR bit is reset at the end of the INTA pulse. Otherwise, the ISR bit remains set until an appropriate end-of-interrupt (EOI) command is issued at the end of the interrupt subroutine.

If no interrupt request is present at step 4 (the request was too short in duration), the 8259A will issue an interrupt level 7. Both the vectoring bytes and the CAS lines will look like an interrupt level 7 was requested.

When the 8259A PIC receives an interrupt, INT becomes active and an interrupt acknowledge cycle is started. If a higher-priority interrupt occurs between the two INTA pulses, the INT line goes inactive immediately after the second INTA pulse. After some time the INT line is activated again to signify the higher-priority interrupt waiting for service. This inactive time can vary between parts.

## Cascading

The 8259A can be interconnected in a system of one master with up to eight slaves to handle up to 64 priority levels. The master controls the slaves through the three-line cascade bus (see Fig. 8.4). The cascade bus does the chip selecting to the slaves during the INTA sequence. The cascade bus lines are normally low and contain the slave address code.

In a cascaded system, the slave interrupt outputs are connected to the master interrupt request inputs. When a slave request line is activated and acknowledged, the master can enable the slave to release the device routine address.

Each 8259A in the system uses a separate initialization sequence. An end-of-interrupt (EOI) command is issued twice: once for the master and for the corresponding slave. An address decoder is used to activate the Chip Select (CS) input of each 8259A. The cascade lines of the master 8259A are active only for slave inputs; nonslave inputs leave the cascade line inactive (low).

## Cascade Buffer/Comparator

A cascade buffer/comparator is used to store and compare the ID codes of 8259As used in the system. There are three I/O pins (CAS0–2) that are outputs when the 8259A is used as a master and inputs when the 8259A is used as a slave. The master 8259A sends the ID code of the interrupting slave device on the CAS0–2 lines. The selected slave sends the subroutine address to the data bus during the INTA* pulses.

## EISA Application

In the 82351 Local I/O EISA chip the interrupt control logic selects and enables the parallel port, serial channels, keyboard, and mouse interrupts by programming their configuration registers. The keyboard interrupt to the 8259A core of the chip is IRQ01. It is generated from KBFULL of the keyboard controller. IRQ01 is cleared by an I/O read or by a reset.

The mouse interrupt (MSIRQ) is enabled by a configuration register and activated with ABFULL by the keyboard controller. It is deactivated by an I/O read, a reset, or when a bit in the configuration register is written as a zero.

The chip supports two separate serial ports that allow each interrupt source (VARTINTA, VARTINTB) to be assigned to one of the four interrupt outputs (COM1IRQ, COM2IRQ, COM3IRQ, and COM4IRQ). The inputs OUT2A# and OUT2B# provide tristate control to the selected interrupt output in a PC/AT-compatible manner. The parallel port of the system can generate an interrupt on either LPT1IRQ or LPT2IRQ from the ACK number signal. A configuration register controls the interrupt operation mode.

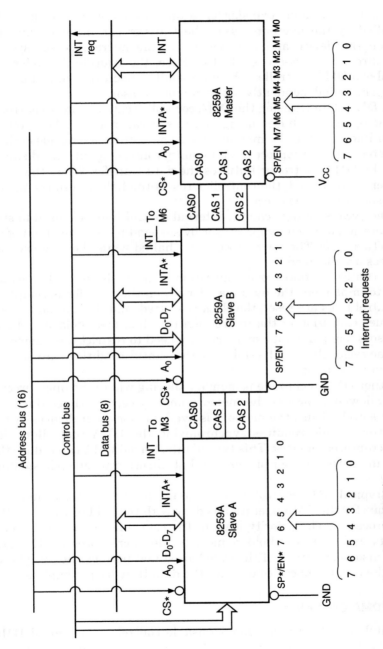

**Figure 8.4** Cascading the 8259A.

341

### Direct-Memory-Access Techniques

When I/O devices must transfer large amounts of data too quickly to be controlled by the microprocessor, the transfer can be made directly between the device and the memory of the microprocessor system using direct-memory-access (DMA). Here, the transfer is under the control of a DMA controller which is usually a dedicated chip or circuit that operates independently of the microprocessor.

In a DMA data transfer, the DMA controller can take over control of the microprocessor buses using one of several methods. An external control line can stop the microprocessor after the current bus cycle is completed. The microprocessor's memory-control signals are disabled while the DMA controller initiates the data transfer. When the DMA transfer is completed, the controller resets the halt line so the microprocessor can resume execution.

In the cycle-stealing scheme, external control lines are used to stop the operation of the microprocessor by suspending the execution of an instruction cycle. The microprocessor is halted while the memory control lines are disabled.

The controller takes over operation and steals several machine cycles to implement the data transfer. When the transfer is complete, the control lines are reset, the clock is started, and the microprocessor continues execution of the instruction that had been delayed. Microprocessors using dynamic memory may need to restrict the number of machine cycles that can be stolen, so that status conditions are not lost between refreshing.

Another DMA technique is memory sharing where the microprocessor is allowed to access the memory only at certain times during a machine cycle. Thus, the memory is available for other devices at the other times. This requires synchronizing the DMA controller with the microprocessor clock. This type of interleaved DMA can reduce the delays in microprocessor processing that can occur when cycle stealing is used.

In a typical DMA controller chip like the Intel 8257, the acquisition of the bus for the DMA operation is done with the hold function for the microprocessor. The priority logic in the controller is used to resolve conflicts and issue the hold request to the microprocessor. The controller also keeps track of the cycles used and notifies the peripheral when the number of cycles used for the data transfer is complete.

### 8237A DMA Controller

The Intel 8237A provides enable/disable control of individual DMA requests for four independent DMA channels with independent autoinitialization of all channels. It allows transfers up to 1.6 Mbytes/

second with the 5-MHz version and is directly expandable to any number of channels. The controller comes in a 40-lead Cerdip or plastic package.

The 8237A peripheral interface circuit is designed to improve system performance by allowing external devices to directly transfer information from the system memory. Memory-to-memory transfer capability is also provided.

The 8237A is used with an external 8-bit address latch. The channels are expanded by cascading additional controller chips (Fig. 8.5). There are three basic transfer modes.

### Registers

The 8237A has 344 bits of internal memory in its registers as shown in the following:

4 Base address registers of 16 bits each

4 Base word count registers of 16 bits each

4 Current Address registers of 16 bits each

4 Current Word Count registers of 16 bits each

1 Temporary Address register of 16 bits

1 Temporary Word Count register of 16 bits

1 Status register of 8 bits

1 Command register of 8 bits

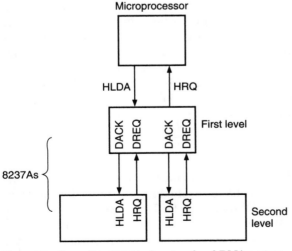

**Figure 8.5**   Cascading 8237As in a two-level DMA system.

1 Temporary register of 8 bits

4 Mode registers of 6 bits each

1 Mask register of 4 bits

1 Request register of 4 bits

### Base Address and Word Count Registers

Each channel has a pair of Base Address and Base Word Count registers. These 16-bit registers hold the original value of their associated current registers. During autoinitialize these values are used to restore the current registers to their original values.

The base registers are written simultaneously with their corresponding current register in 8-bit bytes in the Program Condition by the microprocessor. These registers cannot be read by the microprocessor.

### Current Word and Address Registers

Each channel has a 16-bit Current Address register. This register holds the value of the address used during DMA transfers. The address is automatically incremented or decremented after each transfer. The intermediate values of the address are stored in the Current Address register during the transfer. This register is written or read by the microprocessor in successive 8-bit bytes. It can also be reinitialized by an Autoinitialize back to its original value. Autoinitialize takes place only after an EOP occurs.

Each channel also has a 16-bit Current Word Counter register. This register sets the number of transfers to take place. The actual number of transfers is one more than the number programmed in the Current Word Count register. The count is decremented after each transfer and the intermediate value of the word count is stored in the register during the transfer. When the value in the register counts out, a TC will be generated. This register is loaded or read in successive 8-bit bytes by the microprocessor in the Program Condition. At the end of a DMA it can be reinitialized by Autoinitialization after an EOP occurs.

### Other Registers

The status register holds information about the status of the devices. This includes the channels that have reached a terminal count and the channels that have pending DMA requests. Bits 0 through 3 are set when a TC or external EOP* occurs. These bits are cleared with a Reset and by each Status Read. Bits 4 through 7 are set when their channel is requesting service.

The 8-bit Command register controls the operation of the chip. It is programmed by the microprocessor in the Program Condition and is cleared by Reset or a Master Clear instruction.

The temporary register holds data during memory-to-memory transfers. At the completion of the transfers, the last word moved can be read by the microprocessor in the Program Condition. The temporary register holds the last byte transferred in the previous memory-to-memory operation, unless it is cleared by a Reset.

Each channel has a 6-bit Mode register associated with it. When the register is being written to by the microprocessor in the Program Condition, bits 0 and 1 determine which channel Mode register is to be written.

Each channel has a mask bit which can be set to disable the incoming DREQ. A mask bit is set when the associated channel produces an EOP* if the channel is not programmed for Autoinitialize. Each bit of the 4-bit mask register can be set or cleared separately with software. The complete register can be set by a Reset. This disables the DMA requests until a clear mask register instruction allows them to occur.

The 8237A can respond to requests for DMA service which are initiated by software as well as by a DREQ. Each channel has a request bit associated with it in the 4-bit Request register. These are nonmaskable and controlled by the Priority Encoder.

Each register bit is set by software or cleared with a TC or external EOP. The complete register is cleared with a Reset. In order to set a bit, the software loads the proper data word. To make a software request the channel must be in the Block Mode.

### Special Software Commands

There are special software commands which are executed in the Program Condition. These do not depend on any bit pattern on the data bus. The following software commands are used:

1. *Clear First / Last Flip-Flop.* This is executed before writing or reading new address or word count information. It initializes the flip-flop so accesses to the register contents go to the proper upper and lower bytes.

2. *Master Clear.* This works like a hardware Reset. The Command, Status, Request, Temporary, and Internal First/Last Flip-Flop registers are cleared and the mask register is set. The 8237A goes into the idle cycle.

3. *Clear Mask Register.* This clears the mask bits of all four channels and allows them to accept DMA requests.

### Control Blocks

The 8237A has three control logic blocks. The Timing Control block generates internal timing and external control signals for the chip. The Program Command Control block decodes the commands sent by the microprocessor for servicing a DMA Request. It also does the decoding of the Mode Control word used to select the type of DMA used. The Priority Encoder block handles the priority contention between DMA channels that request service at the same time. The Timing Control block gets its timing information from the clock input. This input is usually the phase 2 clock from an 8224 or the CLK signal from an 8085AH or 8284A.

## DMA Operation

The 8237A uses two major cycles called the *idle* and *active cycles*. Each cycle is made up of several states. The chip can be in one of seven states. Each state lasts for one clock period. The inactive state is used when there are no DMA requests pending. In this state the DMA controller is inactive but it may be in the Program Condition, being programmed by the processor.

In the first state of DMA servicing, called the S0 state, the 8237A has requested a hold but the processor has not yet returned an acknowledge. The chip may still be programmed until it receives an HLDA from the CPU. An acknowledge from the CPU allows DMA transfers to begin.

S1, S2, S3, and S4 are the working states of DMA servicing. If more time is needed to complete a transfer, wait states (SW) are inserted between S2 or S3 and S4 using the Ready line. The data is transferred directly between the I/O device to memory with IOR* and MENW* or MEMR* and IOW* active low at the same time.

Memory-to-memory transfers use a read-from- and a write-to-memory for each transfer. These states are similar to the normal working states and use a two digit number for identification. Eight states are needed for a transfer. The first four states, S11 to S14 are used for the read-from-memory and the last four states, S21 to S24, for the write-to-memory part of the transfer.

## Idle Cycle

When there are no requests for service, the chip goes into the idle cycle and performs S1 states. In this cycle the chip samples the DREQ lines every clock cycle to check if any channel is requesting service. The device will look at CS*, which indicates when the microprocessor tries to read or write any internal registers of the 8237A. When CS is low and HLDA is low, the 8237A enters the Program Condition. In this mode the CPU can set or check the condition of the internal registers. Address lines A0 through A3 select the registers to be read or written to.

The IOR* and IOW* lines select and time the reads and writes. An internal flip-flop is used to generate an additional bit of address. This bit determines the upper or lower byte of the 16-bit Address and Word Count registers. The flip-flop is reset by a Master Clear, Reset, or a software command.

## Active Cycle

When the 8237A is in the idle cycle and a nonmasked channel requests a service, the device sends an HRQ to the microprocessor and goes into the Active cycle. The DMA servicing will take place, using one of the following four modes.

### Single transfer

In the single transfer mode the device is programmed to make one transfer only. The word count will be decremented and the address decremented or incremented following each transfer. When the word count goes through zero, a Terminal Count (TC) will cause an autoinitialize if the channel has been programmed for this.

### Block transfer

In the block transfer mode the device is activated by a DREQ and continues with the transfer until a TC, caused by the word count ending or an external End of Process (EOP). An autoinitialization will occur at the end of the service if the channel has been programmed for it.

### Demand transfer

In the demand transfer mode the device continues with the transfer until a TC or external EOP occurs or until DREQ goes inactive. This allows the transfer to continue until the I/O device has no more data ready to transfer. When the I/O device has more data to transfer, the DMA service is reestablished with a DREQ. During the time between services, the values of address and word count are stored in the Current Address and Current Word Count registers. An EOP is needed to Autoinitialize at the end of the service. The EOP may be generated by either a TC or by an external signal.

### Cascade

The cascade mode is used to cascade more than one device for system expansion. The HRQ and HLDA signals from the additional device are connected to the DREQ and DACK signals of a channel of the initial device. This allows the DMA requests of the additional device to propagate through the priority circuits of the preceding device.

The priority chain is preserved and the new device must wait for its turn to acknowledge requests. Since the cascade channel of the initial device is used only for prioritizing the additional device, it does not output any address or control signals of its own. These could conflict with the outputs of the active channel in the added device. The 8237A will respond to DREQ and DACK but all other outputs except HRQ are disabled. The ready input is ignored.

This results in a two-level DMA system. More devices could be added at the second level by using the remaining channels of the first level. Additional devices may also be added by cascading into the channels of the second level device to form a third level.

### Types of Transfers

Each of the three transfer modes can be used to perform three different types of transfers. These are Read, Write, and Verify. Write transfers move data from an I/O device to the memory using MENW* and IOR*. Read transfers move data from memory to an I/O device using MEMR* and IOW*.

Verify transfers act as pseudo transfers. The device operates like it is in a Read or Write transfer, but the memory and I/O control lines are inactive. The ready input is ignored in the verify mode.

### Memory-to-Memory Transfers

A block move of data can be made from one memory address space to another. This is done by programming a bit in the Command register to select channels 0 and 1 to operate as the transfer channels. The transfer is started with DREQ. The device requests DMA service and after HLDA is true, four state transfers in the Block Transfer mode are used to read data from the memory. The channel 0 Current Address register holds the address and is decremented or incremented. The data byte read from the memory is stored in the 8237A internal temporary register.

Channel 1 then does a four-state transfer of the data from the temporary register to memory using the address in its Current Address register and incrementing or decrementing it. The channel 1 current Word Count is decremented. When the word count of channel 1 terminates, a TC is generated and an EOP output terminates the service.

Channel 0 can be programmed to retain the same address for all transfers. This allows a single word to be written to a block of memory. The device responds to external EOP signals during memory-to-memory transfers. Data comparators in a block search can use this input to terminate the service when a match is found.

## Autoinitialize

A bit in the mode register is used to set a channel in Autoinitialize. This means the original values of the Current Address and Current Word Count registers will be automatically restored from the Base Address and Base Word count registers in that channel after an EOP. The base registers are loaded simultaneously with the current registers by the microprocessor and are not changed during the DMA servicing. The mask bit is not changed when the channel is in Autoinitialize.

## Priority Encoding

There are two types of priority encoding. Fixed Priority fixes the channels in a priority order based upon the descending value of their number. The channel with the lowest priority is 3 followed by 2 and 1, and the highest priority channel is 0. After a channel is selected, the others are prevented from interfering with the service until it is completed.

In Rotating Priority, the last channel to get service becomes the lowest priority channel while the others go into a rotation. In a single-chip DMA system, any device requesting service will be recognized after less than three higher-priority services have occurred.

## Compressed Timing

More throughput is allowed by compressing the transfer time to two clock cycles. State S3 is dropped and the read pulse width is set equal to the write pulse width. The transfer uses state S2 to change the address and state S4 to perform the read/write. S1 state is still used if A8-A15 needs updating.

## Address Generation

The 8237A multiplexes the eight higher-order address bits on the data lines. State S1 is used to output the higher-order address bits to an external latch from which they can be placed on the address bus. The Address Strobe (ADSTB) is used to load these bits from the data lines to the latch. Address Enable (AEN) is used to enable the bits onto the address bus through a three-state enable.

During Block and Demand Transfer modes, including multiple transfers, the addresses generated are sequential and in many transfers the data held in the external address latch will remain the same.

This data only changes when a carry or borrow from A7 to A8 takes place in the sequence of addresses.

The 8237A executes S1 states only when updating of A8-A15 in the latch is needed. This means that in long services, S1 states and Address Strobes can occur only once every 256 transfers, resulting in a savings of 255 clock cycles for each 256 transfers.

# 9

# Timekeeping

Time is one of the most important of measurements and often it is important to interface a microprocessor to some type of timekeeping circuits. Microprocessors use information about two types of time: relative and absolute. Relative time marks the intervals between events. The updating of a video display every second is an example of relative time.

Relative time measurement is concerned with the time between events rather than when an event occurred in real time. When we say an event happened two days ago, rather than saying it happened on Monday, we are using relative time.

Absolute time fixes an event to a specific time and date. It gives you no indication of how long it has been since a previous event happened. Absolute time is the common type of timekeeping that we are familiar with. When we say an event occurred at 1:35 p.m. on June 12, 1994, we are making a statement in absolute time.

Absolute-time point lines are unique, they will never occur again. Absolute-time is used in microcomputer systems for dating files with the time and data and for synchronizing timed events in the physical world.

### Timekeeping Circuits

Most circuits used to keep time involve counters (Fig. 9.1a). A fixed frequency is generated in the system, usually with a crystal-controlled oscillator. A counter is used to count the oscillations. If the counter is set for a specific number of counts, it can be used to interrupt the microprocessor after this number of oscillations occurs, this provides a method for relative timekeeping.

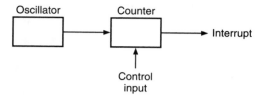

(a) Relative time counting

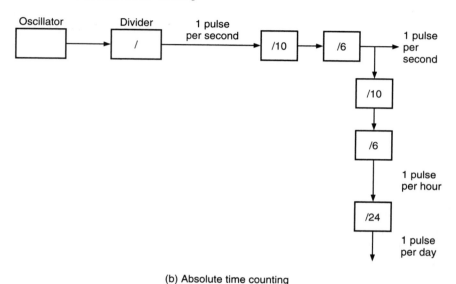

(b) Absolute time counting

**Figure 9.1**   Types of time count circuits.

When the counter reaches its maximum count, called the *terminal count,* it generates a signal. Then the counter returns to zero and starts the count again. The signal from the terminal count is used to generate an interrupt to the microprocessor.

If the oscillator is running at 8 MHz, and the counter can count up to 1000, the circuit will interrupt the microprocessor every 1.25 milliseconds. The microprocessor can then perform an operation such as a peripheral service poll every 1.25 milliseconds. This could be used to scan for a keyboard, check a mouse position, check if a motor is at the proper speed, or measure the temperature of an oven.

These are all applications that involve an I/O process. The use of some type of relative timekeeping circuit allows the computer to relate to outside events, so these are all I/O applications.

If a programmable counter is used, then the time period between interrupts can be adjusted by the microprocessor. The program can change the interval between the interrupts depending on external conditions. This type of interface can be used when different intervals are needed in the system at different times.

## Dividing Counters

Dividers are often used in counter circuits. The oscillator output is counter/divider which is sometimes called a prescaler. This counter accepts the frequency output of the crystal oscillator and divides it down. In an absolute time-counting circuit, or clock-calendar, the first counter/divider would provide an output of one pulse per second (Fig. 9.1b). This signal is then divided by a series of counters to obtain minutes, hours, days, months, and years.

A set of divide-by-10 and divide-by-0 counters counts the seconds and provides a one-pulse-per-minute signal. The output from this set of counters is used for counting hours by a second pair of counters. A set of divide-by-8 and divide-by-3 counters can then be used to count the hours. The other counters must be programmed for the different months of the year and the year counter must change to accommodate leap years.

The contents of the counters can be checked by the microprocessor and if the counters are preset to the time of day, they will reflect the absolute time as long as power is applied. The microprocessor can find out what time it is by reading the counters so this circuit acts as a time-of-day clock calendar. Timekeeping chips are available from several integrated-circuit manufacturers.

## 8253 Programmable Interval Timer

The Intel 8253 Programmable Interval Timer is typical of the counters used in I/O expansion boards. The 8253 chip has three 16-bit programmable counters and uses a 24-pin package. It has eight pins assigned to a bidirectional data bus, a chip select (CS∗), read and write control signals (RD∗ and WR∗), and two address lines. The two address pins are used with the three read and four write registers. Each of the 16-bit counters has an 8-bit write register.

Each counter chip has three I/O pins, two inputs and an output. The inputs include a clock to drive the counter and a gate to control the counting function. The output can be used to control an interrupt or provide a timing function. A write-only mode register allows the processor to configure each of the three counters. The mode register is used to set the mode of operation of each counter.

Two select counter bits (SC1 and SC0) are used to indicate the counter that the mode word will configure. These bits indicate which of the three mode subregisters is to be accessed. SC1 and SC0 form a 2-bit binary number as shown in the following:

| Bit pattern | Counter selected |
|:-----------:|:----------------:|
| 00 | 0 |
| 01 | 1 |
| 10 | 2 |
| 11 | Not allowed |

Each 16-bit counter can be independently programmed, although the counters are 16 bits wide, they use an 8-bit path to the microprocessor.

A set of read/load bits is used to indicate how the microprocessor accesses the counter. These indicate that the microprocessor read or write only the least significant byte of the counter (start at zero). If the microprocessor does not read the lower 8 bits of the counter, then the counter acts as 8-bit counter.

When the microprocessor is set to read and write the full 16-bit counter value, the write is made first to the least significant byte and then to the most significant byte. When a read of the counter contents is made, the counter will supply the least significant 8 bits first, followed by the most significant 8 bits. If this sequence is not followed, then the 8253 can lose synchronization with the program.

## Accuracy

When a counter is actively counting, a read of a counter value may not reflect the current value. There may be ripple delays through the counter and the counter may be changing as the read takes place. A latch can be used to avoid this problem. In the 8253, the microprocessor can latch the current count in a holding register. This register can then be read for a more accurate count.

A BCD/binary control bit in the mode register is used to operate the counter as either a binary or a BCD counter. The counter can operate as a 16-bit binary counter or a four-digit BCD counter. The maximum count is in the 65536 in the binary mode and 10000 in the BCD mode.

## Modes of Operation

There are three mode bits that are used to select one of five operating modes for each counter. The interrupt-on-terminal count mode allows the counter to act as an interval timer which runs once and then stops. The counter output goes low when the mode word is written to the 8253. As the initial count is written to the counter, it starts to count down. As the counter reaches zero, the output of the counter goes true and counting stops. The output goes low when the microprocessor writes a new mode byte or reinitializes the count.

This mode is used when an event must occur after a certain number of time pulses. The microprocessor can start the counter and go to work on other tasks. As the counter reaches zero, it interrupts the microprocessor, telling it that time has run out.

## Watchdog Timers

The interrupt-on-terminal count mode can be used as a watchdog timer to monitor the steps of a certain operation. The watchdog timer is used to ensure that certain steps occur at the right time. If these events do not occur at the specified time, an interrupt is sent to the microprocessor which tells it that something has gone awry and instructs it to stop the operation.

A watchdog timer is useful in many control systems where the computer system is monitoring and controlling some type of process. Noise or some other factor may cause the processor to lose its place in the program and start executing the wrong sections of memory. If this should happen, the processor will not be controlling the process and will not be able to communicate with the watchdog timer at the desired time out. This causes a reset of the processor.

When the interrupt-on-terminal count mode is used as a watchdog, the processor writes the first byte of the count to a counter running in this mode which stops counting. Next, the second byte is written and the counter is reinitialized and starts counting down again. A software routine that tells the watchdog-timer uses for the periodic checks is needed. The main program will call this routine, which writes 2 bytes to the 8253 to prevent the watchdog timer from starting a reset. If the program loop is large, several watchdog-routine calls may be used by the program.

## Pulse and Rate Generation

There is also a programmable one-shot mode, which is used to generate precise pulses. In this mode, the counter output is initially high. The counter starts with a low-to-high transition at the counter's gate input and the counter output remains low until the counter reaches zero. Then it goes back to a high level. When another low-to-high transition occurs on the gate input while the counter output is low, the count starts again. This allows the one-shot operation to be retriggered.

A rate generator mode can generate pulses at precise intervals. The counter continually counts down, reaches zero, and then reinitializes. When the counter is at zero, the counter output is low; at all other times, it is high. This mode can produce a series of short, low-true pulses.

When the gate input goes low, this causes the count to reinitialize and stop counting. When the gate input goes high, the counting starts again. This allows the count to be synchronized with the gate input.

The square-wave rate generator mode operates similarly to the rate generator mode, except that the counter output is high for the first half of the count and is driven low for the second half.

### Strobe Modes

In the software-triggered strobe mode, a pulse is generated after the programmed number of counts occurs. The count starts when the microprocessor loads the count into the counter. The pulse is generated for one clock pulse when the counter reaches zero. This mode is similar to the interrupt-on-terminal count mode, except that the output is low for only one count pulse.

In the hardware-triggered strobe mode, the counter is initialized and a low-to-high transition at the gate input causes the counter to start counting. After the programmed number of counts, the counter reaches zero and the counter output pin is driven low for a single count. This sequence can be retriggered by the gate input. If a second trigger occurs before the counter reaches zero, the counter is reinitialized and the sequence is restarted. This mode can also be used as a watchdog timer.

### 8254 Timer

The Intel 8254 is a similar device that provides three channels of programmable interval timers. The 8254 allows trigger pulses at any rate from 250 kHz to one pulse/hour. Two channels can be operated in fixed divider configurations from an internal 1- or 10-MHz crystal clock. The third channel may be uncommitted. It can provide a gated 16-bit binary counter that can be used for pulse counting, frequency or pulse generation, or delay triggering, and in conjunction with the other channels for frequency and period measurement. The 8254 is a superset of the 8253; the differences in operating modes are shown in Table 9.1.

### Counter/Timer I/O Boards

These boards are available with five channels in a counter-timer interface board that will plug into IBM PC 8-bit expansion slots (Fig. 9.2). The five general-purpose 16-bit counters are part of the AMD 9513 chip. Various internal frequency sources and outputs can be used as inputs for the individual counters. Two of the counters are associated with additional alarm registers and comparators and with the logic for operating in a

**TABLE 9.1  8253/54 Comparison**

| Mode | 8253 Signals | | | 8254 Signals | | |
|---|---|---|---|---|---|---|
| | Low or going low | Rising | High | Low or going low | Rising | High |
| 0 | Disables counting | | Enables counting | Disables counting | | Enables counting |
| 1 | | Initiates counting Resets output after next clock | | | Initiates counting Resets output after next clock | |
| 2 | Disables counting | Reloads counter Initiates counting | Enables counting | Disables counting Sets output immediately high | Initiates counting | Enables counting |
| 3 | Disables counting Sets output immediately high | Reloads counter Initiates counting | Enables counting | Disables counting Sets output immediately high | Initiates counting | Enables counting |
| 4 | Disables counting | | Enables counting | Disables counting | | Enables counting |
| 5 | | Initiates counting | | | Initiates counting | |

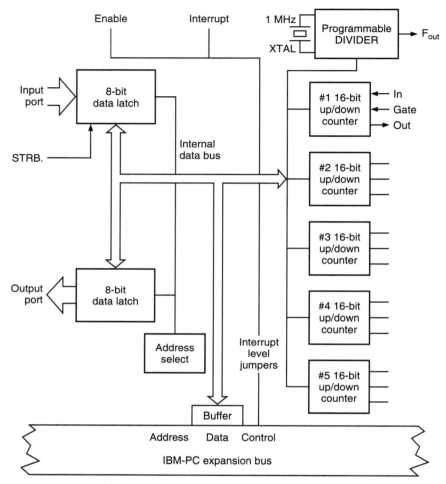

**Figure 9.2**  Counter/timer I/O board.

24-hour time-of-day clock mode. For real-time control applications, the time-of-day logic will accept 50-, 60-, or 100-Hz input frequencies.

Each counter may be gated by hardware or software. The counters can be programmed to count up or down in either binary or BCD. All five counters may be connected together to obtain for an 80-bit counter. Each counter has a load register and a hold register. The load register is used to reload the counter to a predefined value and controls the effective count period. The hold register is used to save the count values without disturbing the count process, thus permitting the microprocessor to read intermediate counts. The hold register can also be used as a second load register to generate complex output waveforms.

Each counter uses a single dedicated output. It can be inhibited when the output is not needed. The input and the gating of the individual counters can be configured using software control. Several counters can use a single input, and a single gate pin can be used to control more than one counter.

## Connector Interface

The counter and digital I/O signals are sent through a standard 37-pin D male connector that projects through the rear panel of the computer. The connector pin assignments are as follows:

| | | | | | |
|---|---|---|---|---|---|
| Counter 2 input | | 19 | 37 | Counter 1 gate | |
| Counter 2 gate | | 18 | 36 | Counter 1 input | |
| Counter 3 input | | 17 | 35 | Counter 1 output | |
| Counter 3 gate | | 16 | 34 | Counter 2 output | |
| Counter 4 input | | 15 | 33 | Counter 3 output | |
| Counter 4 gate | | 14 | 32 | Counter 4 output | |
| Counter 5 input | | 13 | 31 | Counter 5 output | |
| Counter 5 gate | | 12 | 30 | Oscillator out (Fout) | |
| Digital common | | 11 | 29 | IP0 | |
| | OP0 | 10 | 28 | IP1 | |
| | OP0 | 9 | 27 | IP2 | |
| | OP2 | 8 | 26 | IP3 | IP0–7 Digital |
| OP0–7 Digital | OP3 | 7 | 25 | IP4 | inputs with latch |
| outputs with latch | OP4 | 6 | 24 | IP5 | |
| | OP3 | 5 | 23 | IP6 | |
| | OP2 | 4 | 22 | IP7 | |
| | OP1 | 3 | 21 | IP Strobe* | |
| | interrupt enable* | 2 | 20 | +5 V from computer | |
| | Interrupt input | 1 | | | |

Both the 8254 and 8253 Programmable Interval Timers have three 16-bit programmable counters in a 24-bit package. The microprocessor interface of the 8254 and 8253 are also the same. There are eight pins for a bidirectional data bus, a chip select (CS*), two address lines, and the read and write control signals RD* and WR*.

## 6840 PTM

The Motorola 6840 Programmable Timer Module (PTM) has three 16-bit counters and each of these has its own control register. The pin list is shown as follows:

| | |
|---|---|
| V$_{SS}$ 1 | 28 C1 |
| G2 2 | 27 01 |
| 02 3 | 26 G1 |
| C2 4 | 25 D0 |
| G3 5 | 24 D1 |
| 03 6 | 23 D2 |
| C3 7 | 22 D3 |
| RESET 8 | 21 D4 |
| IRQ 9 | 20 D5 |
| RSO 10 | 19 D6 |
| RS1 11 | 18 D7 |
| RS2 12 | 17 E |
| R/W 13 | 16 CS1 |
| V$_{CC}$ 14 | 15 CS0 |

There are eight data lines, two chip selects, an Enable clock, a Read/Write line, an interrupt request and a reset. The chip has three register select lines, but there are nine write and seven read registers so an indirect pointer bit in register 2 is also used to access all of the write registers. The registers are selected as shown in the following, along with the register operations.

| Register selection | | | Register operation | |
|---|---|---|---|---|
| RS2 | RS1 | RSO | R/W* = 0 | R/W* = 1 |
| 0 | 0 | 0 | CR20 = 0 Write control register #3 | No operation |
| | | | CR20 = 1 Write control register #1 | |
| 0 | 0 | 1 | Write control register #2 | Read status register |
| 0 | 1 | 0 | Write MSB buffer register | Read timer #1 counter |
| 0 | 1 | 1 | Write timer #1 latches | Read LSB buffer register |
| 1 | 0 | 0 | Write MSB buffer register | Read timer #2 counter |
| 1 | 0 | 1 | Write timer #2 latches | Read LSB buffer register |
| 1 | 1 | 0 | Write MSB buffer register | Read timer #3 counter |
| 1 | 1 | 1 | Write timer #3 latches | Read LSB buffer register |

## Counters

The three counters have some differences; bit 0 of control register 3 operates a divide-by-eight counter in counter 3. In the three control registers, bit 1 determines the source of clock pulses to the counter. If bit 1 is set to 0, the external-clock-input pin supplies clock pulses to the counter. If this bit is 1, then the microprocessor-enable clock is used.

The enable clock is the master system clock in 6800 systems. The external-clock sources are internally synchronized with the enable clock by the 6840. The external clocks frequencies are slightly less than the enable-clock frequency.

Bit 2 sets the configuration mode of the counter. If bit 2 is 0, the counter operates as a 16-bit binary counter. If bit 2 is 1, the counter is divided into two 8-bit counters and the clock is sent to the least significant 8-bit counter. The output of the least-significant bit counter is sent to the input to the most significant 6-bit counter. This is known as the *dual 8-bit mode*. Both modes have a maximum count of 65536.

The 6840 has one status register and only the four least-significant bits in the register are used; the rest stay at zero. Each counter has an interrupt-status bit in this register as shown in the following:

Bit 0     Counter 1

Bit 1     Counter 2

Bit 2     Counter 3

Bit 3 is an inclusive-OR of these bits, and it acts as a general request bit for the 6840. The function of the interrupt status bit depends on the operating mode of the respective counter.

## Counter Operating Modes

The counter operating modes are determined by bits 3, 4, and 5 of their control register. There are four operating modes and since three bits are used to specify the mode, there is an extra bit for each mode selection. This bit takes a different position for the different modes and is used to modify the operating mode.

Continuous operation is the most basic. First, the microprocessor initializes the counter with an initial count. The counter will count the clock pulses if there is a gate input to the counter. As the counter reaches zero, an interrupt status bit in the status register is set and the initial count is reloaded into the counter for a new count. This mode of operation allows the 6840 to interrupt the microprocessor at programmed intervals, if the interrupt-enable bit (bit 6) of the control register is set.

This mode can be used to generate waveforms using the counter output pin. If control register bit 7 is set, the output pin of the counter is enabled. The counter can be operated as a binary counter to generate a square wave. The frequency is set by the clock input to the counter divided by the counter's initial value plus 1.

If the counter is used in the dual 8-bit mode, the frequency is found as follows. Let the lower 8-bit counter be initialized to L and the upper 8-bit counter initialized to U. The total count is equal to $(U + 1)*(L + 1)$. The frequency is the input clock divided by this value.

The single-shot mode of operation is like continuous operation except that the output has only one cycle. The counter is freerunning and not controlled by the gate input. Only the output pin is affected by the gate input pin. The output is disabled when the counter reaches zero in either the binary or dual 8-bit modes.

This mode generates a single pulse on the output. When the gate input to the counter is set, the pulse starts and the gate input is no longer needed. As the counter reaches zero, the interrupt-status flag is set and the counter reinitializes and continues counting. The output pulse appears only once until the microprocessor reinitializes the counter's initial-count registers or mode register.

In the continuous and single-shot operating modes, bit 4 of the control register determines when the microprocessor can initialize the counter. If this bit is a zero, the counter is initialized when the microprocessor writes a value to the counter latches. The information is written to the latches with the most significant byte of the 16-bit value first.

The 6840 buffers the most significant byte, and writes the full 16-bit initial count value when it gets the least significant byte. This buffer is shared by the other counters, so full 16-bit initial values are needed when writing an initial count, even if the count is less than 256. This must be done to prevent bytes intended for one of the other counters from being accidentally written into the counter currently being addressed.

Frequency comparison is another operating mode of the 6840. In this mode, an input waveform can be compared with the clock period. The counter starts by setting the gate input. When the counter reaches zero, the gate input is checked and the interrupt-status bit is set according to the gate input and the state of control register bit 5.

If this bit is 1, the interrupt-status bit is set if two negative pulses do not occur at the gate input. This means that the frequency applied to the gate input is lower than the cycle of the counter.

If bit 5 of the control register is 0, the interrupt-status bit is set if the frequency applied to the gate input is higher than the cycle of the counter.

Pulse-width comparison is a mode that is used to determine the length of a pulse. This pulse is defined as the time that the gate input is set. The counter is started when the gate input is set, which marks the start of the pulse. When the counter reaches 0, the gate input is checked and the interrupt-status bit is set according to the level at the gate input and bit 5 of the control register.

Pulse-width comparison uses the level of the gate input for testing, while frequency comparison uses the timing between pulse edges. If bit 5 is 0, an interrupt is generated if the gate input is no longer set. This means the pulse is smaller than the cycle of the counter. If bit 5 is 1, the interrupt is set if the gate input is still set. This means the pulse is longer than the cycle of the counter. In both the frequency and pulse-width comparison modes, the counter cycles once and then stops until the microprocessor reinitializes the counter.

## Absolute Timekeeping

In some applications, marking the passage of time is not enough. It may be important to allow the microprocessor to control some operation using the time of day. This could be a heating or cooling control system. One way is to use an interval timer along with software counters to make an absolute-time or real-time clock. By counting the intervals, the microprocessor marks the passage of time. One thousand, one-millisecond intervals makes one second, sixty seconds makes one minute, sixty minutes makes one hour, and twenty-four hours makes one day.

One problem with a software time-of-day clock is that the microprocessor is spending a good part of its time just to keep track of real time. If an interrupt routine is activated each millisecond, just for counting seconds, this subtracts from the ability of the microprocessor to perform other functions. In a simple control system this may be acceptable, but if any amount of data processing is needed it may be prohibitive. If you add the month and the year to the timekeeping task, some microprocessors may not be fast enough to keep track of the time and a faster processor may be required.

Another problem with a software time-of-day clock is that the absolute time is lost when the system is turned off. Even if we stored the last output or most recent time when the computer was turned off, this value would be wrong when the computer is turned back on.

## Absolute Time Clocks

There are integrated circuits that are designed to provide the features of a real-time clock. They are able to keep track of the time without any assistance from the microprocessor. The benefit of placing them in the system is the reduced software burden on the processor.

Most of these time-of-day integrated circuits have a low power consumption so they can be powered by a small battery when the rest of the computer is turned off (Fig. 9.3). Most time-of-day circuits use CMOS technology which is also used for battery-powered digital display clocks and watches.

Other features of these circuits are a microprocessor bus interface along with day, month, and year counters in addition to the second, minute, and hour counters, automatic leap-year correction for February, and alarm functions. An example of such a part is the National MM58174.

## MM58174 Clock/Calendar

This part is like the National MM58167 that also uses an Intel-like interface along with a 32,6768 Hz crystal, but this part is faster since

(a)

(b)

**Figure 9.3**  Batteries used in PC systems. (*a*) Lithium batteries used in some 286 and 386 systems; (*b*) Button-type batteries are used in some 386 and 486 systems.

it uses a 600-nanosecond bus cycle instead of 1 microsecond. Even the 600-nanosecond cycle is not fast enough for some of the newer processors, and wait states are required to interface this device to them.

The data path is four bits wide on the 58174. This means that each counter has a separate address. Four address lines give the processor access to the sixteen locations in the chip. Most of these locations are used for the counters in the chip. The chip can adjust the number of days in February if the current year is a leap year. A code for the current year is stored in the year register.

Setting the chip starts with the microprocessor writing a zero to the stop location in memory to stop the counters. Then the present time is written to the registers which are listed in Table 9.2. The year code is also written but it cannot be read back as part of the time. The clock is started by writing a one to the start location in memory. Reading the time involves reading the counters.

Interrupts are different in the MM58174 compared to the older MM58167. Three interrupt intervals can be selected: 0.5, 5, and 6 seconds. A periodic or a single interrupt can be programmed.

When an interrupt occurs, bit 3 of the interrupt-status register is set. When the processor reads this bit, it clears the interrupt request. The pin list is shown as follows:

| Pin diagram of the National Semiconductor MM58174 | |
| --- | --- |
| CS* 1 | 16 $V_{DD}$ |
| NRDS 2 | 15 Crystal in |
| NWDS 3 | 14 Crystal out |
| $DB_3$ 4 | 13 Interrupt |
| $DB_2$ 5 | 12 $AD_0$ |
| $DB_1$ 6 | 11 $AD_1$ |
| $DB_0$ 7 | 10 $AD_2$ |
| $V_{SS}$ 8 | 9 $AD_3$ |

**TABLE 9.2    58174 Registers**

| | Address bits | | | | |
| --- | --- | --- | --- | --- | --- |
| Counter selected | AD3 | AD2 | AD1 | AD0 | Mode |
| 0 Test only | 0 | 0 | 0 | 0 | Write |
| 1 Tenths of seconds | 0 | 0 | 0 | 1 | Read |
| 2 Seconds | 0 | 0 | 1 | 0 | Read |
| 3 Tens of seconds | 0 | 0 | 1 | 1 | Read |
| 4 Minutes | 0 | 1 | 0 | 0 | Read or write |
| 5 Tens of minutes | 0 | 1 | 0 | 1 | Read or write |
| 6 Hours | 0 | 1 | 1 | 0 | Read or write |
| 7 Tens of hours | 0 | 1 | 1 | 1 | Read or write |
| 8 Days | 1 | 0 | 0 | 0 | Read or write |
| 9 Tens of days | 1 | 0 | 0 | 1 | Read or write |
| 10 Day of week | 1 | 0 | 1 | 0 | Read or write |
| 11 Months | 1 | 0 | 1 | 1 | Read or write |
| 12 Tens of months | 1 | 1 | 0 | 0 | Read or write |
| 13 Years | 1 | 1 | 0 | 1 | Write only |
| 14 Stop/Start | 1 | 1 | 1 | 0 | Write only |
| 15 Interrupt & Status | 1 | 1 | 1 | 1 | Read or write |

## MSM58321 Clock Calendar

The OKI MSM58321 is an improved version of the older MSM5832. A leap-year compensator is built into the 58321. Table 9.3 is a pin list of the MSM58321. A major change is the shift from separate address and data pins to a multiplexed address/data bus. This means the address must be clocked into the device first, with the ADDRESS WRITE, then data access is made using either the WRITE or READ pins. The multiplexing of address and data allows the MSM58321 to use a 16-pin package while an 18-pin package is used for the 5832.

The leap year is set by writing the two most significant bits of the tens-of-days register. Since there are not more than 31 days in a month, these bits are available.

Setting the time in the 58321 involves writing the desired values in the registers. Reading the time involves reading the registers. A BUSY* output indicates that the counters are being updated. This process takes over 180 microseconds. BUSY* is set a few hundred microseconds before the counters start to change. If the processor checks BUSY* and sees that it is not set, it has enough time to read the counters.

### 146818 Clock/Calendar

The Motorola CMOS real-time clock numbered the MC146818, is a powerful real-time clock/calendar (Fig. 9.4). This part even has some storage locations for the system software to use. These locations will hold the information stored in them if the device is powered by a battery when the system is turned off. Table 9.4 lists the pins used for the part.

There is a microprocessor-bus interface, counters for the clock, registers for an alarm function, and a 50-byte, general-purpose RAM storage area.

**TABLE 9.3    Pin list of 58321**

| CS | 1 | 16 $V_{DD}$ |
|---|---|---|
| Write | 2 | 15 XT |
| Read | 3 | 14 XT* |
| $D_0$ | 4 | 13 $CS_1$ |
| $D_1$ | 5 | 12 Test |
| $D_2$ | 6 | 11 Stop |
| $D_3$ | 7 | 10 Busy* |
| GND | 8 | 9 Address write |

**TABLE 9.4    Pin list of 146818**

| NC | 1 | 24 $V_{DD}$ |
|---|---|---|
| OSC1 | 2 | 23 SOW |
| OSC2 | 3 | 22 PS |
| AD0 | 4 | 21 CKOUT |
| AD1 | 5 | 20 CKFS |
| AD2 | 6 | 19 IRQ* |
| AD3 | 7 | 18 Reset* |
| AD4 | 8 | 17 DS |
| AD5 | 9 | 16 NC |
| AD6 | 10 | 15 R/W* |
| AD7 | 11 | 14 AS |
| $V_{SS}$ | 12 | 13 CE* |

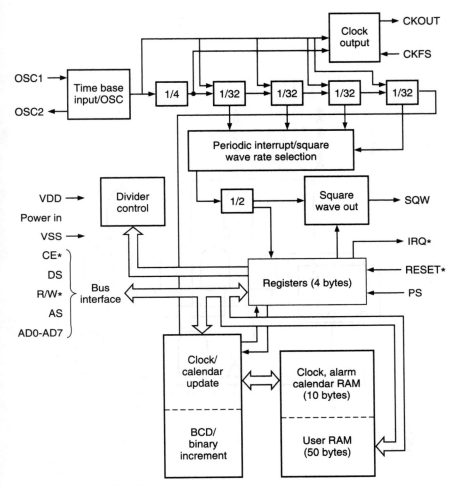

**Figure 9.4**    146818 Clock/Calendar.

The microprocessor-bus interface involves the following pins: a bi-directional 8-bit data bus, an address strobe (AS), a data strobe (DS), a read/write line (R/W), and a chip select (CS). There are no address lines since the part has a multiplexed address/data bus. The address is strobed on the data lines using the AS control line, and the data is transferred using the other control lines.

The 186818 can be interfaced to a nonmultiplexed bus, using a parallel-interface chip to drive the bus interface. An alternative is to use two addresses for the part—when the processor writes to one address, the address decoder sets the real-time clock's address strobe. When the other address is accessed, the data strobe is set.

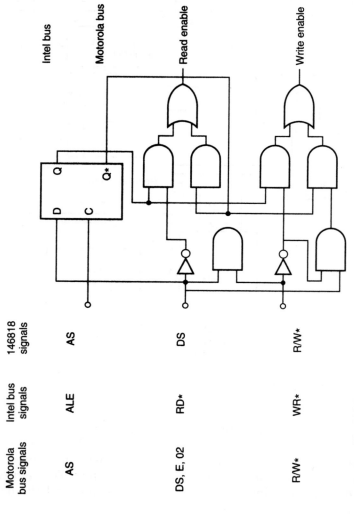

**Figure 9.5** The MOTEL (Motorola/Intel) interface translates Motorola or Intel microprocessor bus signals into read-and-write enables.

Then, access to the registers on the chip takes two steps: first a write is made to the address using one bus address and then the data access is made using the other address.

Along with the multiplexed address/data bus, the 186818 uses a MOTEL (Motorola/Intel) circuit to detect and use either Motorola-bus control lines or Intel control lines. Operation of the MOTEL circuit depends on the fact that, on either bus, the address strobe and data strobes are never turned on together.

On the Motorola bus, AS and DS are never at a high level together and on the Intel bus, when ALE is high, RD∗ will also be high. ALE is positive true and RD∗ is negative true while AS and DS are both positive true.

When the AS input to the MOTEL circuit (Fig. 9.5) goes off, if DS is low, the flip-flop is cleared, setting the Motorola-bus signal. If DS is high when AS falls, the Intel bus signal is set.

The bus signals are used with the gates to decode the DS and R/W∗ inputs to the circuit and generate a read-enable and write-enable signal. In the Intel bus, the read enable is the inverse of RD, and the write enable is the inverse of WR∗.

In the Motorola bus the read enable is generated by an AND of DS and R/W∗. The write enable is generated by ANDing DS and the inverse of R/W∗. The MOTEL circuit does the translation needed for the interface.

The 146818 real-time clock keeps track of the seconds, minutes, hours, day of the week, day of the month, month, and year. It has an alarm function which monitors hours, minutes, and seconds. Each register handles two digits of time and the time can be in either binary or BCD formats. Besides the time and alarm registers, the 146818 has four status and control registers, A to D.

Register A is used to select the time-base frequency and a periodic interrupt frequency. The most significant bit of register A is used to indicate that an update is in progress. This read-only bit is set a few hundred microseconds before the counters start to change. This bit tells the processor when it can read the time. The chip runs at the following clock frequencies; 4.914304 MHz, 1.048576 MHz, or 32,768 Hz. The frequency is selected by writing the proper value to register A.

Register B has a counter-enable bit, interrupt-enable bits for the interval and alarm interrupts, the binary/BCD data-mode-select bit, and a 12/24 hour mode-select bit. There is also a Daylight-Savings-Time-select bit. If this bit is set, the 146818 will advance the hour in April and set it back in October.

Register C is the interrupt-status register and is used to indicate the cause of an interrupt. Reading register C clears the interrupts. Register D has only a single bit; it indicates if the power level is sufficient to allow the 146818 to communicate with the microprocessor. The battery backup system that used real-time clocks generally have lower voltages than the microprocessor power supply. Register D is also used as a power-failure indicator to prevent the microprocessor from accessing the time data when power is low or off.

# Bibliography

Adams, L. F. *Engineering Measurements and Instrumentation.* London: English Universities Press, 1975.

Alford, Roger C. "Dueling DX2s: The First 486 Clock Doublers." *BYTE,* July 1992.

Altman, L., ed. *Microprocessors.* New York: Electronic Magazine Book Series, 1975.

Bade, P., Enggebretson, A. M., Heibreder, A. F., and Niemoeller, A. F. "Use of a Personal Computer to Model the Electroacoustics of Hearing Aids." *Journal of the Acoustical Society of America,* February 1984, pp. 617–620.

Baily, S. J. "Personal Computers Frugal Path to Specialized Control Systems." *Control Engineering,* July 1984.

Basset, Edward W. "First Industrial Pentium PCs." *INTECH,* September 1993, pp. 50–51.

Bell, C., and Newell, A. *Computer Structures.* New York: McGraw-Hill, 1970.

Benedict, R. P. *Fundamentals of Temperature, Pressure and Flow Measurements.* New York: John Wiley, 1969.

Bigelow, Stephen J. *Maintain and Repair Your Notebook, Palmtop, or Pen Computer.* New York: Windcrest/McGraw-Hill, 1994.

———. *PC Drives & Memory Systems.* New York: Windcrest/McGraw-Hill, 1994.

Breuer, M. A., and Griedman, A. D. *Diagnosis and Reliable Design of Digital Systems.* Woodland Hills, Calif.: Computer Science Press, 1976.

Buckley, P. S. *Techniques of Process Control.* New York: John Wiley, 1964. *Burr-Brown Integrated Circuits Data Book.* Tucson, Ariz.: Burr-Brown, 1986.

Burton, D. P. "Handle Microcomputer I/O Efficiently." *Electronic Design,* June 21, 1978.

Caine, K. E. "Personal Computer as an Engineering Tool." *Iron and Steelmaker,* April 1984, pp. 12–16.

Camenzind, H. R. *Electronic Integrated System Design.* New York: Van Nostrand Reinhold, 1972.

Cherncoff, David P. "66MHz PCs a Sound Bet for CPU-Intensive Tasks." *PC Week,* August 17, 1992.

Chintappali, P. S., and Ahluwalia, M. S. "The Use of Personal Computers for Process Control." *Energy Progress,* June 1984.

Chornik, B. "Application of a Personal Computer for Control and Data Acquisition in an Auger Electron Spectrometer." *Review of Scientific Instruments,* January 1983, pp. 80–84.

Chu, Y. *Computer Organization and Microprogramming.* Englewood Cliffs, N.J., Prentice-Hall, 1972.

Coffee, M. B. "Common-mode Rejection Techniques for Low-Level Data Acquisition." *Instrumentation Technology,* July 1977.

Collier, D. "Personal Computers in Industrial Control." *Microelectronics and Reliability* (U.K.), vol. 2, pp. 461–465.

Combs, C. F., ed. *Basic Electronic Instrument Handbook.* New York: McGraw-Hill, 1972.

"Computerland Solutions" Newsletter. January 2, 1990.

Corwin, T. K., Clarke, P., and Frederick, E. R. "Field Application of a Personal Computer for Data Collect and Reduction." *Proceedings of the Speciality Conference on Continuous Emission Monitoring Design, Operation, and Experience,* Air Pollution Control Association, Denver, Colo.: 1982, pp. 293–302.

Crick, A. "Scheduling and Controlling I/O Operations." *Data Processing,* May–June 1974.

Diefenderfer, A. J. *Principles of Electronic Instrumentation.* Philadelphia, Pa.: W. B. Saunders, 1972.

DiGiacomo, Joseph, ed. *Digital Bus Handbook.* New York: McGraw-Hill, 1990.

Dodds, D. E. "Home Energy Simulation Using Personal Computers." *Proceedings of Energex '83, Solar energy Society of Canada* (Winnipeg, Manitoba), 1982, pp. 1020–1025.

Doebelin, E. O. *Measurement System-Application and Design.* New York: McGraw-Hill, 1975.

Eckhouse, R. J., Jr. *Minicomputer Systems.* Englewood Cliffs, N.J.: Prentice-Hall, 1975.

Elliott, T. C. "Temperature, Pressure, Level, Flow-key Measurements in Power and Process." *Power,* September 1975.

Englemann, B., and Abraham, M. "Personal Computer Signal Processing." *BYTE,* April 1984, pp. 95–110.

Farnbach, W. A. "Bring Up Your P Bit-by-Bit." *Electronic Design,* vol. 24, no. 15, July 19, 1976.

Farramce, Rex, and Goodwin, Michael. "486SX PCs: Double-Time Performers." August 1992.

Foley, C., and Lamb, J. "Use of a Personal Computer and DFT to Extract Data from Noisy Signals." *EDN,* April 5, 1984.

Foster, C. C. *Computer Architecture.* New York: Van Nostrand Reinhold, 1970.

Freedman, M. D. *Principles of Digital Computer Operation.* New York: John Wiley, 1972.

Fung, K. T., and Toong, H. D., "On the Analysis of Memory Conflicts and Bus Contentions in a Multiple-Microprocessor System." *IEEE Trans. Computers,* vol. C-27, no. 1, January 1979.

Garland, H. *Introduction to Microprocessor System Design.* New York: McGraw-Hill, 1979.

Gear, C. W. *Computer Organization and Programming.* New York: McGraw-Hill, 1974.

Gilkerson, Tim. "Communicating with Your Computer." *PC Today,* November, 1989.

Gregory, B. A. *An Introduction to Electrical Instrumentation.* New York: Macmillan, 1973.

Gunashingham, H., Ang, K. P., Mok, J. L., and Thiak, P. C. "Design of pH Titrator as a Component Part of a Personal computer." *Microprocessors and Microsystems,* July–August 1984, pp. 274–279.

Harriott, P. *Process Control.* New York: McGraw-Hill, 1964.

Heaton, J. E. *The Personal Computer as a Controller.* Ann Arbor, Mich.: Oracle, 1984.

Herrick, C. N. *Instrumentation and Measurement for Electronics.* New York: McGraw-Hill, 1972.

Hill, F. J., and Peterson, G. R. *Digital Systems: Hardware Organization and Design.* New York: John Wiley, 1973.

Hnatek, E. R. *A User's Handbook of Semiconductor Memories.* New York: John Wiley, 1977.

———. "Current Semiconductor Memories." *Computer Design,* April 1978.

Hodges, D. A. *Semiconductor Memories.* New York: IEEE Press, 1972.

Hodson, Gerri. "Affordable Performance Using Speed-Double Technology." *Microcomputer Solutions,* May/June, 1992.

Holton, M. J. "Programmable Input/Output System Prevents Communication Bottlenecks." *Advances in Instrumentation,* vol. 39, pp. 1001–1010. Research Triangle Park, N.C.: Instrument Society of America, 1984.

Hordeski, M. F. "Digital Control of Microprocessors." *Electronic Design,* December 6, 1975.

———. "When Should You Use Pneumatics, When Electronics?" *Instruments & Control Systems,* November 1976.

———. "Guide to Digital Instrumentation for Temperature, Pressure Instrument." *Oil, Gas and Petrochem Equipment,* November 1976.

———. "Digital Instrumentation for Pressure, Temperature/Pressure, Readout Instruments." *Oil, Gas and Petrochem Equipment,* December 1976.

———. "Innovative Design: Microprocessors." *Digital Design,* December 1976.

———. "Passive Sensors for Temperature Measurement." *Instrumentation Technology,* February 1977.

———. "Adapting Electric Actuators to Digital Control." *Instrumentation Technology,* March 1977.

———. "Fundamental of Digital Control Loops and Factors in Choosing Pneumatic or Electronic Instruments." Presentation at the SCMA Instrumentation Short Course, Los Angeles, Calif., April 6, 1977.

———. "Balancing Microprocessor-Interface Tradeoffs." *Digital Design,* April 1977.

———. "Digital Position Encoder for Linear Applications." *Measurements and Control,* July–August 1977.

———. "Future Microprocessor Software." *Digital Design,* August 1977.

———. "Radiation and Stored Data." *Digital Design,* September 1977.

———. "Microprocessor Chips." *Instrumentation Technology,* September 1977.

———. "Process Controls are Evolving Fast." *Electronic Design,* November 22, 1977.

———. "Fundamental of Digital Control Loops." *Measurements & Control,* February 1978.

———. "Using Microprocessors." *Measurements & Control,* June 1978.

———. *Microprocessor Cookbook.* Blue Ridge Summit, Pa.: TAB Books, Inc., 1979.

———. "Selecting Test Strategies for Microprocessor Systems." *ATE Seminar Proceedings,* Pasadena, Calif., January 1982 (New York: Morgan-Grampian).

———. "Selection of a Test Strategy for MPU Systems." *Electronics Test,* February 1982.

———. "Trends in Displacement Sensors." *Sensors and Systems Conference Proceedings,* Pasadena, Calif., May 1982 (Campbell, Calif.: Network Exhibitions).

———. "The Impact of 16-Bit Microprocessors." *Instrumentation Symposium Proceedings,* Las Vegas, May 1982 (Research Triangle Park, N.C.: Instrument Society of America).

———. "Diagnostic Strategies for Microprocessor Systems." *ATE Seminar Proceedings,* Anaheim, Calif., January 1983 (New York: Morgan-Grampian).

———. *The Design of Microprocessor Sensor and Control Systems.* Reston, Va.: Reston, 1984.

———. *Microprocessors in Industry.* New York: Van Nostrand Reinhold, 1984.

———. "CAD/CAM Equipment Reliability." Paper presented at the Western Design Engineering Show and ASME Conference, San Francisco, Calif., December 5, 1984.

———. "Specifying and Selecting CAD/CAM Equipment." *Proceedings of CADCON West,* Anaheim, Calif., January 14–17, 1985 (New York: Morgan-Grampian).

———. "A Tutorial On COM/Factory Automation." Paper presented at the Western Design Engineering Show and ASME Conference, Anaheim, Calif., December 12, 1985.

———. *CAD / CAM Techniques.* Reston, Va.: Reston, 1986.

———. *Microcomputer Design.* Reston, Va.: Reston, 1986.

———. *Transducers for Automation.* New York: Van Nostrand Reinhold, 1987.

———. *Illustrated Dictionary of Microcomputer Terminology.* (3d ed.) Blue Ridge Summit, Pa.: TAB Books, Inc., 1988.

———. *Repairing IBM PCs and Compatibles an Illustrated Guide.* New York: Windcrest/McGraw-Hill, 1992.

———. *Control System Interfaces Design and Implementation Using Personal Computers.* Englewood Cliffs, N.J.: Prentice-Hall, 1992.

———. *Control Technology and Personal Computers.* New York: Van Nostrand Reinhold, 1992.

———. *Upgrading the IBM PC Family 8088 to 486.* Englewood Cliffs, N.J.: Prentice-Hall, 1993.

Hougen, J. O. *Measurement and Control Applications.* Research Triangle Park, N.C.: Instrument Society of America, 1979.

Hughes, J. S. "Personal Computers: If You Don't Have One Now, You Soon Will." *INTECH,* February 1985, pp. 45–47.

———. "Personal Computers in Process Control." *Advances in Instrumentation,* vol. 40. Research Triangle Park, N.C.: Instrument Society of America, 1985.

"IBM Personal Computers and Compatible Equipment, April 1985–March 1986, Citations from the INSPEC Data Base," Report PB86-859022/XAB. National Information Service (Springfield, Va.), March 1986.

Intel Corp. *Connectivity.* Mt. Prospect, Ill.: Intel Corp., 1993.

————. *8086 User's Guide*. Santa Clara, Calif., Intel Corp., 1976.

————. *1486 Microprocessor Hardware Reference Manual*. Mt. Prospect, Ill.: Intel Corp., 1990.

————. *Intel386 DX Microprocessor Hardware Reference Manual*. Mt. Prospect, Ill.: Intel Corp., 1991.

————. *Pentium Processor User's Manual*. Mt. Prospect, Ill.: Intel Corp., 1993.

————. *Peripheral Components*. Mt. Prospect, Ill.: Intel Corp., 1993.

Ivanov, V. V., Morenkov, A. D., and Oleinkrov, A. Y. "Personal Computers and Measurement-Computation Complexes for Automation of Large-Scale Laboratory Experiments." *Instruments and Experimental Techniques* (English Translation of Pribory I Teknika Eksperimenta), September–October 1984, pp. 1106–1109.

James, D. R., and Grierson, J. B. "Evaluating Personal Computers for Process Control," *InTech*, January 1984, pp. 49–51.

James, D. R., and Griterson, J. B. "Evaluating Personal Computers for Use in Process Control." *Advances In Instrumentation*, vol. 38, no. 707. Research Triangle Park, N.C.: Instrument Society of America, 1983.

Jones, J. C. *Design Methods*. New York: Wiley-Interscience, 1970.

Jutila, J. M. "Temperature Instrumentation." *Instrumentation Technology*, February 1980.

Kay, Alan C. "Microelectronics and the Personal Computer." *Scientific American*, vol. 237, no. 3, September 1977.

Kershaw, John D. *Digital Electronics: Logic and Systems*. North Scituate, Mass.: Duxbury Press, 1976.

Klingman, E. E. *Microprocessor Systems Design*. Englewood Cliffs, N.J.: Prentice-Hall, 1977.

Klipec, B. "How to Avoid Noise Pickup on Wire and Cables." *Instruments & Control Systems*, December 1977.

Knorr, Erick. "486 Times 2." *PC World*, May 1992.

Kobayashi, K., Watanabe, K., Ichikawa, R., and Kato, A. "Personal Computer." In *C & C (Computing and Communications)*, Proceedings of the IEEE, March 1983, 352–362.

Kofler, G. "Personal Instrumentation, A Personal Computer as Part of a Measuring System." *Elekronkschau* (Austria), June 1983, pp. 46–47.

Kohonen, T. *Digital Circuits and Devices*. Englewood Cliffs, N.J.: Prentice-Hall, 1972.

Krigman, A. "Selecting Peripherals for Process I/O." *InTech*, April 1984, p. 49.

Kuck, D. J. *The Structure of Computers and Computations*. vol. 1. New York: John Wiley, 1978.

Lawrence, S., and Marcus, L. S. "Designing PC Boards with a Centralized Database." *Computer Graphics World*, March 1984.

Leibson, Steve. *The Handbook of Microcomputer Interfacing*. (2d ed.), Blue Ridge Summit, Pa.: TAB Books, Inc., 1983.

Levenspiel, O. *Microprocessors: Software, Hardware, Programming*. Englewood Cliffs, N.J.: Prentice-Hall, 1978.

Liptak, B. G. *Instrument Engineers' Handbook*. Radnor, Pa.: Chilton, vol. I, 1969, vol. II, 1970, Supplement, 1972.

Liptak, B. G. *Instrumentation in the Processing Industries*. Radnor, Pa.: Chilton, 1973.

————, ed. *Instrument Engineers' Handbook on Process Measurement*. Radnor, Pa.: Chilton, 1980.

Litton Industries Technical Training Group. *Digital Computer Fundamentals*. Englewood Cliffs, N.J.: Prentice-Hall, Inc., 1965.

Manoff, M. "Control Software Comes to Personal Computers." *Control Engineering*, March 1984, pp. 66–68.

Martin, D. P. *Microcomputer Design*. Chicago: Martin Research, 1975.

Mazur, T. "Microprocessor Basics." Part 4, "The Motorola 6800." *Electronic Design*, July 19, 1976.

McDermott, J. "Personal Computer Add-ons and Add-ins." *EDN*, January 20, 1983, pp. 62–82.

McGlynn, D. R. *Microprocessors*. New York: John Wiley, 1976.

Mehta, Suketu. "Zero-Slot Alternatives." *LAN*, July, 1988, pp. 63–66.

Merritt, K., and Persun, T. "Personal Computers Move into Process Control." *Instruments & Control Systems,* June 1983.

Mills, J. "Use Your Personal Computer for Measurement and Control." *Analog Dialog,* vol. 16, no. 2 (Analog Devices, Norwood, Mass.), 1982.

Mills, M. "Memory Cards: A New Concept in Personal Computing." *Byte,* January 1984.

Milne, B. "Personal Computers: Instruments." *Electronic Design,* September 29, 1983.

Moss, C. E. "Sophisticated Gamma-Ray Data Acquisition System Based on an IBM PC/XT Computer." Report LA-UR-85-3755. Proceeding of the IEEE Nuclear Science Symposium. October 23, 1985.

Motorola Semiconductor. *M6800 Microprocessor Applications Manual.* Phoenix, Ariz.: Motorola, 1975.

————. *MC68000 Microprocessor User's Manual.* Austin, Tex.: Motorola, 1979.

Murrill, P. W. *Automatic Control of Processes.* Scranton, Pa.: International Textbook, 1967.

Nance, Barry. "Intel's Double-Fast CPUs." *BYTE,* May, 1992.

Nick, J. R. "Using Schottky 3-State Outputs in Bus-Organized Systems." *Electronic Design News,* vol. 19, no. 23, December 5, 1974.

Novitsky, John. "32-bit 80386 Chip Will Hasten Development of A1 Systems." *Systems 3X.* October 1986.

Ohkubo, T., and Nakamura, T. "Automated Data Acquisition System of Environmental Radiation Monitor with a Personal Computer." Report INS-TS-24. Tokyo University (Japan), Institute for Nuclear Study, May 1984.

Oliver, B. M., and Cage, J. M. *Electronic Measurements and Instrumentation.* New York: McGraw-Hill, 1971.

Ottinger, L. "Using Robots in Flexible Manufacturing Cells/Facilities." *Automated Manufacturing* (Greenville, S.C.), March 19–22, 1984.

Patterson, D. A., and Seguin, C. H. "Design Considerations for Single-Chip Computers of the Future." *IEEE Trans. Comp.,* vol. C-29, February 1980.

"The Personal Computer as a Measuring Instrument." *Regulacion y Mendo Automatico* (Spain), December 1983, pp. 55–56.

Pinto, J. J. "Evolution of the Industrial Process Measurement and Control Computer." *Advances in Instrumentation,* vol. 38, Research Triangle Park, N.C.: Instrument Society of America, 1983.

Pritty, D. W. "The Potential of Personal Computers In Laboratory Control Applications." *Journal of Microcomputer Applications* (UK), January 1983, pp. 47–57.

"Process Control by Personal Computers." *Wireless World* (UK), September 1983, pp. 54–59.

Quain, John R. "Speed-Doubler Technology." *Personal Computers,* June 16, 1992.

Rafiquzzaman, Mohamed. *Microprocessors and Microcomputer Development Systems.* New York: Harper and Row, 1984.

Reinhardt, Andy. "Pentium Changes the PC." *BYTE,* July 1993, pp. 81–93.

Riley, J. "Process Control for a PWB Facility." *Automated Manufacturing* (Greenville, S.C.), March 19–22, 1984.

Rompelman, O., Snijders, J. B. I. M., and Van Spronsen, C. J. "The Measurement of Heart Rate Variability Spectra with the Help of the Personal Computer." *IEEE Transactions on Biomedical Engineering,* July 1982, pp. 503–510.

Sandberg, U. "Personal Computers in Control and Regulatory Systems: Dream or Nightmare." *Industrielle Dataknik* (Sweden), vol. 47, June 1984.

Saxena, P., and Gupta, L. K. "PCs Provide Low Cost Process Monitoring." *Proceedings of the North Coast Conference.* Research Triangle Park, N.C.: Instrument Society of America, 1986.

Schgor, G. "Personal Computers in the Control of Industrial Plants," *Automazione y Strumentazone* (Italy), November 1983, pp. 93–96.

Schwartz, P. "When Personal Computers Become Measuring Instruments." *Electronique Industrielle* (France), May 1983, pp. 49–53.

Seymour, Jim. "Intel Ups the Ante with Its 50-MHz DX2." *Personal Computers* September 15, 1992.

Sheingold, D. H. *Analog-Digital Conversion Handbook.* Norwood, Mass.: Analog Devices, 1972.

Shinskey, F. G. *Process Control Systems*. New York: McGraw-Hill, 1979.

Singer, A., and Rony, P. "Controlling Robots with Personal Computers." *Machine Design,* September 23, 1982, pp. 78–82.

Sinha, N. K. "Control System Design with Personal Computers." *Proceedings of the 1983 International Electrical and Electronics Conference IEEE,* New York, 1983, pp. 420–423.

Skrokov, M. R., ed. *Mini and Microcomputer Control in Industrial Processes*. Van Nostrand Reinhold, 1980.

Slater, Michael. "Intel Clock-Doubler 486 Debuts as 486 DX2." *Microprocessor Report,* March 4, 1992.

Soisson, H. E. *Instrumentation in Industry*. New York: John Wiley, 1975.

Soucek, B. *Microprocessors and Microcomputers*. New York: John Wiley, 1976.

Stone, H. S. *Introduction to Computer Architecture*. New York: McGraw-Hill, 1975.

Sylvan, J. "Industrial Monitoring with Personal Computers." *Machine Design,* October 6, 1983, pp. 91–95.

Takanishi, I., Tomokiyo, O., and Yokouchi, N. "Personal Computer for Measurement and Control." *Hitachi Zosen Technical Review* (Japan), March 1983, pp. 56–63.

"Take Measurements with Your Personal Computer." *Measures* (France), September 13, 1983, pp. 27–29.

Texas Instruments. *The TTL Data Book for Design Engineers*. Dallas, Tex.: Texas Instruments, 1973.

————. *The Microprocessor Handbook*. Houston, Tex.: Texas Instruments, 1975.

————. *TMS 9900 Microprocessor Data Manual*. Dallas, Tex.: Texas Instruments, 1978.

Toong, H. D., and Gupta, A. "An Architectural Comparison of Contemporary 16-Bit Microprocessors." *IEEE Micro,* May 1981.

Useda, K., and Kinoshita, K. "Data Processing System for the Measurement of Thermal Desorption Spectra Using a Personal Computer," *Journal of the Vacuum Society of Japan,* vol. 26, no. 10, 1983, pp. 764–788.

Vacroux, A. G. "Explore Microcomputer I/O Capabilities," *Electronic Design,* May 10, 1975.

Weir, J. D., and Weir, C. J., "Personal Computers For Machine and Process Control: Fast, Inexpensive, Easy Automation." *Elastromerics,* August 1983, pp. 17–18.

Wolf, S. *Guide to Electronic Measurements and Laboratory Practice*. Englewood Cliffs, N.J.: Prentice-Hall, 1973.

Yourdon, E., and Constantine, L. L. *Structured Design*. New York: Yourdon, 1975.

Zaks, Rodney. *Microprocessors*. Berkeley, Calif.: Sybex, 1979.

Zaks, Rodney, and Lesea, Austin. *Microprocessor Interfacing*. Berkeley, Calif.: Sybex, Inc. 1979.

Zilog CORP. *Z8000 User's Guide*. Cupertino, Calif.: Zilog Corp., 1980.

Zimmerman, Michael. "Vendors to Flood Market with 66MHz DX2 PCs." *PC Week.* August 10, 1992.

Zimmerman, Michael, and Boudette, Neal. "2 Intel Chips to Double Speed *PC Week.* February 17, 1992.

# Index

## ABOUT THE AUTHOR

For more than 30 years
industry and governmen
areas as systems and re
networks, microcompute
tems, automated manuf
is a prolific author and l
design and applications
automation and commu
Hordeski has also serve
Pomona and San Luis C
sis, electronic devices, p
design, industrial and n
design, engineering test
statistics.